Anna Wacławek began researching graffiti and street art
in the late 1990s, travelling extensively in Canada and
the USA as well as Japan, China, Poland, Germany, the
UK, France and Spain to conduct first-hand analysis. She
holds several professional qualifications in art history
and currently works at Concordia University, Montreal,
in the Department of Art History.

Thames & Hudson world of art

This famous series provides the widest available range of
illustrated books on art in all its aspects.

To find out about all our publications, including other titles in the
World of Art series, please visit **thamesandhudsonusa.com**.

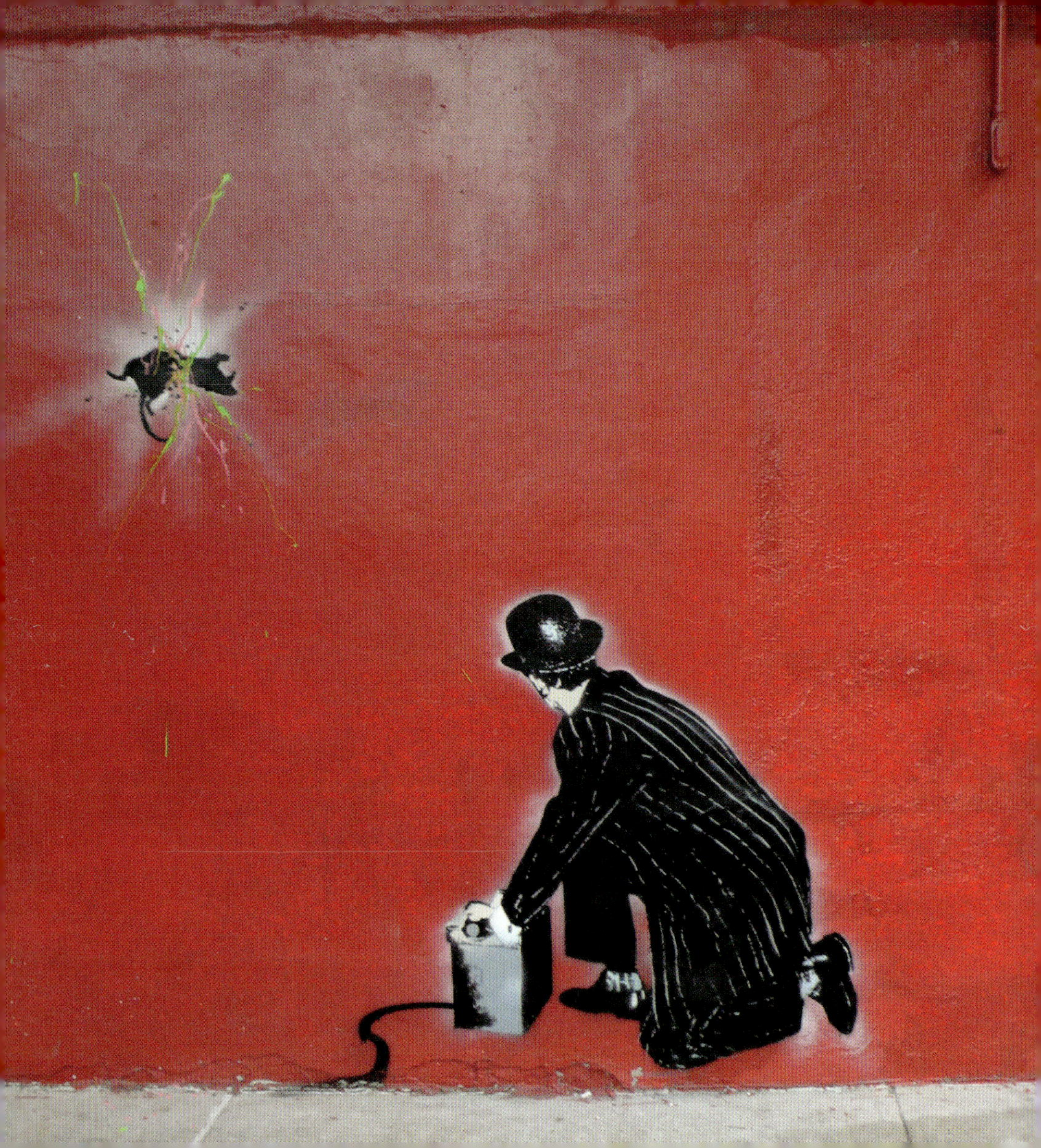

Anna Wacławek

Graffiti
and Street Art

211 illustrations

Thames & Hudson *world of art*

For Piotr Wacławek (1949–2010)

Acknowledgments

I extend my deepest gratitude to Piotr, Grażyna and Justyna Wacławek for their tireless encouragement. Dr Johanne Sloan, Dr Cynthia Hammond and Dr Catherine MacKenzie, thank you for your exceptional support and profound insight. Heartfelt thanks to my friends and colleagues, whose support – intellectual or otherwise – has resulted in the timely completion of this book. Sincere thanks to Zoë Tousignant, Sharon Murray, Rachel Lauzon, Federico O'Reilly Regueiro, Megumi Komatsuzaki, Mariana Vidal and Napoleon Soberanis for translation, technical assistance and moral support. Many thanks to the students of 'ARTH 3981: Graffiti and Street Art' (Summer 2010) for your enthusiasm. Special thanks to all graffiti writers, street artists and supporters of renegade art projects worldwide. Finally, I reserve a special place of gratitude for everyone involved at Thames & Hudson, without whom this book would not have been possible.

Frontispiece: Nick Walker, *Ratatouille*, New York City, USA, 2008
Page 196: Faile, New York City, USA, 2010

This book is a documentary record and critique of a form of artistic expression including graffiti and street art. Neither the author nor the publisher in any way endorses vandalism or the use of graffiti and street art for the defacement of private and public property.

First published in 2011 in paperback in the United States of America by Thames & Hudson Inc., 500 Fifth Avenue, New York, New York 10110

thamesandhudsonusa.com

Library of Congress Catalog Card Number 2011922587

ISBN 978-0-500-20407-8

Printed in China through Asia Pacific Offset Ltd

Contents

Preface 7

Chapter 1   **From Graffiti to Post-Graffiti 10**
Signature Graffiti Writing *12*; The Tag *14*; Throwies *16*;
Pieces *18*; Tools of the Trade *19*; Kings, Toys and Crews *26*;
Urban Painting *28*; Stencils *33*; Logos *37*; Characters *38*

Chapter 2   **Graffiti's Genealogy 43**
Writing Style *44*; Graffiti in Motion *48*; A Necessary Crime *54*;
'Hip-Hop Graffiti' *56*; Forays into Galleries *58*; Basquiat and
Haring *62*

Chapter 3   **Street Art and the City 65**
Street Art as Public Art *65*; Contesting 'Public' Space *73*;
Defining a Community *79*; The City as Context *84*; Here
Today, Gone Tomorrow *91*; Performing Street Art *96*;
Identity Politics *102*

Chapter 4   **Post-Graffiti, Site and Space 112**
The Liminal *114*; But What Does It Do? *122*; Same Work,
Multiple Sites *132*; Location, Location, Location *139*;
The Material Support and the Work Itself *147*

Chapter 5   **Urban Visual Culture 157**
Visual Culture and Art History *159*; Street Art off the Streets
169; In the Gallery *174*; On the Internet *178*; Reclaiming the
Streets: Remixing, Culture Jamming and Subvertising *185*;
Urban Painting Today *190*

Artists' Websites *197*
Select Bibliography *198*
List of Illustrations *204*
Index *206*

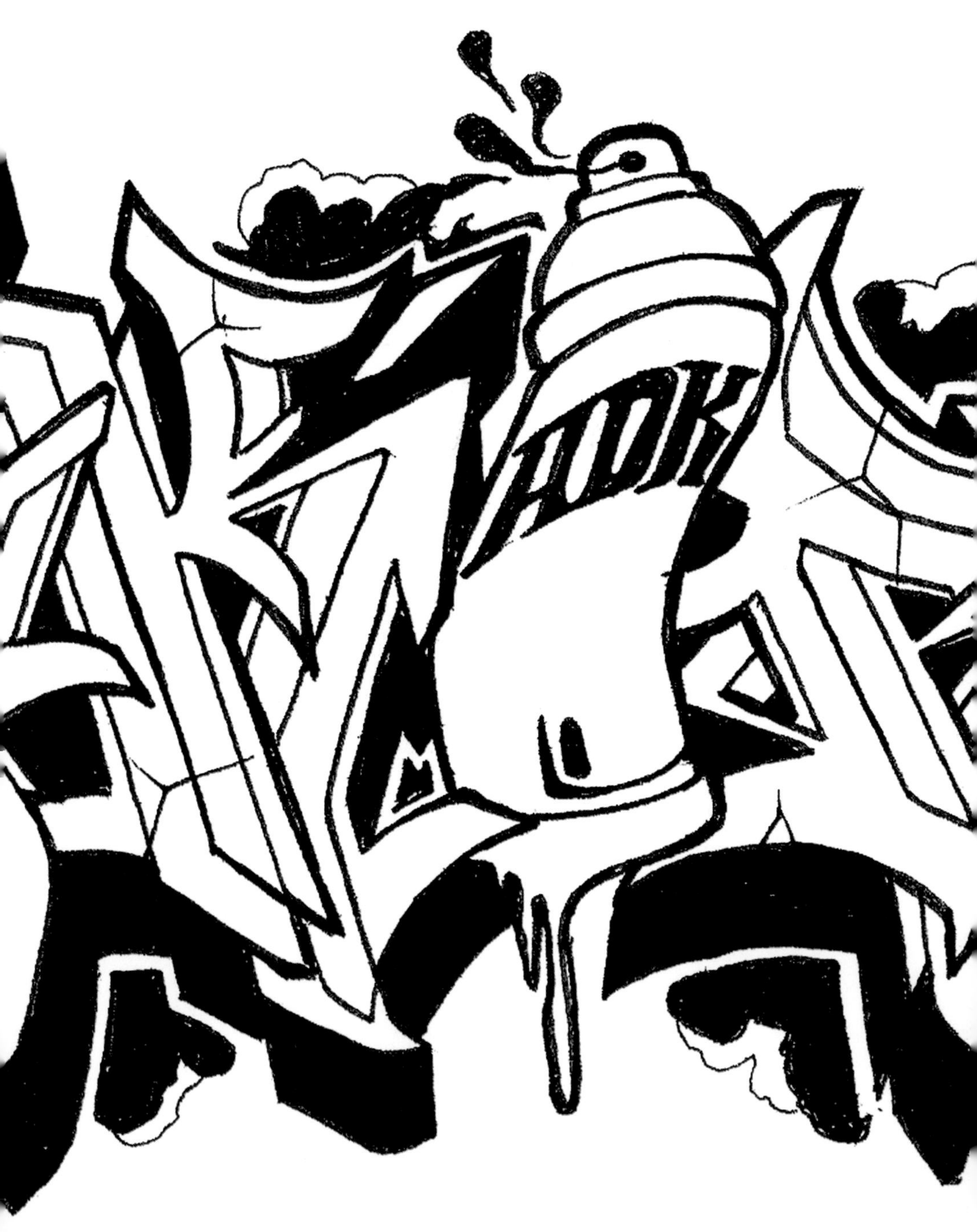
ADK

Preface

A curious phenomenon can be observed in university and public libraries: the graffiti and street art books that are part of library catalogues are often classified as missing or are long overdue; and when they can be found, pages have generally been torn out, and personal remarks scribbled in the margins. This ongoing trend reflects the buzz surrounding these art forms. Conversations with those who write graffiti ('writers'), street artists, curators, gallery assistants, academics and students, or other professionals directly involved in some aspect of graffiti production, exhibition or research, invariably turn to the significance of this art movement. After all, a visual tradition that has subsisted for over forty years and continues to evolve worldwide is unsurprisingly ripe with discourse. Most remarkable, however, are the conversations about graffiti and street art, also commonly known as post-graffiti, involving people uninitiated in graffiti cultures. No matter what the social context or city, it seems people want to talk about illegal urban painting. Although the dialogue may not always be in favour of graffiti, it is typically passionate. People want to talk about graffiti and street art because these art forms, which exist in the city, are accessible to everyone and are simultaneously mysterious and controversial.

At a recent conference, Scott Burnham said: 'The street is a huge cultural laboratory.' Burnham, who in 2003 established and directed 'Ill Communication', one of the largest street art biennials, expressed the value of surveying the ongoing materialization of art at street level as a foreshadowing of the coming trends in leading cultural institutions. A few months after Burnham's lecture, Tate Modern held the first major museum exhibition of street art in London, displaying work by six artists on the façade of the iconic building. This is but one indication that street art is being recognized by mainstream art institutions as a movement worthy of the art world's

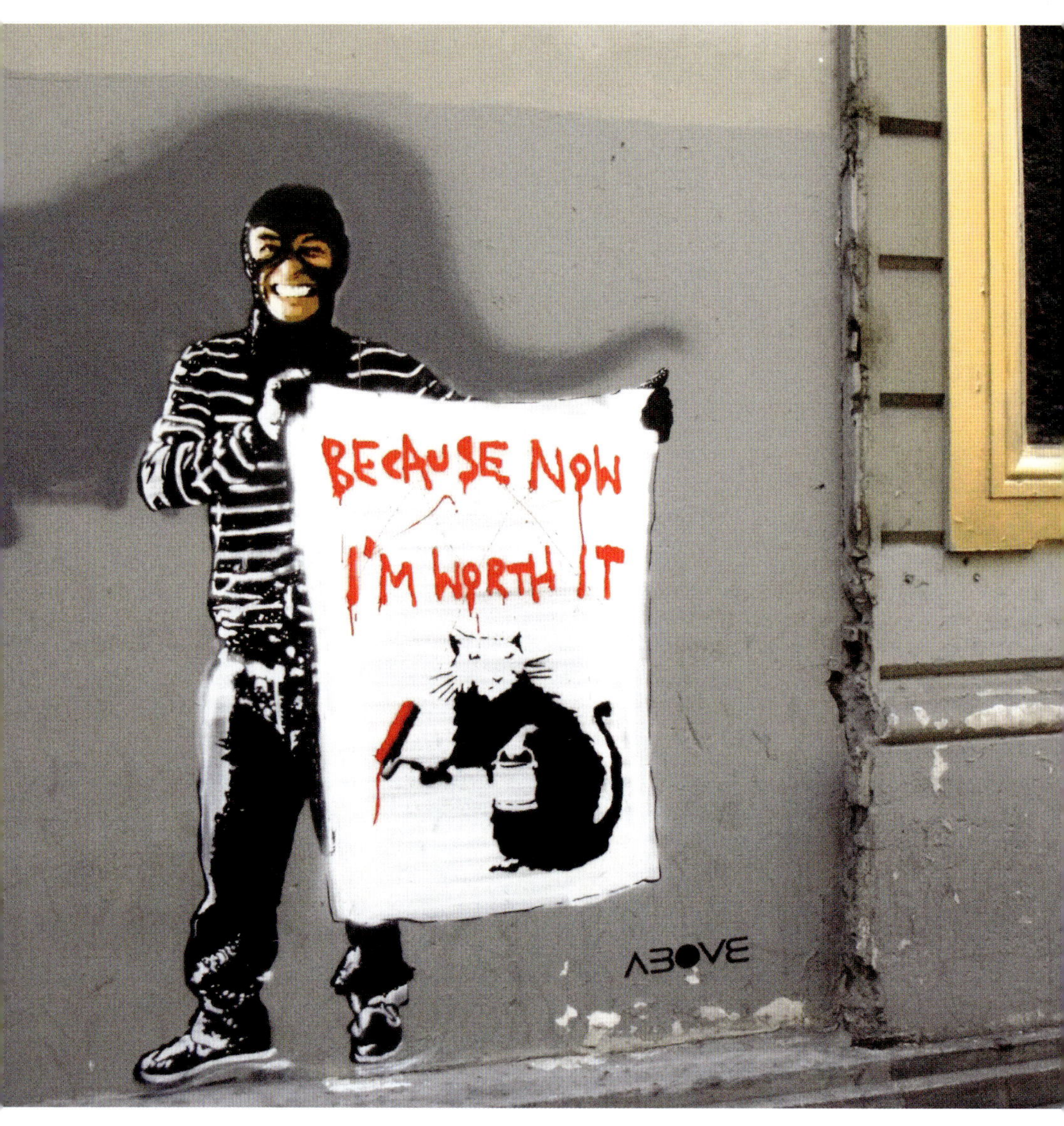

2 **Above**, *Because Now I'm Worth It*, Paris, France, 2010. Above uses a familiar image – Banksy's 'because I'm worthless' rat stencil – as the centrepiece of this work to comment on the theft of street art pieces. Playing on the 'worthless' tagline, he reflects on the cultural and economic value of street art and on the irony of stealing free art.

attention. A major study of graffiti and street art grounded in visual art analysis, however, has yet to be published. This book aims to fill this gap, first by examining the pioneering work of graffiti writers, and second by positioning street art as the quintessential art movement of the twenty-first century.

Whether abhorred or adored, graffiti and street art provoke passionate debate, reflecting the prominent role they play in the cultural landscape and consciousness of a city.

To experience art as part of one's navigation of the urban environment is not uncommon in major cities worldwide. Graffiti and street art are exceptional, however, for three key reasons. First, as unsanctioned interventionist practices, they challenge the art institution and commissioned public art, which both typically involve numerous decision-makers in a project from conception to fruition. Second, street art practices are guided by and guide a city's visual aesthetic in that they both assimilate that environment and recreate it. And finally, graffiti writers and street artists fundamentally question the ethos of ownership through the process of creation and thus approach the city from an alternative perspective. Both graffiti and street art practices illuminate the city with signs of life. The walls, streets, billboards and all manner of structural details that make up a city are brought to life with the addition of urban painting. The function of illegal urban art, and whether it should be supported or penalized, remains open for discussion. However, one thing is certain: when it comes to contemporary international art movements, the writing is on the wall.

Chapter 1   From Graffiti to Post-Graffiti

3 (*below*) **Thundercut**, *Thundercut*, New York City, USA, 2004. Graffiti writers focus on deconstructing the alphabet and creating it anew through the individualized and stylized letters of their tag. Often working with woodcuts, New York duo Thundercut add their spin on tagging to a graffiti-covered wall, making the distinction between signature graffiti writing and street art abundantly clear.

4 (*opposite*) **Puppet**, *Graffiti Girl*, 'Classics' series, Spain, 2009. Characters are a fundamental element of graffiti, and writers have been incorporating them into pieces since the early days of the movement. This example by Swedish writer Puppet is a fresh take on classic graffiti.

Writing signature graffiti, or graffiti focused on both letters and names, began in the mid- to late 1960s in Philadelphia, exploded as a subculture in New York City in the 1970s, and has over the past forty years become an undeniable ingredient of street cultures worldwide. Since the 1990s, a handful of academic texts have been published about the subway graffiti phenomenon in New York and graffiti subcultures in various cities around the world. These were preceded and continue to be succeeded by an impressive number of studies focused on documenting and describing graffiti cultures, often in the artists' own words. What is often missing is an exploration of the function, meaning and impact of illegal, ephemeral art within the contexts of cityscapes, art worlds and urban visual cultures. Beginning with a review of the genealogy of graffiti, this book examines the contribution of graffiti and street art to the experience of urbanity and the role of both art forms in the history of art.

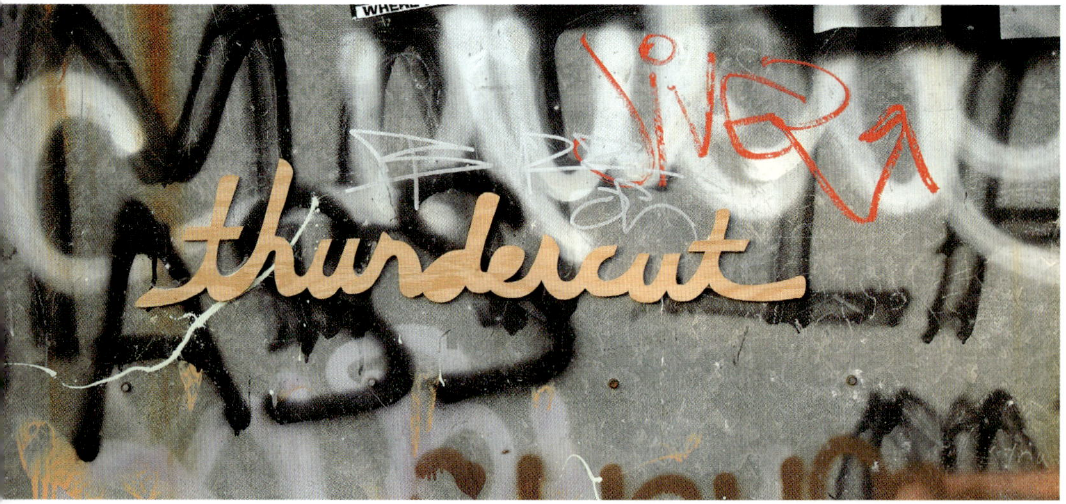

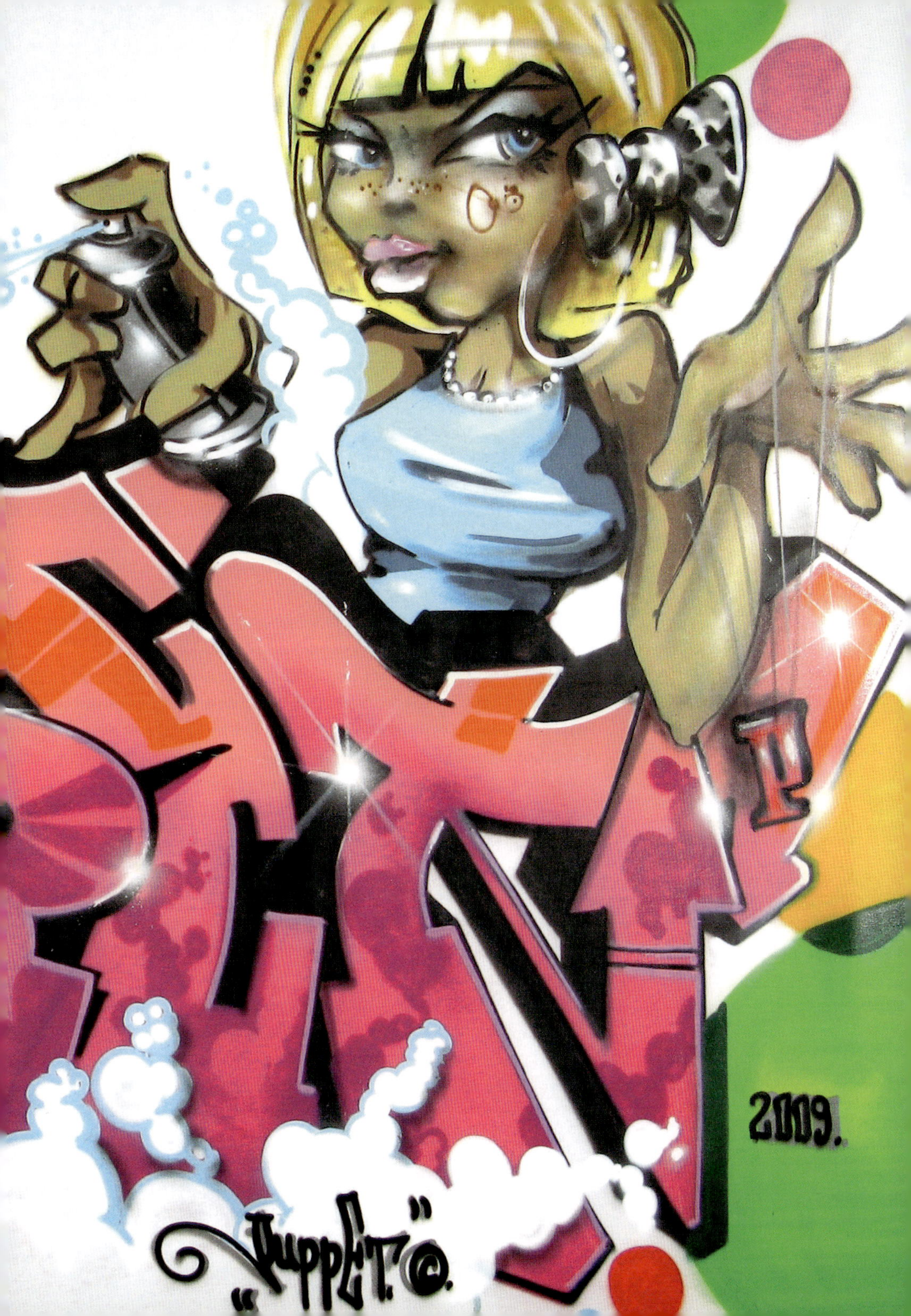

2009.
„Juppet"

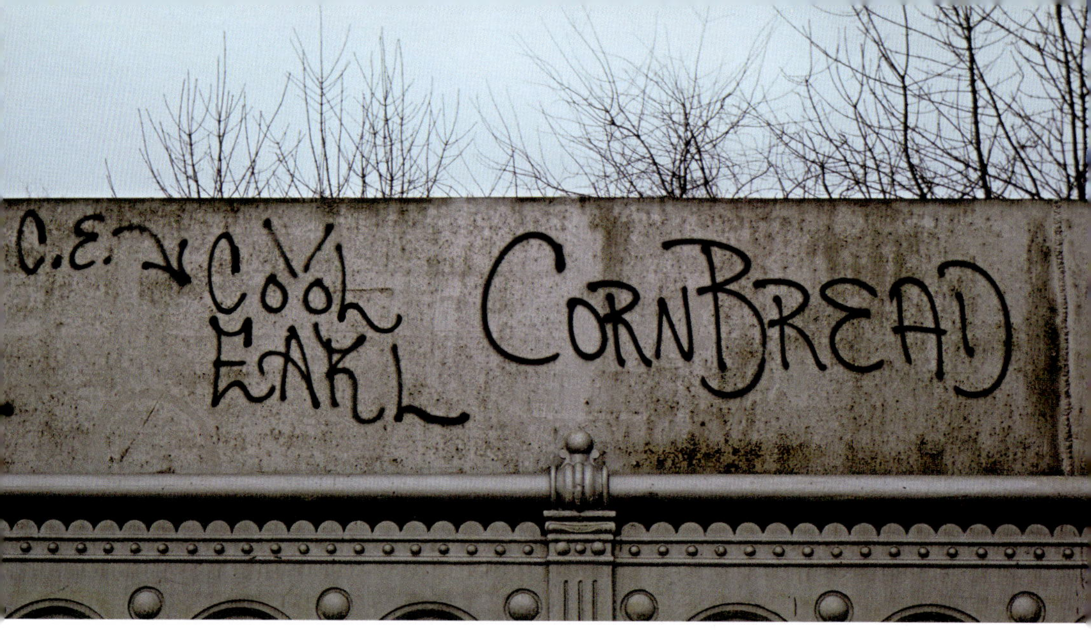

5 **Cool Earl and Cornbread**, Philadelphia, 1960s. Cool Earl and Cornbread have gone down in history as originators of the tradition of signature graffiti writing. Gangs in many cities had been writing their names to mark out territory for years, but both Cornbread and Cool Earl had a different motivation: they disseminated their signatures everywhere they could with no other purpose than to establish an identity for themselves. Although their signatures were unstylized and legible, they were instrumental in setting in motion a movement that revolves around spray-painting one's tag.

Graffiti writing is unique in three main regards: it is an art movement begun and sustained primarily by youth, a visual vocabulary whose subject is the signature, and a pictorial tradition that developed and continues to flourish illegally. Meanwhile, post-graffiti art practices, or the diverse forms of urban art that have arisen since the 1990s as a result of graffiti, have come to epitomize contemporary urban visual culture. Together, as graffiti and street art foster exchanges with the material and built environment of a city, commercial imagery, and canonical movements within art history, they take their place within the matrix of visual culture.

Signature Graffiti Writing

Alongside political, bathroom and gang graffiti, the practice of individuals writing their names or pseudonyms on city walls with spray-paint first developed in Philadelphia during the 1960s. Legendary writers such as Cornbread and Cool Earl [5] set the tradition of signature graffiti writing, or tagging, in motion and unexpectedly introduced a trend that would become a lifestyle for millions of young people around the world. By the time tag writing reached New York, it had gained incredible momentum, especially as writing famously assumed visual control over subway trains during the 1970s.

The letter-based style of graffiti writing centres on the writer's name, and its basic formal elements came to include 'tags', 'throw-ups' and 'pieces'. Each component, no matter how ornate, depicts the writer's pseudonym, which is sometimes adorned with images. The rendition of each of these forms asserts the writer's graffiti identity, one that paradoxically is largely centred on anonymity. Writers frequently refer to and recognize each other solely by their nicknames, often not knowing each other's real names. The practice of writing graffiti thus constitutes a unique dynamic between authorship and anonymity. On the one hand, writers' graffiti names allow them to visually assume the walls of a city in an anonymous fashion. On the other, the very act of writing tags in the cityscape implies authorship. The execution of the stylized name is momentous as it is inextricably linked both to a writer's identity and to his or her status within the subcultures that developed around this visual practice. Although graffiti writing is potentially accessible to everyone because of its dissemination in the city, writers are not interested in communicating with the general public; they are only concerned with creating an internal dialogue with each other. A graffiti name consequently allows the writer to be recognized throughout a city while maintaining anonymity and at the same time gaining notoriety within the subculture through stylized execution.

In accordance with the defiant nature of graffiti, writers typically renounce the classification 'artist'. Their visual language, although undeniably artful and contingent on an exploration of the elements of art and design, is also reflective of an entire culture that involves more than artistry. The art of graffiti occurs in the dismantling of the building blocks of art and design and in their reformulation through the individualized signature. Influenced more by commercial imagery than canonical art movements, the language of graffiti is in essence conceptually simple and visually complex.

Today, the graffiti movement is propelled by a number of graffiti subcultures around the world. These subcultures present graffiti writers with a supportive, albeit competitive, social network complete with unwritten rules, hierarchies, alternative identities, friendship and the impetus to prove oneself on the graffiti scene. Stylistic and formal innovation – restructuring the traditional appearance of letters and, in a way, rewriting the alphabet – is a writer's primary goal. The techniques, artistry and styles developed by those who practise graffiti writing worldwide have not only sustained these subcultures, but have also ensured that they continue to progress, challenge and provide visual thrills.

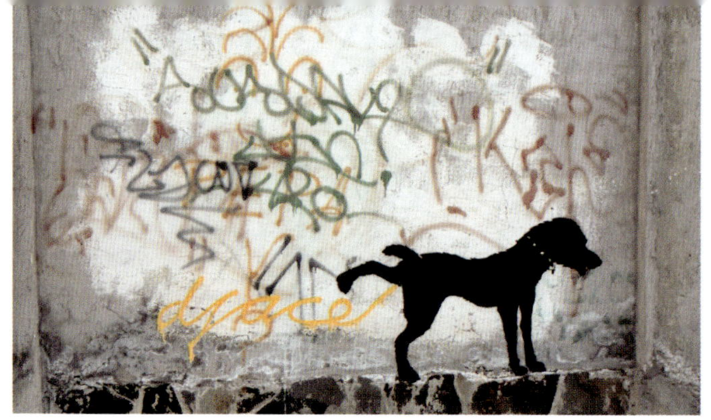

6 **D*Face**, *Dog Tag*, Ecuador, 2010. In questioning the commercial visual culture of the city, D*Face consistently aims to provoke reactions. Commenting on the recurrent idea of tagging as marking one's territory, he cleverly makes the perception literal by displaying a dog relieving itself with his signature.

The Tag

The earliest, simplest, most elemental form of graffiti writing, the tag is a quickly executed, monochromatic rendering of a writer's graffiti name [7]. Tags are typically short, sometimes clever words that, when drawn, are no bigger than standard paper size and take only a few seconds to execute. A graffiti tag represents a pseudonym that the writer devises or acquires.

In New York, early tags frequently appeared as a combination of the writer's real name and his or her numerical street name. In this way, others knew not only whether the writer was male or female, but also in which neighbourhood he or she resided. When Taki183, Julio204, Eva62 and other early taggers were writing prolifically or 'bombing' the city, they were neither preoccupied with style nor technique. Their intention was to get their name out on the street as a visual demonstration of existence and an assertion of their alter ego. Although tags have nowadays become stylized and abstract, in the early 1970s they were clearly written and could be read by anyone. By the mid-1970s, writers were gradually moving away from the established 'name – street number' approach in favour of words that made a visual impact.

Taggers understand their names as representations of the self and have therefore evolved their tags into individualized logos. When settling on a tag, writers consider both how the letters look together when drawn and how the word sounds when spoken. Therefore, names sometimes appear as nonsensical words whose letters work well in sequence to create rhythm and a sense of motion or visual flow, such as Merz or Spie. In other cases, writers may choose a meaningful word for their tag but give it an alternative spelling, such as Revok or Kase. A tag name can also serve to convey an attitude or describe how writers want to represent themselves within

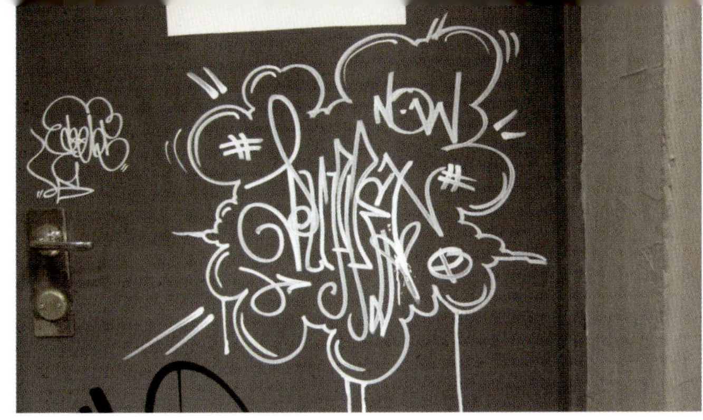

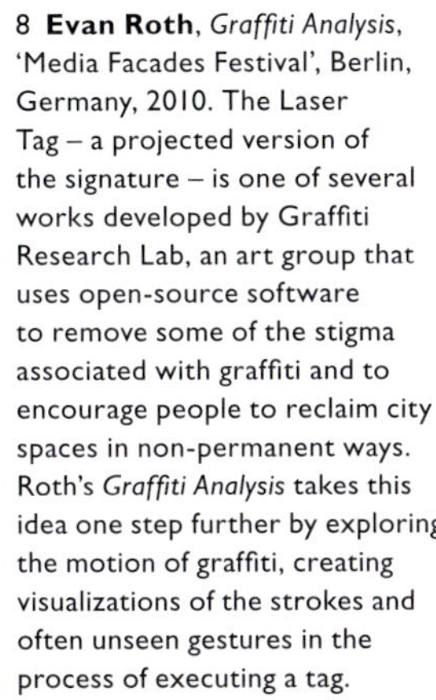

7 **Puppet**, Sweden, 2011. Arrows, quotation marks, clouds, bubbles and painted drips are among the key symbols and flourishes that activate a graffiti tag and provide it with a sense of dynamism and movement. This example in pen is an updated version of an earlier tag of 1985 by Puppet.

8 **Evan Roth**, *Graffiti Analysis*, 'Media Facades Festival', Berlin, Germany, 2010. The Laser Tag – a projected version of the signature – is one of several works developed by Graffiti Research Lab, an art group that uses open-source software to remove some of the stigma associated with graffiti and to encourage people to reclaim city spaces in non-permanent ways. Roth's *Graffiti Analysis* takes this idea one step further by exploring the motion of graffiti, creating visualizations of the strokes and often unseen gestures in the process of executing a tag.

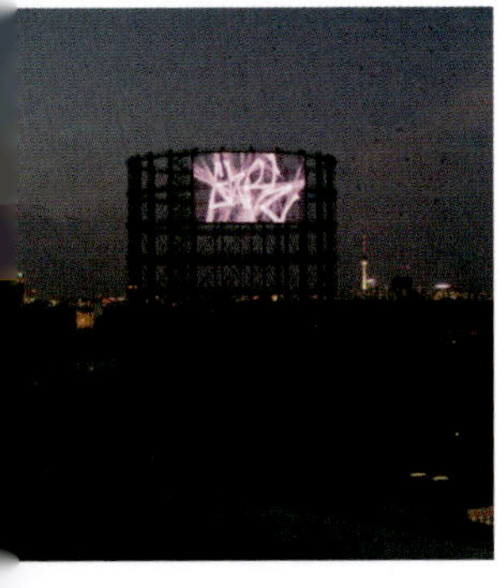

the subculture, as in the case of legendary tagger StayHigh149 (New York). Beyond the development of a tag's letters into personalized versions of the alphabet, taggers also typically add flourishes or symbols to their names. Arrows, intertwined with the name to facilitate a sense of motion, direction and energy, were an early development and continue to be a staple icon for contemporary writers worldwide, including Caru (Argentina), Prisco (Puerto Rico), Falco (South Africa) and Blef (Italy). Quotation marks, employed by many early writers such as Mare139 (New York), and stars, popularized by legendary New York writers Iz the Wiz and Cope2, continue to be standard elements of writing culture and are prominently employed by the Tats Cru (New York) and Great & Bates (Denmark), among others. Essentially, a personally stylized tag is the first step to affirming a writer's identity within the graffiti subculture.

Writers' preoccupation with the stylistic interpretation of letters also means that they ordinarily write more than one tag. This strategy provides the writer with versatility and greater security. They can name-switch if they come to prefer working with a specific combination of letters or if the name by which they are best known becomes too easy for the police to track. Celebrated New York writer Dondi [43], for example, used a number of aliases, including Naco, 2Hot, 2Many, White761 and Asia. Switching between tags or decreasing the number of letters in one's tag – letter-dropping – is both a method of self-protection and a tool for stylistic innovation. Name-switching provides writers with a fresh combination of letters to explore and contort, while letter-dropping allows them more time to paint their tag and make it more visually compelling. Zephyr (New York), for example, often used Zeph as an abbreviation [12], while Revolt (also New York) would sometimes drop the 'e' and 'o' from his tag and write Rvlt.

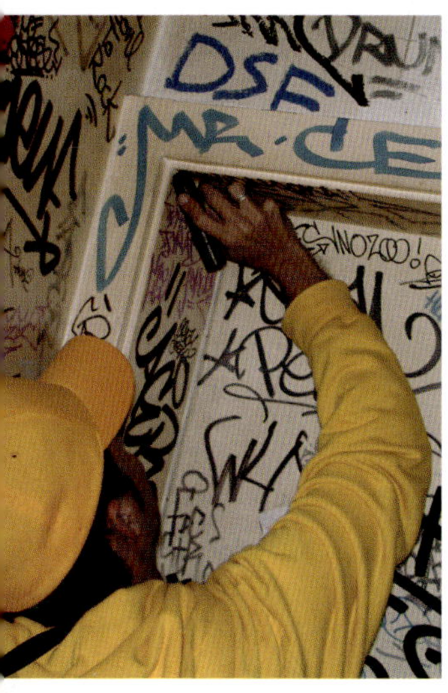

9 (*above*) **Kero**, Berlin, Germany, 2007. By adding one's tag to a wall that has been activated by other taggers, a writer enters into a visual conversation with others and asserts his or her place within the subculture.

10 (*opposite, above*) **Chas**, Kumasi, Ghana, 2011. Graffiti writers often find themselves in unpredictable situations. For this piece, Dutch artist Chas had to improvise with a bucket of rollerpaint and old spray cans after his package of supplies went missing en route from the Netherlands to Ghana.

11 (*opposite, below*) **MadC**, Leipzig, Germany, 2009. Writers practise various articulations of their names, using stylistic elements such as interconnected lines, overlaps and blending to make each rendering unique. The letters often attain such abstraction that reading a signature becomes practically impossible for those outside the graffiti culture. In this way writers fashion a sort of secret language that, while articulated in the public sphere, effectively excludes the passer-by.

Tagging is usually executed at a frenetic pace as a way of publicizing and potentially making a name for oneself on the graffiti scene. To this end, taggers utilize a common advertising strategy: overexposure. Writing a tag hundreds or even thousands of times may assure a tagger some credibility among taggers, but not necessarily in the subculture as a whole, where tagging is not seen as intensely challenging. Still, some writers who have no aspirations of becoming 'piecers' (associated with big, complex and colourful murals) remain taggers for their entire graffiti careers. The highly addictive nature of graffiti writing within an unrestricted terrain, as well as the potential respect gained from within the community, ensures that taggers can spend years tagging without losing interest in their competitive activity. In essence, writing tags is like a game whereby the entire city is the playing field.

Throwies

As the number of taggers in New York grew from the mid-1970s onwards, writers realized that to get noticed they had to develop their tags both in colour and in size. Originally describing pieces that were unsuccessful, by 1975 'throw-ups' or 'throwies' had come to define a new development in the graffiti form. One of New York's most prolific writers during the later 1970s, In aka Kill3, even made a name for himself as 'the king of throw-ups' thanks to the estimated 10,000 throwies he painted on subway trains. Essentially larger versions of tags, throwies – consisting of outlined, traditionally 'bubble' letters, which are grouped together and sometimes filled in with a different colour – are rendered or 'thrown up' on a train or wall in a brisk manner. At least twenty times bigger than tags, more time-consuming, and more involved in terms of colours, shadows and styles, throw-ups are typically composed of an outline, a fill and 'glow'. If a throwie features three colours, one might be used to outline the letters and form shadows, the second to fill in the outlined letters, and the third to create glow – emphasizing the whole drawing and making the name pop.

Throw-ups, not unlike tags, hinge on the writer's design ability, yet they are relatively simple to execute, especially if they are represented as block letters or in the iconic, readable bubble or 'softie' style credited to New Yorker Phase2. Like tags, throwies are essentially about quantity, since they are not traditionally evaluated according to style or quality. They represent another manifestation of the writer's name that

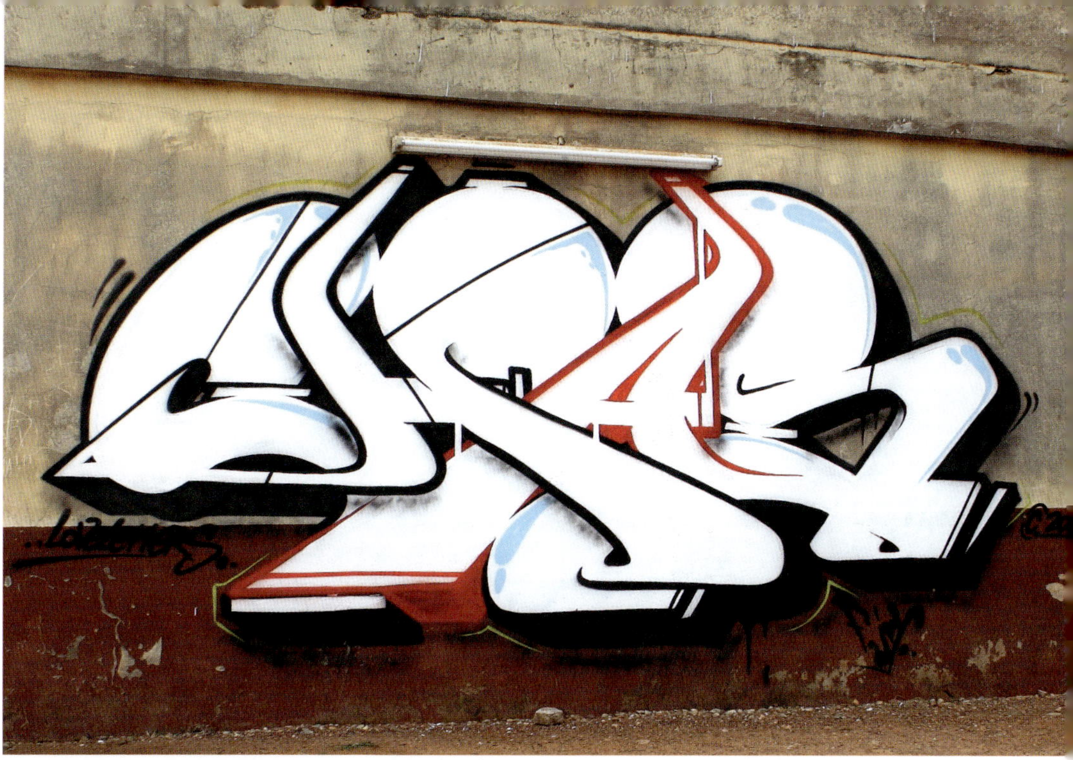

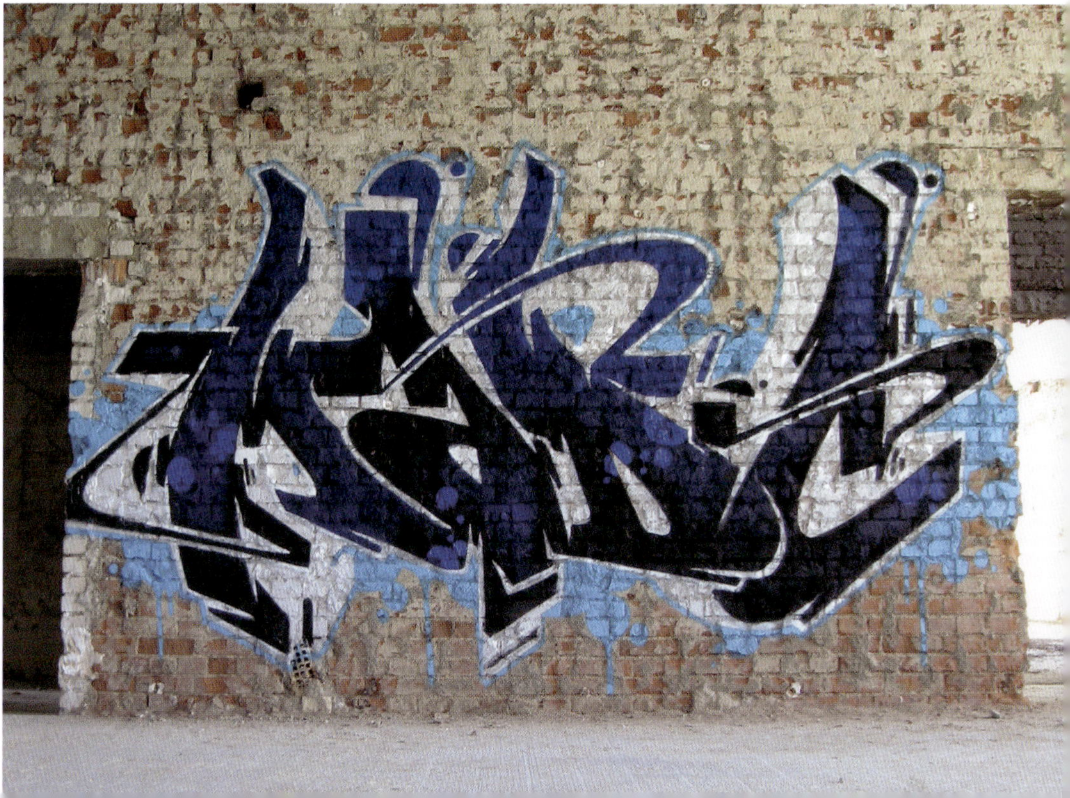

appropriates more space, thus making the writer increasingly visible within the subculture and the cityscape. Often writers use throwies as a springboard for more complex letter experimentation, which leads to the creation of abstract or 'wildstyle' pieces.

Pieces

While the general public largely considers tags and throwies to be a nuisance, pieces tend to impress. Short for 'masterpieces', these large, colourful, elaborate and stylistically challenging works require a greater amount of time to create and earn a writer the most respect. As opposed to tags and throw-ups, these works are assessed within the community on the basis of quality and technical expertise. By 1975–77, while the era of throwies was peaking, pieces had plateaued in terms of innovation, only to be revitalized between 1978 and 1981 in New York through the work of writers such as Case2, Mare139, Duro, Zephyr [12], Revolt, Daze and Crash [48]. Pieces are like murals; whether on a wall or the outside of a train, they sometimes convey a message and combine words with another fundamental graffiti element – characters [13]. When early New York writers such as SuperKool223, Tracy168 and Lee163d [45] began experimenting with scale and design, they set in motion a tradition in graffiti writing that continues to ensure the evolution of the movement to this day. The focus remains on letters and the name, but it is through the stylistic components, elements of art and design,

12 **Zephyr and Noc167**, New York City, USA. During the 1970s, the culture of graffiti writing flourished on the New York subway. Legendary writers Zephyr and Noc167 started writing at an early age and by the end of the decade were producing highly stylized pieces on trains. They were respected above all for their burners (expertly executed pieces) and stylistic innovation.

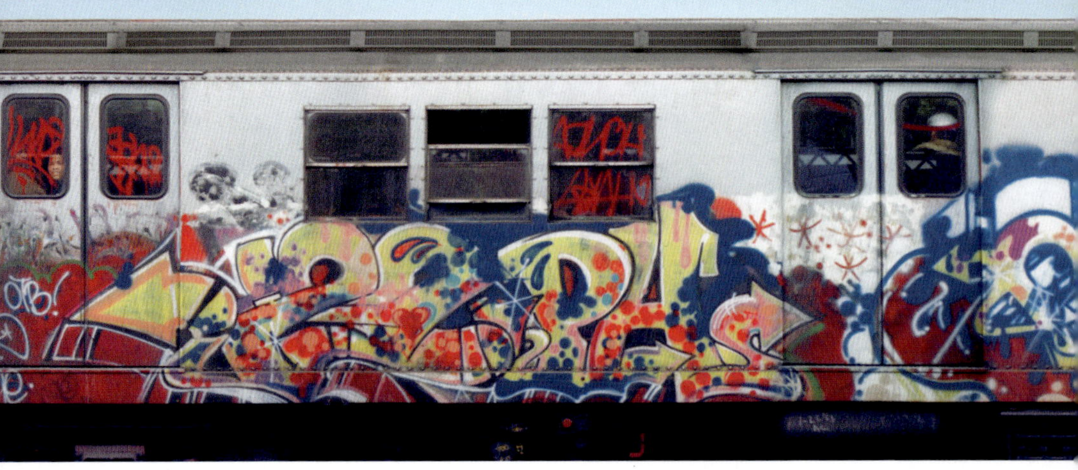

and expressive iconography that pieces convey the vitality and rich artistic tradition of graffiti writing [14]. It is also through the specialized visual vocabulary most discernible in pieces that writers have fashioned their subcultures.

Before attempting a piece, writers typically spend many hours planning its visual composition and the practical aspects of its dissemination. Whenever possible, writers begin a piece by priming their chosen wall with house paint. Prepping the wall in this way makes sense economically and aesthetically. Economically, a coat of house paint impedes the absorption of expensive spray-paint by old walls. Aesthetically, it not only provides writers with a monochromatic backdrop, but also outlines the piece and allows for the rendition of sharper lines. Pieces are typically composed of numerous vivid colours and appear in a variety of styles. Most significantly, they depict endless re-articulations of the alphabet.

Early writers developed a number of piecing styles that became popular within the subculture. For example, Philadelphia's TopCat126 introduced the elegant, slender 'broadway' lettering style, which gave way to blocky, square 'blockbuster' letters and Phase2's softie style. Still, no other style of writing has had as much influence over the entire graffiti culture as wildstyle, the development of which is credited to Tracy168. In the mid-1970s, the term 'wildstyle' came to designate energetic pieces with interlocked, highly stylized letters. Virtually unreadable, especially to non-writers, wildstyle letters are characterized by their ruptured, interwoven or twisted appearance, and are enhanced by arrows, lines that give the style a sense of movement, as well as an assortment of items that highlight parts of the design. The illusion that the stylized letters are in motion is part of the energy expressed through graffiti. As writers develop their styles and learn the ropes, from tagging to piecing, they master reshaping the letters in their names to such a conceptual and abstract state that each individual letter becomes a work of art. In the development of letterforms that are illegible, sometimes even to other writers, the graffiti culture has successfully constructed a visual language that, while performed in the cityscape, is reserved for and fuels the subculture.

Tools of the Trade

Markers, spray-paint and spray-can tips are the staple materials of graffiti production. Spray-paint is a fitting medium for the

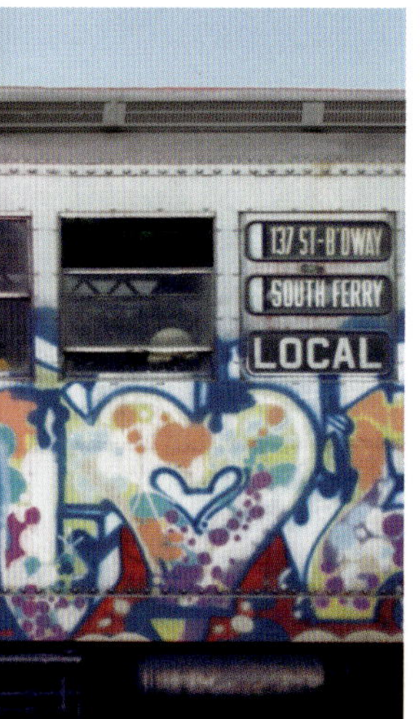

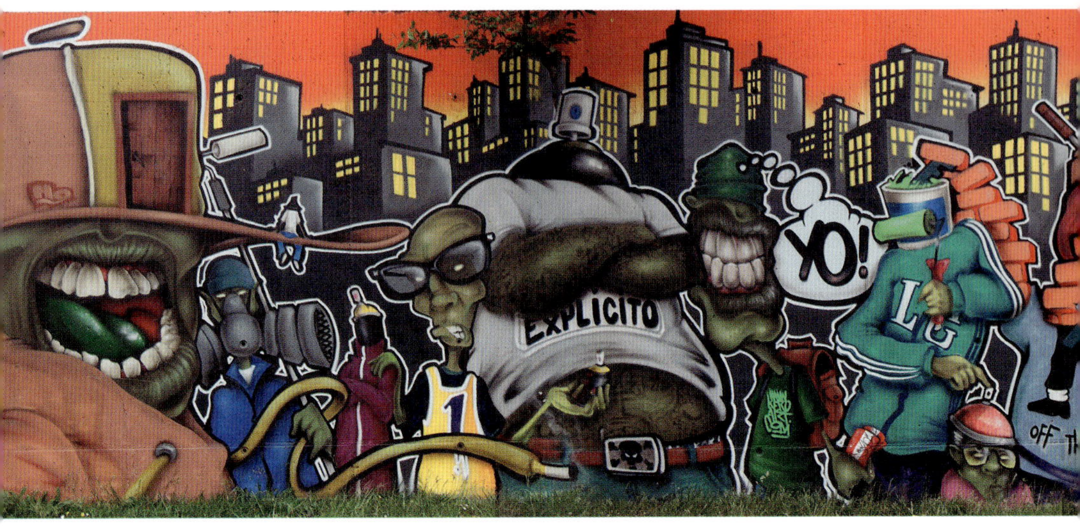

13 **Kero**, *lavidalooka*, Bilbao, Spain, 2010

propagation of graffiti: it is portable, affordable and available in a wide variety of colours, but it also reflects writing's urgency. Painting under pressure, and typically constrained by time, early writers appropriated a commercial paint medium and transformed it for their own use.

The spray-paint can, an archetypal symbol of graffiti, is modified by writers to serve as both paint and brush. Nozzles, known as 'tips' or 'caps', are essential to graffiti production because they, like paintbrushes, allow for varying thickness of line. Initially removed from other aerosol products such as household cleaners and hairsprays and affixed to paint cans, caps specifically designed for graffiti writers are now widely available. 'Fat', 'skinny', 'outline' and 'fill-in' caps are vital tools for any dedicated writer. As the name indicates, fat caps, sometimes called 'softballs', emit a thick, soft spray and are habitually employed to fill in throw-ups or parts of pieces. Skinny caps, on the other hand, produce thin lines and are suited to the precise work of detailing.

As writers work with spray-paint and experiment with caps, they become skilled at calculating the appropriate distance to leave between themselves and the wall in order to create the perfect drip-less line. Learning to work with a can of spray-paint is an art form in itself. From the speed of paint application and proper can grip to the movement of one's hand and wrist to create gradient fills, crisp outlines, layers and blending, writers have plenty to master in order to achieve 'can control'.

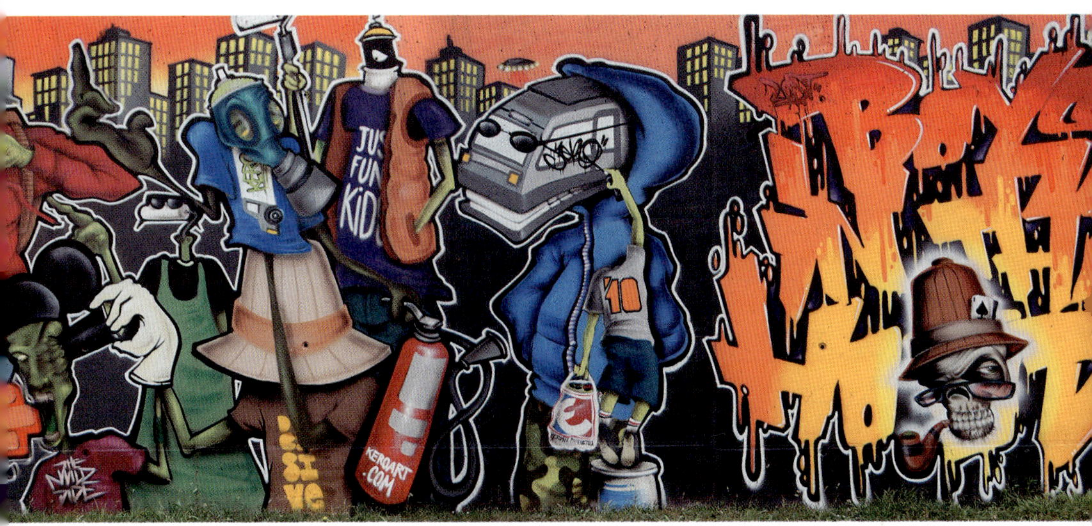

Since spray-paint is a difficult medium with which to work, most writers practise and perfect their names for quite a while before fashioning a successful piece. To this effect, tags and throw-ups are not only necessary in order to establish oneself on the graffiti scene, but are also an essential part of learning to spray-paint on challenging surfaces. In other words, the pieces for which writers are often admired by the general public would not exist without the practice of tagging.

Wide-tip or fat-tip markers are a tagger's preferred tools. Compared with spray-paint, markers are silent and easily concealed, dry faster, are simpler to control and quicker to use, emit fewer fumes and, as such, enable writers to be more

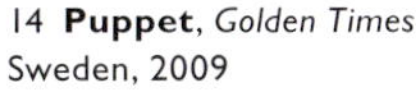

14 **Puppet**, *Golden Times*, Sweden, 2009

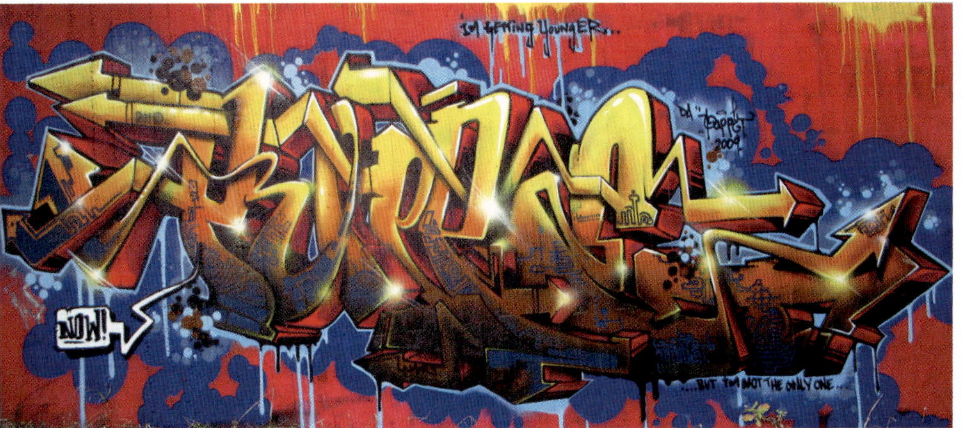

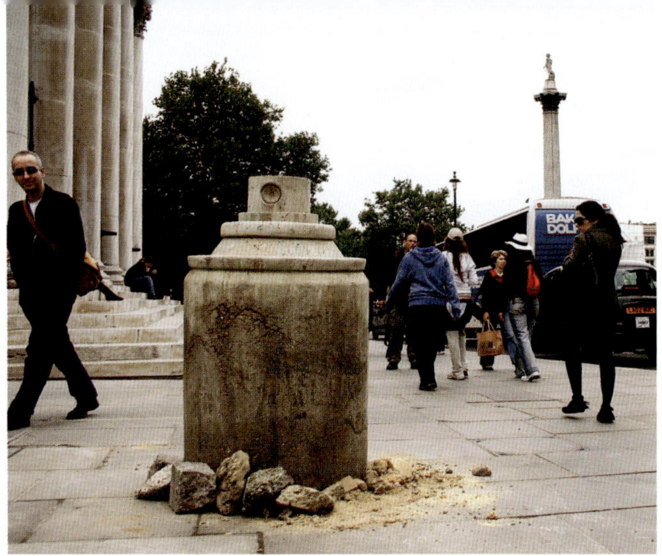

discreet when drawing tags. Like spray-paint cans, markers
are often tailored to meet a desired effect. Markers that are
cut diagonally, as opposed to those with a rounded tip, are
especially popular because they allow writers to produce
a sharper calligraphic tag. The ability to control a marker
effectively in order to accomplish an aesthetically pleasing tag
is referred to as 'handskills'. What may look like a scribble to
the general public is in fact the result of a laboured practice in
terms of originality, style and design.

In addition to spray-paint and markers, another critical
material for writers is the sketchbook [16, 17, 18, 19]. Called
'piecebooks' or 'blackbooks', hardcover, leather-bound
sketchbooks are used to sketch pieces that will be transferred
onto city walls. The development of letterforms on a small-
scale is an essential step in figuring out what works aesthetically
and in its eventual large-scale format. Piecebooks are also an
invaluable way to record works that eventually disappear from
public view. Moreover, they function as a writer's portfolio and
as a collective tool of creativity. Writers sign and draw in each
other's piecebooks, and also collaborate on pieces together
inside a single book. More than just a record of writers' work
and evidence of their skills, piecebooks also confirm a writer's
identity. They are thus essential, not only because they reveal
a writer's commitment to his or her art, but also because they
function as educational reference tools.

Aside from having an encyclopedic knowledge of spray-
paint, whether they choose to do so or not, contemporary

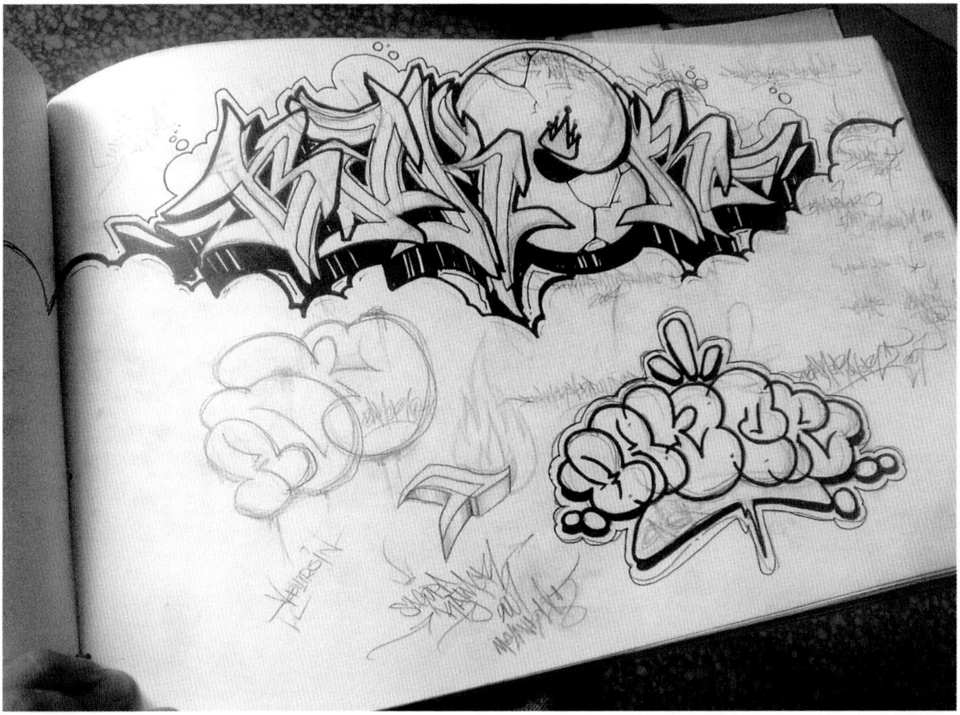

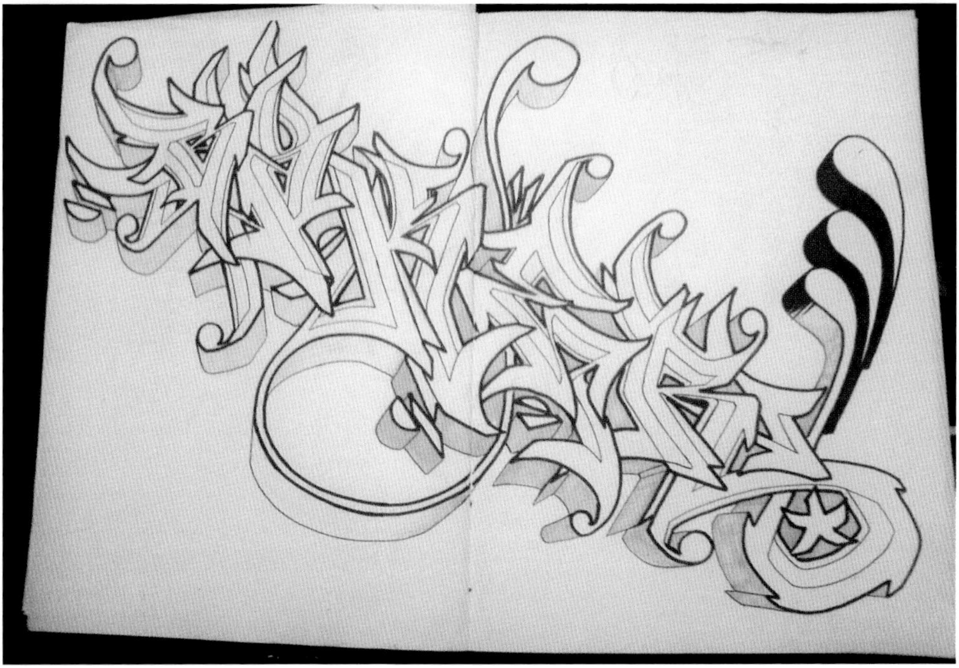

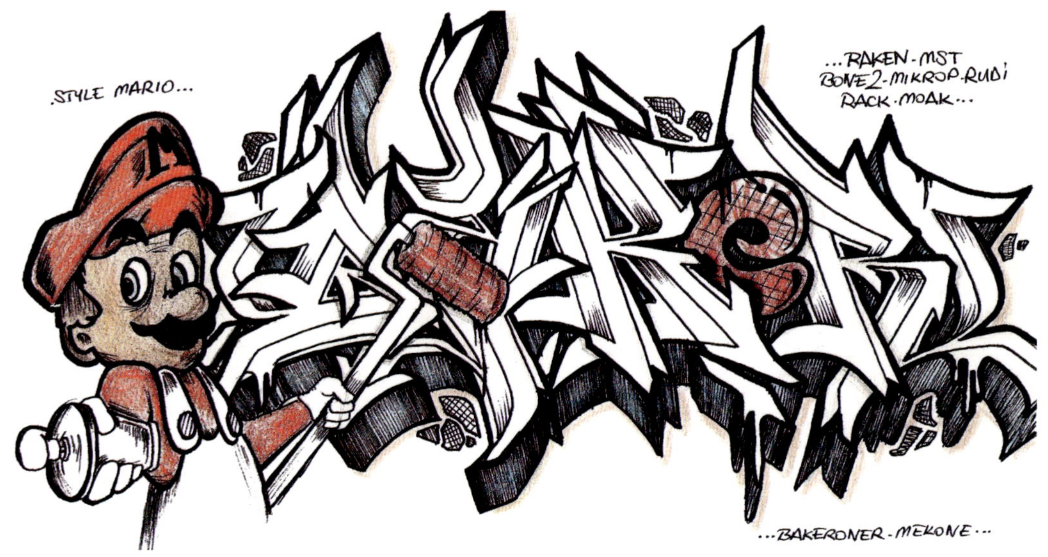

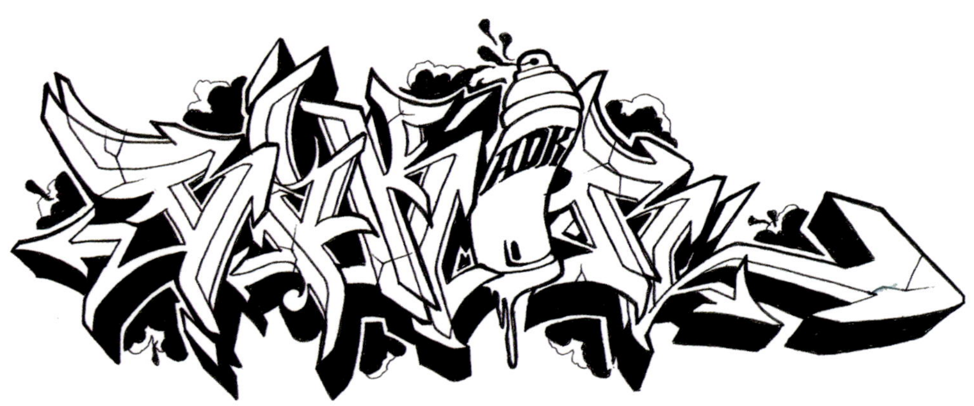

18, 19 (*top and above*) **Baker**, 2008. Writers spend many hours working out the stylistic details of their signatures in sketchbooks. The incorporation of recognizable cartoon, video game or pop culture characters as well as representations of the tools actually used for graffiti writing – in this case, the spray can – is a common strategy in decorating the name. When pleased with the elements of art and design in a sketch, writers often recreate the piece in large format on a city wall. Every detail, from shadows to colours to composition, is carefully planned before getting up on a wall.

writers also know to protect themselves with latex gloves and masks. Gloves shield the skin from harmful exposure to paint, and also protect caps from sticky paint-covered fingertips. Spray-paint is neither good for the environment nor for the human body, and masks that prohibit the inhalation of fumes are therefore an excellent preventative measure.

Taken together, the basic elements used to construct graffiti's imagery operate as a form of resistance. The creation of a graffiti identity through the circulation of a tag is both a form of camouflage and what identifies the writer as part of an underground culture. The reconstruction of the alphabet, the use of spray-paint, and the proliferation of names that are meaningful only to those who participate in their diffusion all point to the fact that, like some contemporary art practices, the culture of graffiti writing rebels against established art forms and modes of communication.

20 **Vexta**, Bogotá, Colombia, 2009

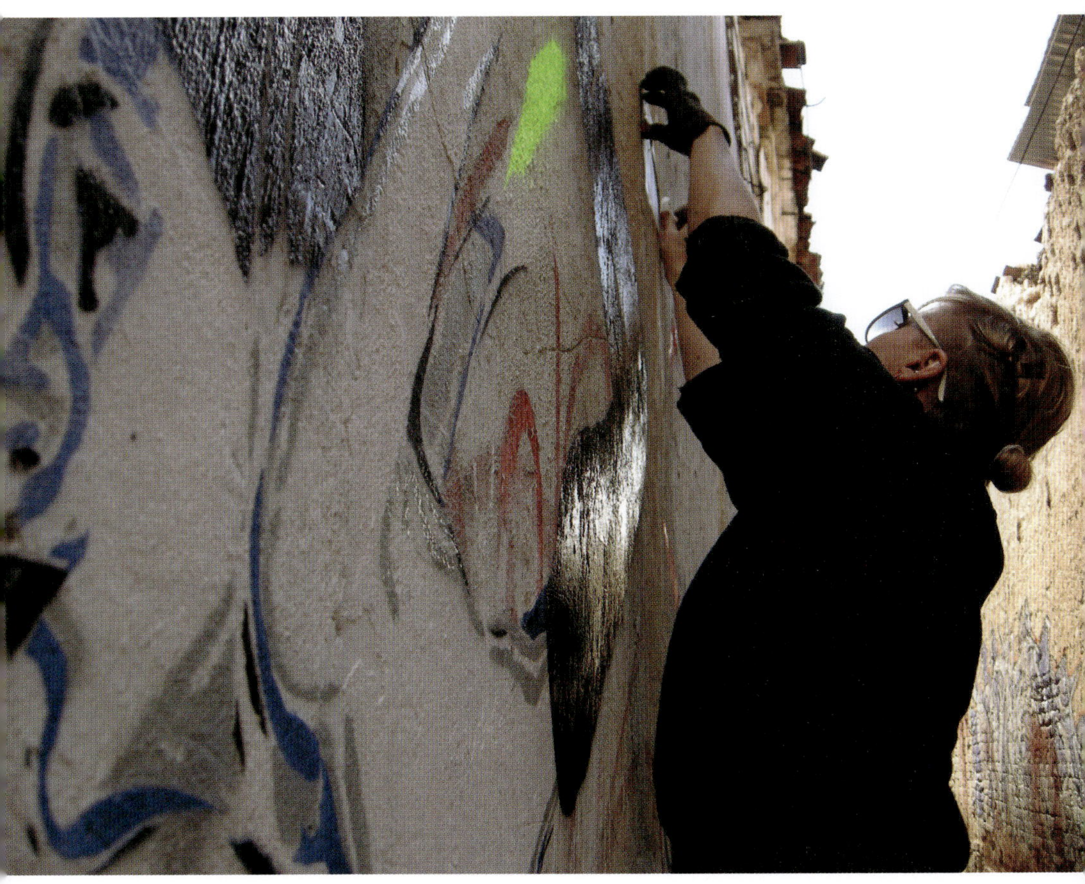

Kings, Toys and Crews

During the development of the graffiti-writing phenomenon, writers furthered their aesthetic vocabulary through a sort of visual competition and became organized as a subculture complete with unwritten codes of conduct and hierarchies. The term 'king' came to be used by writers in the 1980s to signify an accomplished and prolific writer or a master of style and technique. Similarly, the word 'queen' would define a female graffiti virtuoso. These coveted titles have written writers into graffiti history. For example, Lee [47] was known as 'king of style', In was the 'throw-up king', and PB5 was the 'king of the As' (meaning the trains of the 'A' subway service in New York). Although writers usually have to achieve the title of king through a display of talent – king of a particular style or a specific subway line, for example – sometimes writers claim the title for themselves either by drawing crowns above their names or by referring to themselves as kings in conversation. Proving oneself in the field, however, must support such a self-declaration. In opposition to king, the term 'toy' designates considerably less competent or less skilled writers who do not garner as much recognition for their work.

In the culture's early days, younger or less experienced writers often apprenticed under more knowledgeable, veteran writers, helping with their projects while learning the trade. In this way, the writing community passed down its traditions. Toys were educated by their mentors on which markers and spray-paint brands were best, which effects were produced with which nozzles, and how to control paint without dripping. In New York, where in the 1970s the culture of writing exploded on subway trains, kings, who were typically fifteen or sixteen years old, were often helped by toys, who were between nine and fourteen, in the less precise work of filling in their pieces.

Writing crews or groups, as they were initially called, typically consist of writers with equivalent levels of skill and make writing a fun, communal practice. Crews are loosely organized and function as a peer group of friends who paint together in order to share ideas and innovations, and to aid each other in the field. It is not uncommon for a writer to be associated with multiple crews. Deliberating on a crew name, most often tagged as initials, is as vital as choosing an individual tag, as the reputation of a crew is linked with the notoriety of its members. When working in crews, writers either each paint their names, one next to the other, or they write their

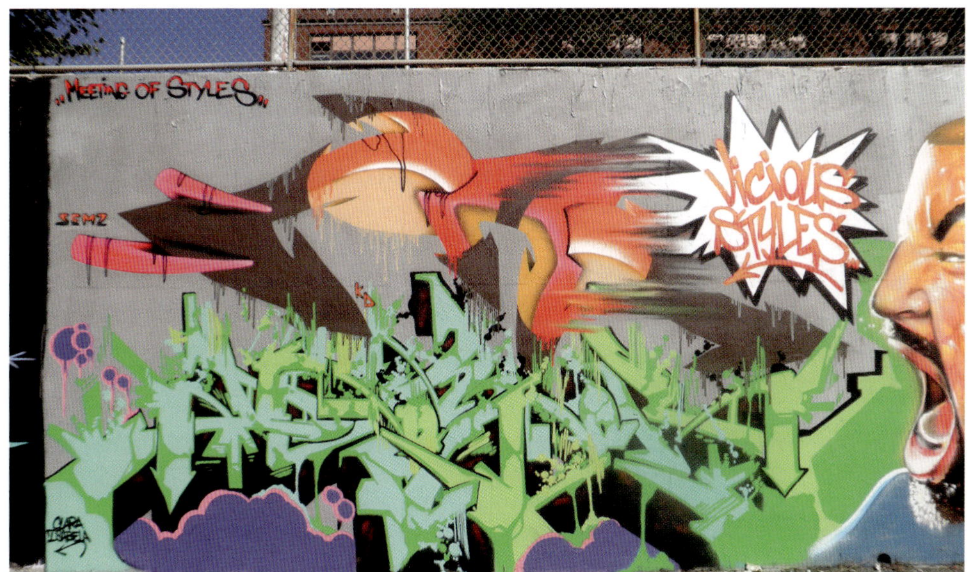

21 **Demer, Col and Kasso** of the Vicious Styles crew executed this piece for 'Meeting of Styles New Jersey' in 2010 – one of more than seventy-five events staged internationally since 2002 by a network of graffiti writers under the 'Meeting of Styles' banner. Crews – groups of writers who work together – have always been an integral part of graffiti and make it a fun, communal practice. Although members have a competitive approach to other crews, writers are often associated with multiple crews.

crew's name and add personalized embellishments [21]. A crew provides a learning environment that fosters cooperation and communal education among writers.

Whether affiliated with a crew or not, a writer's main goal is to be respected and famous within the writing community. Typically writers gain recognition thanks to either copious tags and throw-ups or artistic talent and skilful pieces. Moreover, the more outrageous, dangerous or inaccessible a tag's location, the more respect the writer acquires. The path to success within the writing subculture is neither spontaneous nor arbitrary. Acquiring status is a slow process whereby writers have to convince their peers that their work is both original and noteworthy. Bypassing these strategies, writers can also gain 'cheap fame' if immortalized by the media. Newspaper stories with photographs and television shows or films that immortalize a name can earn a writer status. However, although this sort of instant fame is prized, it is not as respected as working hard to get up – in other words, to diffuse one's name anywhere and everywhere. Shortcuts, in the graffiti world, neither guarantee nor sustain recognition.

Graffiti writers also abide by a set of unwritten rules and ethical codes. The most critical of these rules is that 'going over' or crossing out another writer's work is disrespectful and should generally be avoided unless initiating a writing battle. Going over refers to the partial or complete covering of someone's name with your own. In the graffiti subculture, this gesture is interpreted as aggressive. When writers are acknowledged as kings, it is unlikely that their work will be covered over. If a toy has occupied a prime space with a piece, it will in all probability be covered up by the work of more skilled writers who, through the act of repainting, assert their rule.

Plagiarism or 'biting' refers to stealing or copying another writer's style. Although graffiti writers appropriate images from popular culture, borrowing from each other is theoretically not an option. Since personal style is so highly valued, copying someone else's innovations is viewed in graffiti circles as forgery. While to the untrained eye all graffiti might look similar, in reality each writer has a signature technique. Working within their established pictorial framework, writers produce individual variations through form, design and colour. Most often, if writers bite someone else's style, they reproduce a character, a specific arrangement of letters or a trademark combination of colours made famous by another author. In spite of the fact that biting can be interpreted as a sign of respect or as a way to develop one's own style by reproducing someone else's, it is negatively received on the whole.

For signature graffiti writers, layering or juxtaposing their work on a given wall reveals a dynamic appropriation of terrain and constructs a specific site as socially valued by the subculture. Writers follow rules of etiquette when it comes to the placement of their work. For example, when tagging, if writers paint their name directly above or encircle another writer's tag, they convey their sense of superiority. On the other hand, adding a signature, sometimes with a supportive phrase, next to another writer's piece is a sign of respect – a visual compliment. Whether positive or negative, this sort of visual exchange functions as a site of collective identity negotiation that is meaningful to those initiated in the subculture. The layering and juxtaposing of graffiti at a given location configure that space into an active site of communication.

Urban Painting

During the 1980s and 1990s, the signature style of graffiti writing developed exponentially as it spread internationally as a result of travel, graffiti-laden trains, underground magazines, movies, exhibitions, popular and hip-hop culture, and, eventually, the internet. Today, numerous graffiti scenes thrive worldwide and push both the technical and aesthetic boundaries of graffiti writing. As writing subcultures continue to evolve, they have had to learn to co-exist with other forms of urban art. Post-graffiti art, commonly referred to as 'neo-graffiti', 'urban painting' or simply 'street art', exists as a new term in the graffiti literature to identify a renaissance of illegal, ephemeral public art production. The emergence of post-graffiti art does not imply that signature graffiti writing has been surpassed or left behind, but rather that it flourishes alongside the varied interventions conventionally typified as street art.

In contrast to the easily recognizable letter-based graffiti style, the post-graffiti art movement boasts greater diversity and includes art produced as an evolution of, rebellion against or an addition to the established signature graffiti tradition [22]. A number of street artists began by writing graffiti and, with time, changed their practice to generate a different brand of urban expression for ideas that moved beyond the representation of their names [23]. Some artists, either not satisfied with or explicitly positioned against the ethical, hierarchical and pictorial codes of graffiti writing, resolve to produce a form of public art that stylistically distinguishes itself from signature writing. Others neither start out by writing graffiti nor decide unequivocally to rebel against it, but create art on the street simply through experimentation with different media and contexts of diffusion. The essence

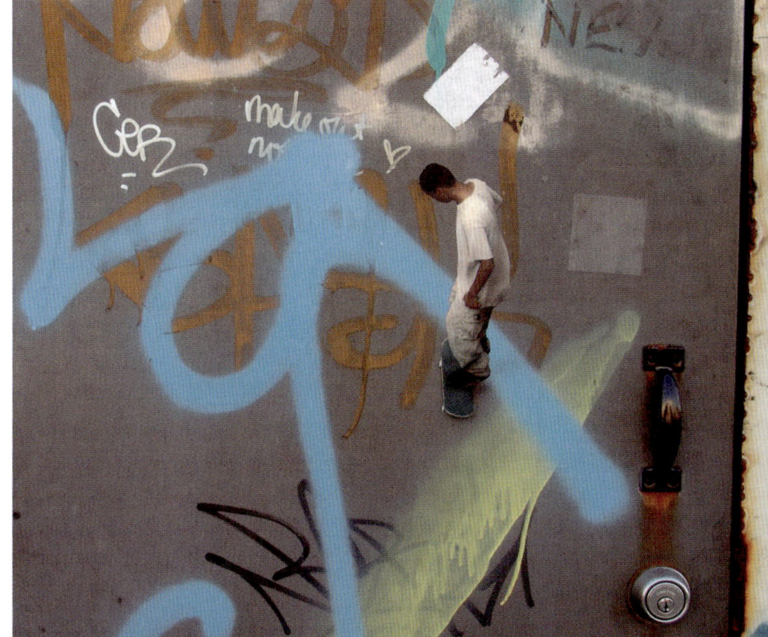

22 **Dan Witz**, *Untitled*, 'Skateboarders Are Graffiti' series, New York City, USA, 2005. The title of this series derives from the idea that skateboarders and graffiti both rely on dissonance and reckless curvilinear lines. Witz uses mixed and digital media to insert lifelike portraits of skaters into graffiti landscapes, thus emphasizing the shared undercurrents of these cultures.

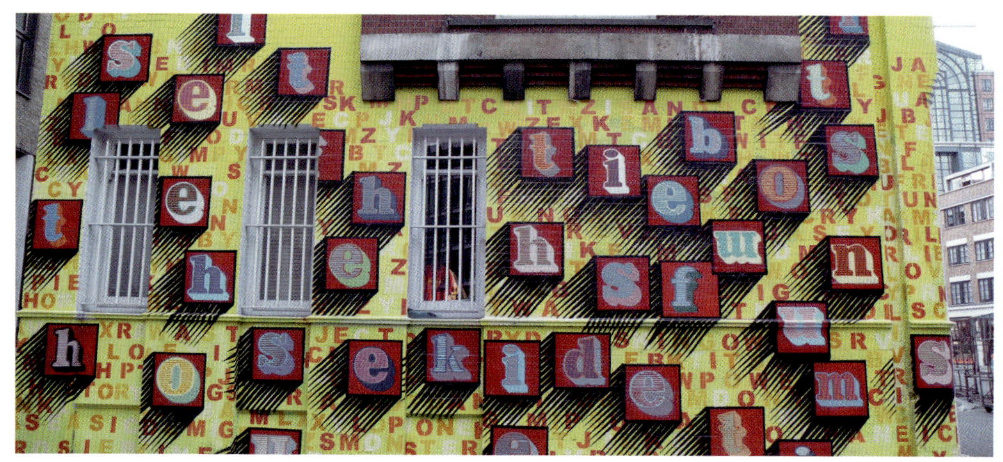

23 **Eine**, *Sell the House, the Kids, the Wife, It's Bonus Time* (detail), London, UK, 2010. Eine has successfully made the transition from signature graffiti writing to street art, using legible, large-scale letters in unique fonts to challenge public space and stimulate debate. The bright colour palette that characterizes his work often masks negative connotations, as shown to great effect by the sardonic phrase spelt out on this wall.

of the post-graffiti movement, thus, and indeed the reason it is referred to as such, derives from the culture of graffiti writing. The addition of the prefix 'post', however, suggests a chronological progression and distancing from the established visual tradition and principles of signature graffiti.

The post-graffiti movement is characterized by wide-ranging stylistic, technical and material innovations, which place less emphasis on lettering with markers and spray-paint and more weight on fashioning varied artistic interventions into the cultural landscape of a city. Unlike signature graffiti, produced predominantly by young men, post-graffiti art is typically disseminated by somewhat older men and a great number of women. Although street artists have fostered communities that are founded on their artistic passion and contempt for laws and institutional conformity, they tend to work autonomously and do not constitute a veritable subculture.

Apart from a more inclusive and less organized membership, the street art movement that exists alongside the signature graffiti movement differs from it mainly in visual terms. In the post-graffiti era, the reliance on letters that characterizes traditional graffiti has been transformed into an exploration of figures, abstraction and symbols. Most notably, street artists exploit more formal art techniques such as stencilling, printmaking and painting to create largely figurative works, which range from realistic portraits [24] to cartoonish characters [25]. Whereas signature graffiti writers bomb cities with their tags, indicating their presence, subcultural status and sometimes crew affiliation, post-graffiti artists are more

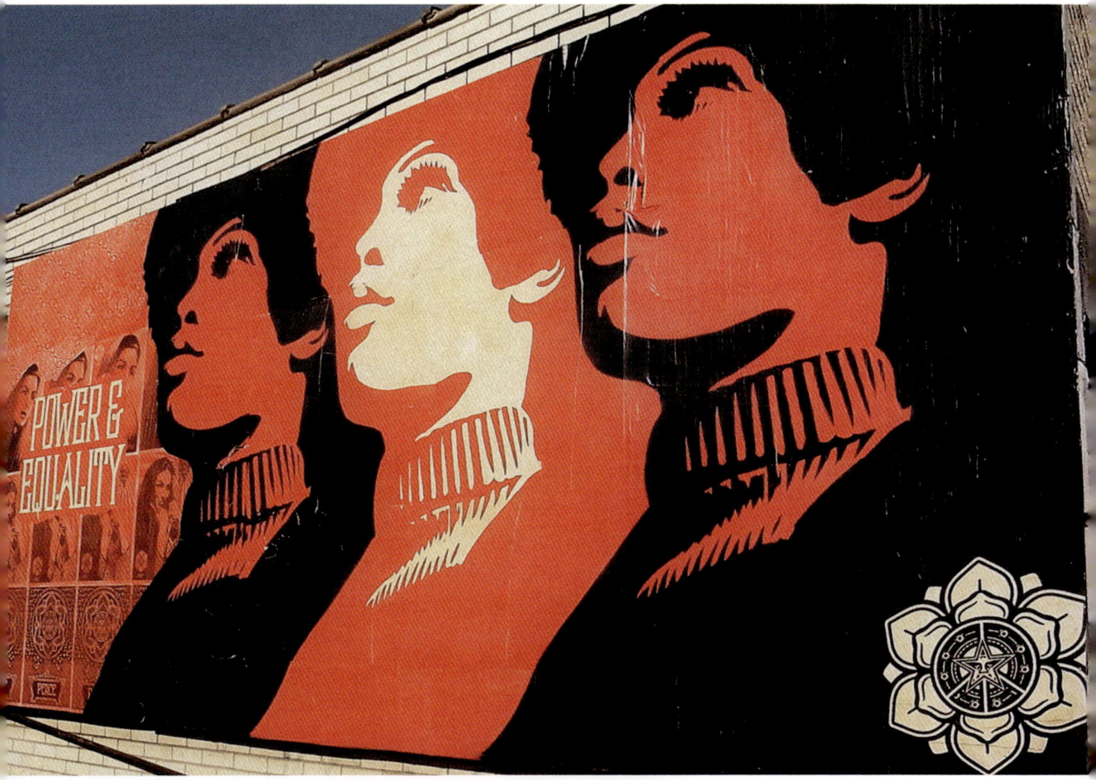

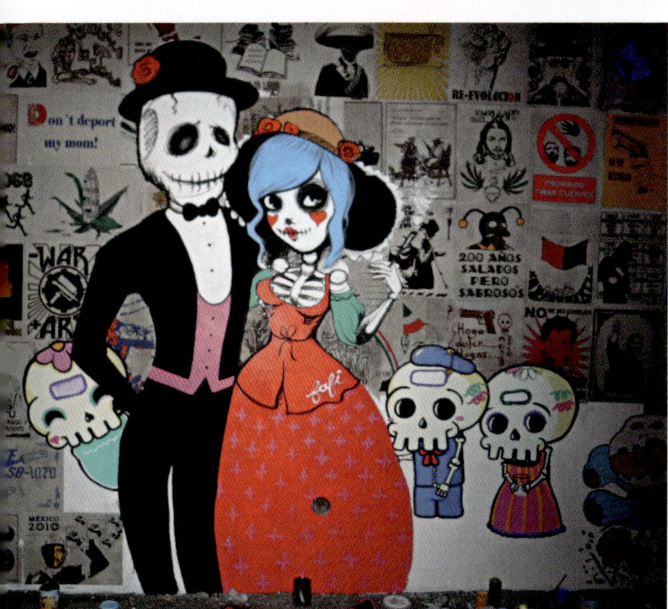

24 (*above*) **Shepard Fairey**, *Power & Equality.* This monumental portrait of Black Panther activist Angela Davis, a key figure in the American civil rights movement, epitomizes Fairey's use of clear and poignant imagery to address social issues and communicate with a wide audience. The artist stays true to his propaganda colour scheme and aesthetic, 'signing' the work with the 'Obey' mandala.

25 (*left*) **Fafi**, *Untitled*, Mexico City, Mexico, 2010. Fafi's characters are instantly recognizable as hers: they form part of the artist's signature. Here, to commemorate the Day of the Dead in Mexico, she tailors her aesthetic to the occasion, infusing it with skull imagery and phoney political posters.

eclectic in their methods of delivering messages through art. The spray can continues to be a key tool in the dissemination of illegal street art, but other media, such as oil and acrylic paint, oil-based chalk, charcoal, stickers, posters, stencils, mosaic tiling and even open-source technologies involving lights and projectors, are also now widely used [8].

Today's street art is just as visible as traditional graffiti in the landscape of a city, but much less visually cryptic. The greatest distinction between graffiti and post-graffiti is the substitution of the letter for the logo or the figurative image. Street artists replicate and subvert the signs and symbols of urban environments, sometimes with an overtly political agenda. As it is typically rendered in accessible locations and is not aimed primarily at other street artists, urban painting is an interventionist tactic that reaches a larger segment of the population than signature graffiti writing. By replacing the stylized written word with the graphically designed image, street artists have expanded the communicative potential of their visual language [26]. While street art practices are diverse and categorized under a multitude of subheadings, stencils, logos and characters tend to be the most prevalent visual and material techniques of urban painting.

26 **Shepard Fairey**, *Duality of Humanity*, c. 2008. Large-scale works displayed on walls accessible to passers-by allow street artists to communicate ideas at street level as opposed to talking down to the citizenry from billboards. This image from the 'Duality of Humanity' exhibition (2008) in San Francisco is a reflection on war and peace through the juxtaposition of symbols of violence and conflict with those of beauty and innocence.

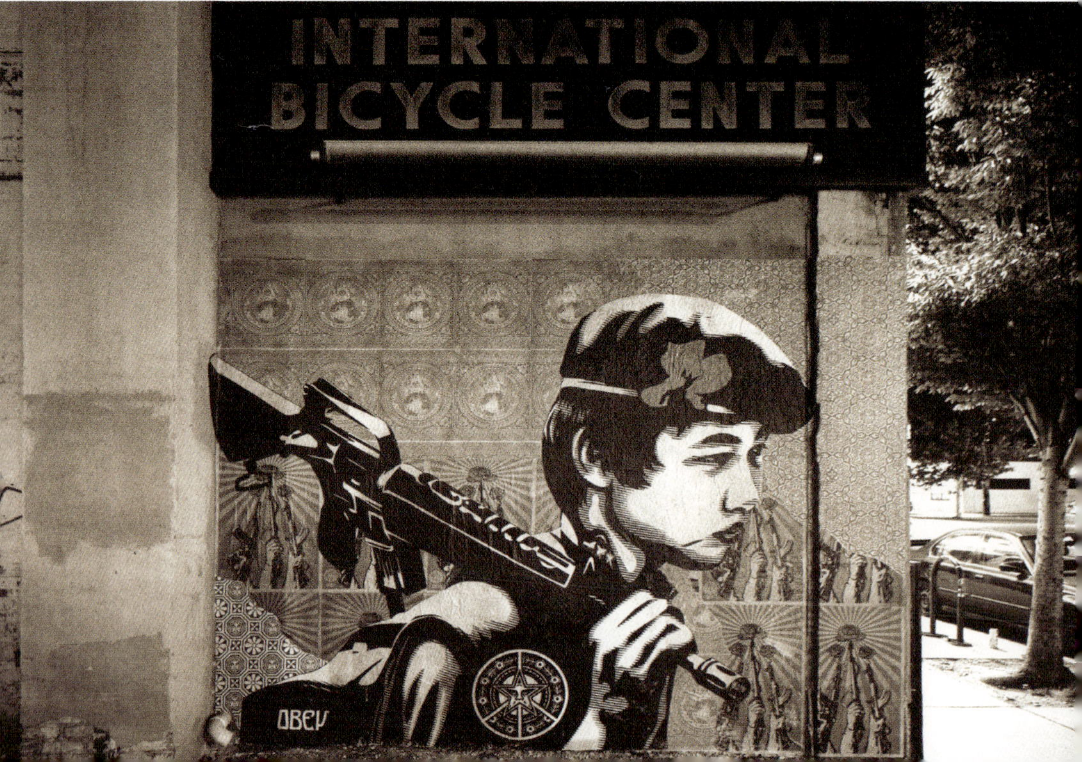

Stencils

Stencilling is one of the most common street art tactics. While a great number of stencil artists are active worldwide, the practices of three prominent street artists comprehensively illustrate the range of this art form: British artist Banksy, Canadian painter Roadsworth and Australian artist Vexta. Each artist's exploration of the stencil as a medium differs from the others' in terms of the sites of diffusion, message and style.

Originally from Bristol, Banksy is revered within the street art community, and more recently within mainstream art circles, as one of the most notoriously witty and palatable contemporary guerrilla artists. His fame has escalated well past his native England to a level many graffiti writers can only dream of. The number, size and clarity of his pieces as well as his humorous and anti-authoritarian style have catapulted him into street art superstardom. His practice is mostly categorized by anti-establishment, anti-war and pro-freedom messages, typically illustrated with figures of rats, policemen, children, monkeys and soldiers [27]. His style is contingent on simplicity: whether he renders a single figure or a narrative scene, the absurdity, clever juxtapositions and meaningfulness of his imagery are immediately apparent. Satire motivates much of

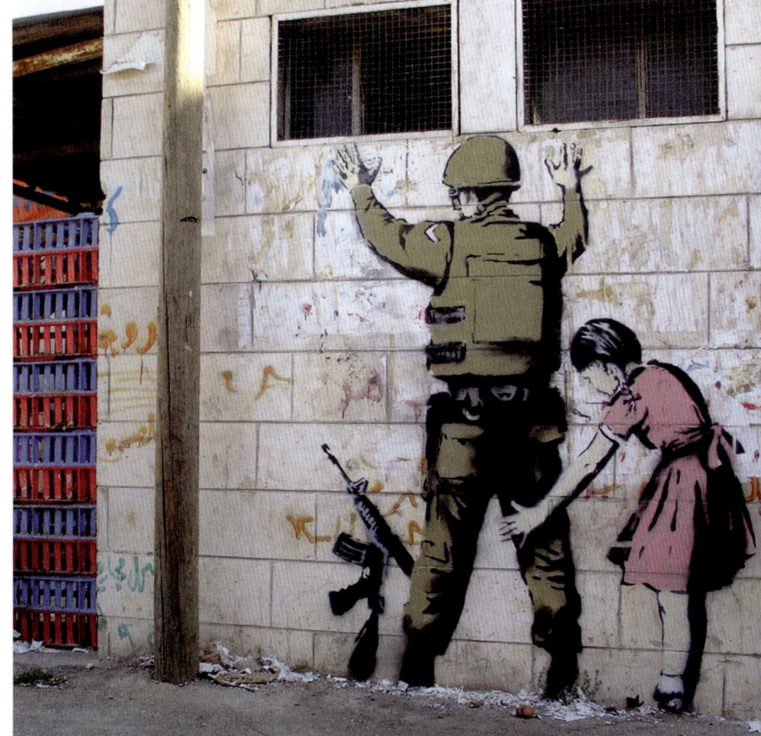

27 **Banksy**, *Untitled*, Israel, 2007. Street stencils are popular both for the ease of reproduction and for their efficacy in conveying impactful or comical ideas. Banksy's subversive, satirical imagery has become synonymous with stencilling as a street art technique. Here, in an improbable role reversal whereby a young girl frisks a soldier, the artist comments on the exaggerated use of power by the military against civilians.

his practice. From the Mona Lisa holding a rocket launcher to a young girl lovingly hugging a bomb, the artist revels in the incongruity of contrasting the innocent – children and animals, for example – with destructive emblems of war. Banksy's imagery represents a trend in street art that is simultaneously tongue-in-cheek and accessible, and deals with contemporary issues [28].

Working with a very different spatial and visual aesthetic, in 2001 Roadsworth initiated a series of stencilled images on the roads of Montreal. The integration of his paintings with official city infrastructure offers a unique opportunity for a dialogue between citizens and the structure of the city. By painting on roads, the artist not only appropriates a non-traditional surface for art diffusion, but also intervenes in a highly structured, functional and systematized formal vocabulary [29]. Roadsworth's practice, uniquely positioned on asphalt, is symptomatic of the sort of jolt that many street artists aim to transmit through their work. The insertion of art into the urban sphere constructs entirely new perceptions of particular locations.

Across the globe, in Melbourne, Australia, Vexta's first street stencil depicted a skeleton with the caption 'this is what a war victim looks like'. While the artist refutes the claim that her work is politically motivated, some of her images reflect the socio-political climate, as demonstrated by the piece

28 **Banksy**, *Untitled*, Detroit, USA, 2010. To impart meaning, street art is often as much about the chosen location as it is about the image: the synthesis of the two generates the significance of the work itself. Displayed on the dilapidated Packard Plant in the Motor City, this work comments on the environmental impact as well as the successes and failures of industrial production.

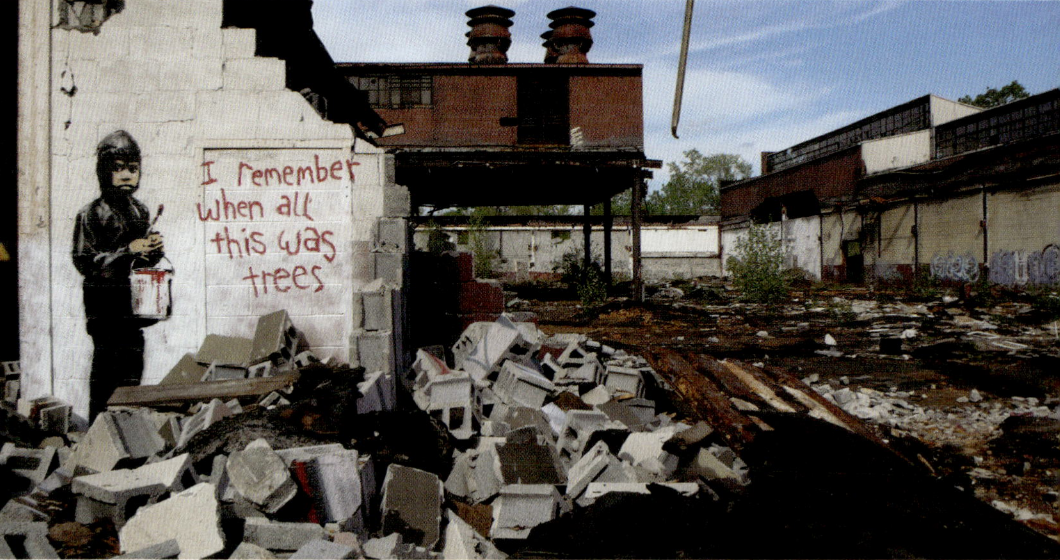

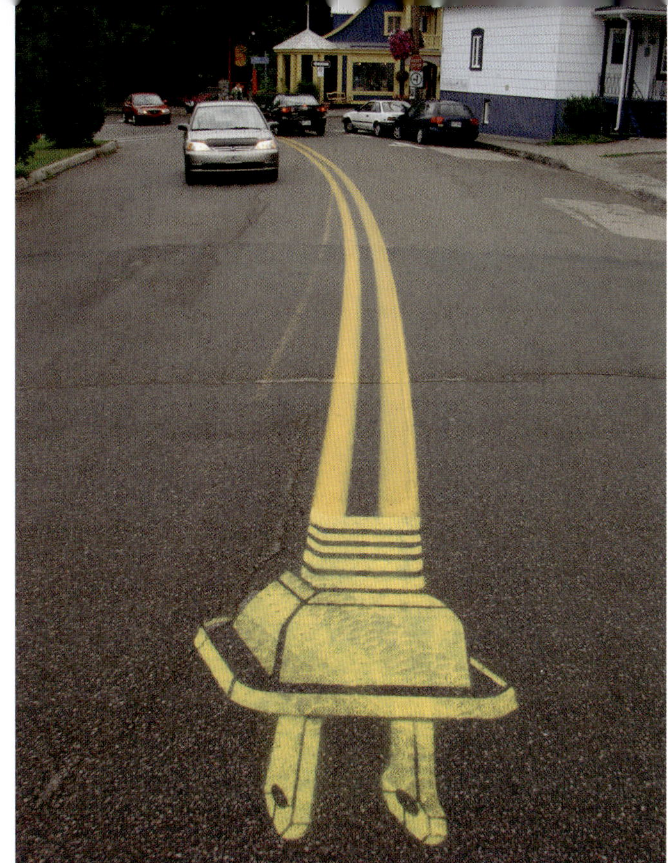

29 (*above*) **Roadsworth**, *Male Plug*, Baie-Saint-Paul, Canada, 2007. A road is an integral constituent in the organization of a city but one that is typically devoid of artistic expression. Roadsworth seamlessly works his stencils into existing road markings to intervene within the regimented urban vocabulary and transform utilitarian symbols into new avenues of meaning.

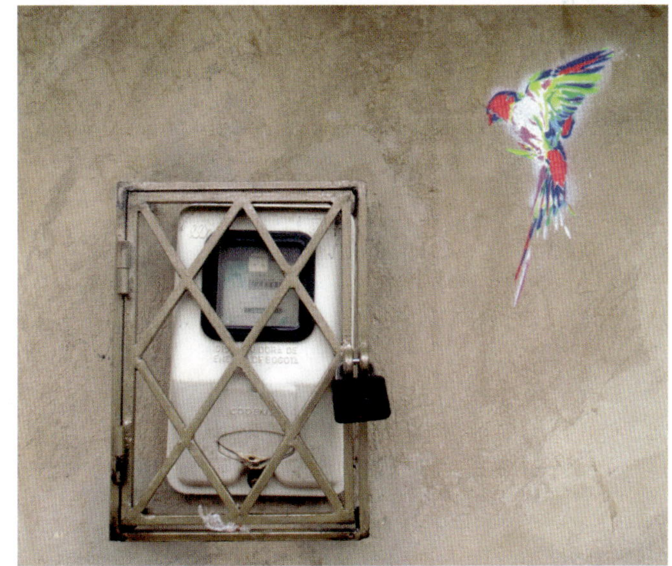

30 (*below*) **Vexta**, *Neon Bird*, Bogotá, Colombia, 2009. Interested in adding colour and playful images to otherwise bland spaces, Vexta breathes life into the urban sphere through non-commercial imagery. This simple image of a radiant bird becomes a symbol of survival in the built environment.

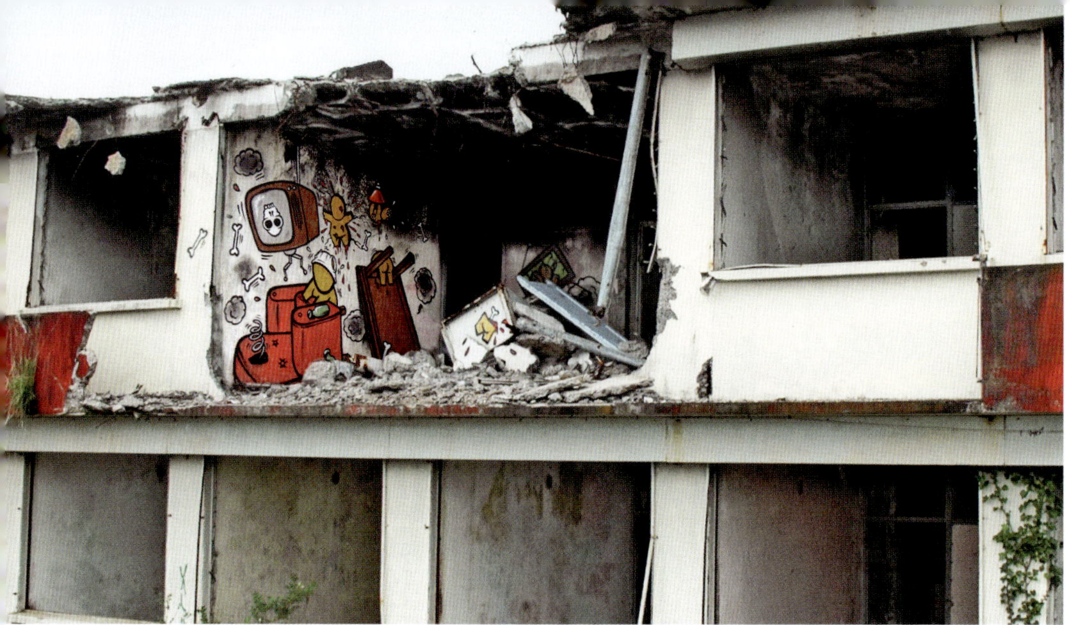

Welcome to Australia (2004) [107]: below the inviting caption, she rendered a large number of armed police officers ready for combat, exposing Australia's strict immigration laws. The overwhelming aim of Vexta's work – according to the artist, to forge a connection with her viewers – relies on her belief that painting on the street is where art can be most influential. Most recently focused on emotionally charged, whimsical portraits, Vexta paints in the tradition of many artists who personalize and poeticize stark places [30].

Stencils, much like signature graffiti writing, require few resources for production: a relatively firm surface, a utility knife and spray-paint. Stencil artists most often utilize cardboard, acetate, metal, wood or plastic laminates to create a durable surface for their designs. Once cut, the stencil can be used repeatedly and in that way operates like a tag. The production of stencil art has become increasingly popular over the past twenty years, mainly because the medium facilitates a premeditated quality to the work as well as rapid dissemination. The greatest difference between stencils and freehand graffiti is, of course, visual. Stencils are also legible and thus able to communicate with a greater number of outsiders than signature graffiti. Stencilled works, even when made by ex-writers whose objective remains to get their names up anywhere and everywhere, legibly tend to represent overtly fun, political or thought-provoking messages.

Logos

While the stylized names of contemporary signature graffiti writers can be considered personal logos, individualized figures and symbols have become a popular practice in street art production. Prominent logo artists include Réunion Islander Jace, Spanish artist Pez and France's Invader. Ex-writers especially favour logos as they both represent the artist by standing for his or her signature and convey an idea. Illegal street logos are materially diverse in that they can be spray-painted, postered, stickered, stencilled or drawn, and unlike corporate logos, an artist's logo, although recognizably his or hers, can vary with each execution. While to an extent graffiti logos advertise the artist, ultimately the goal is not to sell a product, but rather to forge a space in the cityscape for artistic expression.

Jace began writing traditional graffiti in 1984, but in 1992 differentiated his work from that of other writers by devising a character – a logo – as a substitute for his signature. At the risk of alienating himself from the graffiti community, the artist developed his signature 'gouzou' character [31]. Particularly appealing in Jace's practice is his technical experimentation, which includes working with screen-prints, stickers, stamps and wallpaper, as well as his chosen sites. The artist introduces his logo into advertising billboards and into the natural environment, making witty social critiques and simply enlivening a space. Always depicted in mid-action, Jace's logo relays a different message with each execution.

Pez, meaning 'fish' in Spanish, started off tagging during the 1990s in his native Barcelona, and over time formulated a logo to replace his signature. Pez's smiling fish [32], which can be

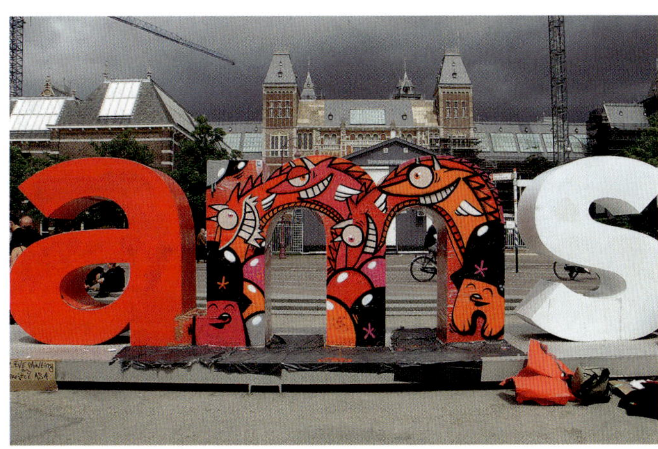

32 **Pez and Flying Fortress**, *Ams Dragons*, Amsterdam, Netherlands, 2010. Just as graffiti writers collaborate on pieces when working with a crew, street artists sometimes join forces to see their logos and characters interact in a shared space. This work, incorporated into the *I Amsterdam* sculpture, combines Pez's fish with the teddy soldier of German artist Flying Fortress.

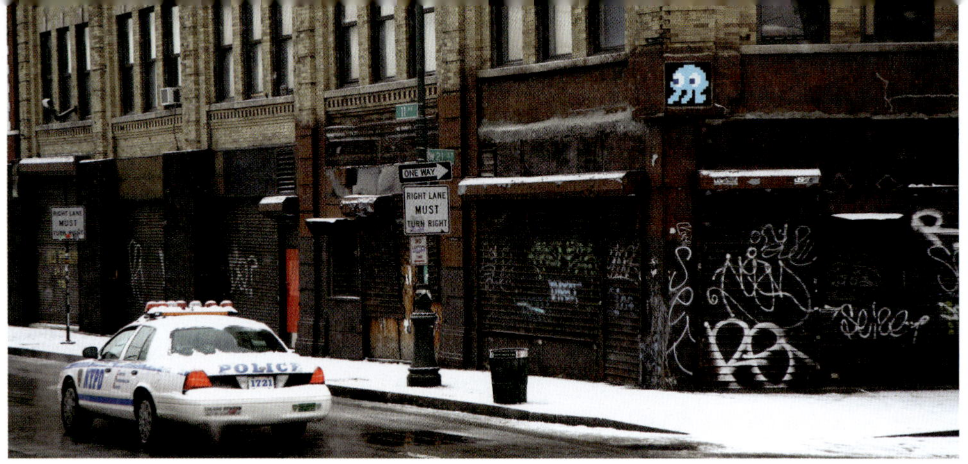

33 **Invader**, *Untitled*, New York City, USA, 2007. Writing graffiti is a competitive practice that motivates writers to outdo each other in terms of location, quantity, size and visibility. Some street artists, such as Invader, also conceptualize their work as urban play. The artist's website functions as a game, whereby locating his logo in photographs that document the invasion of a particular city allows the player to gather points and move on to the next level.

found on city walls worldwide as well as on canvases, T-shirts, stickers and shower curtains, is emblematic of the crossover from a preoccupation with letters (graffiti) to a standardized symbol (post-graffiti). The fish functions to represent the artist visually, as a literal representation of his pseudonym, and symbolically as a logo.

Finally, every one of Space Invader's logo creations, although different, is unmistakably his, since they are cemented rather than painted or pasted. Invader's mosaic interventions pictorially represent the artist's name and simultaneously convey the idea that graffiti and street art invade spaces [33]. Inspired by first-generation arcade games, Invader's pixelated tile characters have sprung up all over the world since 1996. Cataloguing his work through 'invasion guides' and 'invasion maps', available for purchase on his website, the artist retraces the history of a particular invasion, thereby offering a set of potential alternative tourist attractions. In other words, he documents his movements throughout a city through a careful indexing of his work. Conceptualizing his artistic interventions as a game in which every city in the world is a possible target for 'attack', the artist has developed a unique way of initiating a dialogue with city spaces and leaving his mark in the most unexpected places.

Characters

Although a logo could certainly be a character, there are a number of formal, spatial and visual differences between the two. Crisp outlines, a limited colour palette and symbols typify logos. They also tend to be smaller and unsigned. Characters, on the other hand, are visually complex, usually life-size renditions of creatures or personas, often accompanied by legible signatures.

The rendition of characters is well documented in the world of graffiti. Writers have been incorporating cartoon characters into their pieces since the era of subway graffiti in New York. Typically, graffiti characters are either self-created designs used to reflect the writer in some way or appropriated renditions of popular cartoon characters like the Pink Panther or Donald Duck. Writers such as London-based Mode2 and New Yorkers Seen and Lee [47] were instrumental to the development of graffiti writing during the late 1970s and early 1980s through the use of characters in their pieces. The caricatures of urban figures that these writers incorporated into their work further animated the name and generally functioned to make pieces more playful and appealing to the general public.

Street artists, having detached the character from the name, create representations of individuals that are either portraits or imagined creatures. American artist Swoon, French artist Miss Van and the Brazilian duo Os Gêmeos all create characters that function differently from logos. Swoon invites viewers to read her work as an event rather than an object. The artist's diverse, complex portrayals of people, rendered in a variety of media, are intended to reflect the experiences of a city on the fabric of the city itself [34]. Her fragile characters, typically executed in intricate paper cut-outs, represent a material connection to their place of dissemination – an element numerous street artists explore through their practices.

34 **Swoon**, *Temple* and *Alixa and Naima*, Tokyo, Japan, 2009. Swoon's impetus lies in creating art that responds and speaks to the urban sphere in terms of materials and narratives. Her intricate, fragile portraits of family, friends and local characters, executed in paper, linoleum and woodblock prints, decay with time and reflect the immediacy of a city.

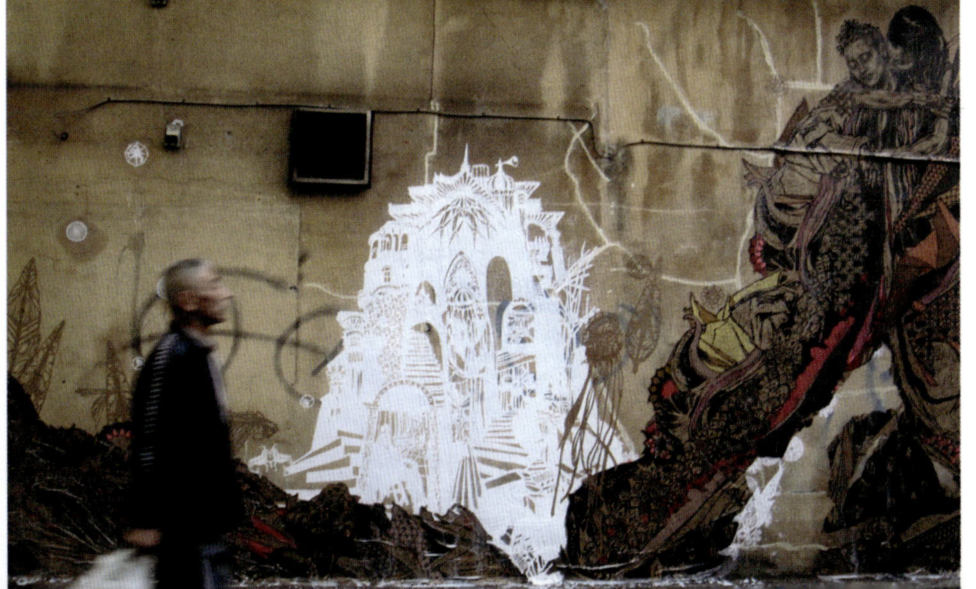

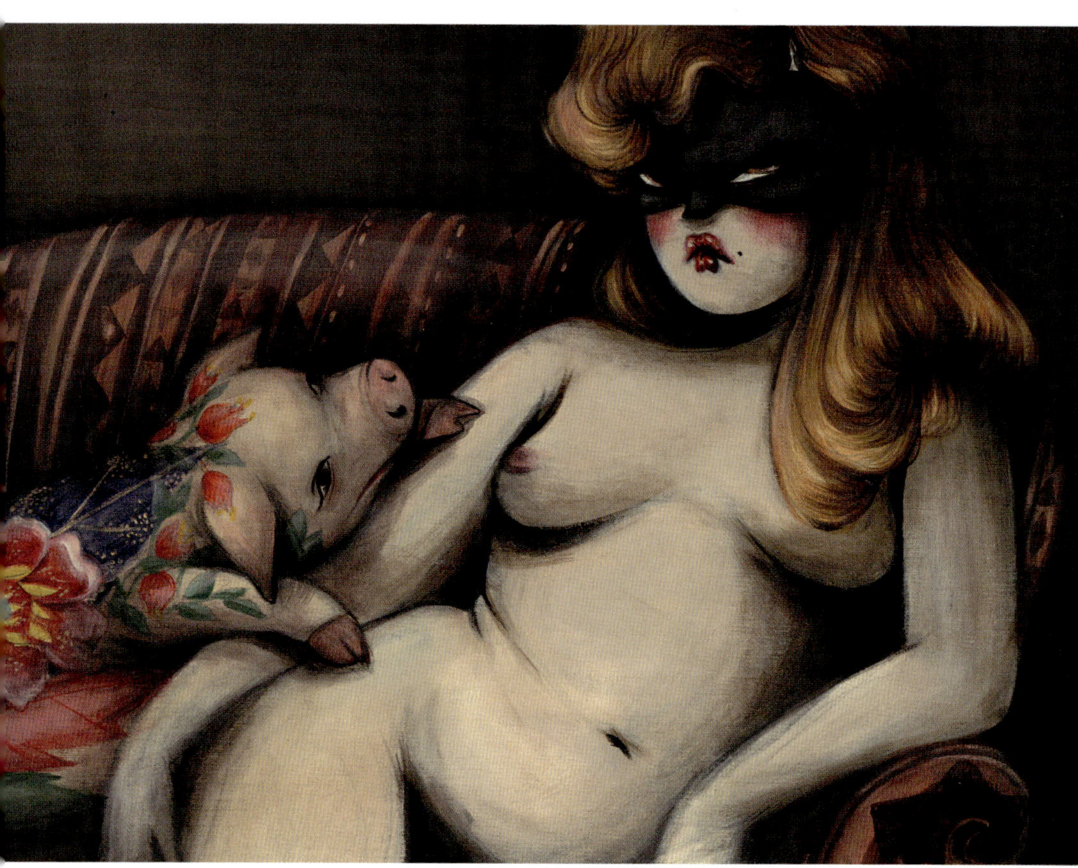

35 **Miss Van**, *Mascaras 8*, 2010.
As with other street artists, Miss
Van's characters have propelled
her from notoriety on the street
to more intimate explorations
on canvas. The 'Mascaras' series,
displayed at the 'Survey Select'
exhibition in San Diego (2010),
reflects the masked intimacy of
the female body, as well as the
animals manifested within.

Working in a dramatically different style, Miss Van began
producing her *poupées* ('dolls') in 1993 in her hometown of
Toulouse [35]. The artist's fanciful characters, often described as
feisty, sexy and glamorous, have since become her trademark and
garnered her international recognition. Although in some ways
representative of the artist herself, the dolls operate as imagined
creatures that aim to inspire fantastical escapes. A great variety
of art on the street is positioned to facilitate this sort of playful
escapism amid the urban noise.

Painting in a traditional graffiti style since 1986, brothers Os
Gêmeos, meaning 'the twins' in Portuguese, are pioneers of the
Brazilian street art scene. Working with latex and spray-paint in
a distorted comic-book style, the pair have greatly influenced,
challenged and redefined the face of street art. Whether
painted on city walls, canvases or made into sculptures, their
characteristically yellow figures act out scenarios inspired by

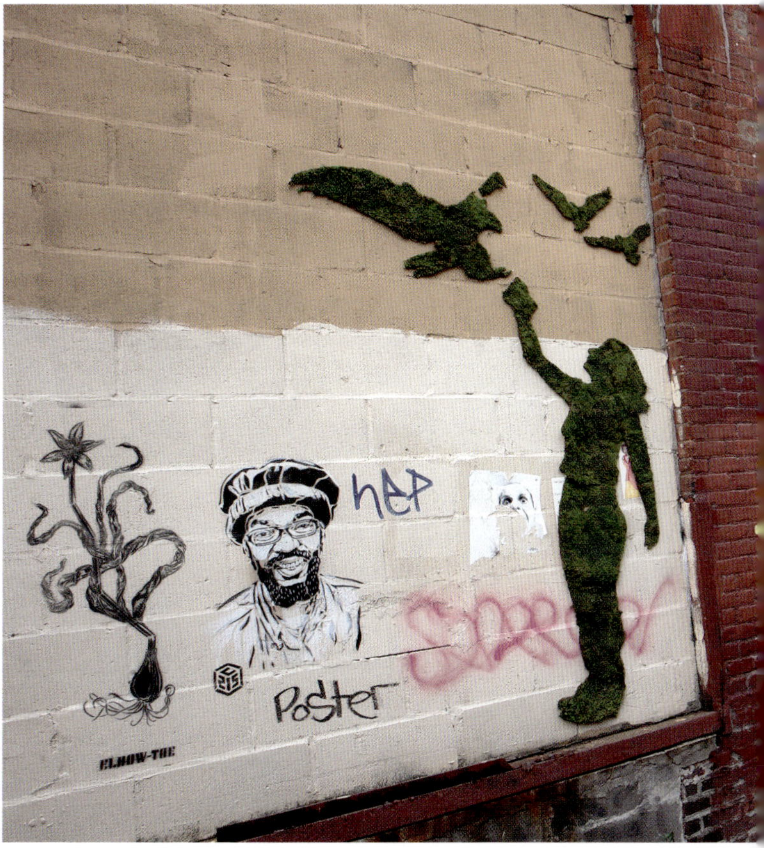

37 (below) **Os Gêmeos**, *The
Youth Are No Longer Young*

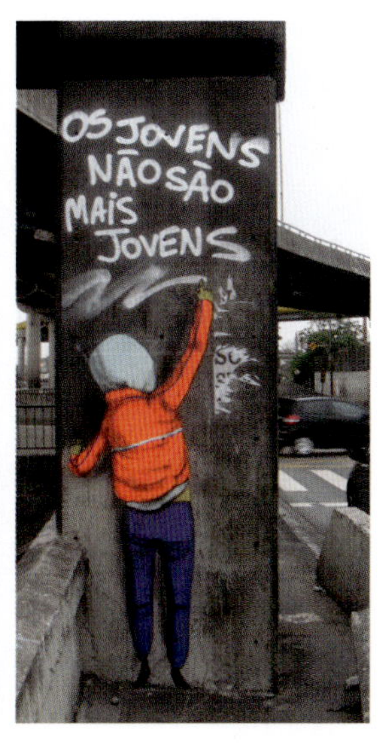

city life [37]. Their characters are representative of a desire to reflect narratives in a way that speaks about the city directly to its inhabitants.

While visually and structurally different, graffiti and post-graffiti practices overlap in a number of ways. Many urban painters may have replaced letterforms with logos, characters and stencils, but the subversive nature of graffiti continues to be reflected in post-graffiti interventions. What has come to be known as street art signals an expansion in the types of graffiti circulated in the urban environment [36]. While contemporary urban painting is undeniably more accepted as an art form, in large part due to its willingness to invite city-dwellers into the conversation, it owes much to the original culture of graffiti writing, which paved the way for the creation of unsanctioned art in the city.

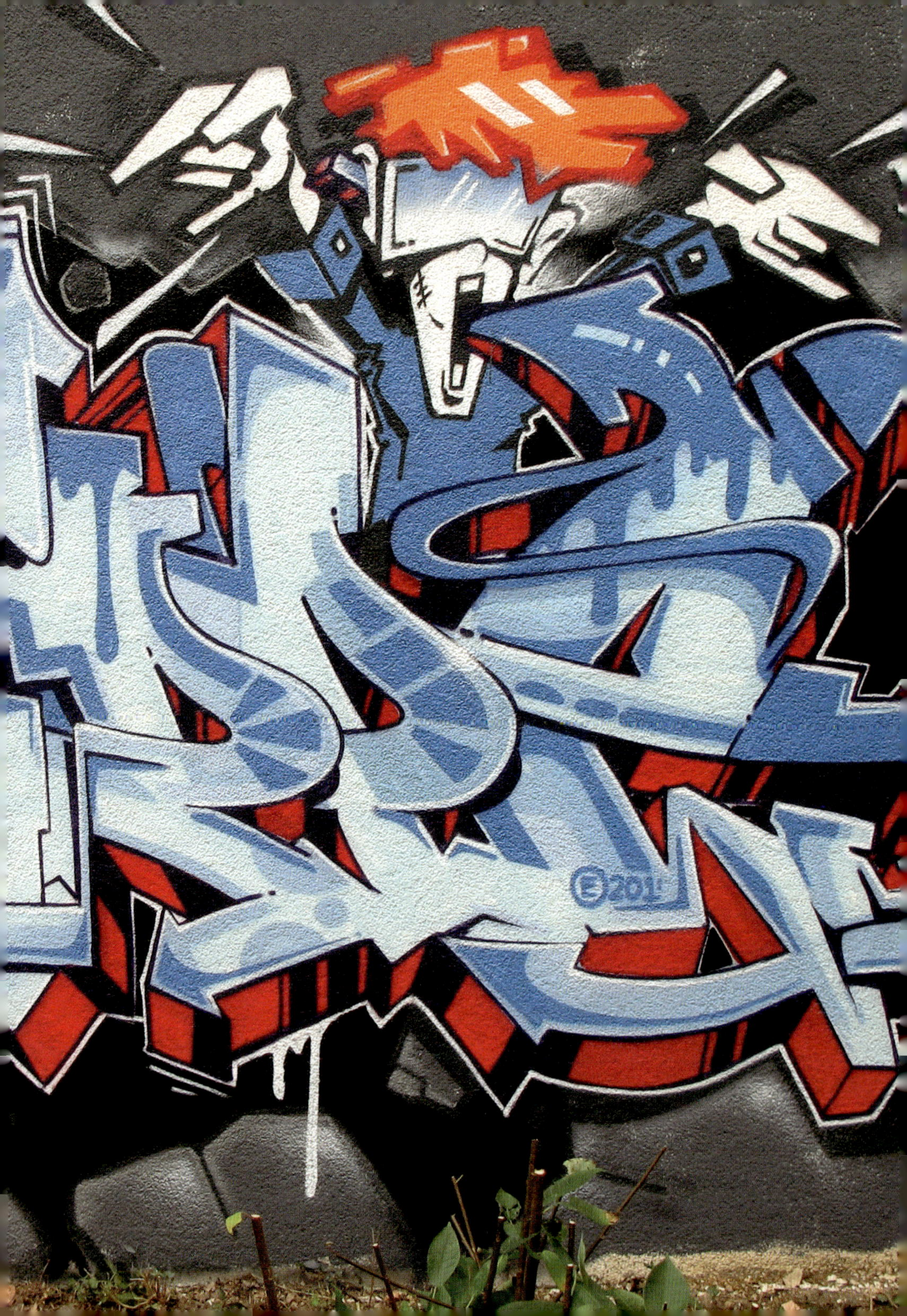

Chapter 2   Graffiti's Genealogy

The practice of writing on walls has had a long and varied history. Writing any form of graffiti, whether it be political, personal or gang-related, responds to a variety of social needs. Expression through words, symbols and figures on city walls can be a reaction against oppression, a mode of protest, an anonymous way to be heard, an act of personal or group empowerment, or a secret language. In one way or another, the graffiti-writing phenomenon that took New York by storm in the 1970s encompasses all these needs.

During its inception in Philadelphia and later in New York, graffiti was largely associated with gangs whose members wrote on walls in order to demarcate their territory. Philadelphia gangs such as Dogtown and The Moon as well as New York gangs such as the Black Spades and Tomahawks had a tradition of writing their gang name in their neighbourhoods so as to represent their presence and control over a particular turf. The connection between graffiti and gangs is unsurprising, especially since writing emerged at a time when gangs dominated many social networks among urban youth. Eventually some non-gang-members, hoping to gain fame and recognition in their neighbourhoods, started writing their names on city walls. These adolescents were not concerned with protecting their territory, but rather with self-expression. Most early writers agree that in many ways graffiti writing became an alternative to gang membership.

Ultimately, while the genealogy of graffiti writing may be linked to several originating influences, it is most significantly connected to the pervasiveness of consumer culture. Adding tags illegally into the official framework of a city relays a number of ideas. First, it implies a desire to belong to a city's visual culture, which is theoretically inclusive but in practical terms exclusive. Second, it disrupts the corporate logic of naming by introducing unsanctioned, unknown names into

38 **Puppet**, *Blue Graffiti With B-boy*, 'Classics' series, Germany, 2009. Puppet has found long-standing success as a graffiti writer over almost three decades on the scene. Although he is best known for signature graffiti pieces such as *Blue Graffiti With B-boy*, like many writers he has also crossed over into street art, depicting twisted, gridlike forms and characters in unexpected places.

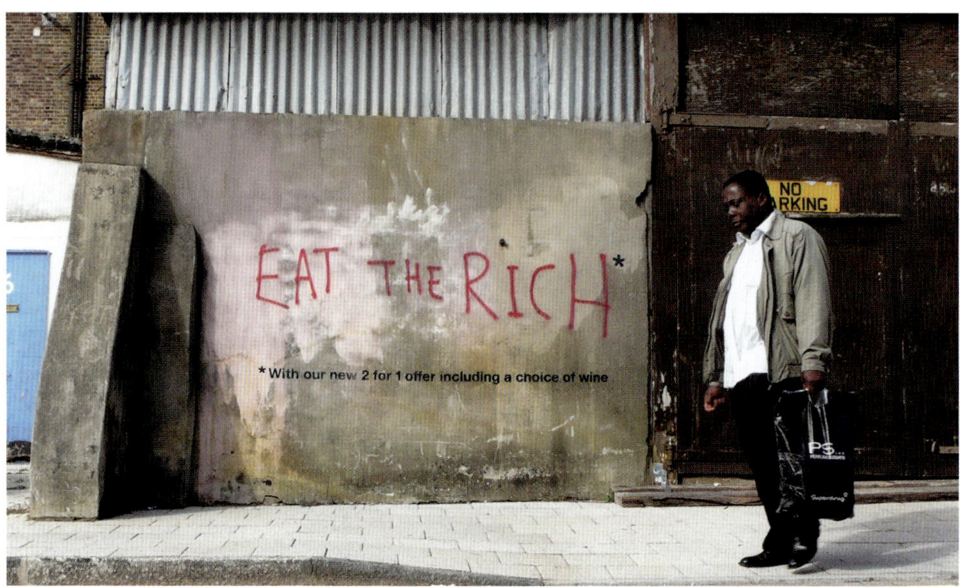

39 **Banksy**, *Untitled*, London, UK, 2009. Whether reconstructing the alphabet through the painting of a name or communicating ideas anonymously, graffiti writers and street artists are in the business of reclaiming public space. Banksy's version of anarchist slogan 'eat the rich', which includes the subtext 'with our new 2 for 1 offer including a choice of wine', comments on the commodification of revolutionary ideals.

the cityscape. To this effect, it uses an existing language as a basis for subversion. Third, it exposes a city's underbelly. The sanctioned names that circulate in the cityscape represent companies that employ thousands of unnamed people. By contrast, unauthorized tags represent real people. Fourth, it reclaims space for a more diverse public, essentially questioning the notion of public space [39].

Writing Style

In both popular and academic studies of signature graffiti, one word continually resurfaces: style. Writers consider style to be paramount because the hierarchies of the graffiti world – whether a writer is respected or not – are evidenced through the details of one's personally stylized tag. For graffiti writers, style equals skill and is inseparable from the name. It can lead either to fame or to irrelevance within the community. The manner in which a name is written, how letters are represented and reshaped, the colours employed, and the flow of the design are all judged when appraising a writer's style.

A writer's subcultural status and identity are rooted in the adherence to and development of the stylistic principles of graffiti writing. Moreover, style is also what defines the conflict between writers and authorities, since graffiti as a style of expression clashes with and disrupts the otherwise controlled

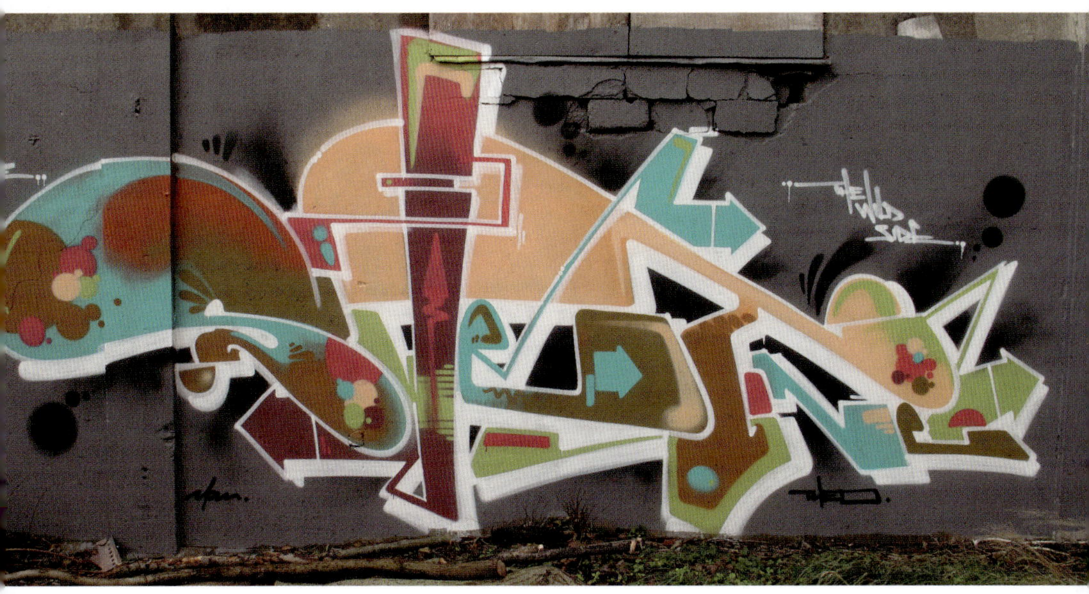

40 **Swet** This piece by Danish writer Swet showcases numerous elements traditionally employed in signature graffiti. Crisp lines are thinly outlined in white, demonstrating can control, while three-dimensional shadows provide the piece with a sense of depth. The use of a broad palette and multiple arrows infuses the work with energy and movement.

aesthetics of the cityscape. Fame, respect and status are driving forces for writers who want to prove themselves on the scene. The common visual language shared by the members of this subculture, which is articulated through style, allows writers to embrace and invert letters to create an alternative culture of signs. Therefore, subcultural status and identity hinge not only on the amount of subcultural participation, but also on the formal quality of that participation – the level of skill displayed in one's style as well as how often one gets up.

Writing graffiti creates a type of secret language that sustains the subculture, while elements of art and design vivify this language. Writers employ various effects, symbols and punctuation to enliven their signatures. In terms of effects, they commonly use fading, pulling, highlighting and overlapping [40]. Fading and shading create areas of light and shadow by blending colours together. Pulling refers to a distortion of the pictorial space by extending or stretching letters to create a sense of movement. Highlighting and overlapping the letters of a piece are effects used both to make the name increasingly effervescent and to add to the cohesive interconnectedness of the lettering style. Writers also blend and connect letterforms, outline their letters, and emphasize them by adding 3D effects. Often letters overlap in a transparent manner and include little pieces that resemble chunks broken off the letterforms, known as bits, cracks for accentuation, as well as a display of glitter or shine to create a shimmering effect. Writers also animate the serifs of their letters by adding flourishes, and create breaking points or small cuts that interrupt the flow of the letters to produce dynamism.

As for symbols, writers customarily paint stars, hearts, crowns, haloes and arrows [41, 42]. The arrow is widely used in wildstyle to shape visually, provide direction and move through the name, while stars, crowns and haloes all imply authority. Although stars are most often decorative, crowns may indicate that writers are considered or consider themselves proficient at their craft. In terms of punctuation, writers are fond of exclamation and quotation marks as well as full stops and underlining: exclamation marks provide the name with a sense of volume or intensity; quotation marks frame and emphasize the name; full stops suggest that with this name the writer has said it all; and underlining the name visually supports it, once again highlighting it.

In addition to these elements, writers are also interested in formal qualities such as line, texture, composition, mass and colour. By modelling the letters – giving them a sense of three-dimensionality – writers allow the piece figuratively to move. In the creation of a piece, writers are not only painting their name in a reformulated alphabet but are also careful to include elements that support, highlight, frame and aestheticize their letters. To this end, backgrounds are painted and characters or symbols, which sometimes stand in for letters, are added.

When critiquing a piece, writers focus on the flow of letters, the design's originality, the method of paint application, the

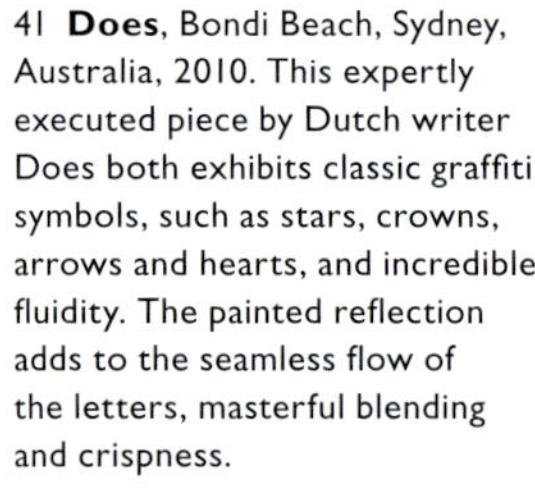

41 **Does**, Bondi Beach, Sydney, Australia, 2010. This expertly executed piece by Dutch writer Does both exhibits classic graffiti symbols, such as stars, crowns, arrows and hearts, and incredible fluidity. The painted reflection adds to the seamless flow of the letters, masterful blending and crispness.

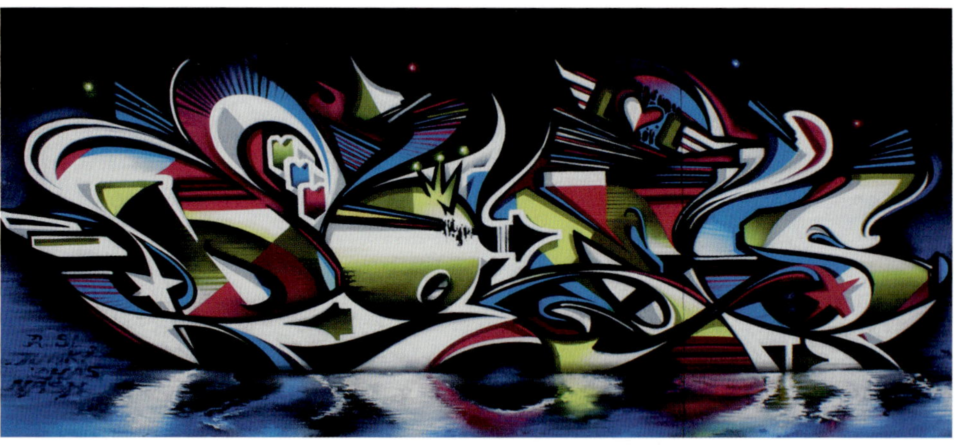

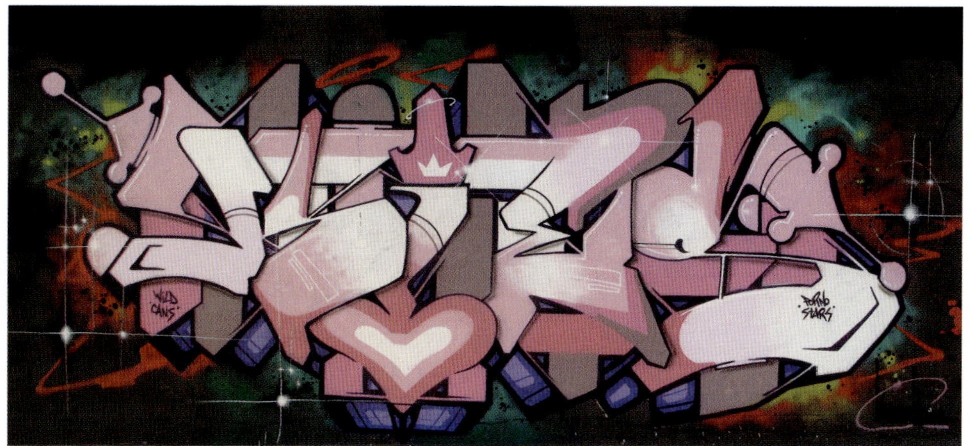

42 **Kies**, Santa Pola, Spain, 2010. This large-scale piece by Spanish artist Kies, painted in an abandoned swimming pool near Alicante, combines strokes of varying widths with traditional graffiti symbols such as arrows, crowns and haloes. Writers typically use arrows to shape the letters of their name visually and provide a sense of movement, while crowns and haloes suggest authority.

rendition of detail and the sharpness of lines. They also pay attention to the use of highlights, shadows, fading and three-dimensionality, and deconstruct all the graphic trimmings. However, the most significant indication of quality lies in the artist's use of letters. The letters create the general design of the work and should ideally represent energy. Whether merged or divided, or a combination of both, the letterforms essentially carry the piece. Stylistically successful letters are neat with drip-less outlines, sharp lines and aesthetically pleasing connections. While drips are typically seen as a sign of inexperience, they are sometimes purposefully incorporated into a piece. Contemporary writers often employ both the 'controlled drip' (letting the paint drip in a stylized manner) and the 'painted drip' (whereby they draw dripping paint to mimic dribble) so as to imply chaos or sloppiness or to assert witty comments on their stylistic ability. Apart from good can control to produce high-quality lines, writers also pay particular attention to how the outline of the letters is filled in. Often the fill accentuates the letterforms; however, at times it is used to challenge the letters, as though the fills stand in visual opposition to the letters themselves.

Beyond style, a critical element of graffiti writing is its appropriation of various aspects of pop culture. Graffiti writing is most obviously inspired by the advertisements, posters, billboards and brand names that bombard the lives of city-dwellers. In short, writers look to the popular culture that shapes their lives, and from it fashion their own culture, subverting the clarity of message to create distorted, illegible brands that represent the individual.

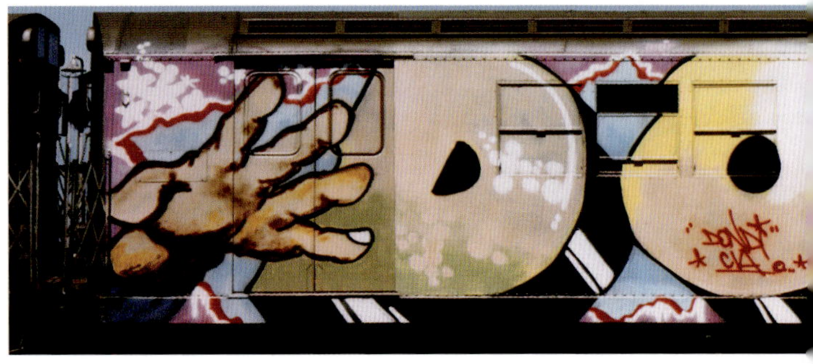

Graffiti's connection with popular culture through icon appropriation suggests integral parallels between the graffiti world and the media-saturated world. Cities are filled with names that promote someone or something. Names, logos and signage of all kinds are naturalized within the cityscape and drive consumer culture. Advertisements in the public arena are in dialogue with each other and with us, the consumers. Names are continually competing for notoriety. Shop names, brand names, corporate names, celebrity names – all have become ubiquitous. For graffiti writers, mixing their names into the fray is a logical extension of the dominant commercial ideology: if your name is recognized in the urban realm, then you are somebody. Illegally adding your name to the public arena, of course, indicates that you are disrupting the system, rebelling against social norms and making your presence felt, albeit subversively.

Graffiti in Motion

During the 1970s in New York, where graffiti gathered the most momentum before spreading to other parts of the country and then the world, the culture of writing flourished on subway trains. Writing on trains responded to every need of the graffiti writer – offering prestige, fame, spontaneity, danger, communication and competition – and was undoubtedly the critical factor in the growth of the subculture. Trains permitted the signature graffiti style to advance both visually and technically by facilitating a communication network between writers from every neighbourhood, as well as giving writers an opportunity to gain 'all-city' fame as their tags literally travelled across the city and were seen by a large audience [45].

Although train graffiti originally referred to the dissemination of tags inside the train cars, the practice promptly evolved into

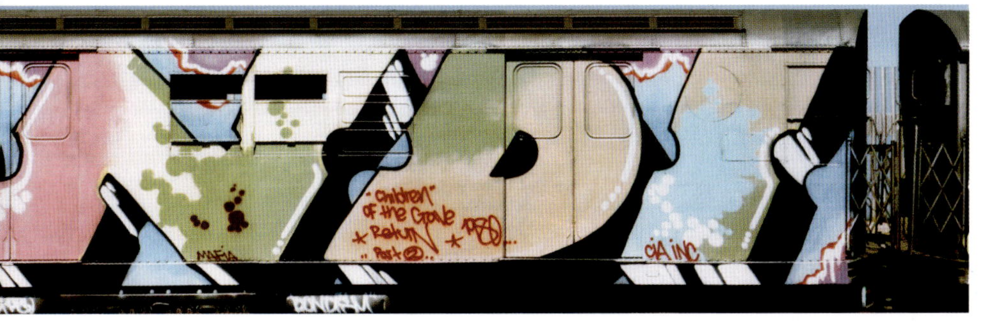

the more dangerous, demanding and visually expressive feat of painting train exteriors. Writers such as Seen, Dondi [43], Tracy168, Iz the Wiz and Lady Pink, among others, were incredibly active in terms of shaping and popularizing the subway writing scene. The risks associated with writing graffiti on subway trains included evading guard dogs and police officers, electrocution and getting hit by moving trains. Getting up on a train thus signalled to others that the writer had executed the work under duress.

The fact that trains are mobile, and thereby dangerous to paint, injected a great deal of excitement and energy into the writing culture and greatly impacted the composition of the works. The graffiti on subway trains was executed with urgency and was designed to be appreciated from a distance and in a flash: the characters were fun, the letters were large and for a long time decipherable, and the colours chosen were bright and bold. The vibrancy and dynamism of graffiti were ideally suited to a surface that is, by nature, in motion. Painting trains was a means of popularizing a tag beyond a neighbourhood and exchanging formal and stylistic ideas with a large number of writers. This mobility ultimately shortened the distance between writers' works in the various boroughs and, in turn, created an informal dialogue through which writers could both share their work and receive feedback.

Over time, pieces on train exteriors became subdivided into four main categories: top-to-bottoms, end-to-ends, whole cars and whole trains. As the name might suggest, top-to-bottom (T-to-B) referred to a piece that covered a subway car from top to bottom, but not the full length of the car. When a piece extended the full length of a car, it was known as an end-to-end (E-to-E) [46, 48]. Unlike T-to-Bs, E-to-Es did not cover the train from top-to-bottom and were usually composed of the signatures of multiple writers linked together, filling the entire space. T-to-Bs and E-to-Es eventually merged [49]; a piece that completely covered the full length and width of a subway car – windows and doors included – was known as a whole car [47]. These massive undertakings were generally executed by a group of writers who shared in the construction of the preliminary design and in obtaining the spray-paint needed for the completion of the piece. When a whole car was painted, the hierarchy between kings and toys was exercised as the less-skilled writers were appointed simply to fill in the backgrounds, while more experienced writers painted the outlines and characters. At times, two subway cars were painted as a single work or 'married couple', or writers managed to paint an entire train from top-to-bottom and end-to-end – the highest possible achievement of subway graffiti writers. Whole car and whole train murals were so impressive, time-consuming, costly (owing to the amount of paint required) and dangerous that they would play a significant role in boosting a writer's or a crew's reputation.

In many ways, trains authenticated the writing culture for both insiders and outsiders, which drew more attention from the authorities. The first anti-graffiti alliance (1971–73), organized by the then-mayor of New York John Lindsay, was unsuccessful. The second attempt at the 'war on graffiti' (1980–83), led by Mayor Edward Koch, however, resulted in a mass transposition of graffiti from subway trains to city walls.

The city's first attempt to eliminate subway graffiti failed primarily because the initial plan focused on repainting graffiti-laden trains. This solution backfired for two important reasons. First, repainting the trains provided graffiti writers with fresh canvases, thus creating new spaces on which they could paint. As writers painted newly clean trains, the scale of their works increased dramatically. The culture's visual and social history had been erased, encouraging new attempts at fame and new competitions for the title of 'king'. Throw-ups became the tool of choice for writers wanting to advance their name, since they are bigger than tags and quicker to execute than pieces.

The second reason that repainting trains backfired was that the task of removing graffiti was often imposed as a sentence on convicted writers. The idea that 'buffing' or chemically removing graffiti could work as a punishment for writers was misplaced: instead of teaching young people a lesson, this clean-up sentence proved to be an excellent opportunity for graffiti

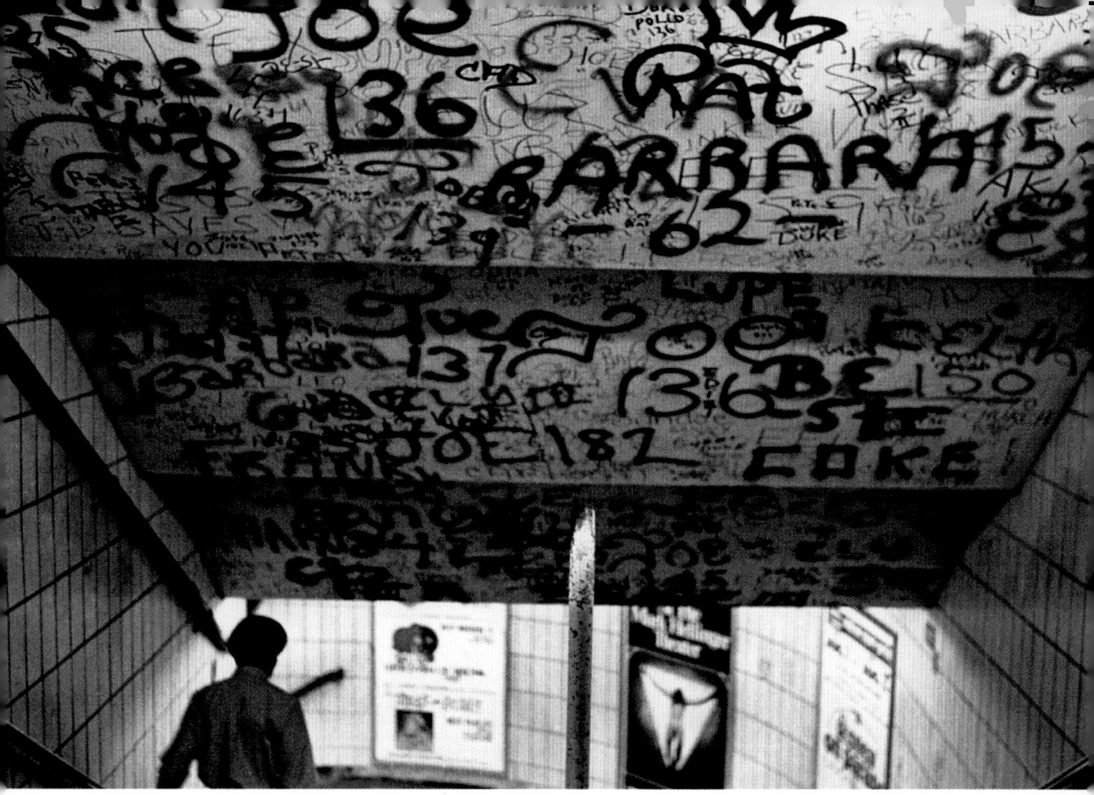

136
BARBARA
62
JOE 182
136
BE 150
COKE

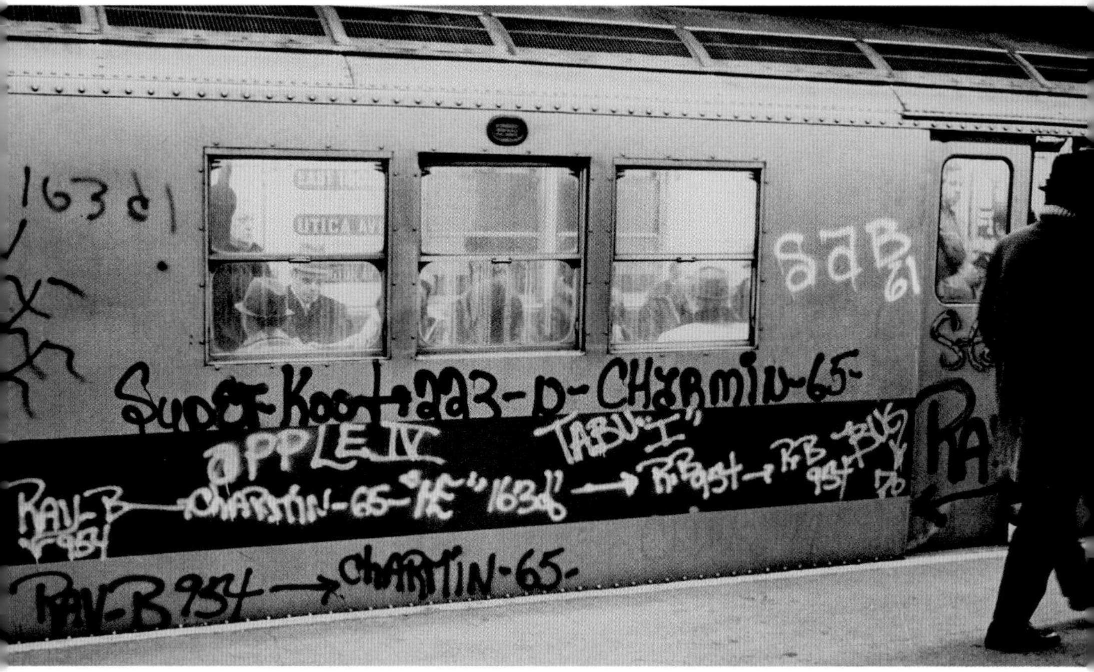

UTICA AV
CHARMIN-65-
APPLE IV
TABU I
RAV-B 954
CHARMIN-65-

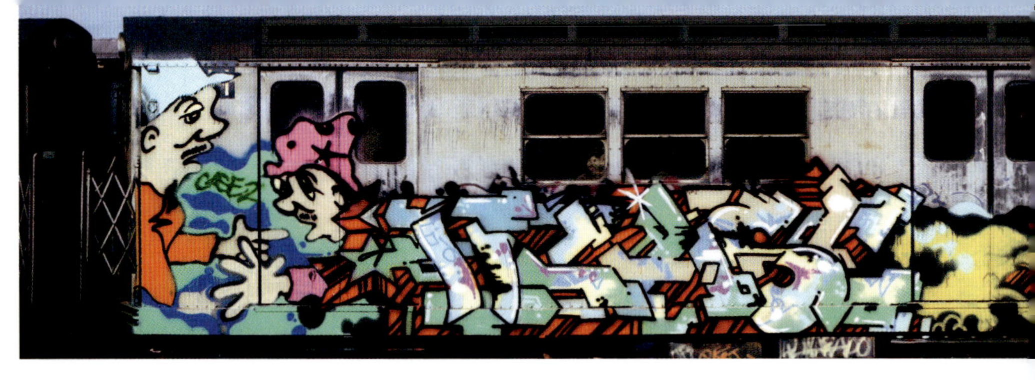

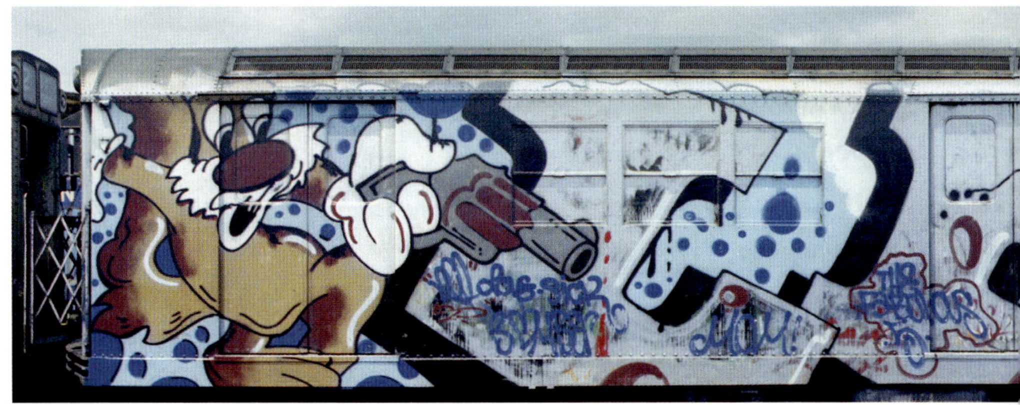

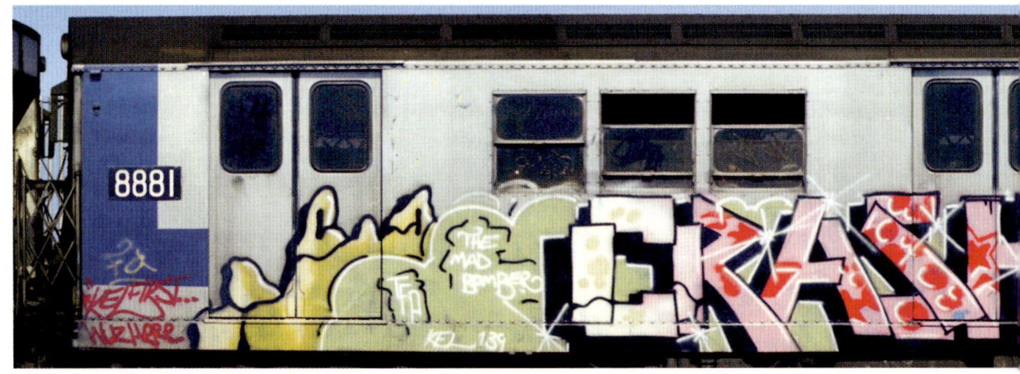

8881

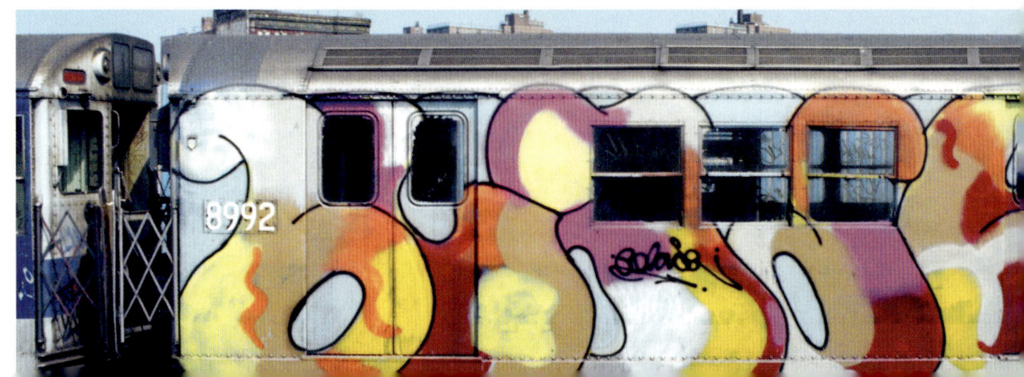

8992

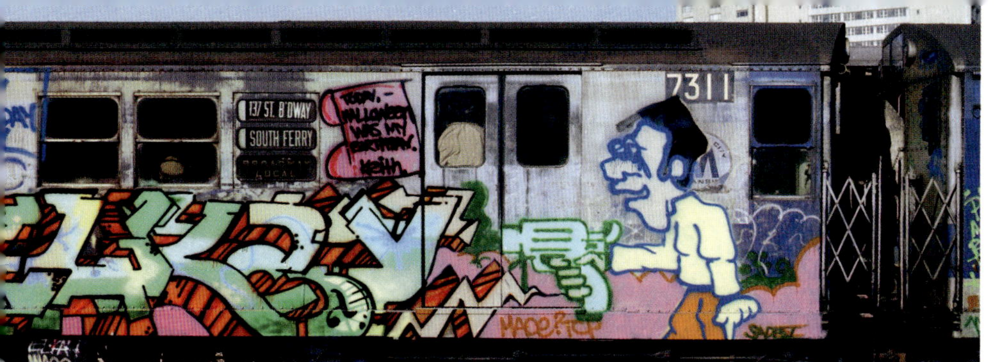
137 ST. B'DWAY
SOUTH FERRY
7311

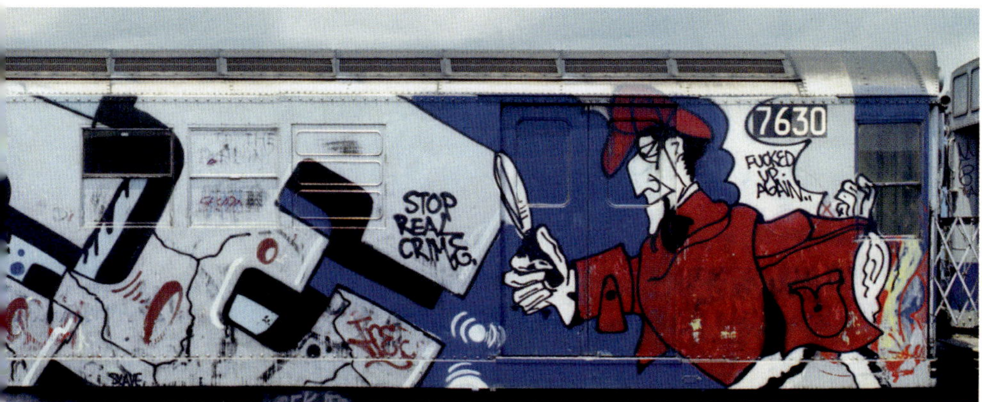
7630
STOP
REAL
CRIME.
FUCKED
UP
AGAIN...

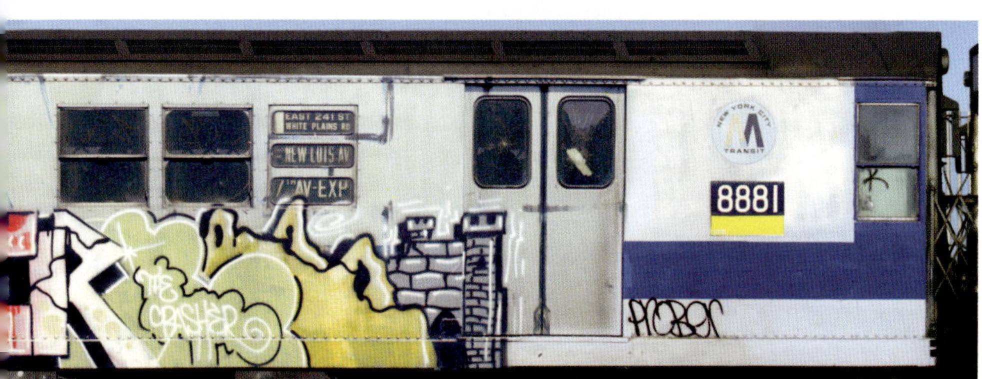
EAST 241 ST
WHITE PLAINS RD
NEW LOTS AV
7TH AV-EXP
NEW YORK CITY
TRANSIT
8881
THE CRASHER

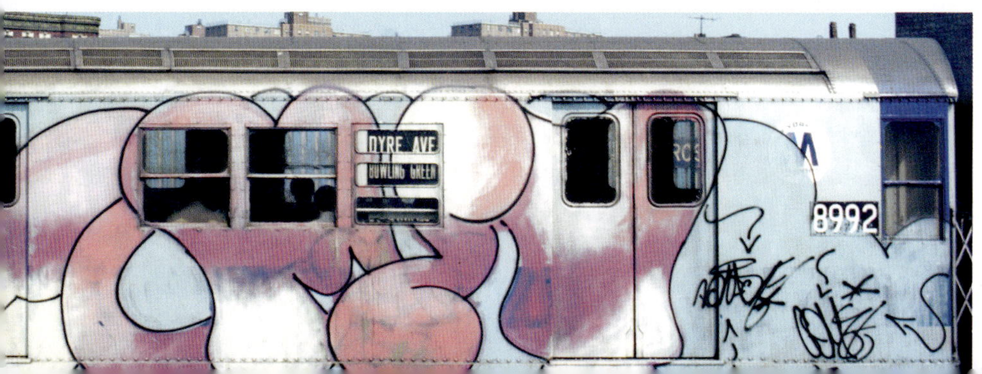
DYRE AVE
BOWLING GREEN
8992

writers to meet others from all over the city and make plans to paint together. In retrospect, the first anti-graffiti alliance failed to obliterate subway graffiti because the manpower, measures employed and sentencing were not altogether severe enough to hinder hundreds of young, determined and resourceful writers.

Koch's war on graffiti characterized writing as a major contributing factor to New York's elevated crime rate and general lack of civic order. The official argument against graffiti rested on the notion that citizens were frightened by it because it represented an unlawful disruption of the urban environment, which encouraged other, more severe crimes. By getting rid of graffiti, the city would emerge as the picture of law and order and raise the morale of New Yorkers. This campaign suggested that the mere appearance of order would improve the quality of life in the city.

The Mayor worked diligently to implement a successful 'clean car programme', which committed subway staff to clean the trains after each run. Although the subway system was actually facing perilous maintenance problems and Koch was eventually forced to admit that graffiti was not one of them, he succeeded in repositioning graffiti not only as a crime, but also as a metaphor for New York's crisis. Eventually, Koch's strategies proved successful, making the second major attempt at getting rid of graffiti one that forever changed the writing culture in New York. The tactics used – guard dogs, video surveillance, a task force and razor fences – worked to deter writers from trains and back onto city walls.

A Necessary Crime

Within the graffiti world there exists a lack of consensus regarding the production of legal pieces. The impetus for the division is straightforward. Some wish to keep graffiti ideologically hidden and inaccessible to mainstream audiences, arguing that its illegality and sense of mystery are empowering and make writing more pleasurable; as a subversive act, graffiti writing must remain illegal. Others, such as Lady Pink and Lee Quinones [47] – both instrumental figures in the New York subway graffiti movement – pushed their art form in new directions and now make a living from it, asserting that graffiti can still be meaningful when disseminated legally and serve as a gateway for successful careers.

The most common starting point for writers is to get up illegally. The risks, thrills and bravado of painting illegally are

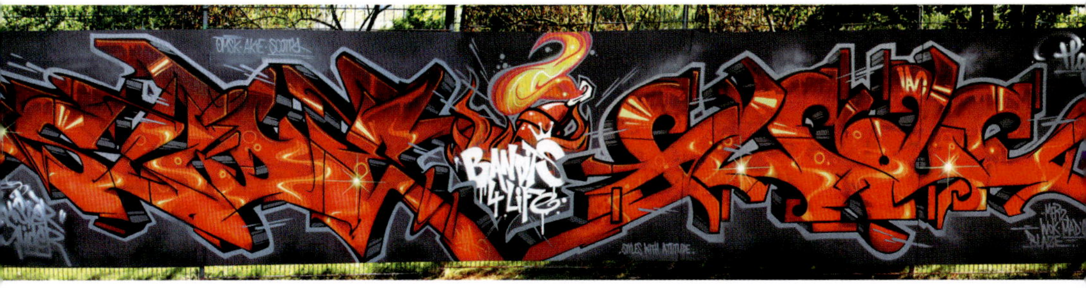

50 **Slider**, *Bandits 4 Life*, Dresden, Germany, 2010

addictive and part of the energy expressed through writing. Being part of a world that functions like a secret society – an alternative community through which one can create a different identity in the public sphere – is enticing. Most writers value the subcultural authenticity, fidelity and control that illegal writing facilitates. Working autonomously to their own schedules and on their own terms, writers have the freedom to paint whatever they want, wherever they want. The fact that their art form is indecipherable and against the law affords writers a unique place in the cityscape and allows them to identify with an exclusive culture that thrives in the face of opposition. For many, writing legally strips away the very reason for doing graffiti.

The graffiti subculture is a part of society, but also stands apart. In terms of its place of dissemination, its visual language and its subsistence as an alternative culture, it is firmly tied to mainstream cultures. The subculture necessitates these ties in order to position and define itself beyond the parameters of the dominant order. Graffiti is at once physically accessible and functionally inaccessible to outsiders [50]. The fact that the general public makes contact with graffiti but has no direct path of entry into its meaning and purpose gives writers a sense of power. By creating a world of their own, neither easily penetrated by non-writers nor intended to be understood, writers can exclude mainstream audiences from accessing their work, thus reinforcing the vitality of their world. The knowledge that most people cannot read their graffiti positions writers as members of an exclusive scene – a scene that is visible to everyone but insignificant to most. Through the construct of the subculture, writers participate in an alternative way of experiencing the city. The graffiti subculture equips writers with structure and collegial encouragement, but also offers roles that foster discipline and models of behaviour.

'Hip-Hop Graffiti'

The commonly acknowledged fundamental elements of hip-hop culture evolved on street corners in the form of recreational, creative and good-natured 'battles'. Battles in hip-hop denote lyrical (between MCs), musical (between DJs) or physical (between breakdancers) competitions. Because hip-hop culture did not require the purchase of expensive instruments or sound systems as prerequisites for participation, it was accessible to urban youth. Aside from energy and talent, a ghetto blaster, turntables and a cardboard box – used as a makeshift dance floor – were the building blocks of hip-hop in the 1970s.

That a youth movement would be fuelled by modes of expression accessible and often driven or made popular by music, dance and fashion seems relatively straightforward, but what is graffiti's role in this? Why is writing so often coupled with the culture of hip-hop? There were several important factors at play: historically, both cultures blossomed at the same time in New York; socially, this art form has been linked with territorial gang graffiti, and gangs, in turn, are associated with the South Bronx and the birthplace of hip-hop; stylistically, graffiti visually renders a similar energy and impulsiveness as hip-hop and it can be argued that writers 'battle' with spray-paint; ethnically, it has been incorrectly stipulated that adherents of both cultures were primarily black and Hispanic, although the writing culture was always ethnically diverse; symbolically, each cultural form can be interpreted as a tool for identity negotiation and self-assertion; and commercially, graffiti fitted perfectly into the marketing of hip-hop culture, which came to define the urban youth experience in New York.

In the 1980s, writing became an international movement partly through its marketed connection to hip-hop. In reality, however, the link between hip-hop culture and the culture of graffiti writing is largely symbolic. The elements of hip-hop all originated in a localized setting, and graffiti writers were at best tangentially involved with the emerging scene. Of course, some graffiti writers were involved in both hip-hop and writing, but, generally speaking, the idea of 'hip-hop graffiti', while a commonly used phrase, is founded on a fabricated reality. The commonalities between these cultures have been defended in the literature, but the simplistic link between graffiti and hip-hop is often taken for granted, thus negating the distinctive nature of each.

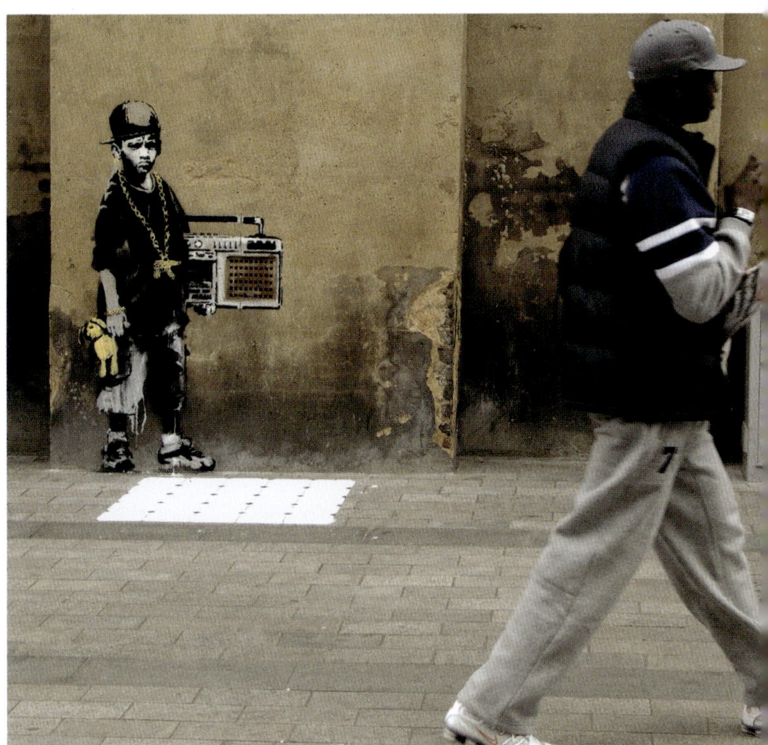

51 **Banksy**, *Untitled*, London, UK, 2009. While historically linked to hip-hop culture, graffiti writing has its own distinct history, language and traditions. In this rendition of a young b-boy, Banksy fashions an existing grate into an old-school boom-box. Outfitted in conventional hip-hop wear, complete with bling, the boy clutches his teddy bear, suggesting his naive emulation of a cultural attitude and style.

As hip-hop culture gained popularity, especially through rap music, it required a visual form of representation that was as new, hip and 'street' as rap itself. Graffiti was the logical choice. Hip-hop already embodied a visual culture represented through fashion, album covers and posters. However, graffiti's illegality (conveying a sense of danger), its indecipherable aesthetic (suggesting a secret society), its reliance on the name (signifying self-empowerment) and its roots (most notoriously linked to New York) could aptly reflect rap's energy. Moreover, much like hip-hop, graffiti writing was also associated with disenfranchised and rebellious youth. All the key elements were in place to make a smooth if not predictable connection between graffiti writing and hip-hop. Both cultures were understood as alternatives to gang membership, both required few instruments and promoted self-expression, and both were created for youth by youth as a way to socialize while engaging in creative endeavours.

Ironically, while hip-hop theorists argue that hip-hop culture has been co-opted and exploited by mainstream multinational companies to sell products, hip-hop has used the culture of graffiti writing in a similar way. Exploited to sell numerous hip-hop products, from CDs to T-shirts, writing continues to be associated with hip-hop, especially as the cultures spread outside the USA and were packaged as one entity.

Forays into Galleries

During the late 1970s and early 1980s, attempts were made by the New York arts community to decriminalize graffiti by framing it as art. These efforts involved graffiti writers and gallery curators, as well as high-end art dealers and gallery owners, who worked to validate graffiti writing as an art form. For commercial gallery owners, bringing graffiti inside was predominantly an exercise in capitalizing on a new art trend. Graffiti first found its way into galleries on a small scale during the early 1970s. During the 1980s, however, and specifically between 1980 and 1983, the work of graffiti writers was promoted as an exciting new trend in the art world in New York. Over a short period of time graffiti was transfigured as a canvassed commodity, responding to the demand of commercial galleries. This process of commodification began with the advent of an organization called United Graffiti Artists (UGA).

Formed in 1972 by Hugo Martinez, a City College sociology student, UGA's mandate was both to aid writers in developing their creativity in a decriminalized setting and to redirect graffiti writing as a legal and profitable enterprise. Martinez's primary goal was for the mass media to reinterpret graffiti as art. He encouraged writers to produce graffiti on canvases so that he could popularize a new art movement by bringing graffiti into galleries. In the end, this organization did not include enough members to provoke any large-scale changes.

After frequenting UGA's exhibitions, Jack Pelsinger, another graffiti aficionado, decided to start an alternative graffiti organization. The Nation of Graffiti Artists, or NOGA, was founded in 1974 and functioned as a type of community arts workshop for all those interested in writing graffiti. While Pelsinger was instrumental in giving writers a place to meet and share knowledge with younger generations, the organization did not produce any significant exhibitions. Both UGA and NOGA formed with a view to empowering writers and redirecting their practices into more conventional forums.

Following the first gallery show by UGA members at SoHo's Razor Gallery in 1973, a number of small-scale graffiti exhibitions were organized as graffiti production on subway trains increased. Early graffiti shows offered writers the opportunity to meet, collaborate and realize the potential of their work and the strength of their community. The experience of painting together in legal spaces was vital in allowing writers to see themselves as artists.

During the early 1980s, graffiti was frequently exhibited at the Fun Gallery and Fashion Moda. The Fun Gallery, owned by Patti Astor and Bill Stelling, opened in 1981 and was the first art gallery in the East Village as well as the first gallery space to give solo exhibitions to graffiti writers. Fashion Moda, founded in 1978 by Stefan Eins, became an informal gathering place for many South Bronx writers. Eins encouraged writers both to spray-paint directly onto the gallery walls and to experiment with canvas.

The approach of these gallery owners made writers more comfortable with the idea of showcasing their work in a more formal and permanent way. In fact, their galleries functioned as links, which connected the street with the art world. The shows hosted by these galleries allowed graffiti writers to experiment with their visual tradition much as they had on the streets, without restriction.

In June 1980, Fashion Moda collaborated with the artists' collective Colab to produce the 'Times Square Show'. This exhibition was held in a dilapidated former massage parlour near Manhattan's porn district and included an amalgam of punk art, graffiti and erotica. While the 'Times Square Show' is habitually considered as the official introduction of graffiti to the high art world, it was not purely a graffiti show, nor was it held in a formal gallery space. This month-long exhibition of politically and socially conscious art included a few works by graffiti writers, but essentially the show featured a mix of conceptual work, neo-expressionism and all manner of revolutionary and anti-establishment practices.

The 'New York/New Wave' show at the PS1 gallery – now MoMA PS1, an affiliate of the Museum of Modern Art – subsequently opened in February 1981. Curated by Diego Cortez, 'New York/New Wave' included graffiti works on canvas and was critical in setting the stage for the solidification of graffiti as art. Pairing the work of writers with that of artists such as Robert Mapplethorpe and Andy Warhol was a telling and ambitious framing.

This exhibition was followed in late 1983 by the 'Post-Graffiti' show at the Sidney Janis Gallery. 'Post-Graffiti' constructed graffiti as art partially by way of name. The inclusion of the word 'post' signified that in the gallery graffiti had undergone a transformation into a movement worthy of art world attention. The name signalled the conversion of graffiti from illegal urban iconography to legal canvassed art. The term 'graffiti art' allowed for superficial groupings of many different styles into one category. Often what was labelled graffiti art in the 1980s was not graffiti writing. In the 'Post-Graffiti' exhibition, this was manifested with the inclusion of artists such as Jean-Michel Basquiat and Kenny Scharf.

In exhibitions such as 'Post-Graffiti', writers signed their canvas paintings with their tags but labels bearing their real names were also included next to each work. The greatest difference between street and canvassed graffiti was the disappearance of the writer's name as the central object of contemplation. The pieces were not traditional depictions of signatures with accompanying imagery: instead they were images with accompanying signatures. Just as many writers argue that graffiti displayed on canvas is no longer graffiti both literally and symbolically, writing one's name as the focal point of a canvassed artwork loses all meaning. No longer a transformation of the urban environment, nor a subversive addition to the cultural landscape of signage, a writer's name on canvas simply does not have the same socio-cultural, personal or political weight. Because the purpose of the work is different on canvas, the central theme of graffiti writing disappears. Whereas on the street a writer's name is a form of self-affirmation and works to identify the writer on the scene, in the gallery the name has a different function. Instead of communicating with a network of initiates in the most unlikely places, it represents a mysterious culture to a collection of outsiders.

Although 'Post-Graffiti' aided in popularizing graffiti within a different context and in introducing writers to one another, it did not appreciate graffiti for its inherent worth. Presented as just another painting style without analysis of its subcultural affiliations and illegal status, graffiti displayed on canvas lost the sense of movement, immediacy and energy that it held in the public realm. The very rawness that attracted New York's high art scene to graffiti was not transferable to a gallery context.

The new conglomeration of small, independent Lower East Side galleries reinforced graffiti's newfound identity as a vibrant, novel form of visual expression. The galleries that

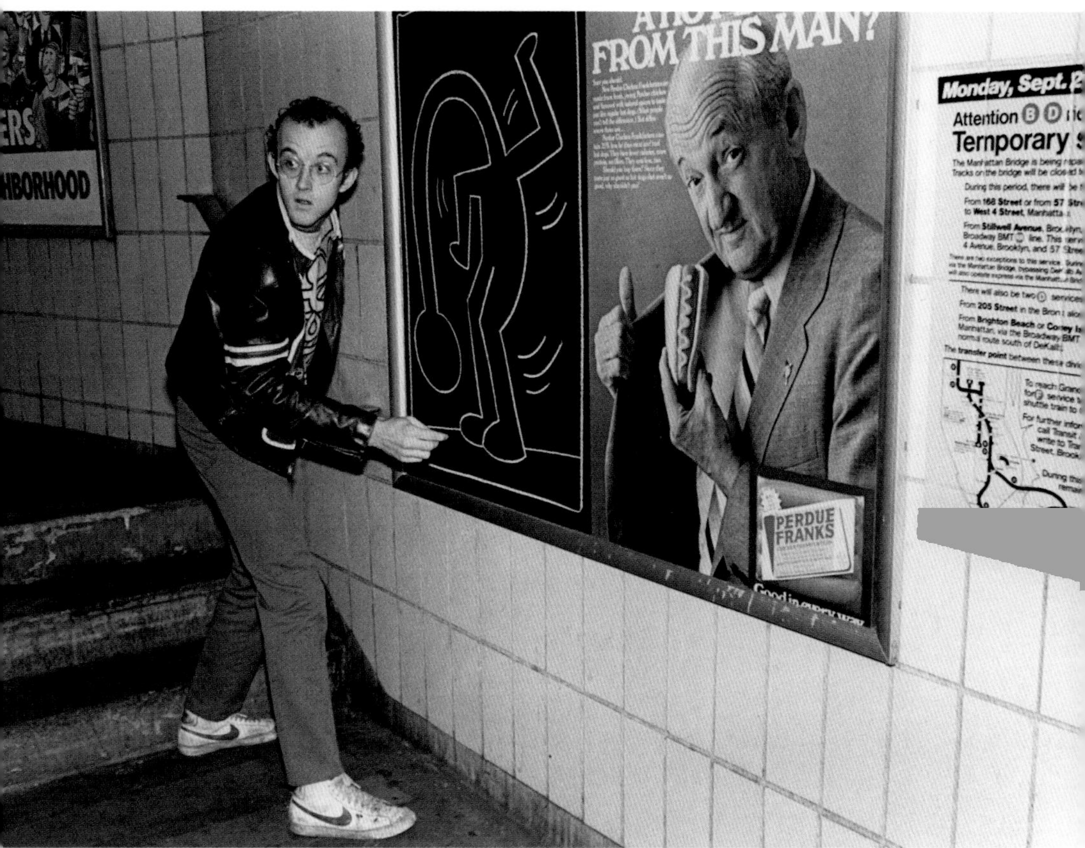

52 Keith Haring, New York City, USA, 1983. Before gaining mainstream acclaim, Keith Haring drew images in chalk on advertising panels in subway stations. Haring's graffiti, characterized by his iconic use of line to create all manner of cartoonish narratives, is observably different from the signature graffiti tradition, yet the artist was often referred to as a graffiti writer and made to represent that culture.

displayed graffiti during the late 1970s and early 1980s sought to communicate the liveliness of this burgeoning art movement and to provide writers with a chance to explore their practices in a legal setting. At the same time, powerful commercial art galleries caught on to the downtown trend and attempted to market graffiti as a new art movement – ignoring its history and imposing limitations on the writers' expression all the while. It is largely thanks to these institutions that artists such as Keith Haring, who drew images illegally, came to be associated with the signature graffiti movement. Within a short period of time, graffiti writing was celebrated within these two different art worlds, each of which had an impact on the movement's destiny. Were it not for the recognition of writing practices in alternative galleries, the big players would not have co-opted the movement. Consequently, the graffiti world's cautious attitude towards exhibitions in decades to come would lead to a vast array of progressive gallery shows, with the writers often taking centre stage as both artists and curators.

Basquiat and Haring

During the 1980s, only a few legitimate graffiti writers who were part of the subway writing culture – including Crash [48], Daze and Lady Pink – sustained art careers and continued to exhibit their work in galleries. In the mainstream media, the output of these writers was often overshadowed by the work of Jean-Michel Basquiat and Keith Haring, who were celebrated as having successfully made the transition from writing illegal graffiti to making high art.

Basquiat first came to be recognized in the art world by the phrases that he wrote on walls in SoHo and TriBeCa. His writings, though legible, were often intriguing and unintelligible – for example, 'Like An Ignorant Easter Suit' and 'Tar Tar Tar (Coal) MCVXLIII' – and were typically signed with a copyright symbol and the name SAMO ('Same Old Shit'). Between 1978 and 1980, Basquiat's graffiti advertised SAMO as a quasi-movement with messages such as 'SAMO as a neo art form', 'SAMO as an end to mindwash religion, nowhere politics, and bogus philosophy' and 'SAMO as an escape clause'. In other writings, SAMO was simply used as a signature to various philosophical musings, such as 'Life is confusing at this point' and 'A pin drops like a pungent odor'. Basquiat's use of legible writings made his graffiti visually and structurally different from that of most signature writers, but his direct approach brought him to the attention of the media as well as prominent gallery owners and dealers.

Basquiat's naive style, his characteristic combination of elements, the extraordinary energy of his paintings, and his street work together provide a number of catalysts for comparisons with traditional graffiti. His use of words, crowns, pop culture references and characters is typical of signature graffiti. Moreover, the movement created through his use of line and paint application to construct an indecipherable yet unified whole is emblematic of the graffiti signature.

Like Basquiat, Haring initially gained notoriety through his illegal drawings in subway stations [52]. Aiming to make his work accessible to the masses, he addressed the public through readable, compelling imagery in highly populated places so as to impart ideas to people outside of institutional boundaries. Haring's brand of graffiti featured cartoonish drawings of people, explosions, televisions, spaceships and dogs, which he rendered in chalk on subway station advertisement panels that had been covered in black paper in preparation for new promotions – a practice he began in 1981 and abandoned in 1985. Although he developed a recurring visual aesthetic and style that made his work identifiably his, in much the same way as graffiti writers, there was a marked difference between his line-drawn figures and the appropriated pop culture characters that writers sometimes depicted: his characters, such as the well-known radiant baby, were decidedly his creations.

Haring's style depends on the rendition of movement through the action of lines, the repetition of a logo that invariably functions as the artist's signature, and numerous pop culture references. Haring's tendency to completely cover a surface with thick, animated lines that frame, compose and give rise to the work itself is perhaps the most obvious point of comparison with graffiti.

The overarching reason for Basquiat's and Haring's links to graffiti, aside from their illegal writing and drawing in the public sphere, was the style and subject of some of their paintings. However, the categorization of Basquiat and Haring as graffiti writers was problematic both for these artists and for members of the writing culture. Although they wrote illegal graffiti, neither utilized the prevalent graffiti iconographical style and visual vocabulary, nor followed the ethics of the graffiti world; nor were they associated with any particular crew. Moreover, both Basquiat and Haring were selective in terms of locations and audiences. While graffiti writers also selectively choose their locations, they do so with the prospect of maximum exposure within the scene. In contrast, Basquiat wrote graffiti largely as a way to arouse interest in his art among curators and dealers, while Haring formulated his own pictorial vocabulary of simplified icons primarily, like advertisers, to address the citizenry at large. The fact that they drew illegally on downtown walls (Basquiat) or in subway stations (Haring) prior to their successful art world careers was of little consequence to the culture of writing.

In the context of art criticism, graffiti as an art form continues to be most often associated with these two artists, but this connection is as problematic as the relationship between the cultures of writing and hip-hop. Through the construction of a correlation between divergent art practices, graffiti is essentially written out of its own history.

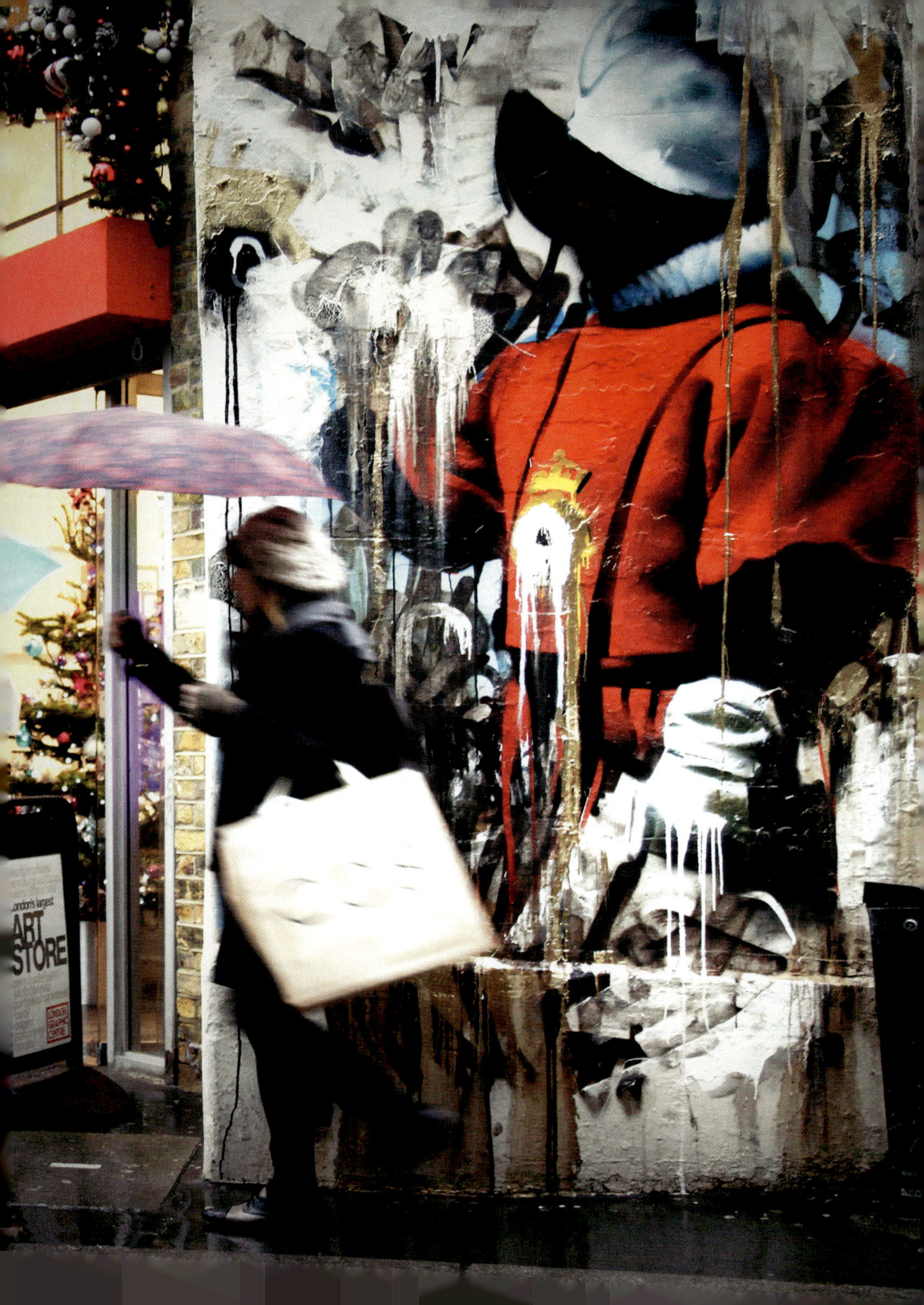
London's largest
ART
STORE
LONDON
GRAPHIC
CENTRE

Chapter 3 Street Art and the City

Much like public art, which functions as a place-making tool in its engagement with and transformation of the cityscape, street art is also part of the process of a city. Street art responds to the environment of a city inasmuch as it partakes in the creation of its visual culture. Contemporary public art projects and street art can both be playful, critical explorations of the cultural structures of a city. In this sense, street and public art practices are not entirely different, even if street artists rarely acknowledge 'official' public art, and public art discourse is all but devoid of street art analysis. Both models are conceived and contextualized within a city – a complex realm that can be understood as a set of relationships between objects, places, people and time. However, necessary differences do exist. Illegality, motivation, medium and place of diffusion are the foremost aspects that differentiate street art as a separate entity from public art. While both public and street art necessarily explore the very meaning of public space, the nature of that interaction is different.

Street Art as Public Art

Public art refers to a vast assortment of art forms and practices, including murals, community projects, memorials, civic statuary, architecture, sculpture, ephemeral art (dance, performance, theatre), subversive interventions and, for some, graffiti and street art. Encountered in both outdoor and indoor environments, public art can be experienced in a multitude of places – parks, libraries, public squares, city streets, building atriums and shopping centres. Public art projects are often commissioned in order to enrich an environment with an artwork that is intended to integrate with the surrounding architecture, urban design and landscape, with the aim of enhancing the socio-cultural context of a specific site. While these types of projects continue to exist, there are many other

53 **Conor Harrington**, *Surveillance*, London, UK, 2009. As with official public art projects, street art practices draw attention to city spaces by transforming them into places of interest. Focused on the stoic male as a comment on the masculinity of urban culture, Conor Harrington inserts his dignified figures into unremarkable places and in so doing makes those spaces remarkable.

public art practices that are not disseminated in the interest of a governing or commissioning body and that question this idea of seamless interjection.

There have been several attempts to categorize public art. The most prominent grouping encompasses works, typically modernist abstract sculptures, that have been placed outdoors to decorate the plazas fronting governmental or corporate buildings. As this form of public art is often perceived as having been 'plopped' in the public sphere without any consideration of the surroundings, it has come to be known as 'plop' art or simply 'art-in-public-spaces'. To counter 'plop art', 'art-as-public-spaces' projects were conceived as more site-conscious and context-driven works that sought integration with the surrounding architecture and cityscape. Instead of simply enlivening a public space, these projects aim to respond to or interact with their sites of display. New genre public art, another key grouping, takes this concept one step further by working with the communities among which the art is placed and incorporates temporary city-based programmes focused on social issues. New genre public art, also known as 'art-in-the-public-interest', is more concerned with the process of democratic dialogue based on audience collaboration than a tangible end product. This aspiration is problematic for some who consider these collaborations to maintain a degree of paternalism towards their audience. The seemingly democratic process of collaboration seeks to define a community as a unified and distinguishable group and does not account for the fact that the artist and the governing body ultimately still make the decision regarding what constitutes the project.

The difficulty with the notion of public art is a lack of consensus about what defines 'public space'. Indeed, art in public places that are not defined as art-viewing spaces, such as museums, functions and is received differently from art produced for gallery display. Whereas in the context of formal exhibitions visitors expect to view art, in the urban environment the artwork may be experienced unwillingly, in other words by people who did not expressly set out to encounter art. This sort of accidental meeting can engender a negative response. The notion of public art implies that certain spaces, which are effectively public, facilitate an experience of art within that realm. In reality, art in public spaces is often simply not recognized as such, as is often the case with graffiti and street art.

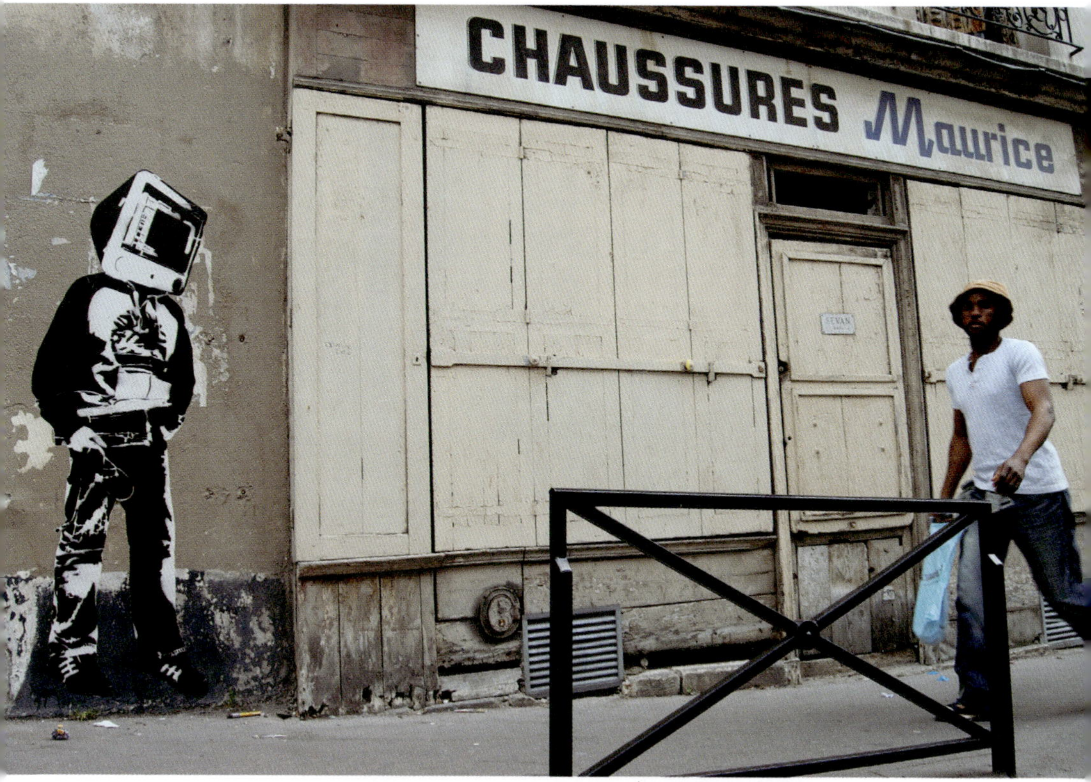

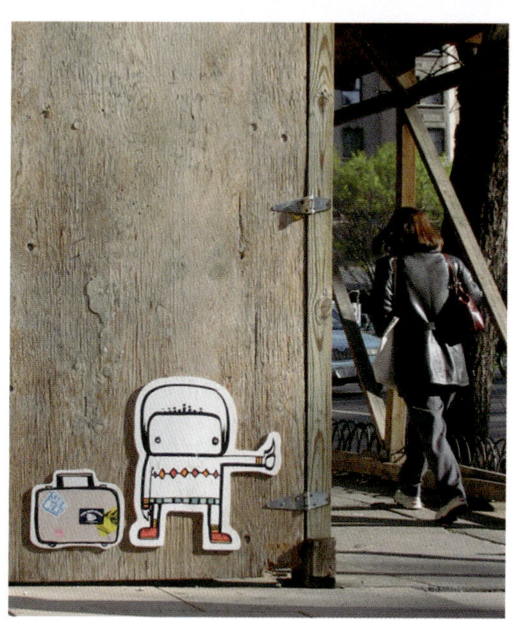

54 (*above*) **Blek le Rat**, *Computerhead*, Paris, France, 2007. Art in the public sphere questions the notion of public space, especially when it is put up without permission. The substitution of the human head for a computer monitor signals our fascination with technology and reliance on computers in our daily operations.

55 (*right*) **Thundercut**, *Out of Here*, New York City, USA, 2006. Street art aids in the creation of urban narratives and engages people in the experience of art in unlikely locations. This simple image of a traveller thumbing a ride may inspire an onlooker to leave behind the daily grind.

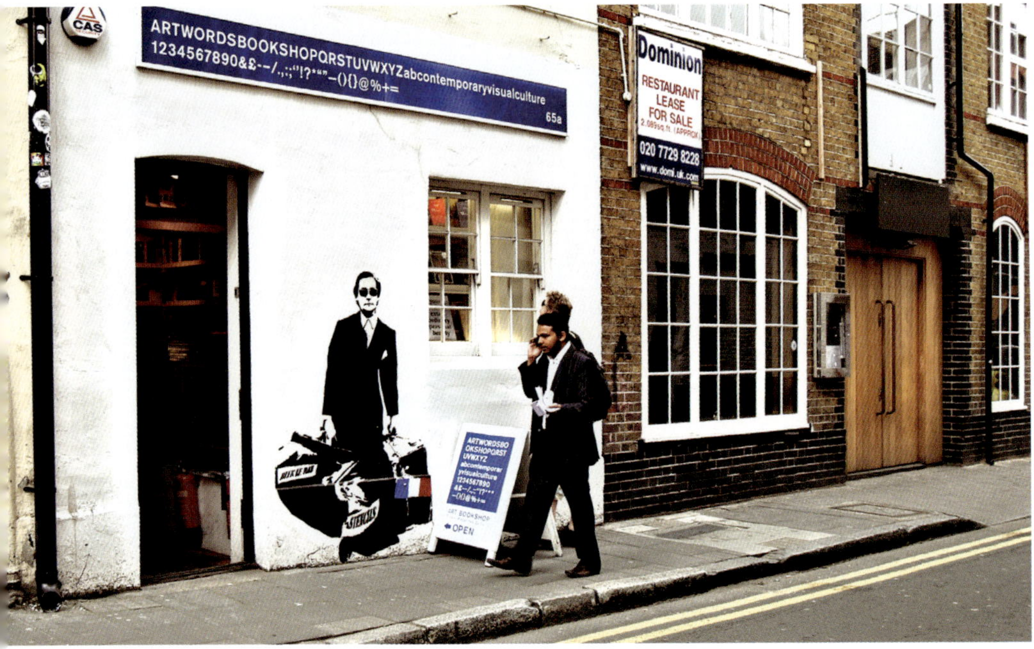

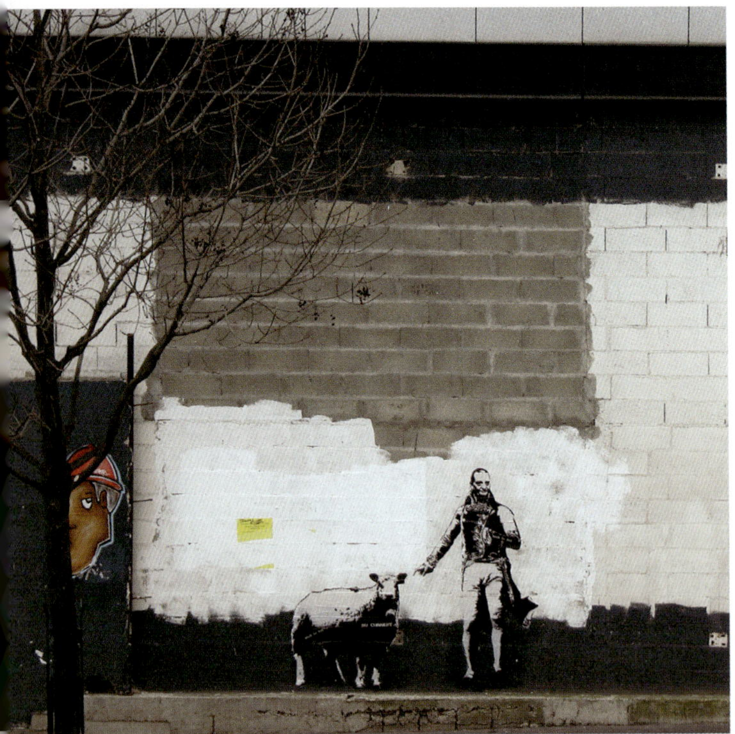

56 (*above*) **Blek le Rat**, *The Man Who Walks Through Walls*, London, UK, 2008. Originally created in 2004, this iconic image is one of several self-portraits that stress Blek's continuing presence in the face of the changing urban environment and the crackdown on urban art.

57 (*left*) **Blek le Rat**, *Napoleon and his Sheep*, Paris, France, 2003. By giving Napoleon the face of a French comedian, Blek transforms him into a figure of ridicule. The sheep, which is often depicted alone, appears out of place in an alien environment.

58 (*opposite, above*) **Blek le Rat**, *Florence Aubenas*, Paris, France, 2005. When journalist Florence Aubenas was kidnapped in Iraq in 2005, Blek pasted hundreds of these portraits as a reminder of her plight and a call for action.

59 (*opposite, below*) **Blek le Rat**, *Homeless in San Francisco*, California, USA, 2010

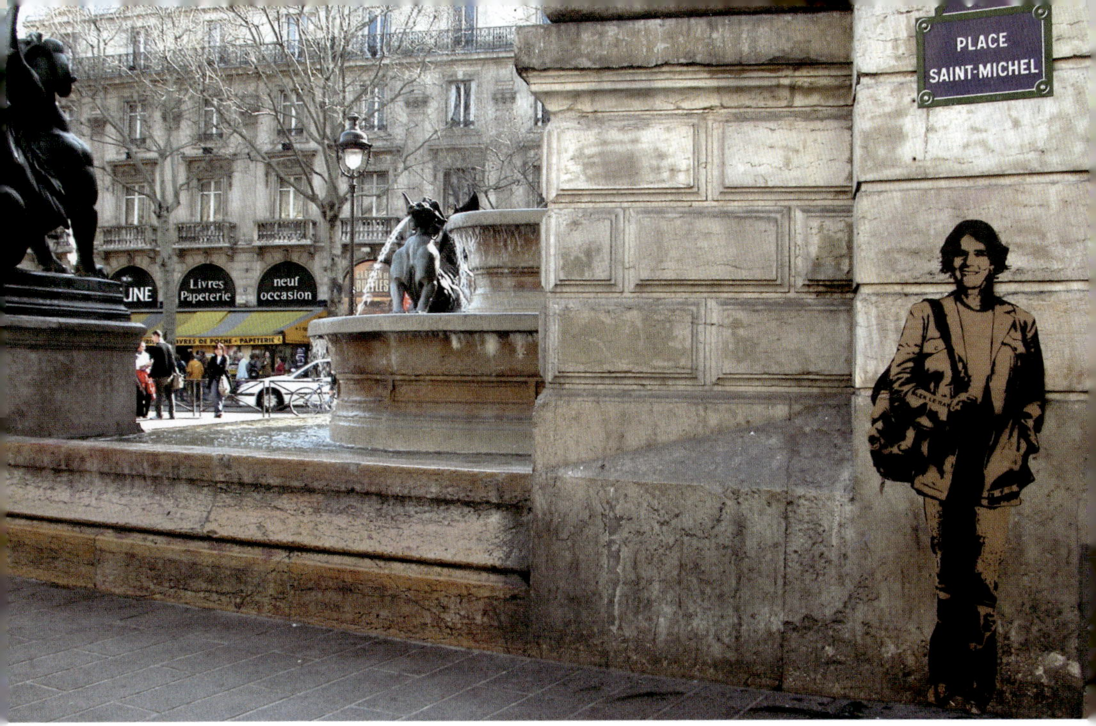

PLACE
SAINT-MICHEL
Livres
Papeterie
neuf
occasion

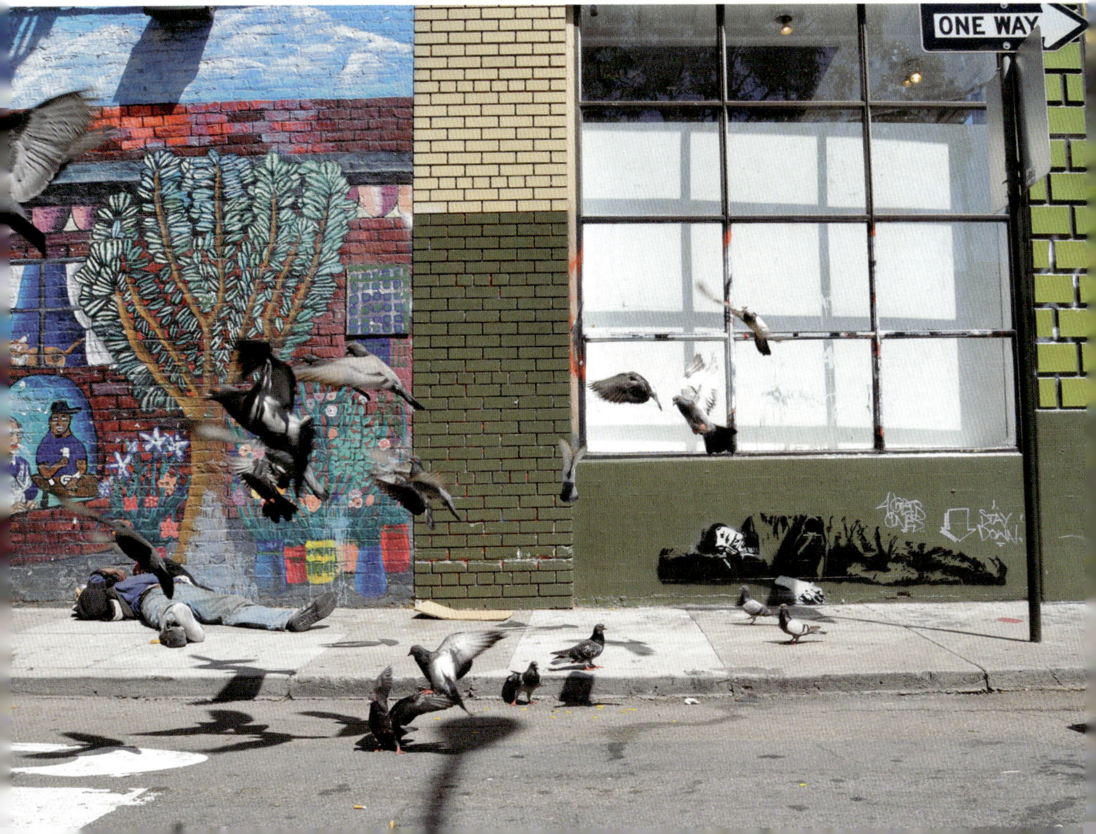

ONE WAY

As unauthorized art forms manifested in public spaces, graffiti and street art suggest that public art is as political as the space it inhabits. Street art aids in the creation of city spaces by occupying a physical location in the cityscape and by engaging people in the experience of art. As unsanctioned projects, street art practices penetrate the city in a way that displaces the boundary between public and private uses of space. Artists whose street practices vividly illuminate the communicative potential of art in the public sphere include Blek le Rat (France) and Magda Sayeg (USA) of graffiti-knitting crew Knitta Please. Like numerous others who display art on the street without permission, these artists are interested in reclaiming the notion of public art and thus public space by making art for the city and its inhabitants.

Blek le Rat, the celebrated godfather of the street stencil, began stencilling small rats on the streets of Paris in 1981 before gradually moving on to full-size figures. His straightforward and compelling imagery includes life-size representations of artists, musicians and political figures as well as socio-political messages. Following a run-in with the law in the 1990s, Blek started to create black-and-white posters and paper cut-outs of his stencils, which he pasted onto city walls. The artist's unwavering interest in creating art on the street as a personal response to a particular situation and location has won him much acclaim within the street art world, while his resolve to diversify his imagery and his methodology vis-à-vis his chosen sites of display has ensured his place as a street art pioneer. Although Blek participates in gallery shows, his passion for working on the street has not diminished over the past thirty years as it allows him to communicate with a much broader audience. As the artist explains: 'The problem with galleries is that 99% of urban artists use urban art as a stepping stone into galleries. It's a fatal error because in galleries they're seen by 40 people, in museums they're seen by 10 people, but in the streets they're seen by 100,000 people. And that's the integrity of an artist's work: to be seen. Not to be sold or to be recognized in a museum – but to be seen by the world.'

Poetic, quotidian and always engaging, Blek's artworks are, in the simplest terms, explorations of humanity. His pseudonym, itself an anagram of 'art' ('rat'), suggests that, through accessible imagery, social issues can indeed be raised to the forefront of urban visual culture. Committed to street art's potential as the future of art, Blek considers his social obligation as an artist to produce imagery with which people

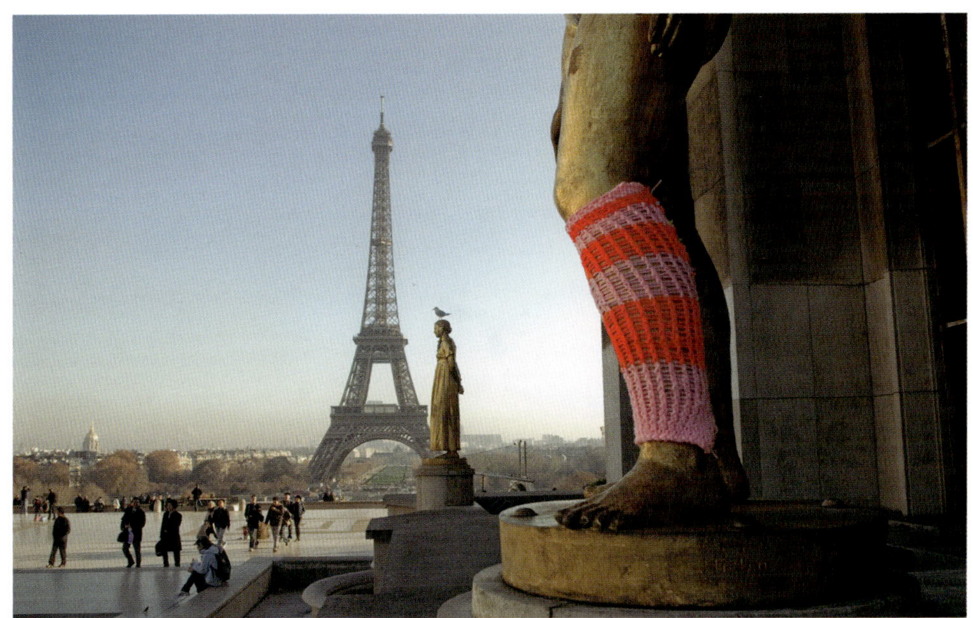

can identify. Whether through self-portraiture, as with
The Man Who Walks Through Walls (first created in 2004)
[56], or the rendition of well-known historical figures, as
with *Napoleon and his Sheep* (from *c.* 2003) [57], Blek creates
images that evoke references to pop culture and contemporary
society in a subtly humorous way. In another project, Blek
pasted images of Florence Aubenas, a French journalist
kidnapped in Iraq, in an attempt to focus media attention
on efforts for her release (2005) [58]. This non-aggressive
form of protest, diffused in locations frequented by Aubenas
in Paris, perfectly showcased the underlying power of art on
the street to facilitate dialogue. Most recently, the artist has
devoted much of his practice to specific social issues such as
homelessness. Pasting images such as *Homeless in San Francisco*
(from *c.* 2006) [59] in areas frequented by homeless people
both raises awareness and symbolically provides the homeless
with a temporary home.

In 2005, Magda Sayeg founded graffiti-knitting crew Knitta
Please in Texas as a way to combine her talent as a knitter with
the aspiration to add a sense of warmth to the urban sphere.
Questioning the gap between art and craft, the abundance of
mass production and the rigidity of urbanity, Sayeg set out to
introduce weaving outdoors. Wrapping otherwise mundane

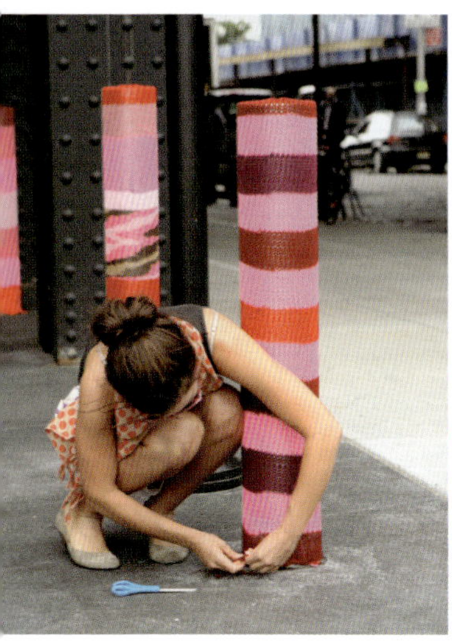

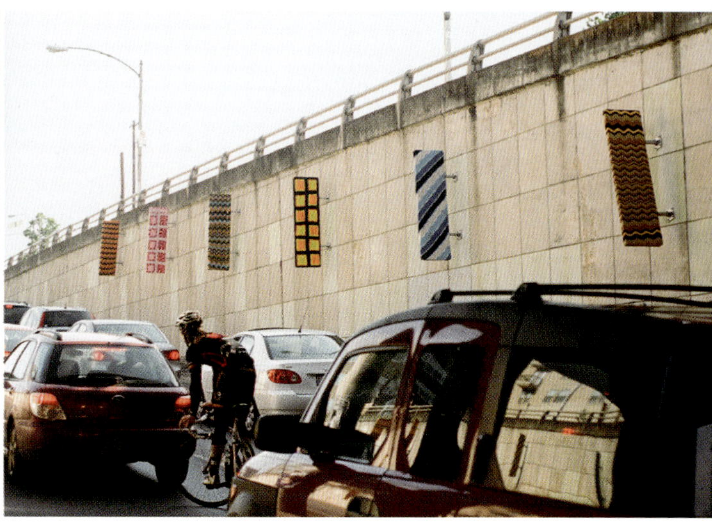

61 (*above left*) **Magda Sayeg** affixing one of her creations

62 (*above right*) **Magda Sayeg**, *Untitled*, Texas, USA, 2010

public objects, such as bike racks, lamp posts and parking meters, with knitted yarn animates the item and by extension its space of residence, softens the severe lines of the concrete urban landscape, and artfully challenges the traditionally functional nature of knitting. Knitta's 'tags', as they are called, are typically read as less aggressive interventions into the public domain – a fact that has encouraged a great number of knitters to get involved in the aptly named movement, yarn bombing. This accessible, textural and brightly coloured type of street art uses graffiti's lexicon to describe its actions, yet stands in direct opposition to its rebellious and stigmatized nature. In terms of function, however, the work of street knitters such as Knitta Please emulates the same ambitions as those of many street artists: to engage with the public and create moments of inquiry in the urban sphere.

Infusing otherwise uniform objects with delicate, crocheted or knitted 'wraps' also brings a conventionally female practice into conversation with a traditionally male movement. Although the work of yarn bombers is more akin to street art, their appropriation of graffiti vocabulary suggests the aspiration of these street knitters to satirize elements of graffiti writing. Whether accessorizing a male nude with leg-warmers [60], wrapping underpass panels with colourfully geometric designs [62], enlivening bike racks [63] or simply decorating an otherwise plain fixture [64], Knitta Please reveals street art's potential to rejuvenate public space.

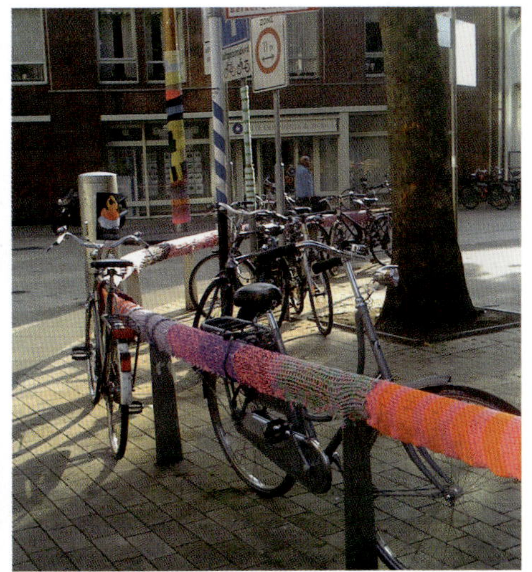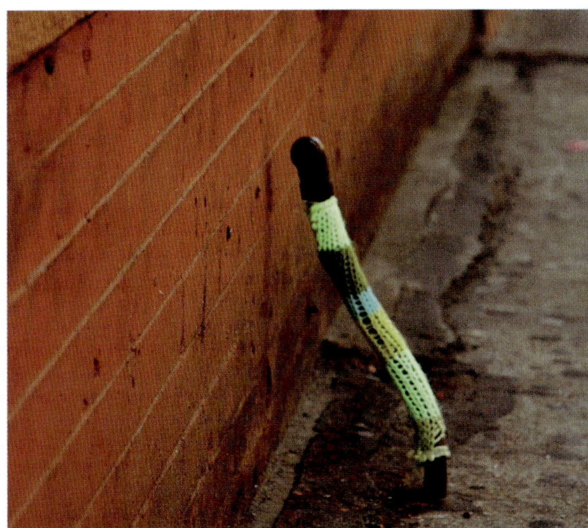

63 (*above left*) **Magda Sayeg**, *Untitled*, Tilburg, Netherlands, 2008

64 (*above right*) **Magda Sayeg**, *Untitled*, New York City, USA, 2008

Contesting 'Public' Space

The criminalization of graffiti, and by extension any form of street art, begs the question: is public space in fact public? Neither politically nor socially neutral, public space breeds conflict – be it physical, socio-political, aesthetic or cultural. Public art, which inevitably occupies public space, naturally evokes the concept of freedom of speech. The term 'public' implies accessibility and, more significantly when it comes to art, connotes a sort of organic integration between the object, its allotted space and the fact that it is singularly positioned to serve the public. Questions relating to whom public art projects benefit or exclude, however, are especially revealing in the context of street art.

While it may seem absurd that art practices grouped together under the umbrella of urban or street art are illegal, it is also a driving force for its practitioners as it allows the artists to work in an unmediated manner. Exercising actual freedom of expression enables artists to contest a city's corporate visual culture by either explicitly responding to it or creating new avenues of visual communication. Regardless of the artist's intention, producing art on the street is in itself a form of resistance to sanctioned imagery and the notion of public space. In other words, the unauthorized visual alteration of city spaces is a type of rebellion against the capitalist construction of space. An illegal mode of expression that subsists on the margins of a city's structure signals an invasion of 'public' space. Unsanctioned art projects

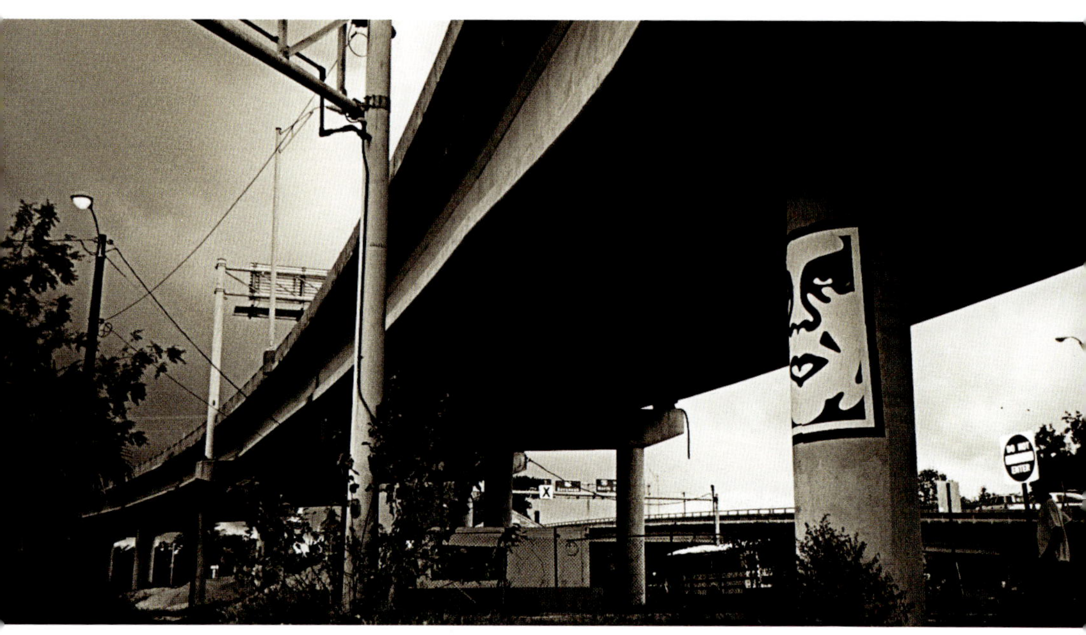

65 **Shepard Fairey**, *Untitled.*
The Andre the Giant 'Obey'
image that launched Shepard
Fairey's street art career over
twenty years ago continues to
be a mainstay in his imagery. Its
purpose – to stimulate curiosity
and encourage a questioning of
one's environment – is a motive
Fairey reinterprets throughout
his oeuvre.

thus infuse the public sphere with moments of fracture, spaces of disruption and subjective uses of territory, and together create alternative forms of urban visual culture. Shepard Fairey (USA), Zevs (France) and Eine (UK) are among a number of artists interested in this dynamic of contestation.

Not unlike Blek le Rat, Shepard Fairey has become synonymous with the street art movement. While the black-and-white Andre the Giant 'Obey' stickers (first conceived in the late 1980s) [65] both supplied the artist with his moniker and launched his street career, his 'Hope' placard design (2008) for Barack Obama's presidential campaign catapulted him to stardom. Screen-printed, painted or collaged, Fairey's wheat-pasted posters have become increasingly rich in their simplicity of design and complex messaging. An interest in propaganda imagery and graphic design propelled Fairey to work initially with a black, white and, on occasion, red palette as well as explicitly accessible images. The complexity in his work comes from the multiple layers of possible meaning abundant in his pieces. Although his initial forays into creating art on the street were overtly nonsensical rather than political, he gained such an impressive amount of feedback for his 'Obey' series that producing art on the street became, for Fairey, a politically motivated act.

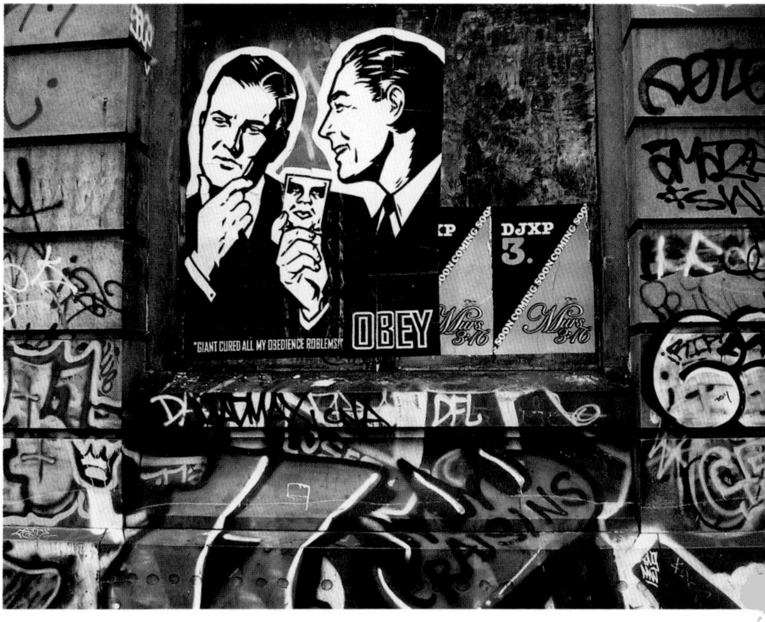

One of the main considerations for Fairey is to ignite a sense of inquiry in people's navigation of their environments. Describing his initial 'Obey' sticker campaign, Fairey explains: 'Whether the reaction be positive or negative, the sticker's existence is worthy as long as it causes people to consider the details and meanings of their surroundings. In the name of fun and observation.' The encouragement of action and reaction is a message convincingly translated through his imagery. The essence of propaganda, to entice people into action by promoting a particular point of view or political cause, is flipped on its head in Fairey's work. In *Giant Cured All My Obedience Problems* (conceived in the late 1990s) [66], for example, Fairey uses characters from 1950s advertisements to 'sell' the idea of his 'Obey' campaign. The jovial exchange between the male figures, centred on an absurd 'product', conveys the witty, self-reflexive notion of nonsensical consumerism and media manipulation. Interested in the power of simple icons and text, the artist makes use of a brainwashing tool – the propaganda poster – but to motivate people to lead and not follow.

While Fairey contests public space by calling attention to the narrative created by billboards and all manner of advertisements and signage that tell citizens what to do, Zevs challenges the urban sphere in a much more subdued way – by working with shadows. The impetus for both artists is similar in terms of aspiring to create a space for reflection and observation in otherwise utilitarian streets and to motivate people to reconsider their environments. However, the challenge that Zevs proposes is based on the intangible. Concerned with calling attention to the unremarkable objects that, in their small way, define urban spaces, the artist contests the mundanity of cityscapes.

Outlining the silhouettes of ordinary urban elements such as traffic lights and mailboxes was a project Zevs developed during the late 1990s. These so-called 'Electric Shadows' play with the notions of appropriation and temporality, and photographic documentation has thus become a significant part of the artist's practice. The act of shadowing objects on the street can be interpreted as a subtle comment on the 'publicness' of public space. While a traffic light, bench or rubbish bin may belong to the city, they are available for public use. Using these objects as the starting point for his art practice – a practice that is at once quietly harmless and illegal – Zevs reaffirms the role of the citizen in the creation of a public space. By drawing attention to a bench (2000) [67] or decorative metro entrance (2000) [68] as everyday fixtures of the cityscape that inspire artistic creation, he emphasizes the aesthetic dimension and potential found in the commonplace. Expressed as outlines, these utilitarian and decorative objects become unrecognizable and are, in essence, transformed into abstract designs that stand apart from their tangible inspirations.

In contrast to Zevs and Fairey, who contest public space through their appropriation of urban objects and images respectively, London's Eine has taken a more traditional route

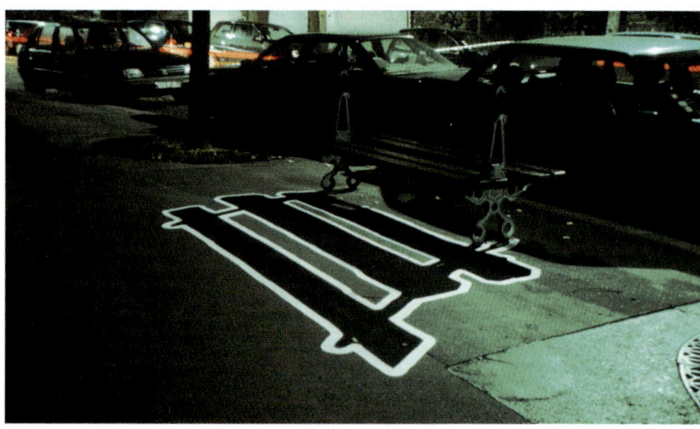

67 **Zevs**, *Public Bench*, 'Electric Shadows' series, Paris, France, 2000. Zevs developed his 'Electric Shadows' series, painting the silhouettes of city fixtures and furnishings, from the late 1990s onwards. Outlining the shadows of ordinary urban elements such as benches, traffic lights and bins both draws attention to the functional and decorative objects that help define the city and creates abstract designs.

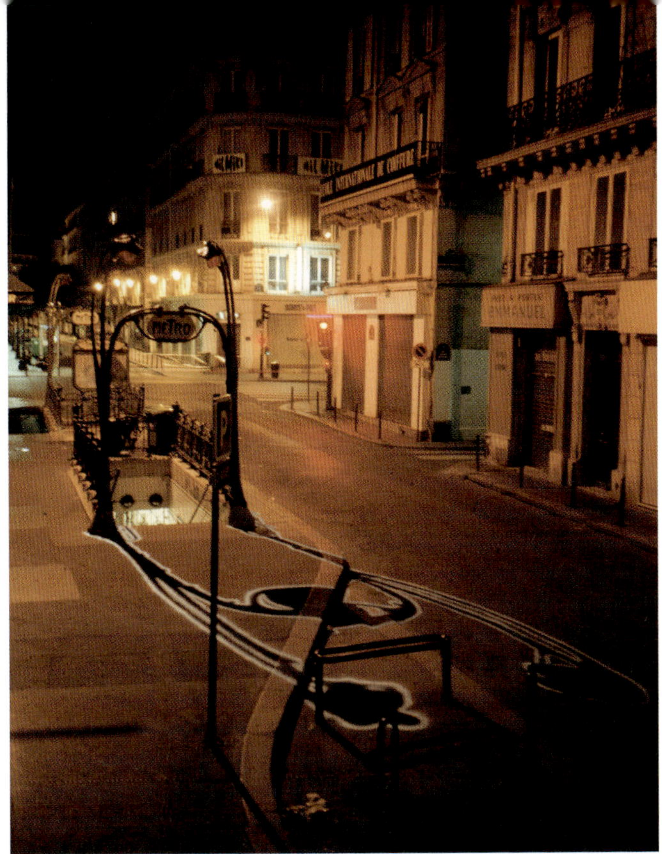

and fashioned a practice based on the writer's primary tool –
letterforms. Working almost exclusively with individual letters
and words, he branched out from a background in graffiti to
explore fonts, typography and the alphabet. While the artist's
fundamental interest in working with letters has remained
a constant, instead of manipulating them into an abstract
form, he works with fonts that already exist. Writing out
the alphabet, letter by letter, on a large scale throughout the
city is an inventive way to challenge public space and people's
conception of graffiti and street art. Eine's colourfully inviting
letters serve both to inspire and to stimulate debate over their
purpose and meaning.

Although brightly coloured, a lot of Eine's paintings have
quite negative connotations through the use of words such as
'scary', 'monster' and 'vandalism'. As the artist explains: 'One
of the reasons I chose "scary" was because of the negative way
graffiti is portrayed in the media… I have often spent hours
with a brush and pot of paint, painting an illegal wall, and if

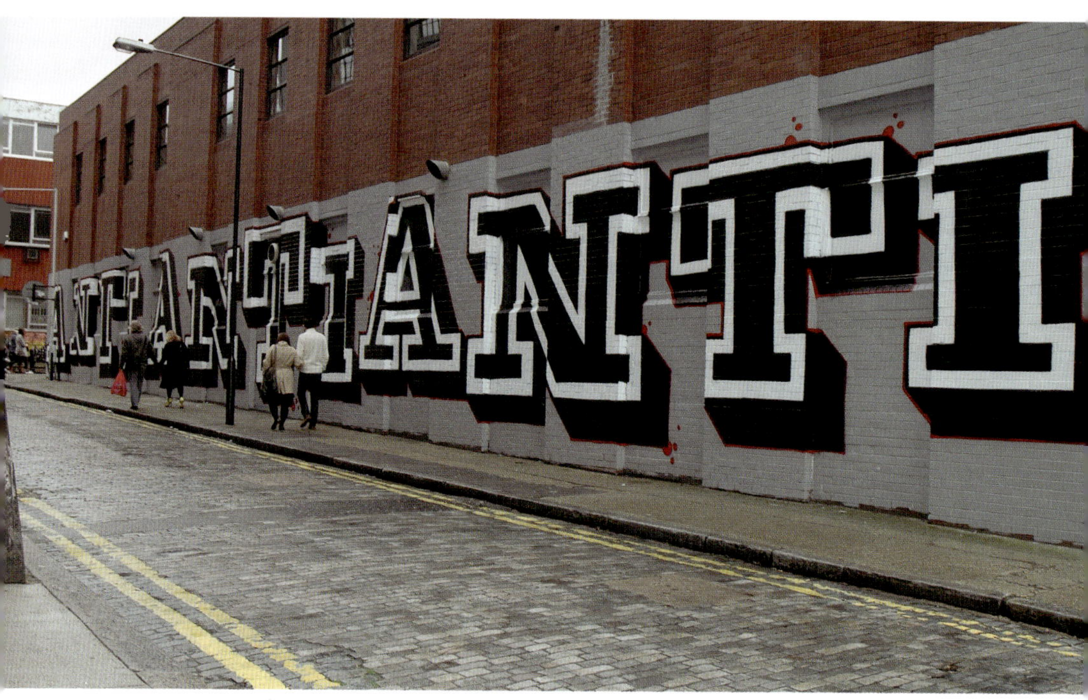

69 **Eine**, *Anti Anti Anti*, London, UK, 2010. Designed to promote the launch of the 'Anti Design Festival' in London, an event that aimed to push the boundaries of creativity and experimentation, this work conveys a straightforward message both through colour palette and meaning. 'Anti Anti Anti' was counterbalanced a week later on the opposite side of the street with a happy, bright 'Pro Pro Pro'.

anyone does say anything, it's positive. But the moment I shake up the can of spray, all heads turn and the public gets nasty: "What's that? Is that graffiti? Do you have permission?" It's quite funny really, and can totally be used to your advantage.'

Writing words that are often used to describe graffiti is a fascinating way of opening up a dialogue regarding illegal art making. The fact that the artist has transitioned from writing stylized, illegible graffiti to painting large legible words – reprimanded for one and celebrated for the other – is in itself a commentary on the double standard that exists in the public's attitude towards art on the street. This is further accentuated by Eine's chosen imagery, which like graffiti pivots on the rendition of letters, and thus succinctly communicates the paradoxical divide between these two worlds. Much like images, words conjure up ideas, emotional reactions and feelings. Writing 'Anti' (2010) [69] successively in massive black letters, outlined in white and highlighted in red, may agitate or unnerve passers-by, whereas colourfully spelling out the word 'Happy' (2010) [70] might be uplifting. Eine's aesthetic vocabulary draws people in through its accessibility, while simultaneously creating a sense of mystery.

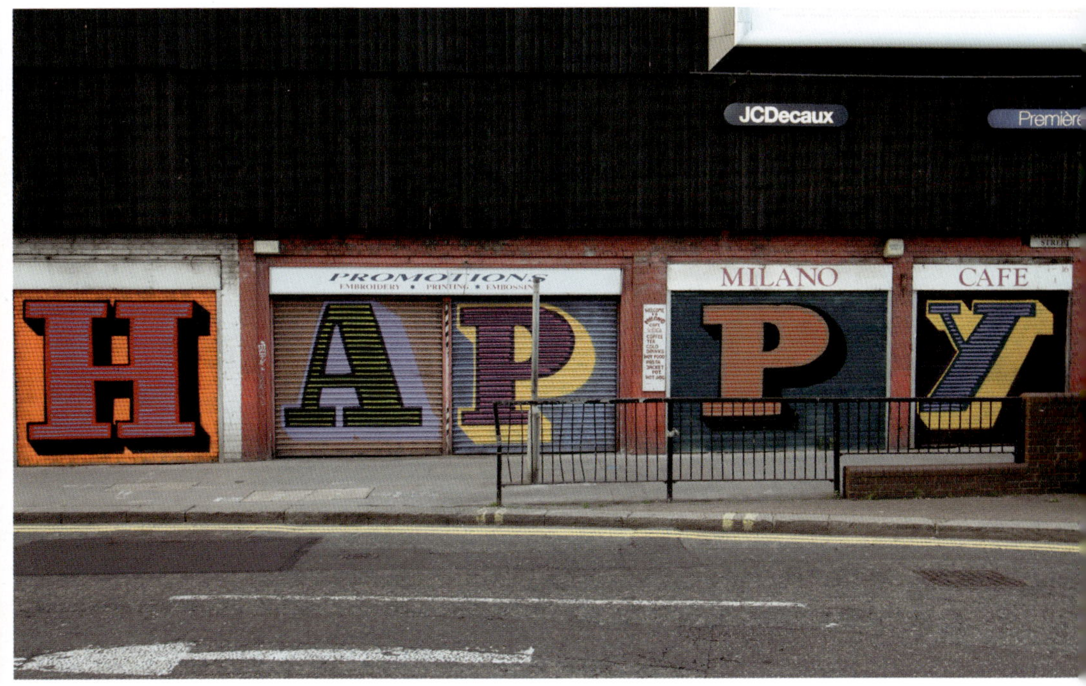

70 **Eine**, *Happy*, London, UK, 2010. This bright, cheerful rendition of *Happy* and the much darker *Anti*, opposite, are likely to conjure up entirely different sentiments. Through font, colour, letter and word forms, Eine expertly displays how the very building blocks of language as well as art and design work together to create a mood and convey an idea.

Defining a Community

In public art discourse, especially in terms of new genre public art, the issue of community representation and engagement is crucial. The 'community' has often, problematically, been regarded as a fixed entity, and thus whom it defines is taken for granted or simply ignored. Instead of being recognized as fluid, the concept of a community is often idealized and to an extent described as a distinct social body.

The ambition behind new genre public art – to represent, interact with or speak to a specific community, in the hope of forging a meaningful relationship between artist and audience – has in some ways moved the discussion away from the work itself to accountability. Public art discourse has thus been transformed from debates regarding aesthetics and design to social accountability, shifting the focus from the site itself to those who occupy it. In the pursuit of issue-based dialogue between artist and community, many questions may arise regarding how a group of individuals becomes identified as a community. Who determines these parameters? What role does each participant play? What issues define the community?

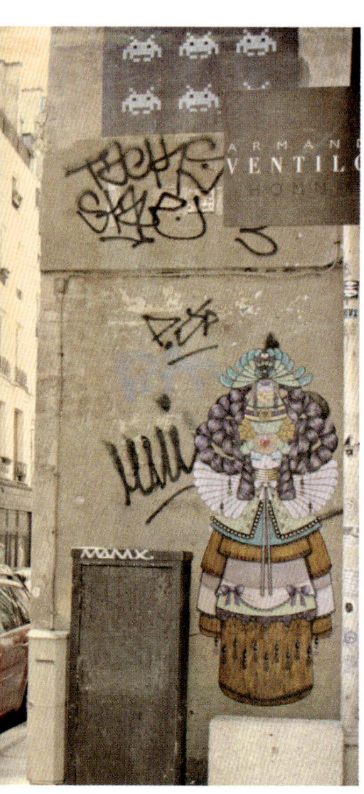

71 **Koralie**, *Untitled*, Paris, France, 2010. Koralie's geisha features alongside graffiti tags and a mosaic by French artist Invader, serving as an example of how visual communication between street artists, manifested on city walls, creates both dialogue and community.

For post-graffiti artists, who produce less visually cryptic art in comparison with signature graffiti writers, the question of communication and community is a valuable one. The city, as an urban community that inspires the production of art, is conceptualized not only as a pivotal constituent of the work itself, but also as a framework for inclusive art practices. Many street artists consider their work to be a reflection of, a response to and an interaction with the citizenry. Rather than fixating on dialogues with specific citizens, they focus primarily on creating work that has the potential to speak to a variety of audiences [71]. The legible medium of stencilling, for example, has become popular with many artists partly because its often text-light and intelligible imagery has the ability to reach a broad public. Other artists such as Swoon create portraits and make these accessible to everyone by pasting them on the street, in the hope of forging a connection with the general public. The artist explains that she 'wanted to make things that were valueless, because they couldn't belong to any one person, and in that way they would belong to everyone'.

Most street artists engage the community at large and not one particular group within the urban crucible. The street artwork necessarily dialogues with its context and at times addresses issues specific to a geographical region, yet in its accessible imagery it aims to communicate with everyone. Through its very existence as a criminalized art form, street art questions to whom the streets belong, and points to the fact that the answer is not only political and economic, but also aesthetic. In this way, it is an unmediated guerrilla art movement which is essentially created by the people, for the people. South African artist Faith47 is interested in this very dialogue with the general public. The artist is on a mission to facilitate empowerment by tackling universal issues such as inequality, poverty and violence through her attractive pieces. Painted in townships, city-centres and abandoned spaces, her work interacts with its material support in a way that makes it seem as though it were part of the original design.

Faith47's imagery is simultaneously varied and unequivocally hers. The lyricism and fluidity of her art is balanced by its strong character. Whether she paints a phrase, a portrait, a real or imagined creature, or some combination thereof, her pieces create a sense of community by speaking of, to and with the people. Pieces such as *A Silent Nation* (2008) [73], painted on a shantytown home, both underline a destitute reality and

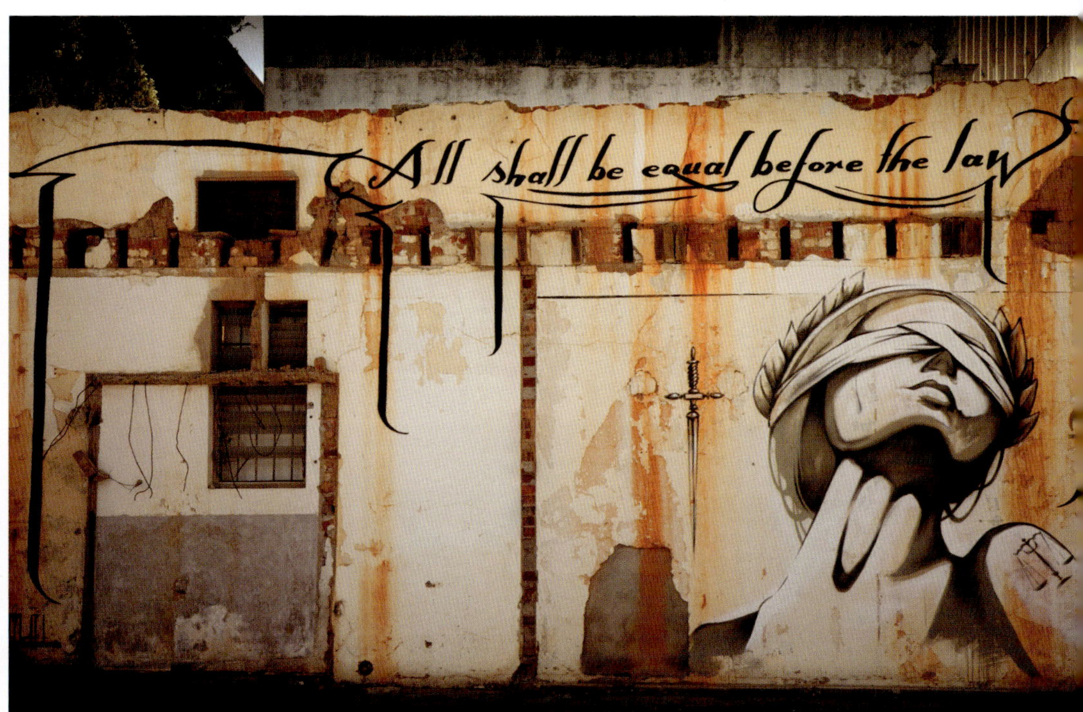

72 **Faith47**, *All Shall Be Equal Before the Law*, Eastern Cape, South Africa, 2009. The symbiosis between Faith47's lyrical calligraphy and corresponding image, seamlessly worked into its site of diffusion, elegantly communicates an ideal that is often not achieved in life. The dilapidated setting underlines the destitute realities of many people and highlights the artist's commitment to making her work accessible to everyone.

directly confront viewers, implicating them in the socio-political reality that numerous South Africans face. *The Hunted* (2010) [74] uses subtler imagery but is another haunting expression of stoic humility in the quest for change. Meanwhile, textual pieces such as *All Shall Be Equal Before the Law* (2009) [72] and *The People Shall Share in the Country's Wealth* (2010) [75] disclose outspoken and straightforward ideals that everyone can appreciate and strive towards. Positioning pieces in decrepit places further accentuates the artist's commitment to bringing art into all manner of spaces, to which anyone has access. Through the aspiration to illuminate these forgotten places with stories that resonate with the people who might come across her work, the artist successfully bridges gaps between people, places and time.

Not unlike Faith47, Brazilian artist Nunca, meaning 'never' in Portuguese, is also interested in visually communicating with as many people as possible to shed light on particular socio-cultural issues. For his part, however, Nunca is focused solely on creating portraits of indigenous South Americans with the aim of giving them a voice within the sprawling metropolis of São Paulo. With

73 (*top*) **Faith47**, *A Silent Nation*, Cape Town, South Africa, 2008. Always mindful of socio-political issues, the artist addresses her audience directly through forthright, candid imagery. Site-specific pieces such as this one, painted on a shantytown home, reinforce the significance of her work and speak directly of and to the people who inspire it.

74 (*centre*) **Faith47**, *The Hunted*, São Paulo, Brazil, 2010. Although this subdued piece is stylistically different from openly confrontational works such as *A Silent Nation*, Faith47 addresses similar issues in each. The quietly haunting imagery of the work serves as a call for action against injustices and civic realities.

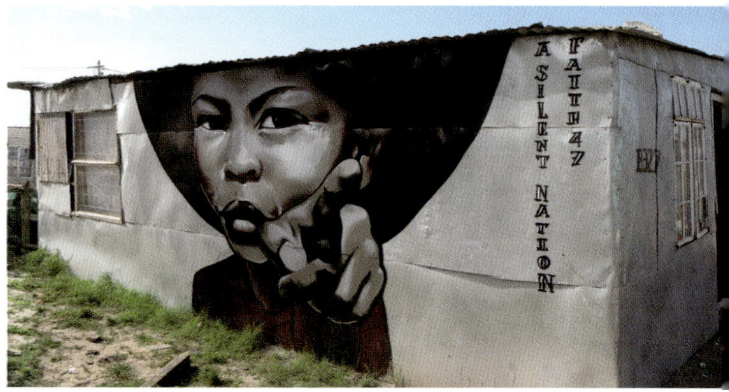

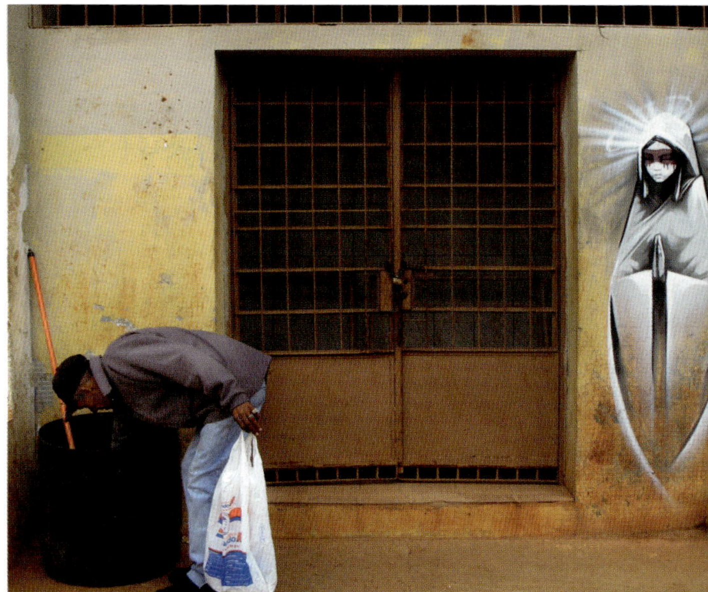

75 (*below*) **Faith47**, *The People Shall Share in the Country's Wealth*, Cape Town, South Africa, 2010

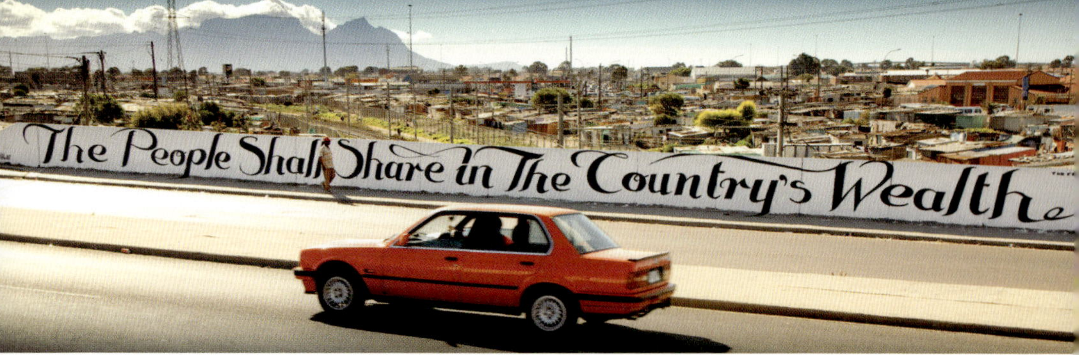

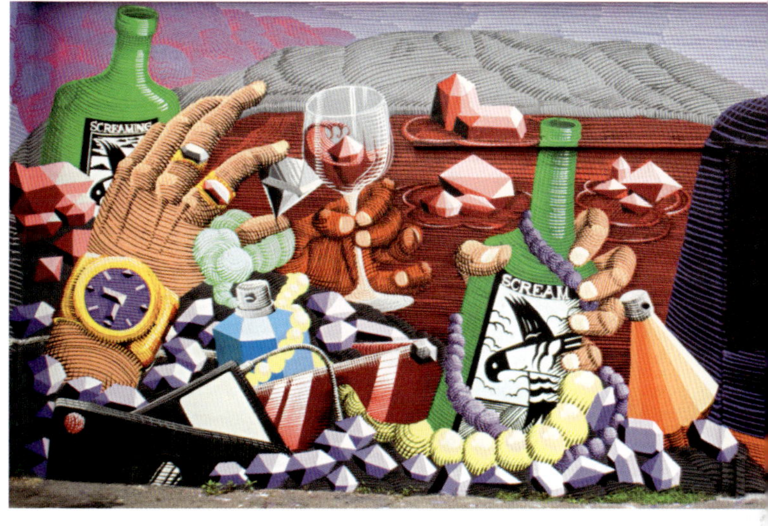

a geometric style of ornamentation by means of figures and a distinctive dark red ochre palette, Nunca's practice questions cultural identity within the context of globalization [76]. The artist's portraits are discernibly influenced by etching techniques to create areas of light and shadow, which provide the work with visual depth. His painted engravings, which resemble woodcuts, deal unmistakably with themes specific to Brazil, but resonate with any population in their exploration of identity and tradition in the twenty-first century. The artist's stoic warriors serve to question the modern world in all its chaotic, technologically enhanced and neurotic actuality. By painting large-scale images of populations that modernity excludes, Nunca calls attention to the dehumanizing effects of streamlining societies.

The political dimension of Nunca's work, although clear, is not alienating. The popularity of his practice reflects the fact that audiences worldwide connect with his point of view, clarity of message and style. Touching on his projects, he explains: 'When I go out to paint on the street, I'm picturing the people that live there – it's for them… The images I use of Indians are a way to depict that this rich culture lives within each Brazilian, but the foreign exploitation in the country diminishes Brazil's self-esteem. An Indian in the city either chooses to maintain [his] roots or to use NAIQUE [Nike] sneakers.' Nunca's fascination with being caught between traditional and modern lifestyles, a timely and politically fraught issue for numerous populations, is clearly conveyed through his introspective imagery.

The City as Context

Street art's raison d'être in the cityscape is in many ways about fostering a relationship between the artist, the viewer and the city. Painting on the street is an entirely different process from painting in a studio. As an uncontrolled environment, the urban sphere necessarily affects the art created in that domain, the finished product and the artist's experiences of the work. Whereas in a studio artists can work quietly and meditatively on a controlled surface in terms of size and texture, and in a controlled environment, on the street this introspection effectively disappears. Thus the city as context for the production of art is necessarily linked to the artwork in question. For some, such as Swoon (USA), urbanity provides all the necessary inspiration and feeds the process of creation. For others, such as Dan Witz (USA), it encourages a wide range of projects that draw attention to unremarkable spaces. For artists such as Thundercut (USA), the city facilitates all sorts of light-hearted, humorous and tongue-in-cheek interventions.

After years of formal art training in various classes and at Brooklyn's Pratt Institute, Swoon became disillusioned with the direction of her work, as well as with the art system for which her creations were destined. She set out first with

77 **Alexandre Órion**, *Metabiotica 05*, São Paulo, Brazil, 2003. The artist describes his 'Metabiotics' project as an inseparable yet incompatible relationship between painting and photography. He relies on the context of the city to create works that are completed only through their documented interaction with the citizenry.

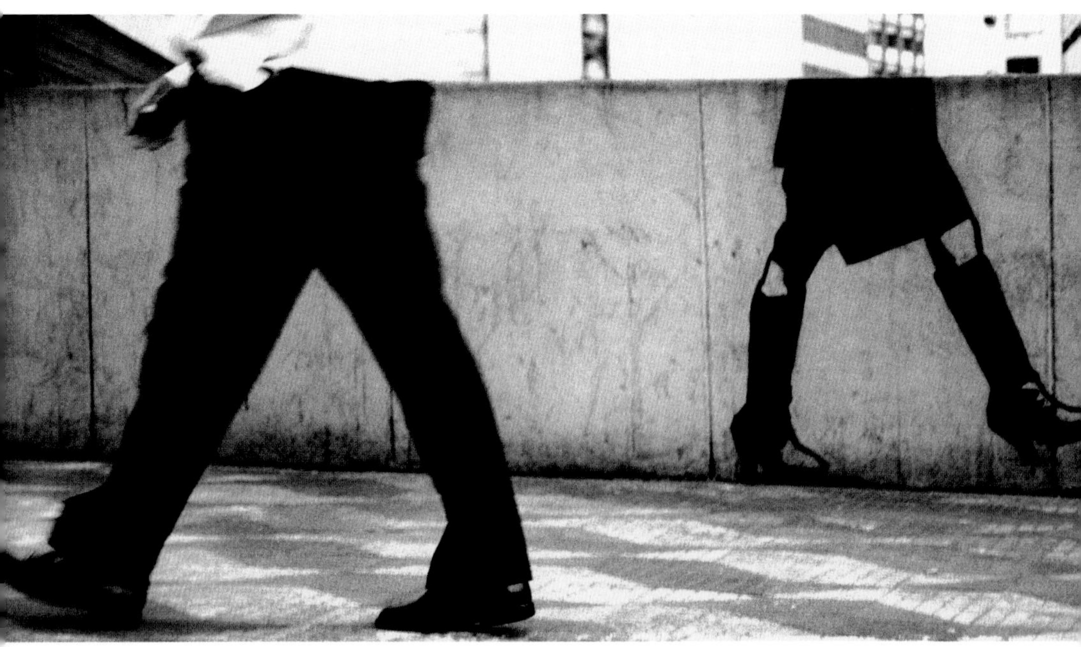

78 Mariusz Waras aka M-City, *M-City 233*, Florence, Italy, 2009. With a focus on urban space, the 'M-City' project reflects the artist's interest in industrial places and the construction of cities. Detailed renditions of the built environment integrated within the physical spaces of the city illuminate the complexity of urbanity on both a macro and micro scale.

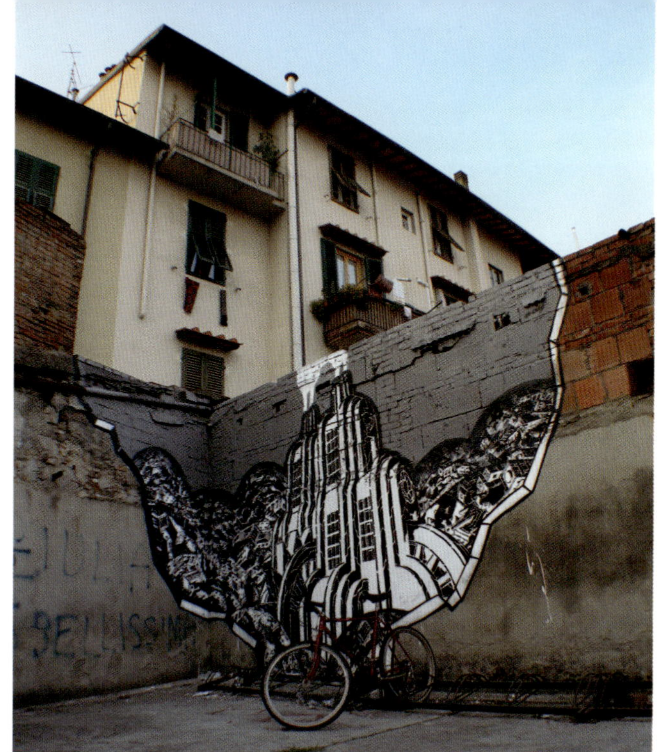

handmade stickers and small collages, quickly moving on to the appropriation of billboards, bus shelters and other spaces reserved for visual commerce, before developing her now trademark cut-outs on city walls. Life-size, realistic renderings of family, friends and neighbourhood characters, the artist's studies are meticulously executed in paper, linoleum and woodblock prints – materials that disintegrate with time and reflect the immediacy of a city. Working from photographs and allowing the image to dictate the medium, Swoon produces her fragile portraits, which take up to two weeks to complete, in a painstakingly precise way. Her works are then wheat-pasted onto city walls, where they willingly surrender to the inevitable process of decay and destruction that awaits them.

The overwhelming attraction of Swoon's work lies not only in the artistry of her practice, but also in the fact that her art seems organically suited to the material complexity of the urban landscape. Like many street artists, Swoon's pieces are envisaged as impermanent processes, whereby the artist's generosity in terms of creativity and labour is effectively donated to the ever-changing interactions with physical environments [79]. When asked what her work signifies,

Swoon answers: 'human connection, paying attention, moments of surprise, participation in the creation of your urban environment'. Through her chosen materials, subject matter and sites of dissemination, these ideals are indeed reflected. Perceiving the street as a space that encourages fleeting connections between people and places, the artist exhibits her ephemeral works typically on abandoned buildings, which nurtures this collaborative process and stimulates a dialogue. As the artist is particularly interested in the physicality and experience of a city, she often seeks to populate places that are integral parts of a city but at the same time peripheral [80]. In her own words: 'Advertising is always trying to place itself a million miles above us, looming down with the shiniest, flashiest, most disconnected depictions of beauty, just out of reach like the rest of its promises, and I find myself trying to get down below that, at eye level, where people are walking, and to depict the life that exists here at the bottom edge, our ordinary reality as it remains connected to the ground.'

Playing with wall texture as well as positive and negative space, Swoon's complex portraits function as interactive spaces where urban dwellers and the cityscape are reflected back onto the surface of a city as though it were a mirror. Particularly through the artist's use of cut-outs, these portraits have an organic quality both in terms of production and narrative. The measured openings of the works expose the material surface beneath them, while simultaneously relaying something about the experience of everyday life in a city – that it is fractured, disjointed, convoluted. As a realm occupied by individuals that are for the most part anonymous to one another, a city is a dynamic, temporal, permeable space. Swoon's visual language asserts that exact temperament. Her portraits open themselves to a city, literally and figuratively, and so are gestures, which materially translate the experience of a city and symbolically facilitate a connection between the individual and the collective. The unrefined character of her art is much more 'of the street' than most of the imagery in the urban landscape. Swoon's practice accentuates the permeability and intricacy of the city and is, in essence, a detailed exploration of that realm.

Dan Witz began painting on the streets of New York at the same time as subway trains were being bombed with graffiti and the culture of writing was expanding in size and scale. In direct contrast to the quickly executed, often large-scale names that were appearing across the city, Witz painted tiny, elaborate

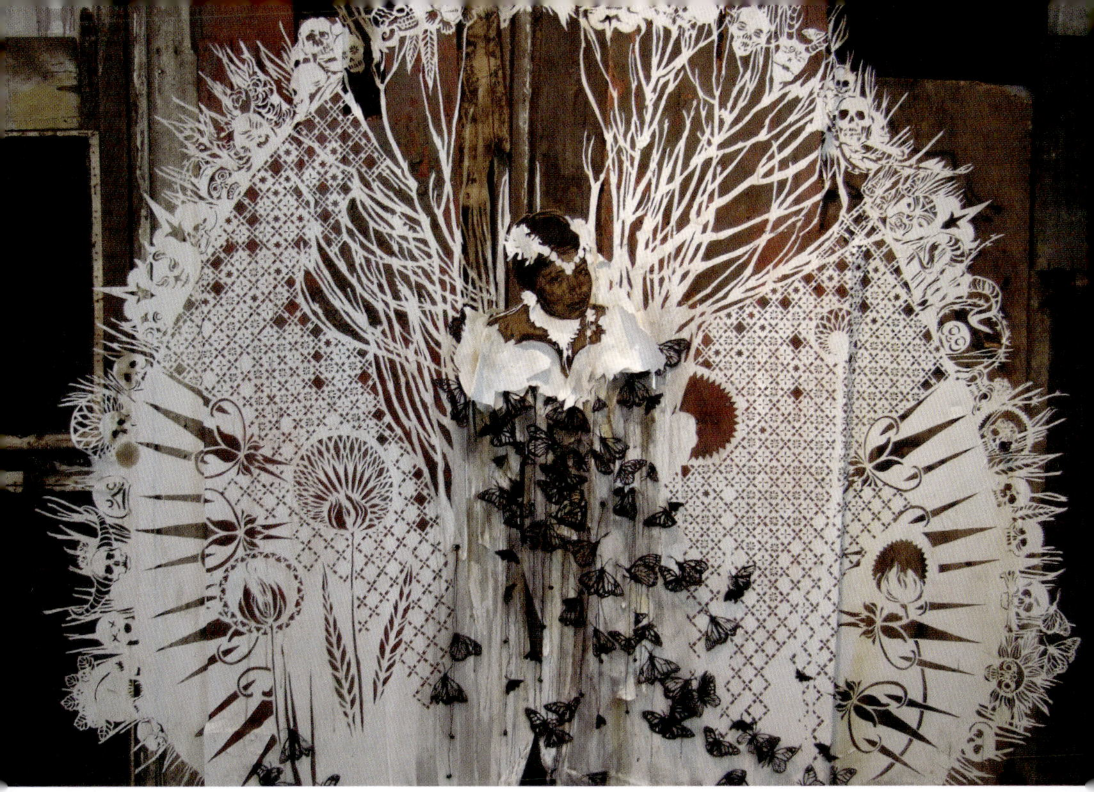

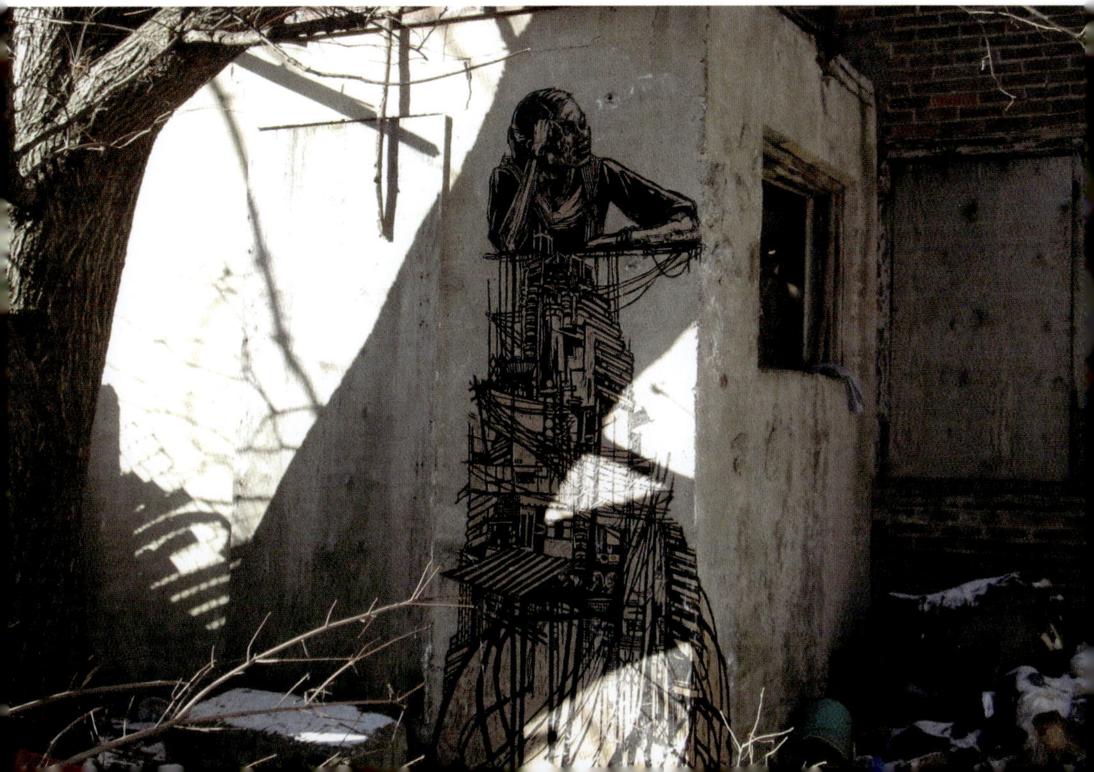

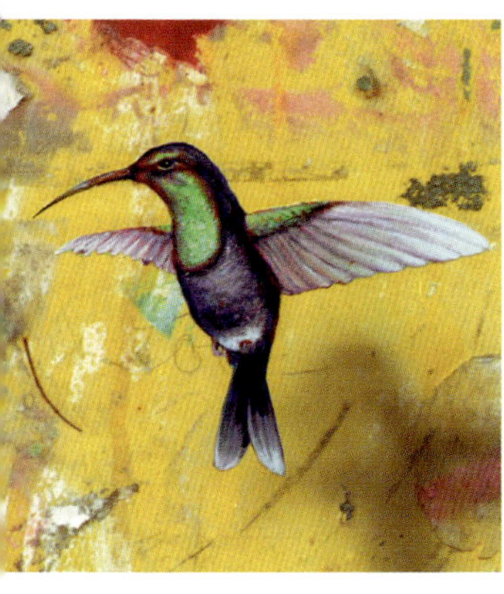

hummingbirds that took a long time to create [81]. Reflecting on his career, the artist muses: 'For me, painting on the street – doing anonymous, free, non-permissible works – was a very satisfying way of expressing my youthful disenchantment with the art establishment. And the lucky break was that there was a lasting humility lesson in it for me: ever since then I've wanted the impact of the work to be felt first, and only after that should you begin to wonder who did it and why.'

Since the late 1970s, his art practice has significantly expanded, yet it continues to be motivated primarily by a mutual exchange between the artwork and its environment. Recently, Witz has been using a trompe-l'œil technique to create artworks that seamlessly fit into all manner of otherwise commonplace urban spaces. His realistic depictions of people trapped behind vents, grids or bars are one such venture [82]. Working with sculpture, silk-screening, photography and oil painting, Witz varies his media as frequently as he varies his projects. Creating moments of surprise in the city allows him truly to intervene into otherwise unexceptional spaces.

Witz's pieces, like Swoon's, are inspired by everyday life and best experienced in person. Fascinated with realism, the artist has increasingly pushed the envelope in terms of producing life-like works that have the capacity to startle and jolt passers-

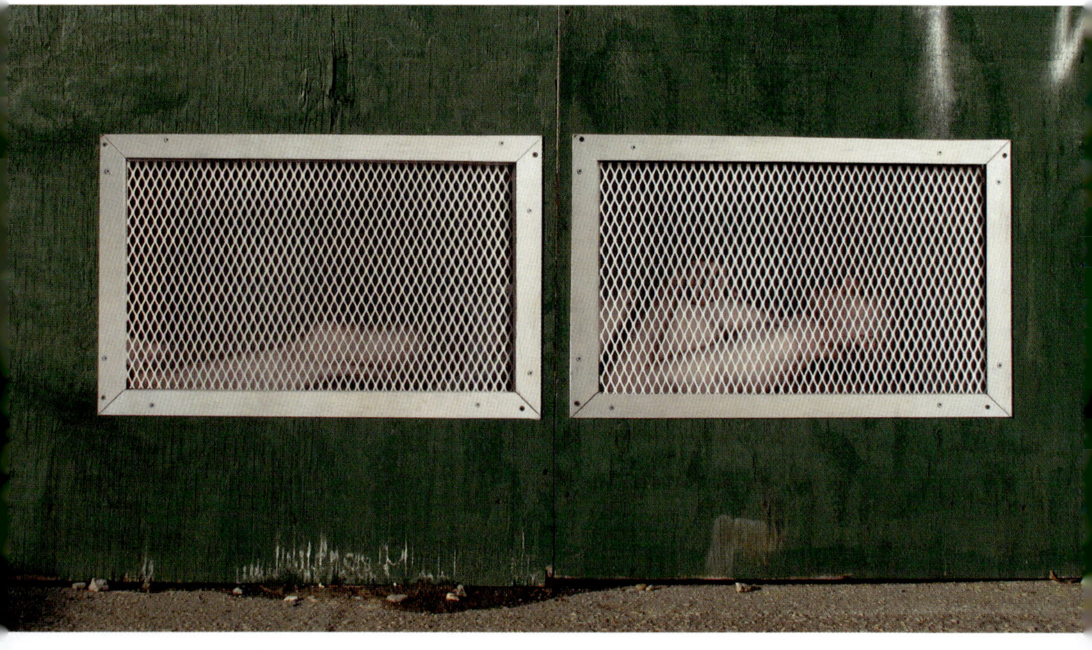

81 (*above*) **Dan Witz**, *Untitled*, 'Birds 2000' series, New York City, USA, 2000. In the late 1970s Dan Witz created his first extensive street art project, anonymously painting small hummingbirds in Lower Manhattan to contrast with the large-scale signature graffiti pieces. In 2000 he revisited his initial forays into street painting by inserting these fragile birds into the city's core.

by from oblivion. Making art accessible, especially to non-art audiences, has prompted Witz to create subtly witty, visually pleasing and incredibly captivating pieces. In his recent 'Ugly New Buildings' series, in digital and mixed media, he diffuses sculptural and trompe-l'œil images of human bodies or body parts on the condos that are taking over his New York neighbourhood. The pieces, which include sculpted hands coming out of a vent (2008) [83], are bold, eerie, comical and, above all, unexpected. The fact that a pair of manicured hands is striving to escape their owner's condo-life ideally conveys the architectural and social agenda that Witz is satirizing. Impeccably executed and always entertaining, the artist's practice continues to inflict moments of surprise in the context of the city.

While Swoon's work responds to the material structure and experience of the city, and Witz encourages site-specific accessibility through his practice, the collaborative venture known as Thundercut has created a series dependent on an emblematic city feature – the lights at pedestrian crossings. Although the work of this duo encompasses many different styles, they are best known in New York for altering the 'walk' symbol of crossing signs. Thundercut jovially call attention to an otherwise utilitarian feature of the cityscape by clothing the 'walkers' in hand-cut vinyl outfits, and in so doing give

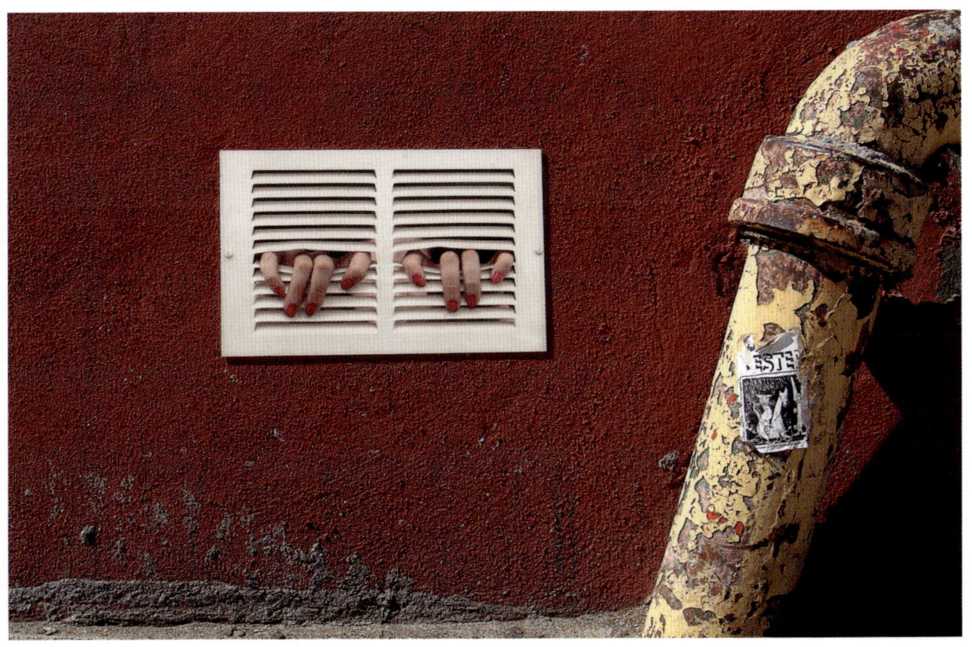

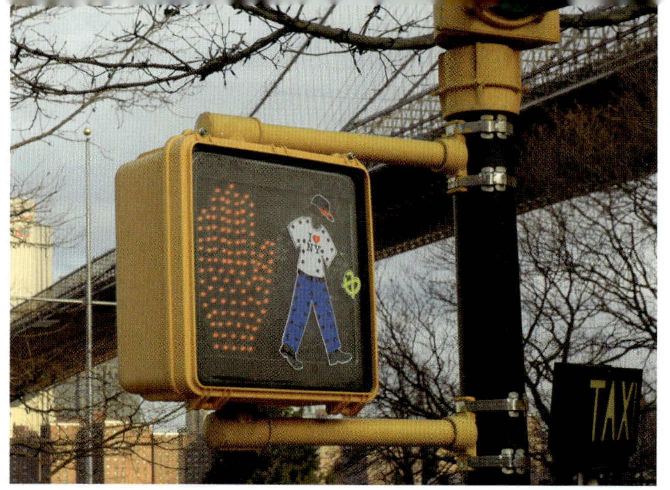

84 (*above*) **Thundercut**, *Tourist Walker*, New York City, USA, 2009. Thundercut's well-known 'Walker' series draws attention to a utilitarian urban feature, pedestrian crossing lights, by playfully outfitting the 'walk' symbol in original vinyl clothing that showcases different fashion styles and personality types. The walkers are typically dressed in attire that responds to their immediate location.

85 (*below*) **Thundercut**, *Graph Walker*, New York City, USA, 2008

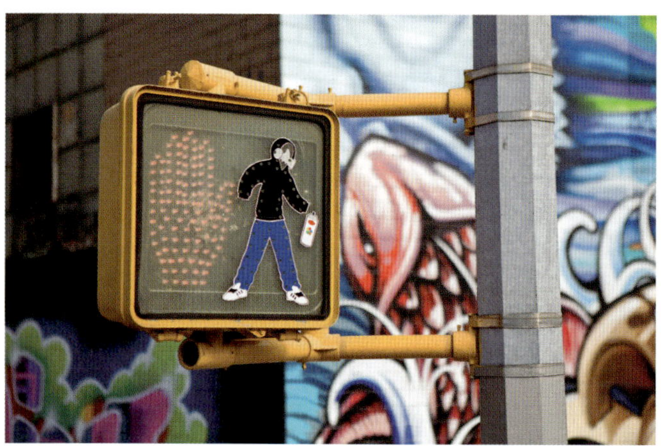

them personalities and urban styles. The walkers also typically reflect their immediate surroundings. For example, the *Tourist Walker* (2009) [84], sporting a baseball cap and an I ♥ NY T-shirt and with a pretzel in hand, is positioned near a taxi stand and the Brooklyn Bridge, while the *Graph Walker* (2008) [85], outfitted in Adidas trainers, a hoodie and a face mask, clutches his Krylon spray-paint next to a graffiti-covered wall. Such a simple act as modifying crossing lights vividly showcases the understated and ingenious power of street art. While not overtly political, this type of work perfectly exemplifies the thought-provoking, amusing, alternative and poetic potential of street art practices. Although fundamentally significant for the possibilities of creating unmediated responses to socio-political and cultural situations, art on the street is also valuable for the playful, momentary pauses it often encourages.

Here Today, Gone Tomorrow

The process of an artwork's birth and death in the complex of a city appeals to many urban painters for conceptual and structural reasons. Using the city as a canvas to recreate otherwise anonymous spaces and working with ephemeral materials accentuates the energy of the work (and the city) itself. When a work of art is fleeting, it engages concerns specifically linked both to its lifecycle and to its site of dissemination. The experience of urban painting as a transitory process is inextricably tied to the work's meaning as an element of a city's changing composition. For example, as paste-ups and posters age, rot, curl, tear and disappear, they reflect the cycle of life and generate a relationship between the audience and the work, the work and its context, and the everyday life of a city. The temporality of much street art thus visually translates the experience of being part of a city's fabric. Making art on city streets is both an anonymous expression of artistic freedom and a form of participatory performance, which facilitates the personalization and re-articulation of the visual cityscape.

Street art's ephemeral nature in the context of a city is typically an ingredient of the work itself. In its interactions with a changing environment, the artwork is created anew on a daily basis. For the most part the materials that artists use are not durable and the urban environment, which subjects the work to weather, pollution and buffing, emphasizes this fact. The illegality of graffiti and street art impacts considerably on both their transient nature and the intentions of many of their producers, who want to establish a connection with the city without necessarily getting permission to do so.

Hungarian-born Mosstika, aka Edina Tokodi, brings the natural world into the heart of New York through street art. Working with plant matter, the artist introduces organic vegetation on city walls and in so doing temporarily reminds city-dwellers of life beyond the concrete jungle. The large chunks of moss that Mosstika fashions into animal, human and vegetal shapes have their own expiration dates. Like Andy Goldsworthy, who works with natural elements such as twigs and rocks found in situ to create ephemeral sculptures, Mosstika reshapes organic matter to produce images. Unlike Goldsworthy, however, her manipulated moss figures populate the city rather than the country. With her urban greenery, Mosstika reflects the cycle of life, advocates sustainable living and artfully participates in the creation of urban visual culture.

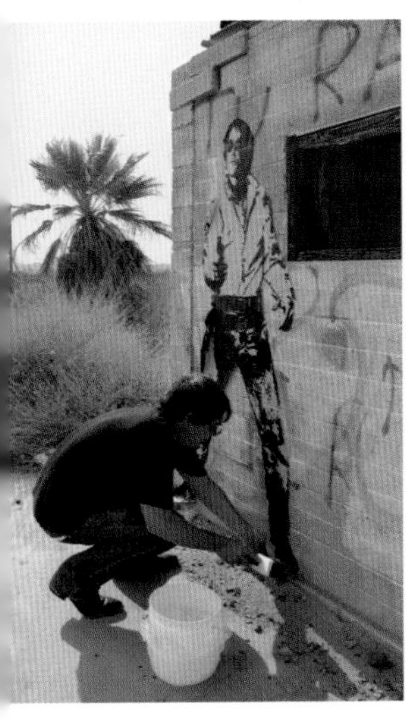

86 **Blek le Rat**, *The Spaceout Cowboy*, Arizona, USA, 2007

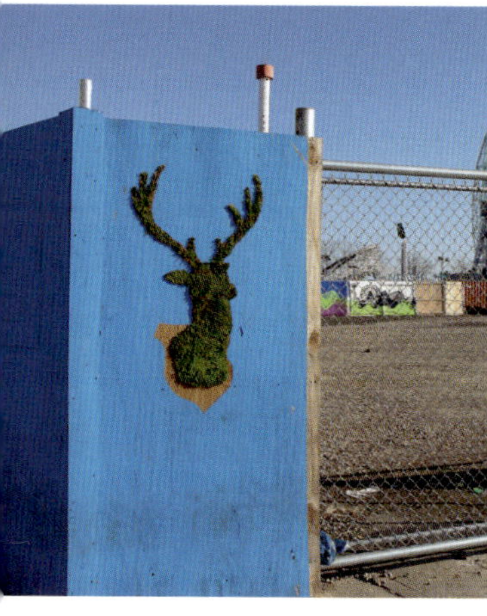 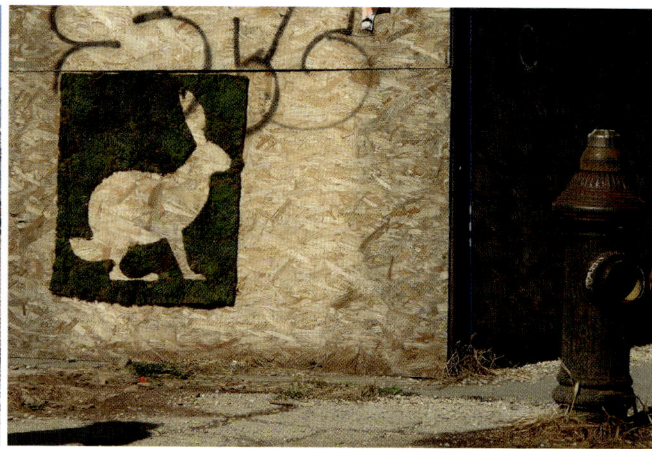

Mosstika, aka Edina Tokodi, is on a mission to remind city-dwellers of the natural world by introducing organic plant matter, shaped into all manner of images, into the heart of the city. The artist's manipulated moss stands out in the world of street art by virtue of its live materiality.

87 (*above left*) **Mosstika**, *Coney Island Moss*, New York City, USA, 2008

88 (*above right*) **Mosstika**, *Brooklyn Moss Rabbit*, New York City, USA, 2009

By working with living materials that continue to grow in their recontextualized states, the artist deals with the question of ephemerality in a unique fashion. Often displayed on scaffolding, which is in itself a temporary medium, the artist's moss stencils celebrate the natural world while suggesting our part in its destruction. *Coney Island Moss* (2008) [87], depicting a deer head on a plaque next to Coney Island's amusement park, for example, conjures up the idea of hunting for game. Through cut-outs or reverse cut-outs of animal silhouettes in a vegetal medium, Mosstika quietly insinuates nature's troubled survival in otherwise industrialized locations. *Brooklyn Moss Rabbit* (2009) [88], representing the disappearance of a rabbit from its leafy terrain, proposes more generally the extinction of animals, while *Wunderbaum* (2009) [89] is a witty commentary on the dematerialization of the natural world. With pieces displayed in unlikely places, such as a heart cut out of moss in a subway car (2008) [90], Mosstika advocates green love and respect for nature.

While Mosstika works with living materials that will inevitably die, artistic collective Faile grapple with impermanence as a symptom of the urban experience. Executed in a variety of media including wood, stencilling and wheat-pasted posters, their creations typically include an amalgamation of images, symbols and text. Overlapping, contrasting and layering – the strategies adopted by Faile – are representative of urban culture as a whole. Working from comic books, signage, novel cover-art, newspapers and photographs, Faile visually reproduce the fragmented reality of our experience of the city. Their poster

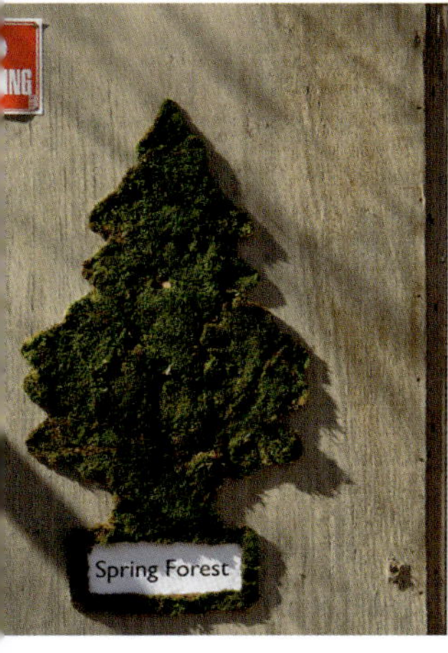

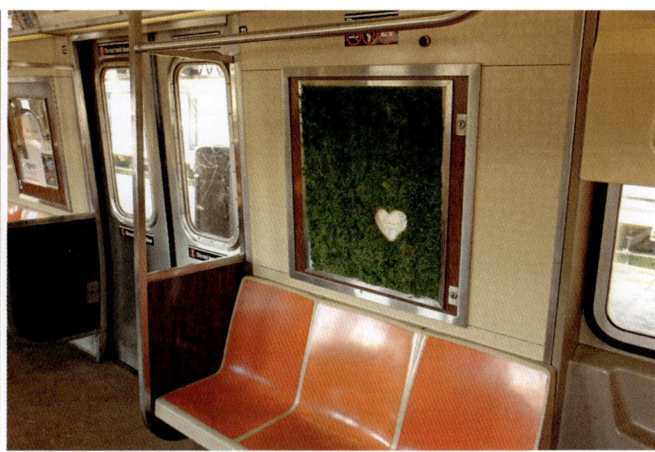

89 (*above left*) **Mosstika**, *Wunderbaum*, New York City, USA, 2009

90 (*above right*) **Mosstika**, *Metro*, New York City, USA, 2008

collages are neither politically motivated nor meant to convey a specific message, but instead tactfully relay the story of the city [91]. Although they might trigger an emotional response, the narratives that the artists create through the process of appropriation and assemblage are overwhelmingly fractured and at times nonsensical. Faile's overall vision is far less lasting than the objects and subjects that infuse their works. At a glance their work seems to advertise an event, but ultimately it advertises Faile itself.

Save Your Stilettos, Faile's a Comin' (2010) [92] exemplifies the playfulness of Faile's work. Reminiscent of band posters, the work's combination of image and text is emotive and meaningful in its meaninglessness. These sorts of illogical combinations of image and text, which often deal with a sense of longing, wonder and anticipation, function like event posters – notices that have a limited material lifespan and fulfil their role for a finite period of time. Playing with the essence of the show poster as a form of promotion, Faile effectively strip it down to its material and visual function. As an element that appears and disappears within the visual culture of the city, such posters reflect the vibrancy of urban life: they advertise that something is happening. Advertising the collective through this ephemeral medium, Faile humorously emphasize the experience of art as a fleeting moment in the experience of the everyday.

The process of disintegration is a common concern in street art production. The Graffiti Research Lab (GRL) seeks to facilitate transitory street art through technology. Based in New York, but with sister organizations worldwide, GRL

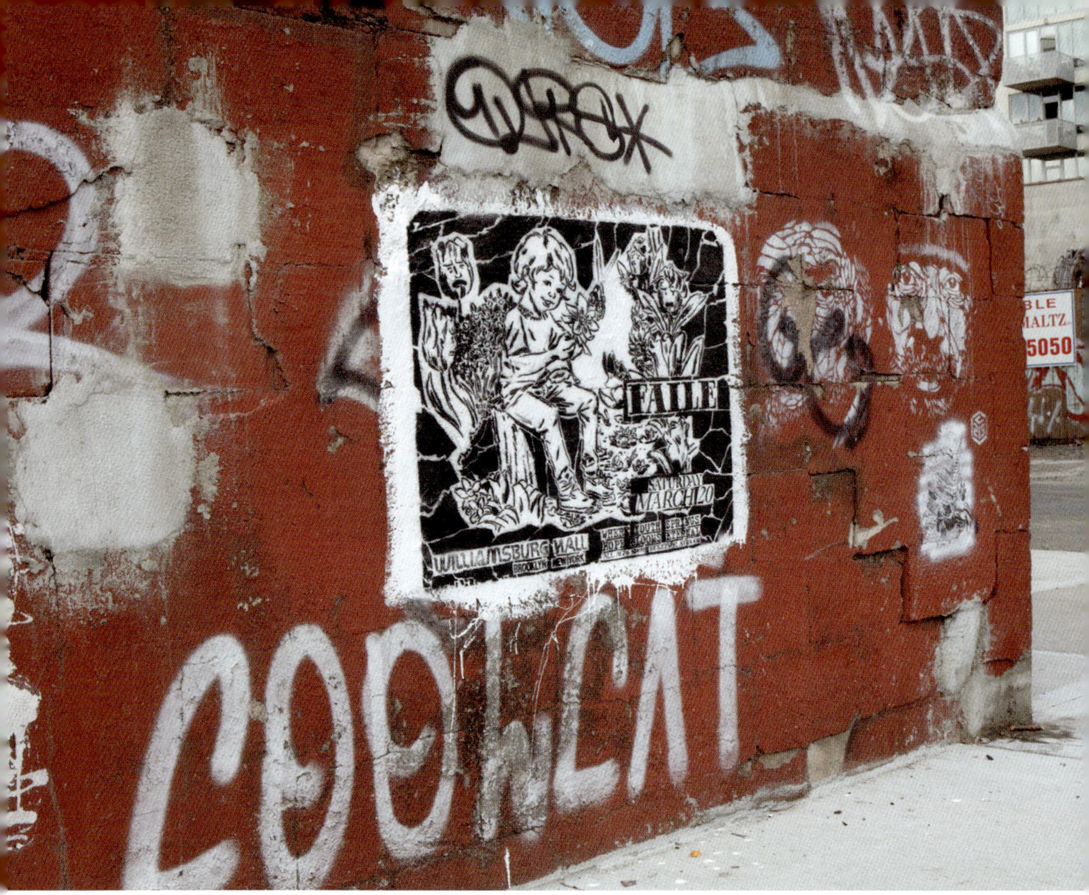

91 (*above*) **Faile**, *Untitled*,
New York City, USA, 2010.
The poster collages for which
artists' collective Faile is best
known reflect our fragmented
experience of the urban
environment. Drawing from
comic books, signage, novel
cover-art, newspapers and
photographs, the results are
reminiscent of event posters
but are fractured, apparently
meaningless and at times
nonsensical. Stripping down the
advertising poster to its material
and visual function allows Faile
to comment on the experience
of art as a fleeting moment in the
bustling, layered city.

92 (*right*) **Faile**, *Save Your
Stilettos, Faile's a Comin'*, New
York City, USA, 2010

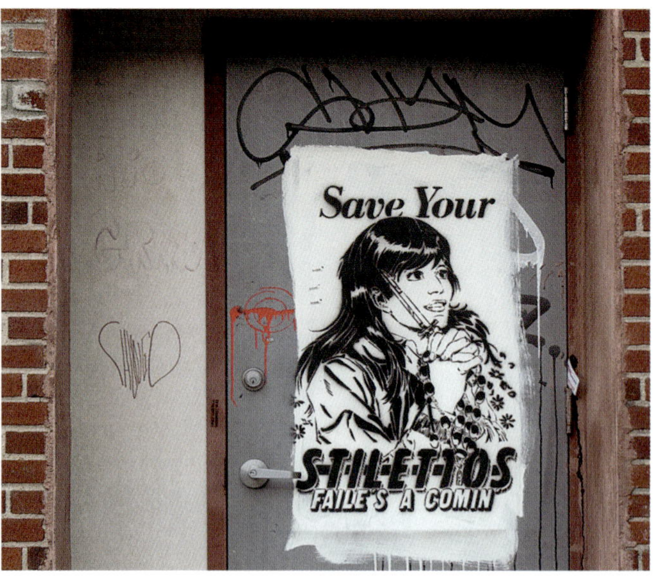

helps graffiti writers, street artists and urban activists to produce temporary works with inexpensive everyday devices by providing open-source tools and technological how-to information through their website. Through the promotion of various projects, including LED throwies and Laser Tags, GRL not only makes all manner of graffiti more user-friendly but also a great deal more temporary. Developed by Evan Roth, James Powderly and Theo Watson, Laser Tag involves the use of a computer, projector and laser pointer to project tags on desired locations. As well as maximizing street artists' access to technological templates, GRL is primarily concerned with destigmatizing an illegal art movement.

Fuelled by the artist's interest in the diverse styles of graffiti writing, Roth's own projects such as *Graffiti Taxonomy* and *Graffiti Analysis* deconstruct the practice and artistry of writing. In *Graffiti Taxonomy* (2004–present) [93], Roth takes isolated letters from various graffiti tags – 'S', for example – and presents them at a similar size in a grid 'to show the diversity of styles as expressed in a single character', to use the artist's own words. The ongoing study *Graffiti Analysis* [94], on the other hand, captures an artist's motions during tagging to create digital visualizations of the original strokes. Roth's repositioning of graffiti writing in the language of information analysis, 'offering a system for greater understanding of a highly coded form of creative expression', effectively tracks the creative gesture of writing. These sorts of analytical projects not only combine new media with graffiti and street art, but also put forward these art forms as a technological object of inquiry. Using new media for graffiti diffusion is a growing sub-genre of street art, which suggests continued developments in this renegade art movement.

93 (*right*) **Evan Roth**, *Graffiti Taxonomy: 'S'*, New York City, USA, 2004. Roth has isolated letters from a variety of graffiti tags in order to explore the diversity of style expressed through a single letter – 'S', for example. The ongoing study reveals the importance for graffiti writers of personal style as manifested through letterforms.

94 (*far right*) **Evan Roth**, *Graffiti Analysis: 'Hell'*, New York City, USA, 2005. Tracking the motion of graffiti writing enables Roth to analyse the creative gesture through technological means. This open-source project intends to archive graffiti in code, thus bringing together two worlds that are both interested in hacking systems.

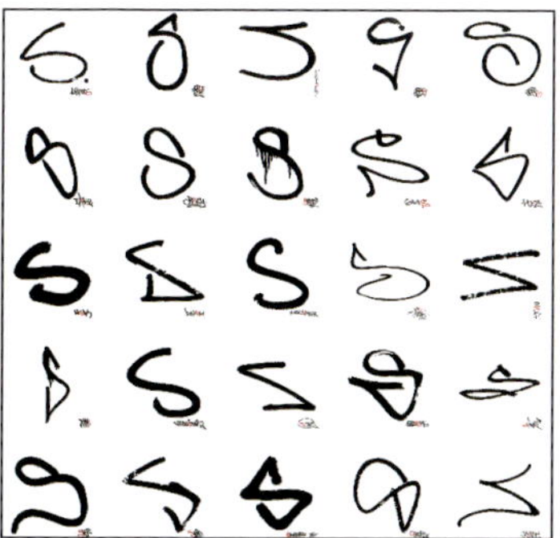

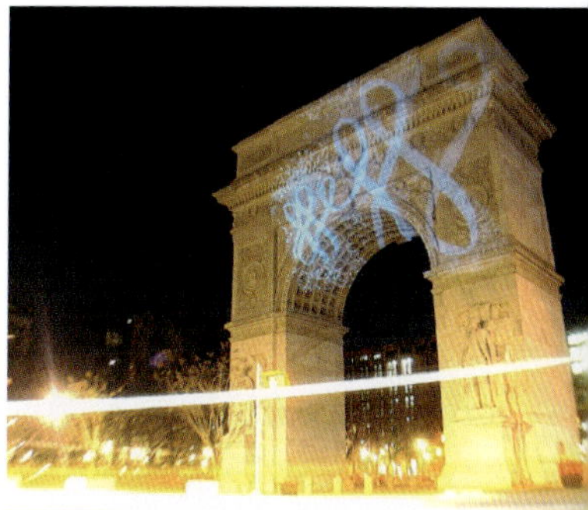

Performing Street Art

The unexpected, in terms of placement and imagery, is one
of street art's greatest qualities. However, exhibiting work
in spaces that are part of people's everyday lives invites two
key questions: how implicated is the spectator in the work's
significance? And, can we assume that, simply because of its
presence on the street, post-graffiti art is somehow more
accessible or more meaningful to people's lives?

At the most basic level, art practices diffused in the urban
realm are arguably more accessible because of the inability by
any one individual to purchase or own them, since they are
displayed for the citizenry. The placement of art in streets
navigated on a daily basis by hundreds of people attests to its
accessibility. Although we cannot measure whom street art
reaches or affects, just as we cannot assess the true impact of
the plethora of advertising and signage in the public sphere,
we can assume that street art operates from a unique vantage
point in a city. Its illegality and diversity of style ensure that
neither its production nor its consumption is limited by private
taste or financial reward. On the margins of what is designed
for us to see and consume in our cities, street art responds to
the needs of its makers and those who experience it as an art
world of resistance. In other words, although we might see it
without really looking at it, street art challenges the art system,
consumer culture and media-saturated urban environments,
while promoting freedom of thought and expression and often
advocating social consciousness.

The intersection between the work, the street and the viewer
is one that cannot be taken for granted. This junction creates
an element of surprise on the artwork's discovery and, in that
moment, also facilitates the work's transitory completion.
The meeting point of art, place and person can be envisaged
as its own space, something Swoon describes as 'a moment
of recognition, a wink from another human presence which is
there but not there, like a little reflection of self embedded in
the wall'. The space of communication created by street art is
accommodated by the work's interaction with other physical
and visual elements, as well as its socio-cultural context. It is a
performative space in the sense that the artist, the work, the
viewer and the location all play a part: the artist through the
process of diffusion, the work and viewer by virtue of reception,
and the location by providing the site of confrontation on which
the myriad performances of the piece are dependent. Directly

95 (*above*) **Buff Monster**, *Untitled*, Los Angeles, USA, 2010. By virtue of its mere presence in the cityscape, street art challenges consumerism, advertising and the art system while promoting freedom of thought and the expression of unmediated political or playful ideas for free. Buff Monster serves as a good example, spreading happiness, joy and a love of the colour pink through his mischievous monsters.

96 (*below*) **Shepard Fairey**, *Zapatista Woman*

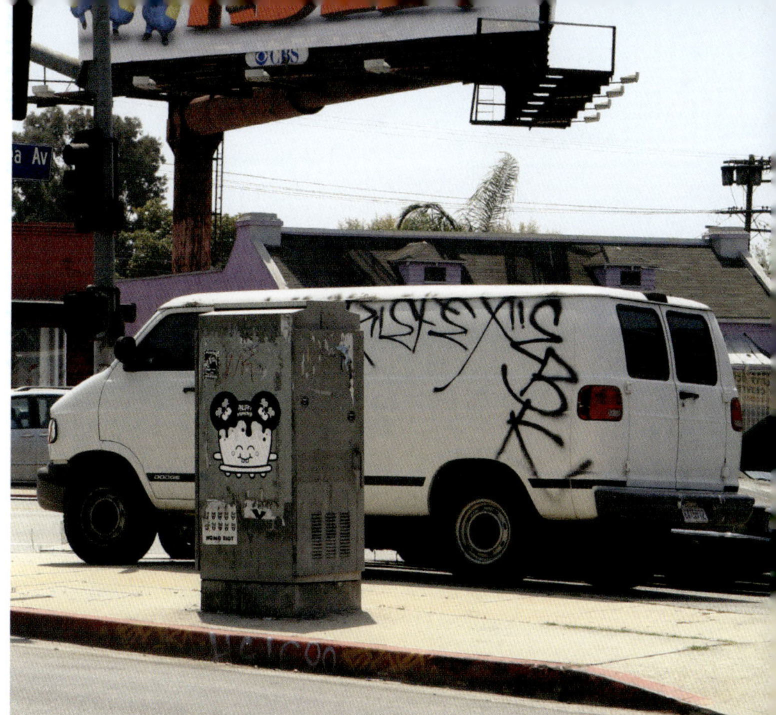

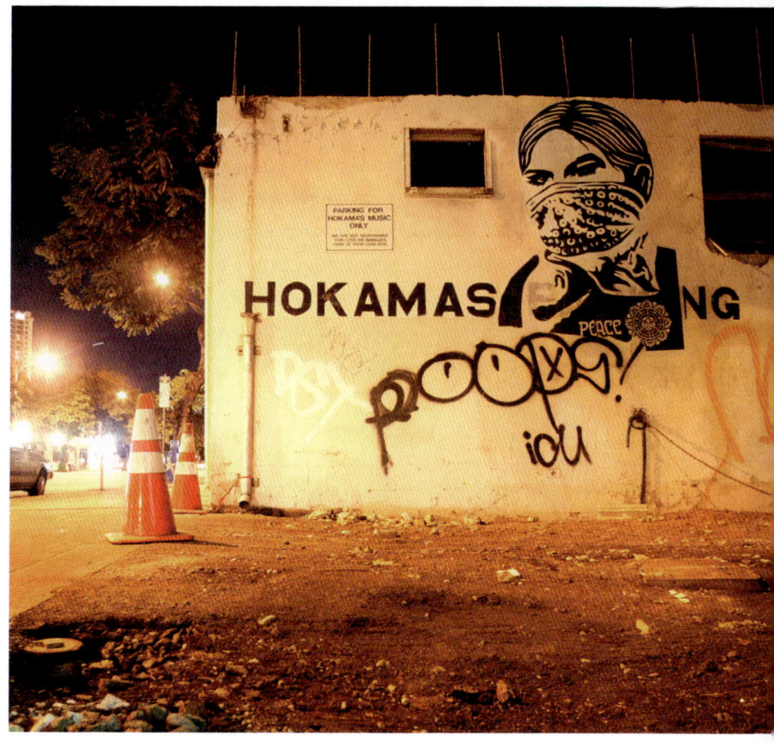

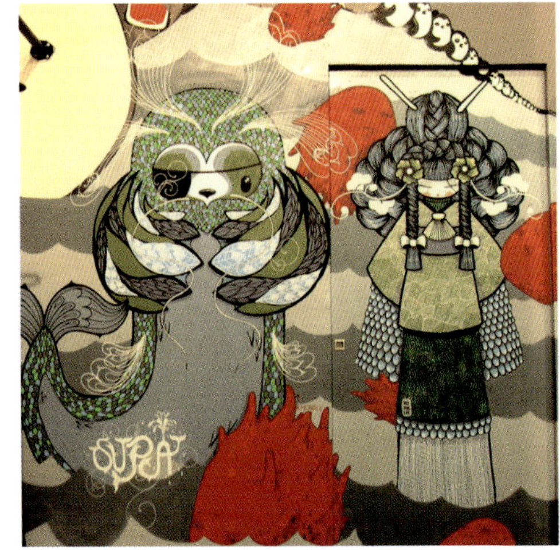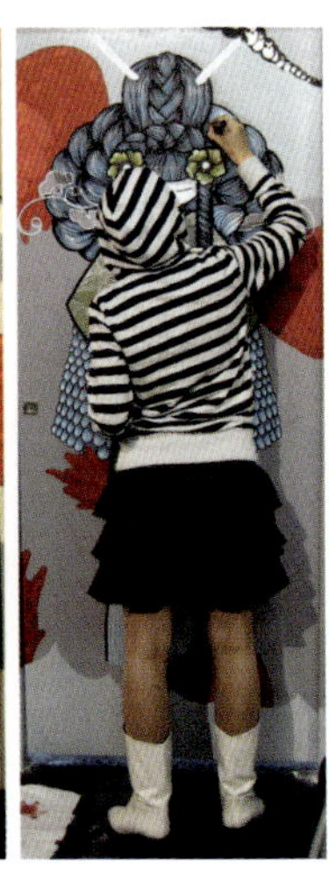

linked to the everyday life of a city, these works propose powerful crossovers between the artist's expression and the viewer's experience of the urban environment.

This concept is effectively illustrated with the art of Miss Van. Boldly colourful, her *poupées* create seductive and mischievous spaces in the cityscape. When, in the early 1990s, Miss Van began disseminating her unique brand of street art in Toulouse, her glamorous, feisty creations were certainly not the graffiti norm. Their exaggerated femininity, made explicit by their soft, round shapes, long, flowing hair and sultry make-up, also defines their controversial allure. Fashioned with acrylics and latex paints, the dolls are visually provocative through their suggestive attire, exposed flesh, poses and expressions, which sometimes verge on pornographic. Occasionally they are accompanied by cuddly animals or toys, which are meant as proxies for boys (boy-toys). Interested in provoking spirited reactions by painting sexualized characters in unlikely places, the artist insists that her pin-up inspired women are never vulgar, simply suggestive. Her interest in playing on ambiguities and depicting females as both girls and women has resulted in numerous characters that are vaguely melancholic, arrogant, sweet, erotic, naive and exceptionally alluring.

Through the seductive and disconcerting playfulness of her dolls, Miss Van expresses her fantasies and appeals to the imaginations of her audiences. One piece, a latex painting of 2006 [99], is at once charming and confrontational, whimsical and sensual, cute and dangerous. The doll's loosely arranged

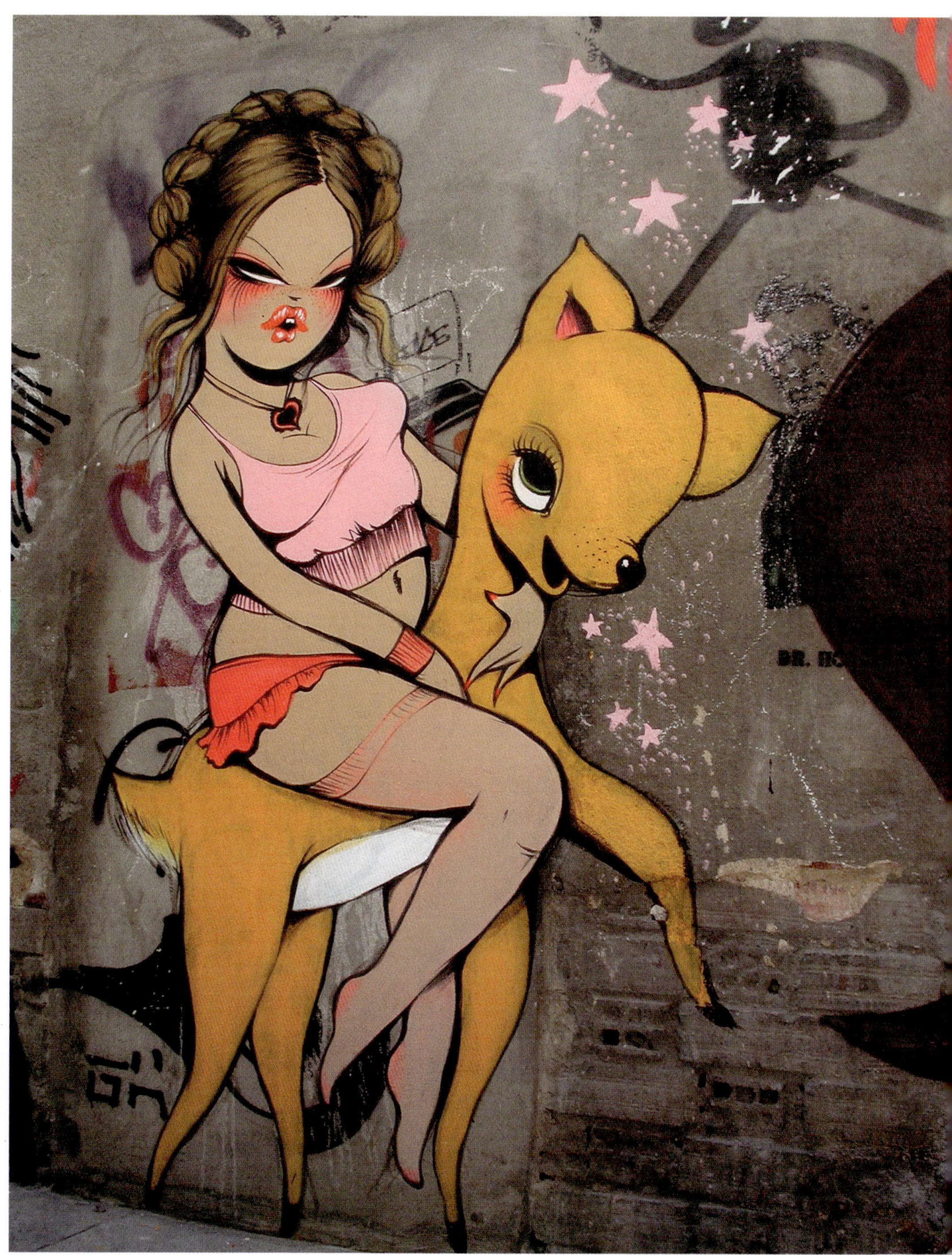

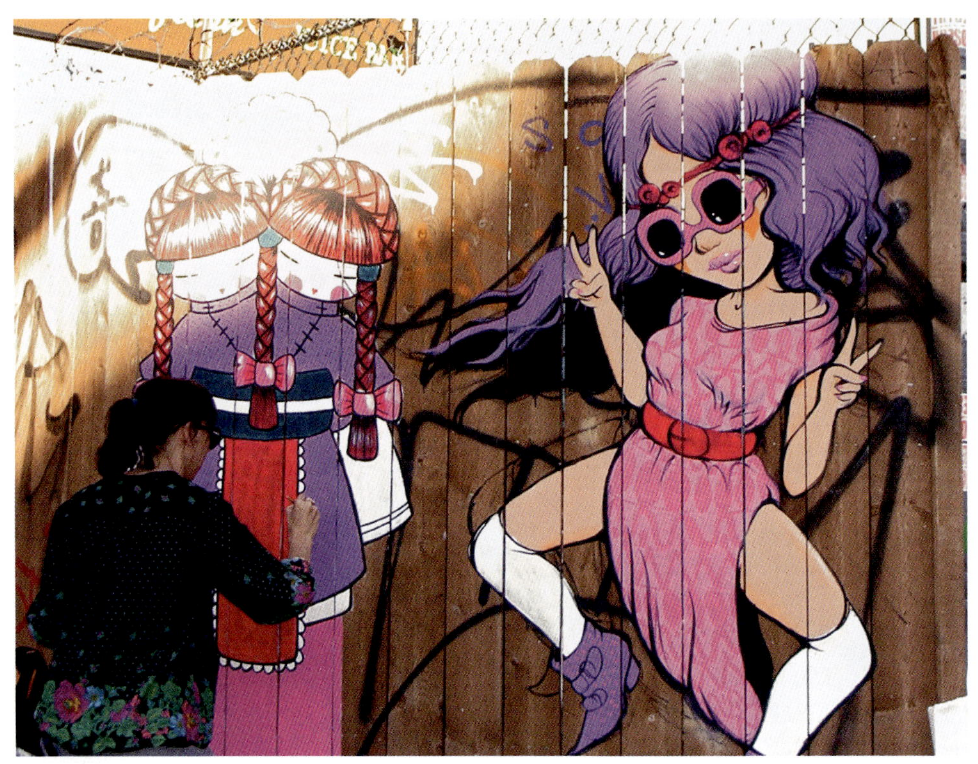

100 **Koralie and Fafi**, *Untitled*, New York City, USA, 2008. The juxtaposition of Koralie's geisha-doll and Fafi's *fafinette* showcases both artists' established styles and, more significantly, plays on opposing female representations. Although painted in strikingly similar colours, one figure is intriguingly demure, the other overtly sexual.

braid, revealing pink attire and a heart-shaped petulant mouth, which is echoed in her necklace, creates a comfortable, dreamy and sexy scene. Her suggestive pose on a deer, with pink stars illuminating the scenario, further implies intimacy and erotica. The scene as a whole is soft, delicate and fanciful, except for the doll's disturbingly direct gaze – a recurring motif in Miss Van's work. The eyes are unsettling because they disrupt the sexual fantasy. Somewhere between the palette's softness, the deer's beckoning stance and the doll's buoyant manner lies the work's true appeal. The carefully rendered scene of innocence and naivety is in fact anything but, given the doll's menacing gaze and her teasingly mischievous pose. As a whole, the image is further complicated by its contextualization in an austere and unwelcoming landscape where grey walls are decorated with more traditionally 'severe' graffiti. Miss Van's dolls, which are ultimately based on some physical and character traits of their author, are neither explicitly portraits of real people nor reflections on a city. Instead, as fantasies pasted on city walls, they are stylistically in keeping with some commercial imagery, but relate personal narratives and ambiguous stories that are left open to interpretation.

In contrast to Miss Van's provocative *poupées*, the geisha-dolls of fellow French artist Koralie are presented fully clothed. While other cartoonish female characters are costumed, accessorized and coiffed to reflect their temperament, Koralie's girls do not depict a certain mood or personality. However, as representations of a specific doll-type, they are inherently performative both in terms of their role as geisha, who are effectively entertainers, and in the theatrical elements that make up their design, particularly their fanciful hairdos and attire. The artist explores the notion of performance through changes in seasons and national costumes, as well as texture and the elements of art and design. Always colour-coordinated and never revealing any part of the body aside from their rosy-cheeked faces, her geometric characters play dress-up in a way that takes the focus away from the female form and accentuates decorative elements, while retaining a seductively calm demeanour in their quiet stance. Their tranquil faces create an elegant counterbalance to their layered clothing and the typically stark backgrounds they inhabit.

Brazilian artist Alexandre Órion's work performs in an entirely different manner. While Órion's stencils function as images on their own, it is through their photographed, in situ representation that he achieves his finished product. The 'Metabiotics' project (2002–5) combines photography, street art and the city-dweller's unwitting participation. Órion must often wait patiently for days before he captures a synchronicity between his work and the passer-by. The theatricality of his practice becomes intelligible through the photograph. Unsuspecting pedestrians, in their navigation of the city, fulfil the role that has been set up for them, and thus the artwork is complete. Whether the scenario is a labourer hard at work while his co-worker takes a rest and looks on (2005) [103], an unsuspecting pedestrian about to have an encounter with a falling flowerpot (2004) [102], or a *pixação* writer's work being painted over before he has finished writing (2004) [101] (*pixação* is a unique form of writing native to Brazil), Órion's participatory narratives come to life through performance. The artist establishes the parameters for this sort of performance first and foremost through the dissemination of crisply angular black-and-white, life-size images. His stencils, when animated by the public, take on another layer of meaning, which in turn

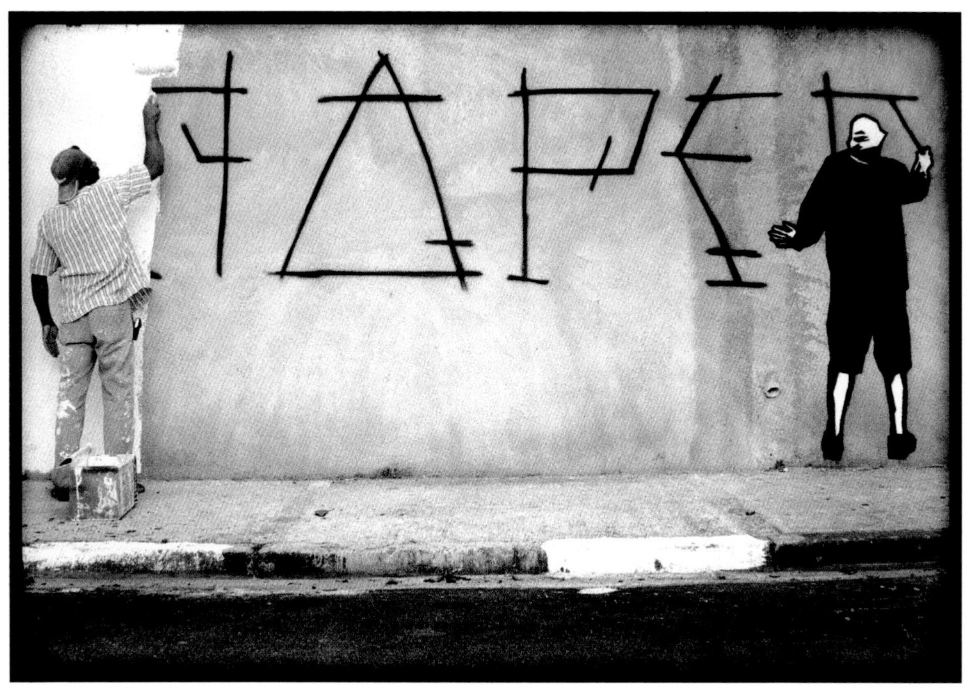

creates a narrative. The interaction between the work, its physical location and members of the public reveals witty, ordinary and poetic tales of life in the metropolis.

Identity Politics

Composed of spaces designed to accommodate the flow of traffic – pedestrian or vehicle – a city, as a planned, architecturally defined realm, is always in flux. By virtue of authorized and unauthorized movement within the cityscape, its make-up changes. Circumventing ordinary expectations of a city's visual imagery, street art's transient interpretations of sites emphasize the uses of public space – particularly as works in progress. As such, the artworks also function as vehicles for identity formation vis-à-vis their sites of dissemination. The place appropriated and subsequently vacated by the artist is marked out as a space to be occupied by the viewer. Of course, any work of art, anonymous or not, can be interpreted as the work of both the artist and the audience through the process of reception. However, this relationship is particularly acute in relation to street art. Owing to its temporal nature, and because the artists work under pseudonyms, the ambiguity of

Alexandre Órion's
'Metabiotics' project, from
which the works on this
spread are taken, effectively
necessitates both the
image and the passer-by to
realize the final product:
the photograph. Only in
the context of the city
can this sort of accidental
performance on the part of
the urban dweller complete
the work of art.

101 (*opposite*) **Alexandre
Órion**, *Metabiotica 16*, São
Paulo, Brazil, 2004

102 (*above*) **Alexandre
Órion**, *Metabiotica 14*, São
Paulo, Brazil, 2004

103 (*below*) **Alexandre
Órion**, *Metabiotica 18*, São
Paulo, Brazil, 2005

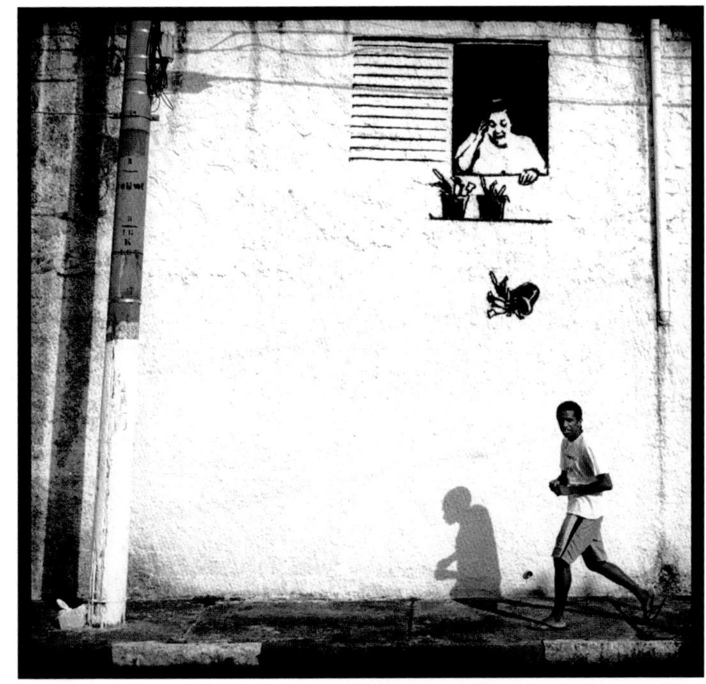

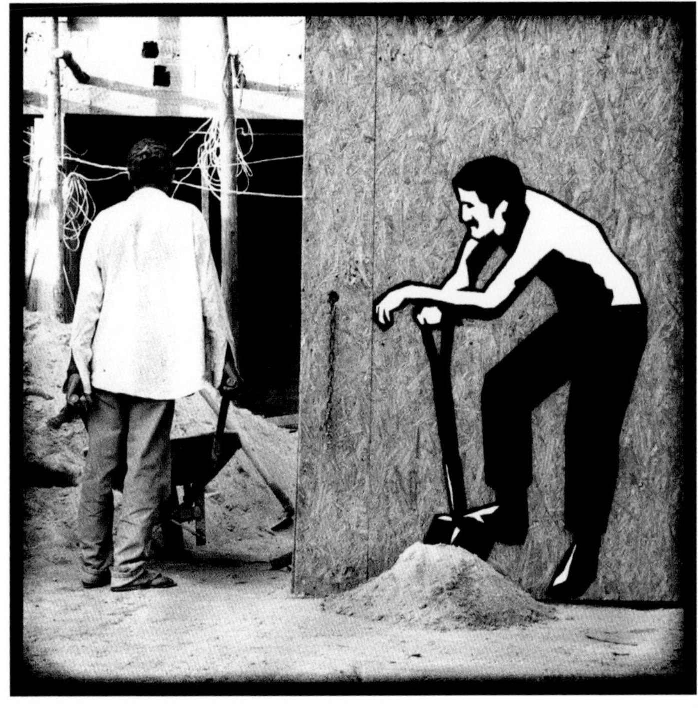

authorship invites the spectator to consider the work in the present moment. Experiencing art on the street often raises the central question of authorship: who made this and why?

The stencilled artworks of Australian artist Vexta reveal the fruitful intersection between authorship and anonymity in the process of identity formulation in the cityscape. Vexta's stencil art focuses on portraits that resonate with members of the public on an emotional level, and is displayed in places accessible to a large and varied audience. Characterized by bold colours in which detailed portraits of friends are juxtaposed with splashes of paint and feathers, or fallen leaves that emulate hands, Vexta's creations tend to represent the joys and sorrows of everyday life [105]. The hand/leaf motif, both ominous and lively, is one the artist returns to continually because hands 'represent a connection of ourselves to our surrounding natural world'. Indeed, contrasting organic elements such as plants, leaves and feathers with playful images of people enables the artist to captivate viewers' attention. Vexta's fascination with 'the way we are motivated by pleasure and pain' is echoed throughout pieces that are frequently explorations of emotional states of being or moments lived [106].

The artist's subject matter is at once personal and universal, which makes the messages of her work relevant to a wide variety of people. Her portraits are colourful expressions of vulnerability, playfulness, tranquillity or action. Armed with an uncompromising interest in painting for the city and its inhabitants, the artist understands her practice as 'intrinsically connected to the city in its medium, message and form'. Identification with specific places thus aids in identity construction and, by the same token, particular places enable

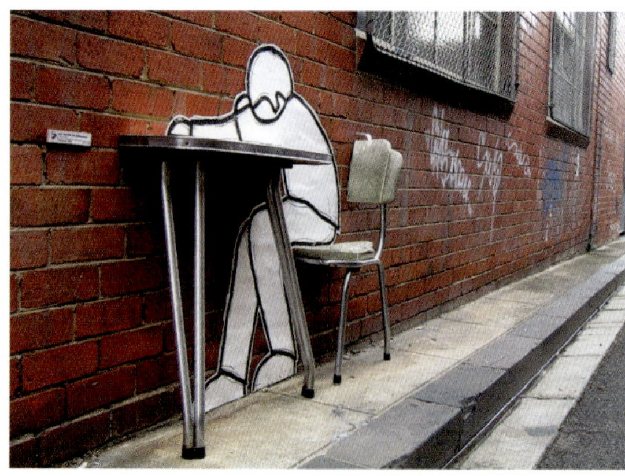

104 **Psalm**, *Bedtime for the Workaholic*, Melbourne, Australia, 2005. Street artists not only stick, stencil, paste and paint images on the walls of the city, but also construct three-dimensional works that amplify the surprise encounter between artwork and audience. Displaying labels with the work's title, as is common in a gallery show, suggests that the street is akin to a giant exhibition hall.

105 (*right*) **Vexta**, *We Are Creatures of the Wind*, Bogotá, Colombia, 2009. Vexta's human–animal hybrids are explorations of confinement within the city through which the artist suggests that we free ourselves from constraint. Her layered use of stencils reveals a painterly aesthetic, accentuated by overlapping neon colours that draw the viewer in.

106 (*below*) **Vexta**, *Ghetto Make-out*, Melbourne, Australia, 2009. Numerous versions of this work appear throughout the world. As a literal unmasking of the human form, this piece lays bare the beauty and fragility of human connections.

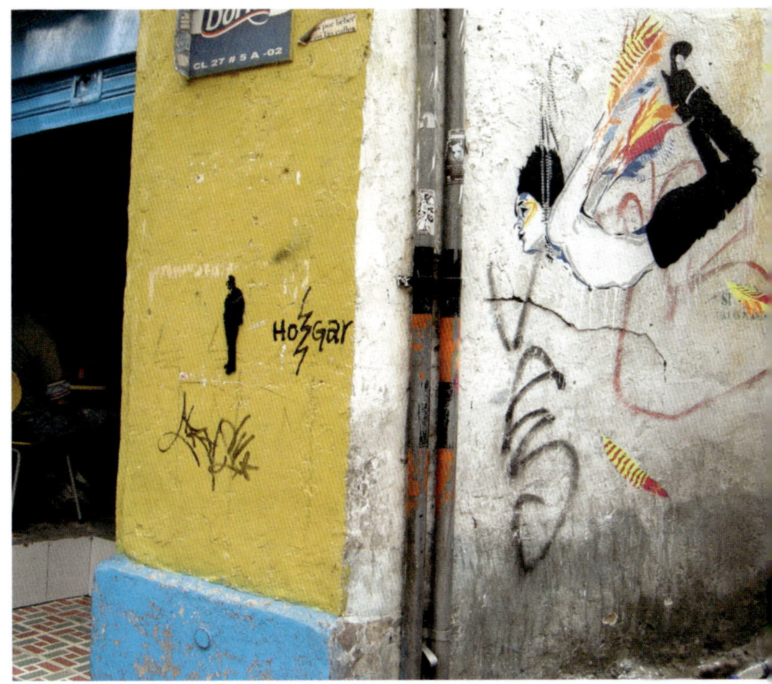

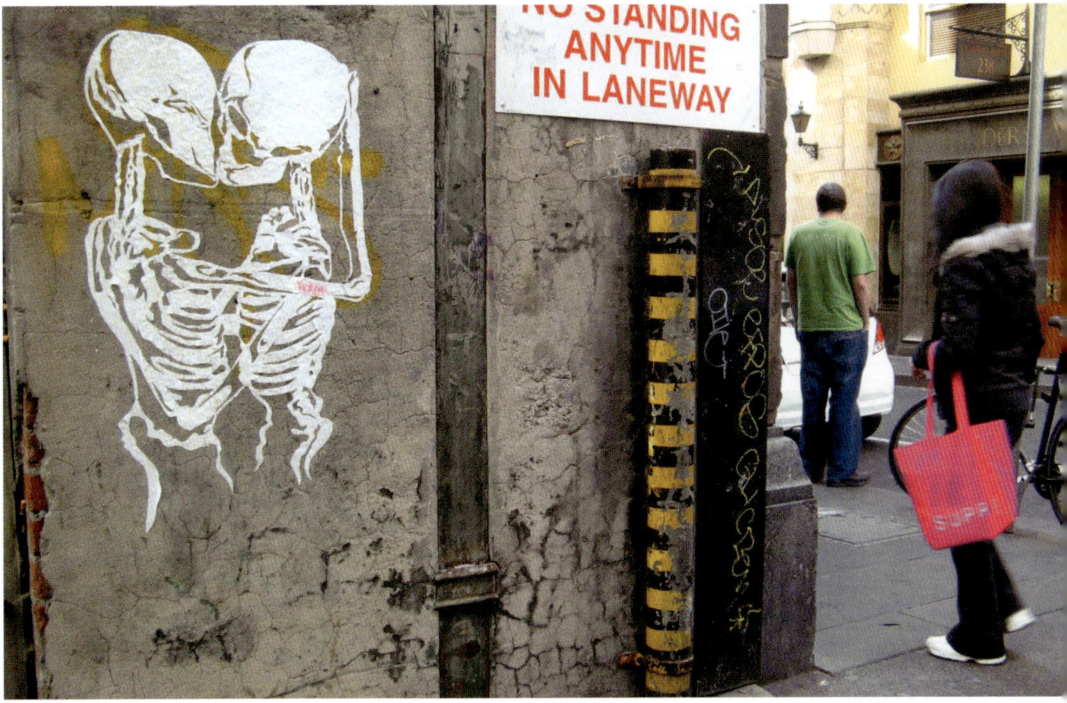

the formation of one's alter ego as a street artist. Through the process of painting throughout the city, street artists are both reconstituting the environment's visual landscape and their own identities. The city thus becomes a framework within which one's identity is made visible and accessible to the rest of the world. Vexta's portraits are motivated not as explorations of the citizenry, but as methods to participate in a city's imagery. The artist's belief in the power of art and her dislike of urbanity's coldness inspire her to paint portraits that in effect explore the soul of a city.

With the piece *Welcome to Australia* (2004) [107], Vexta chose to comment on Australia's severe immigration laws. Painted for a 'Fringe Festival' exhibition on the door of a commercial shed in Melbourne's Docklands, this large work required the artist to be strapped into a harness in order to access the space freely. Vexta's rendition of combat-ready riot police ironically placed beneath a welcoming caption was provoked by a contemporaneous situation. The artist explains: 'A few days before we were to begin painting, I learnt that some refugees who had been broken out of a detention centre had turned themselves in because life was too hard for them with no support. The fact that these people had come to my country asking for help and looking for support and had been met with such hostility, degradation and exclusion made me angry, so I decided to make an artwork showing what I felt was the image that Australia was projecting to the rest of the world. The photo I used to create the stencils of the riot police came from a close friend of mine who went to Baxter detention centre to protest its existence. Incidentally all detention centres in South Australia are now closed.'

Vexta's style successfully expresses a powerful message by offsetting the crisp imagery of riot-suited police officers with dripping paint, and by contrasting the written phrase with the image below. This piece is both meaningful to the Australian artist's own political views and to her national identity. Everything about *Welcome to Australia* feeds the work's significance, but above all its palette, location and size. The black, white and grey set a solemn tone and emphasize the severity of the situation. The fact that this mural is located on the doors of a shed where shipping containers are stored is also emblematic of the inhumane conditions many refugees face to reach their destination. Moreover, the sheer size of the work is daunting, and the officers depicted at ground level

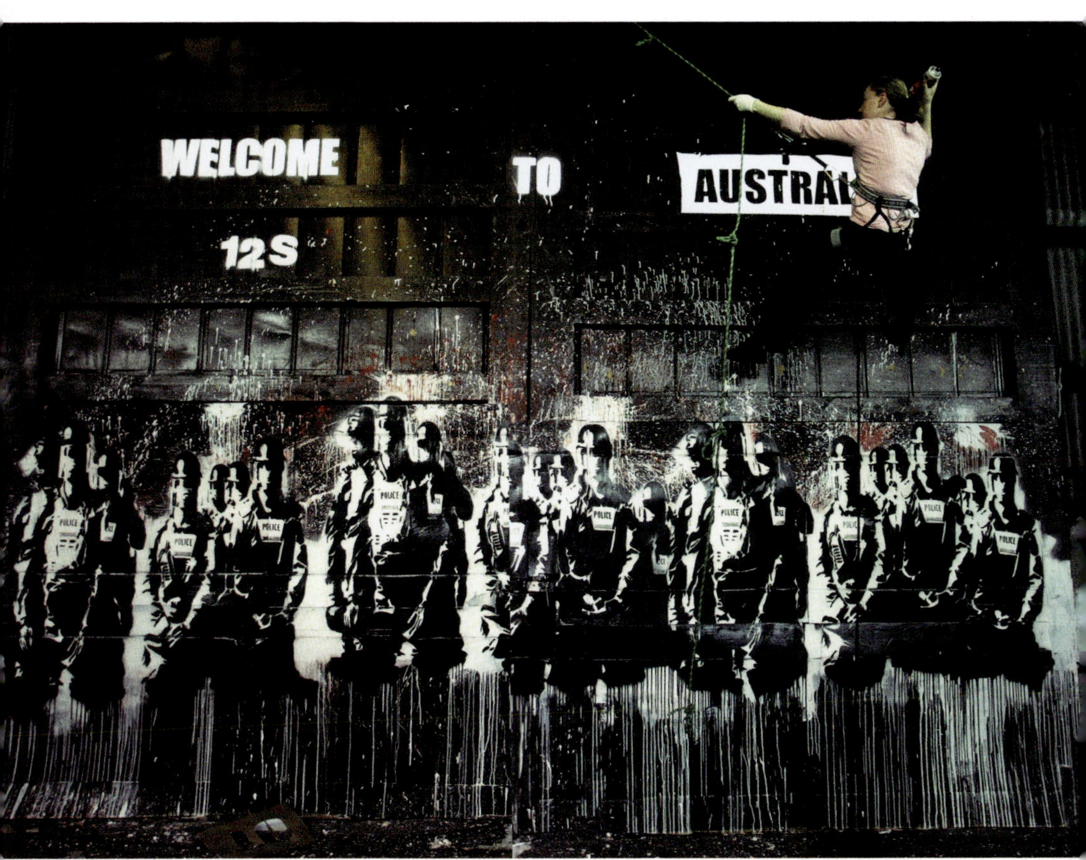

107 **Vexta**, *Welcome to Australia*, Melbourne, Australia, 2004. Vexta's early work was discernibly focused on social and political realities. The contradiction between text and image works well here as a comment on Australia's strict immigration policies.

are placed in direct confrontation with viewers. The immanent violence of the scene is also accentuated by the dripping paint. Painted on the street, this work, now destroyed, was a powerful exploration of controversial governmental policies with regards to refugees and immigrants, and reached a number of people who contacted the artist to express their views on the situation.

Stencil graffiti pioneer Nick Walker seeks to connect with as large an audience as possible with his often humorous street work. When the English artist began combining stencilling with freehand painting in 1992, he tapped into a form of visual expression that speaks to contemporary issues with irony and wit. Walker says: 'Painting is a form of escapism for me and if my work allows the spectator to do the same thing, then I've achieved more than I set out to do.' With his thought-provoking imagery, the artist remarks on modern life

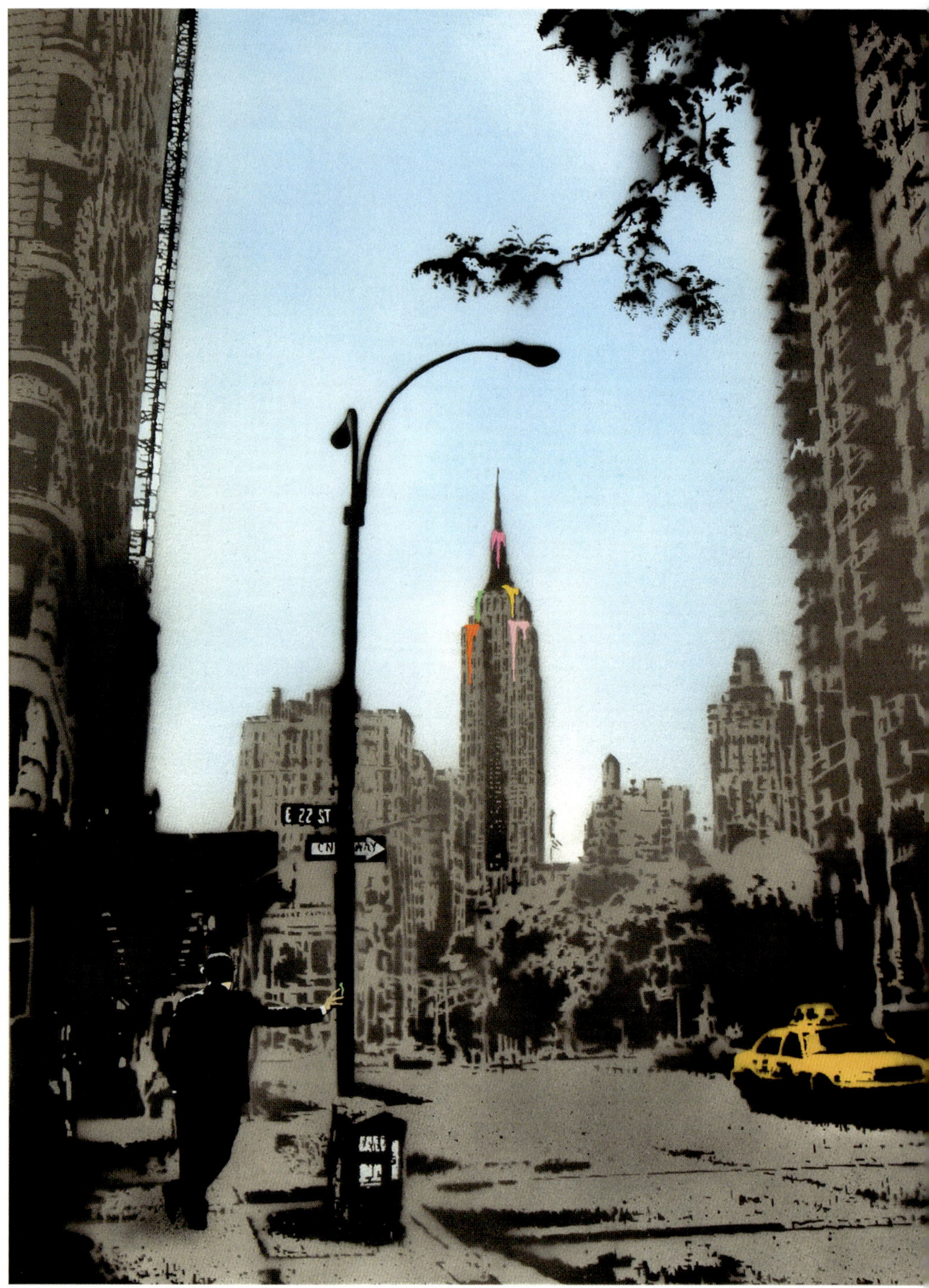

E 22 ST
ONE WAY

in both subtle and transparent ways. For example, an image of a life-size 'brat' doll wondering 'does my head look big in this?' (2009) [110] and an imagined role-reversal depicting a chihuahua as the master of his pursed human companion (2009) [109] are comical reflections on social realities. On the other hand, a miniature representation of a 'graffiti vandal' dressed as a gentleman so as not to arouse suspicion (2009) [108] is a clever comment on first impressions. With their art practices, both Vexta and Walker produce interpretive portraiture that examines emotional states and the actualities of life.

In addition to street artists and graffiti writers, many other contemporary artists, working legally in the city, are interested in the capacity to communicate with societies at large. Krzysztof Wodiczko's politically charged projections on public buildings and monuments, for example, explore history and present-day issues by giving life to otherwise stark public structures and by challenging public spaces. Others working in the public sphere such as Ken Lum address issues of socio-cultural, ethnic and political identity in relation to the culture of a city. Much of Lum's work relates to its urban setting with the goal of challenging conceptions of a national or geographically inscribed

108 (*opposite*) **Nick Walker**, *The Empire's State*, 'The Morning After' series, 2008. The well-dressed 'vandal' character appears in many of Walker's best-known pieces. This example, focusing on the Empire State building in New York, forms part of 'The Morning After' series in which the vandal is depicted in an otherwise grey cityscape, admiring the dripping paint colours adorning iconic structures. London, Sydney and Moscow are among the celebrated skylines featured in this series.

109 (*right*) **Nick Walker**, *Chihuahua*, Los Angeles, USA, 2009. Exhibited in Los Angeles where clichéd preoccupations with fashion and beauty ideals abound, Walker's witty scenarios are both timely and perfectly situated to address the very citizenry his work describes.

110 (*far right*) **Nick Walker**, *Brat*, California, USA, 2009

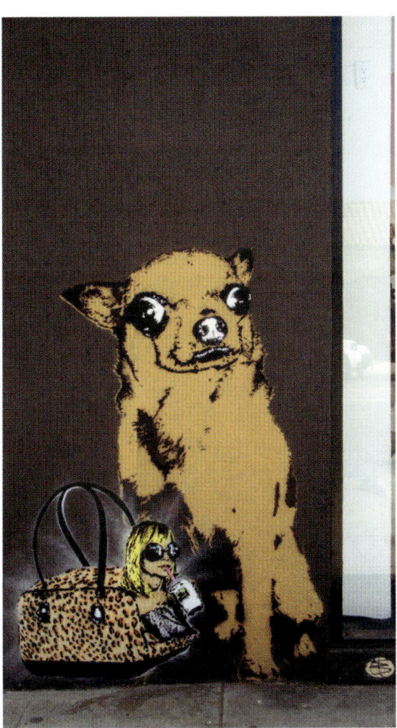

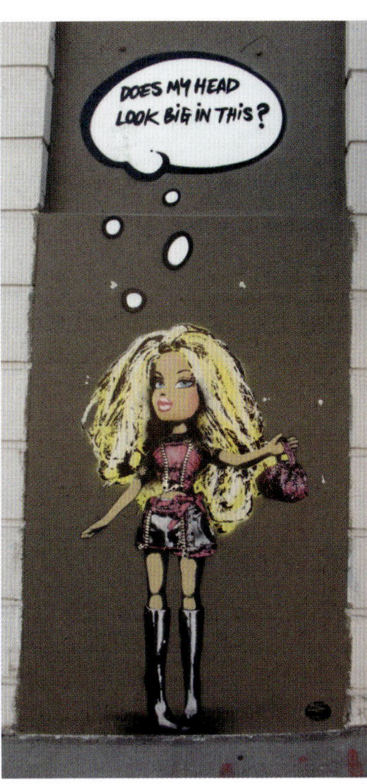

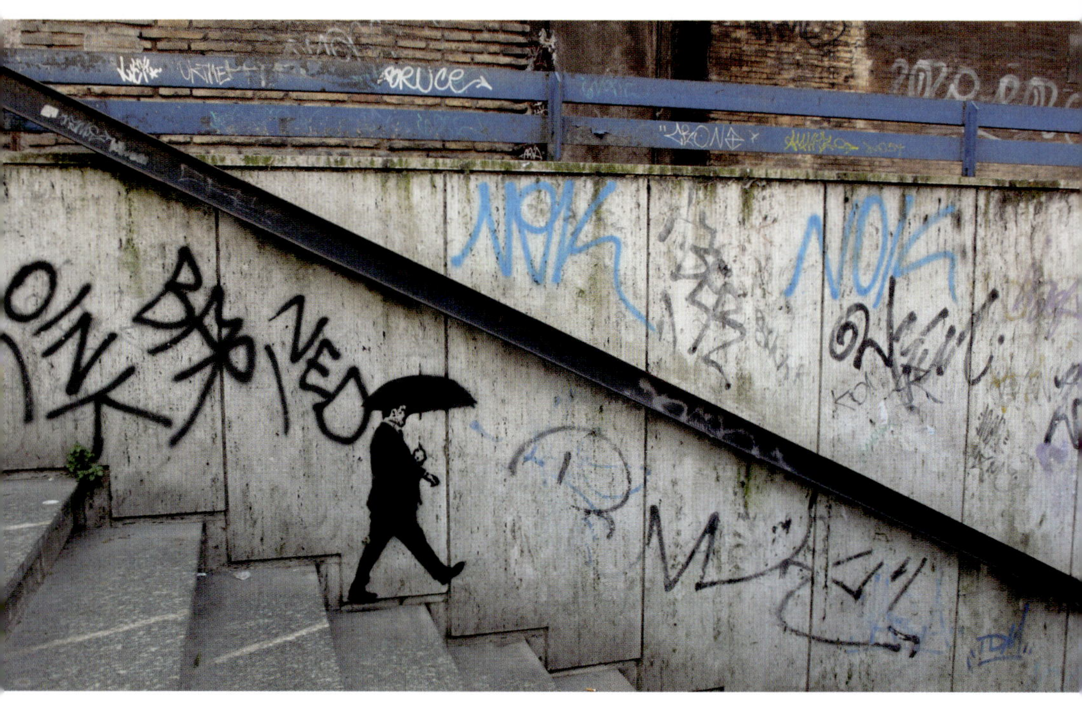

111 **Nick Walker**, Rome, Italy, 2009

identity through cultural and political assimilation. Both public and street art practices can also be read as performances in the urban realm, which capture dimensions of everyday experiences and potentially question the status of high art. Vito Acconci's performances, for example, are at once fiercely personal and examine the relationship between public and private spheres by bringing art into everyday life through direct contact with the general public. Public art projects, much like street art, can also be fleeting and can be executed in liminal or marginal spaces. Andy Goldsworthy's practice, although typically considered as Land rather than public art, is very much a transient exploration of liminal or marginal space. Finally, in their interactions with urban environments both movements can explore banality in a city and create new spaces of meaning by aesthetisizing the street. Gordon Matta-Clark's site-specific series of 'building cuts', whereby the artist removed sections of walls, floors and ceilings from abandoned buildings to create ephemeral works out of unwanted remnants, functioned as performative gestures.

The public artworks created by these artists echo many of the same issues that preoccupy artists working illegally in the urban sphere. Artists around the world have been raising

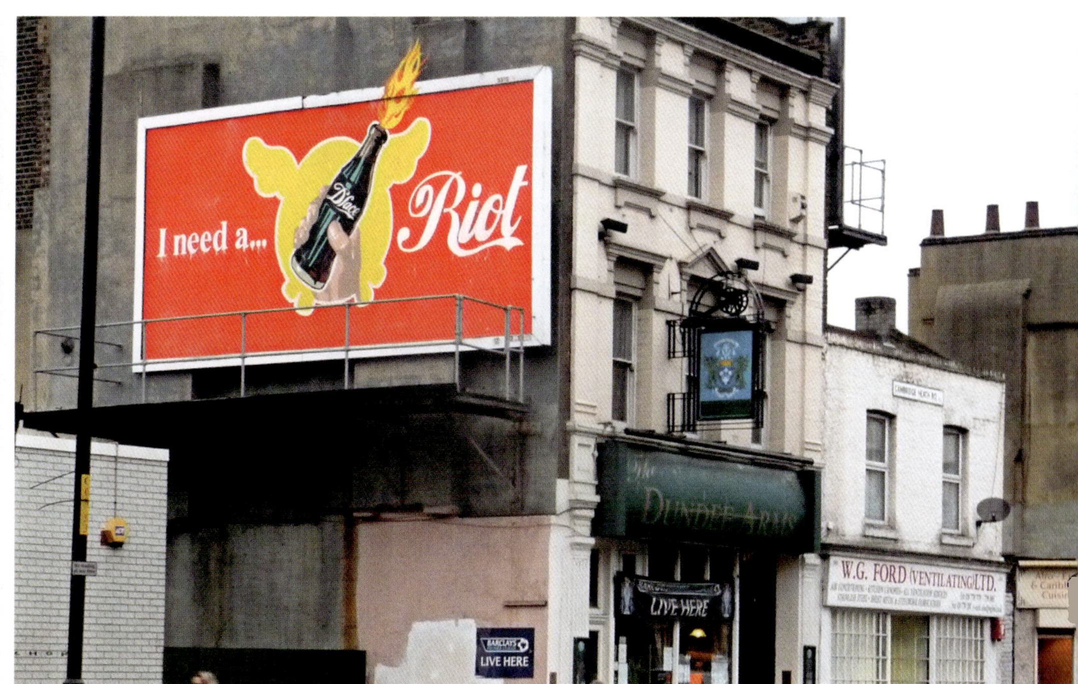

112 **D*Face**, *I Need A Riot*, London, UK, 2010. D*Face has a unique propensity for incorporating his name and most recognized icon, D*Dog, into his pieces while championing social commentary and playing on pre-existing imagery. Like many street artists, his reliance on clear, accessible images and text allows for mass communication.

questions directly tied to some facet of urbanity and public space for decades. The recent illegal art projects contextualized as street art underline the fundamental role of and undeniable fascination with making art on the street. Instead of being sheltered in an institution, artworks at street level have the very real capacity to engage people in the experience of art and foster change.

Chapter 4   Post-Graffiti, Site and Space

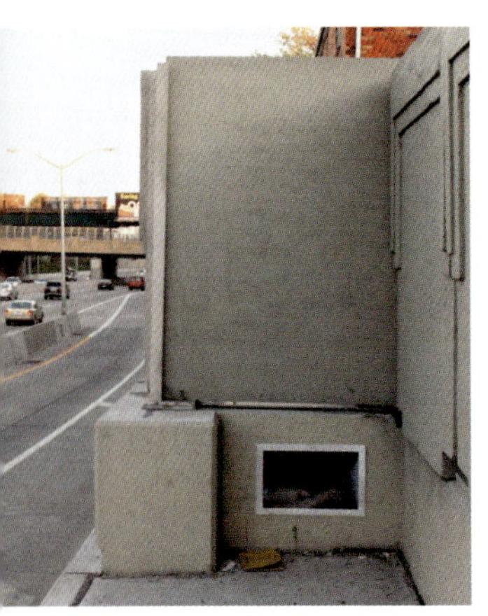

113 (*above*) **Dan Witz**, *Untitled*, 'WHAT THE %$#@ (WTF)' series, New York City, USA, 2010. With this series, Witz discreetly inserts images of realistically rendered human beings trapped behind bars, thus both shocking viewers and facilitating a moment of wonder in otherwise predictably plain city spaces.

114 (*opposite*) **Omen**, *Untitled*, Montreal, Canada, 2009. Omen's painterly use of spray-paint to create meandering, fluid portraits, which merge into abstract and natural elements and fully occupy a given space, illustrates the versatile techniques and potential of aerosol as a medium.

Displaying art on the street is akin to creating time-sensitive performances that contest the 'publicness' of public space. More significantly, however, it also presents an overt challenge to the built and visual environment of the city. Street art is frequently constructed for a particular space and illuminates otherwise marginal places. Moreover, while at times site-specific, versions of the same artwork may also be disseminated multiple times in numerous locations. These realities manifest in art projects that considerably affect the sites and spaces of a city.

On the periphery of mainstream visual imagery, sanctioned public art and the discipline of art history, street art embodies a unique position as a provocative tool. As an illegal form of art, urban painting questions the very notion of public space and the rampant commercialism throughout the cityscape. The infrastructure of a city, dominated by architecture, public art projects, monuments and official signage, commands order and stability and is supplemented by various forms of advertising, which create a type of urban chaos. With colours, lights, flashy designs, attention-grabbing slogans and scale, corporations add a visually muddled scene to otherwise uniform streets. A city is thus not only a functional space through which to move; it is also a strategic space, through which to sell. The introduction of unsolicited art into urban visual culture is a refreshing if not essential act of opposition.

Whether exhibited in marginal spaces, or as modifications to billboards and other sites of visual consumption, urban painting functions as a reminder of free thought, free expression and individuality in networks of conformity. It provokes some people into taking action, as evidenced by the growing number of artists inspired to create as a response to one another's work, and it aggravates the urban landscape.

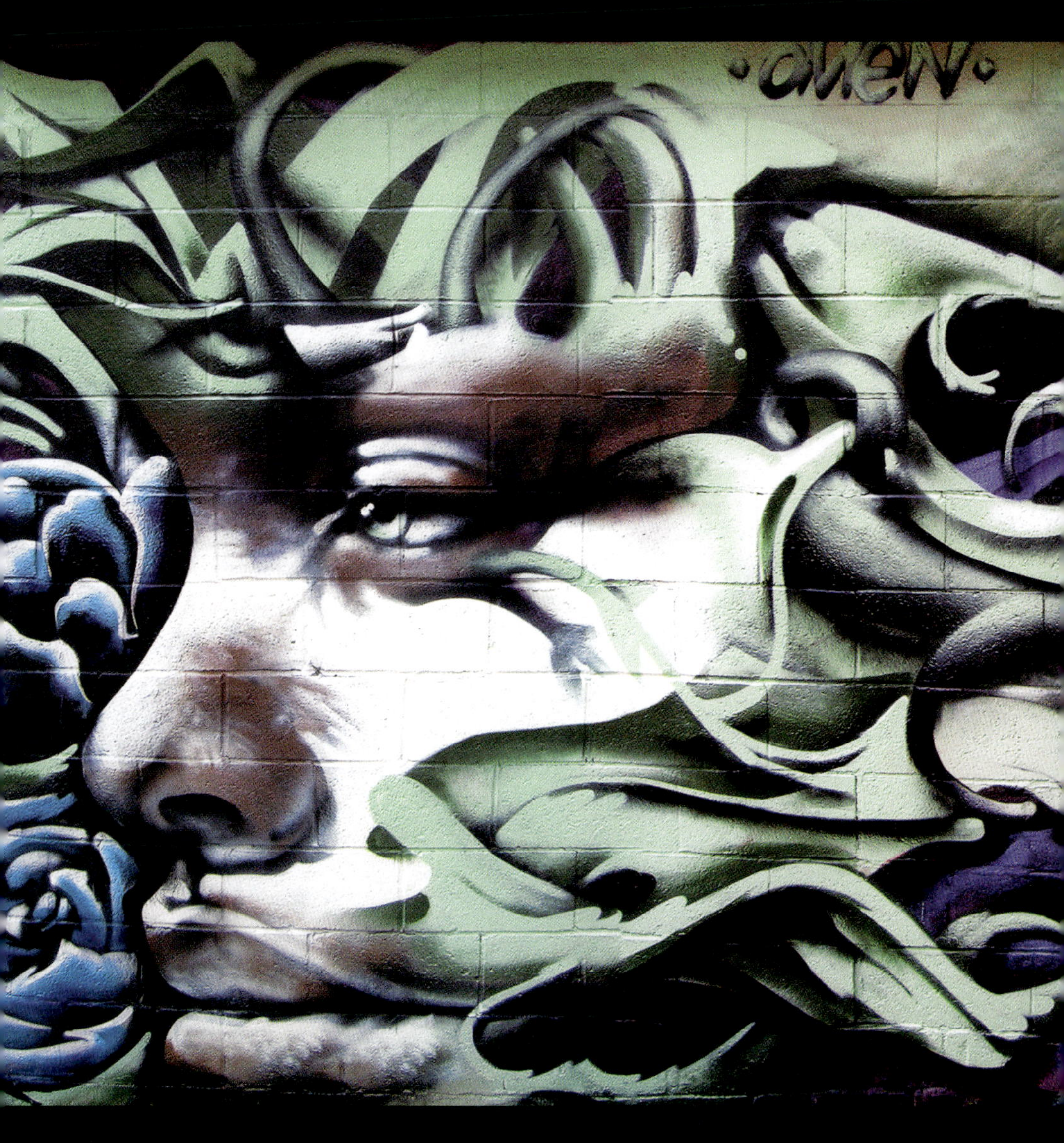

·auEN·

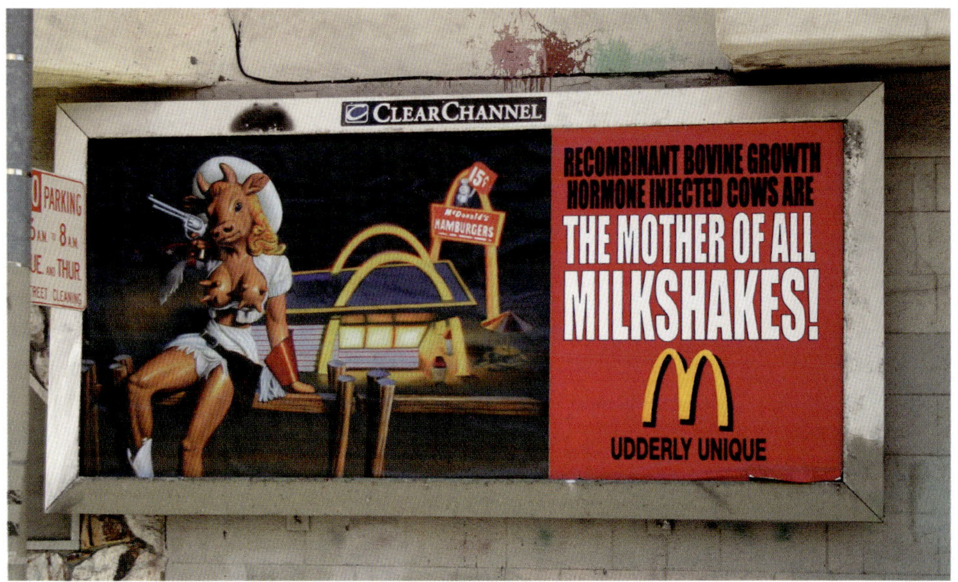

115 **Ron English**, *Udderly Unique*, San Francisco, USA, 2005. Billboards are spaces of commerce within the cityscape. Their occupation by graffiti writers and street artists indicates a clear interest by those making art illegally to disrupt the culture of consumerism by using that space to sell ideas that promote free thought.

The Liminal

As post-graffiti practices demonstrate, no matter how controlled city spaces are, they are also open to subversion. Not every area is monitored, commercialized, depersonalized or functionalized. Some spaces are unrestricted, unobstructed, exposed, empty, isolated, forgotten, unmanaged and bleak. Even within the capitalist economy of space, there are gaps or marginal spaces that, while often neglected, are necessary for the conceptualization of the city as a complex arena. These 'non-spaces' are not necessarily liminal by way of geography, but rather by way of use. Through the process of space reclamation by renegade artists, new layers of meaning are produced in these sites. The activation of a space both reinvents it and connects it to more prominent sites in a city. While some artists choose to put up artwork in spaces that lie on the periphery of a city, many display their work in the liminal spaces of the city's core – amid otherwise mainstream uses of space.

The opportunities that non-spaces offer for freedom of action and expression are especially significant for artists working on the margins of acceptability. Non-spaces such as rooftops, alleyways, car parks, tunnels, bridges, pavements and city walls are part of the infrastructure that creates a city but does not define it – at least not from a consumption-driven, capitalist standpoint. In an almost poetic gesture, street artists,

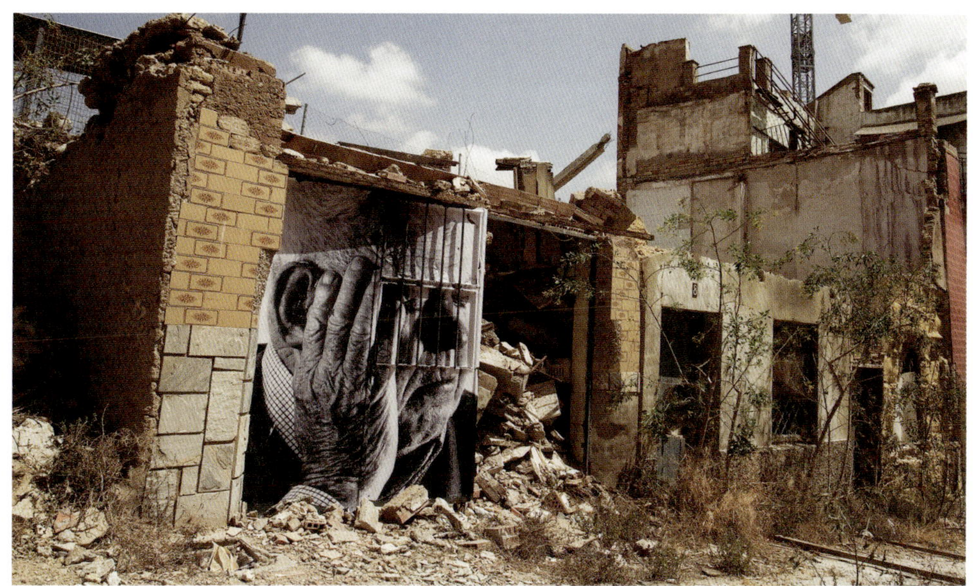

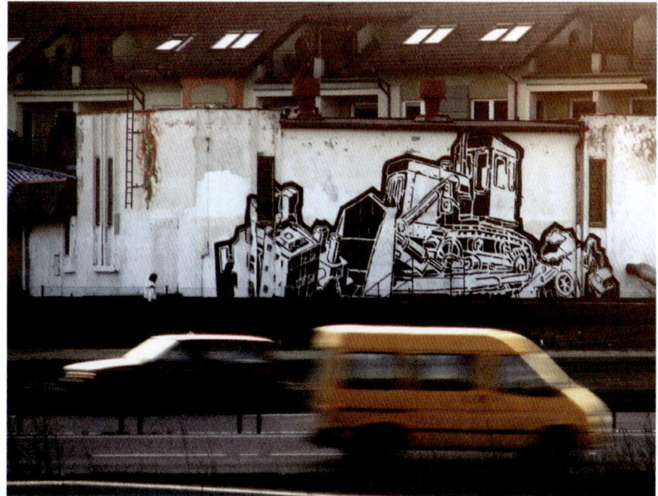

116 (*above*) **JR**, *Wrinkles of the City*, Cartagena, Spain, 2010. With this project, JR's intention was to populate buildings with images of a city's elderly residents in an effort both to honour his subjects and to highlight socio-political, cultural and environmental changes brought about by the passage of time. This series aims to encourage reflection on the past in order to contemplate the future.

117 (*right*) **Mariusz Waras aka M-City**, *M-City 104*, Gdynia, Poland, 2007. Liminal or marginal spaces within a city are necessary for the construction of the built environment, yet peripheral in terms of use. Illuminating these 'non-spaces' with art allows graffiti writers and street artists to draw attention to otherwise drab and utilitarian places and connect them to the liveliness of the city.

who largely conceptualize their work as anti-capitalist and anti-establishment expressions of free speech, transform liminal socio-spatial sites into sites of action, communication and beauty. Partly relegated to such spaces by virtue of illegality, and partly drawn to them as drab canvases, street artists' exploration of interstitial spaces accentuates our experience of the urban environment, as illustrated by the work of Canadian artist Roadsworth.

118 (*right*) **Roadsworth**, *Asphalt Fetish*, Montreal, Canada, 2004. Using road markings as a starting point for his practice, Roadsworth encourages the re-imagining of one's environment while simultaneously transforming mundane spaces into places of beauty or political commentary. His designs, often painted in the same colours as the existing markings, remain within the confines of the language of a city but also break its visual monotony, thus prompting people to question it.

119 (*below*) **Roadsworth**, *Bullets for Oil*, Montreal, Canada, 2001. Here, the artist transforms the markings of a pedestrian crossing into massive bullets, a symbol of war, reflecting his support of pedestrian or bicycle traffic over cars.

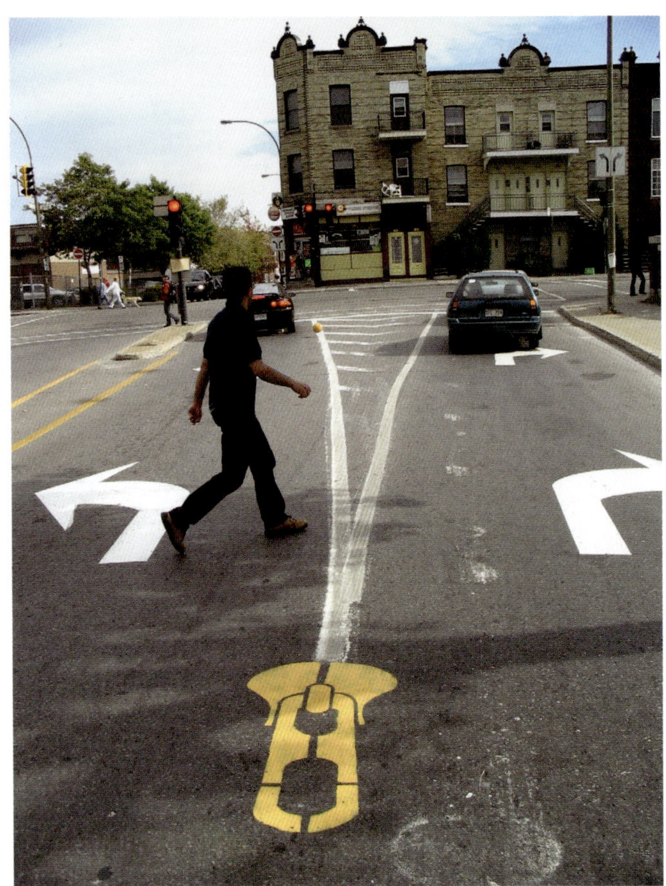

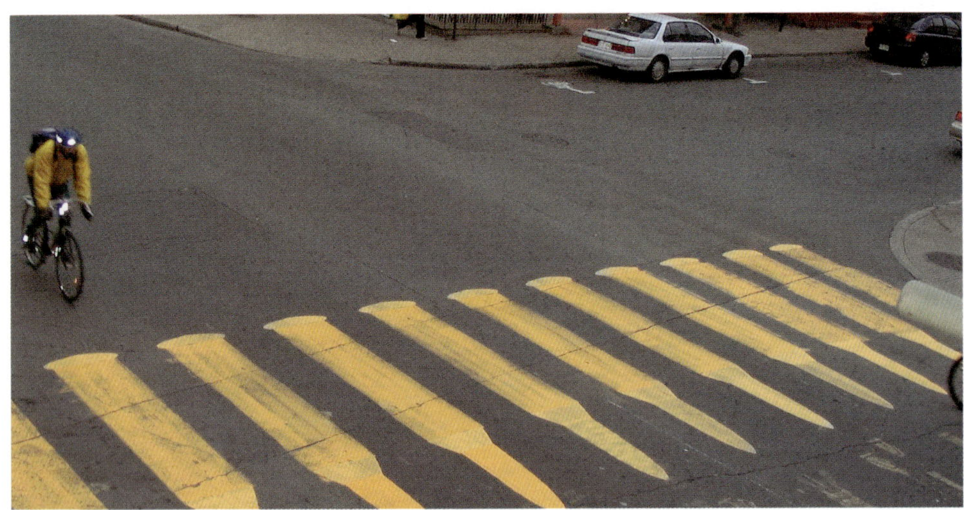

120 (*right*) **Roadsworth**,
Attention All Drivers, Montreal,
Canada, 2004

121 (*below left*) **Roadsworth**,
Asphalt Glory, Montreal,
Canada, 2004. While some of
Roadsworth's stencils make a
loud political statement against
car culture, others beautify roads
with organic elements. Vines and
leaves function as reminders of
the destruction of the natural
world to make way for the
asphalt and concrete structures
that characterize cities.

122 (*below right*) **Roadsworth**,
Fall Leaves, Toronto, Canada,
2008

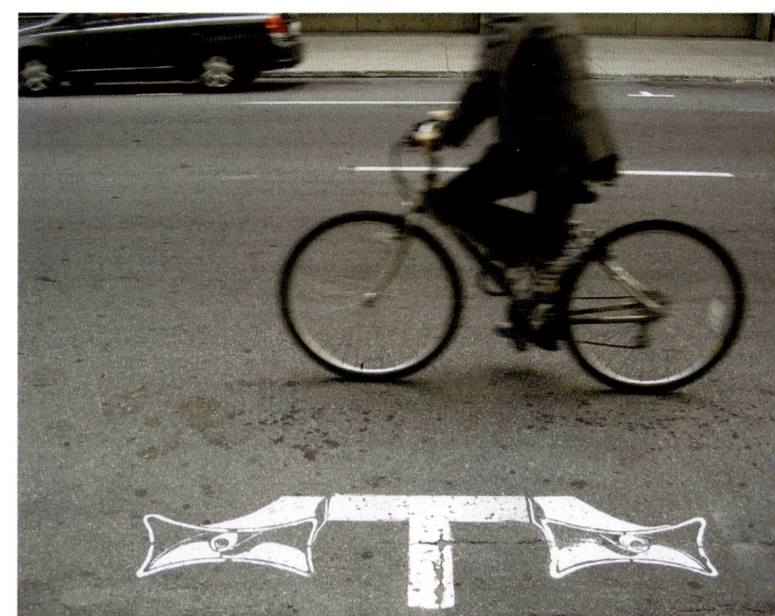

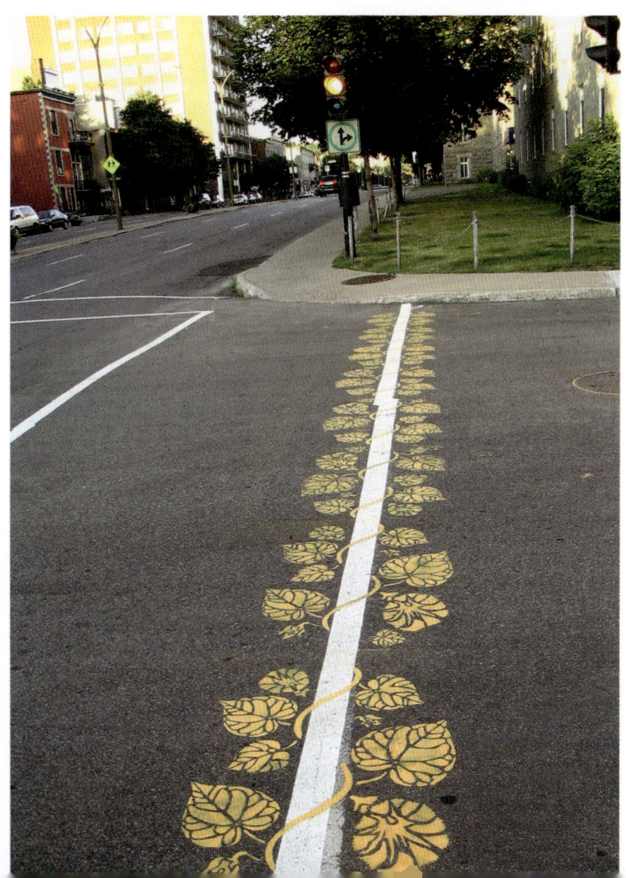

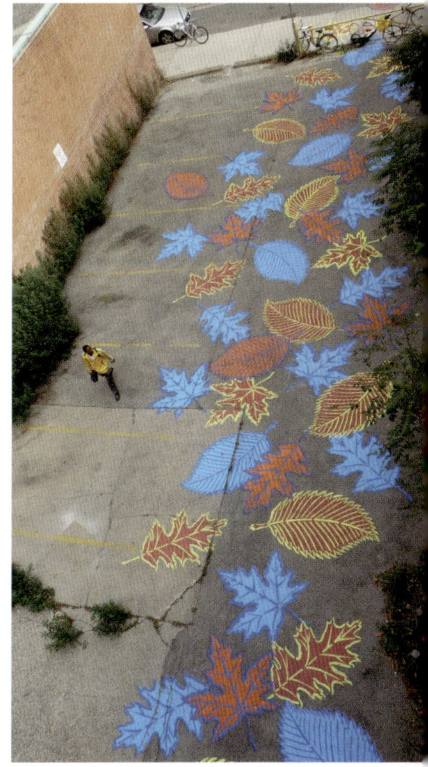

Roadsworth disseminates his work on roads – a space that, while being an invaluable constituent in the organization of a city, is also typically devoid of artistic expression. The artist explains that roads have 'a unique status in that [their] sole purpose is one of transit, of movement. One does not typically dilly-dally on the road. In this sense it is not a location at all but an "anti-location", an intermediary between points A and B.' The space of a road is intriguing for Roadsworth, especially since its markings constitute a language that he finds 'irresistibly ripe for manipulation, subversion, satire and poetry'. Painting on a road allows the artist to stimulate a moment of reflection in an otherwise utilitarian space.

He is best known for his stencils in the Plateau and Mile End neighbourhoods of Montreal, applied directly onto roads using the same yellow and white paint as that of official street markings. Some of his more popular works include the fashioning of a zip fastener out of existing double lines (2004) [118]; the alteration of pedestrian crossing markings into bullets (2001) [119]; and loudspeakers inspired by prison speakers because, much like advertising, they tell people what to do (2004) [120]. Prior to Roadsworth's heavily publicized arrest, these stencils where initially assumed by Montrealers to have been commissioned by the city and were overwhelmingly well received by local residents. Roadsworth's aim, not simply to use the street as a canvas, but to interweave and integrate his designs in and around the existing road markings, works to make people question the language of a city. By using the same paint colours as those of official infrastructural markers, the artist's work remains within the confines of the city's language, but also breaks its visual monotony. The addition of organic elements such as vines to the road (2004) [121] or fallen leaves to a car park (2008) [122] is a reminder of nature pushing through the asphalt and concrete. These stencils, like all the artist's oeuvre, aesthetize the pavement while questioning environmental, social and political conditions. The liminal site of the road allows both for the manipulation of the city's language and for the consideration of the artful gesture as part of the everyday.

Another example of art in non-spaces created in dialogue with its material surface is the work of Spanish artist Nuria Mora. As opposed to layering the street with characters, stencils or visually chaotic posters, Nuria developed her practice based on an element as simple as the line. Her

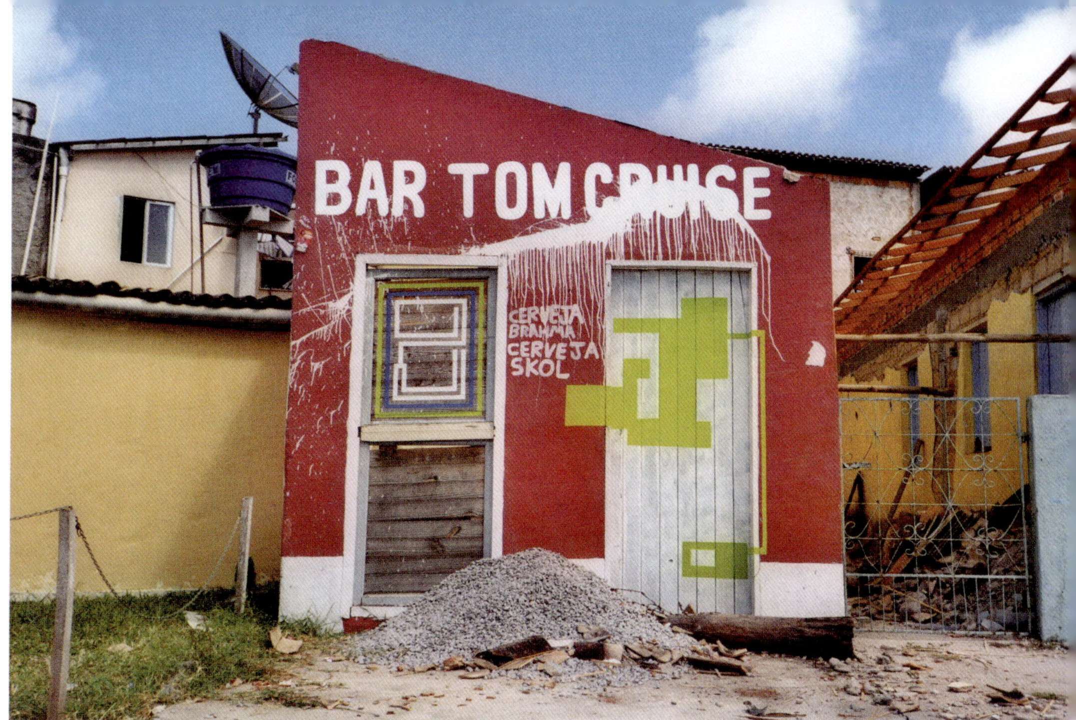

123 **Nuria Mora and El Tono**, *Untitled*, Arraial d'Ajuda, Brazil, 2001. This collaboration with El Tono perfectly showcases Nuria Mora's early work which, like a labyrinth, wraps itself in and around structural elements. Her focus on geometric shapes and lines that echo their material support gently re-articulates all manner of 'non-spaces'.

beautifully simplistic creations emerge from urban and rural architectural forms and are themselves designed in a structural way. With a definite beginning and end, the series of works for which she is best known, such as ill. 123 (2001), like a labyrinth, invite the viewer to follow a path. They accentuate their architectural support and play with the pre-existing framing. Sometimes painting with artist El Tono (known as 'the tuning fork'), Nuria ('the key') has developed a way to communicate with the city through brightly coloured geometric patterns, symbols and crisp, clean lines. In a way, her pieces function like abstracted city plans, with the twists and turns of streets and the demarcation of buildings. A recurring motif, akin to a keyhole, is generally represented as a void in the first – or last, depending on one's perspective – of the adjoined rectangular blocks that typify her work. This symbolic self-representation of the artist suggests that her work unlocks the significance of its material support.

The sense of movement in Nuria's pieces echoes the structures on which they reside, transforming forgotten spaces into beautiful places. The artist explains: 'I start with a pre-defined geometrical structure that has infinite possible shapes because this sign adapts to the surface chosen for the

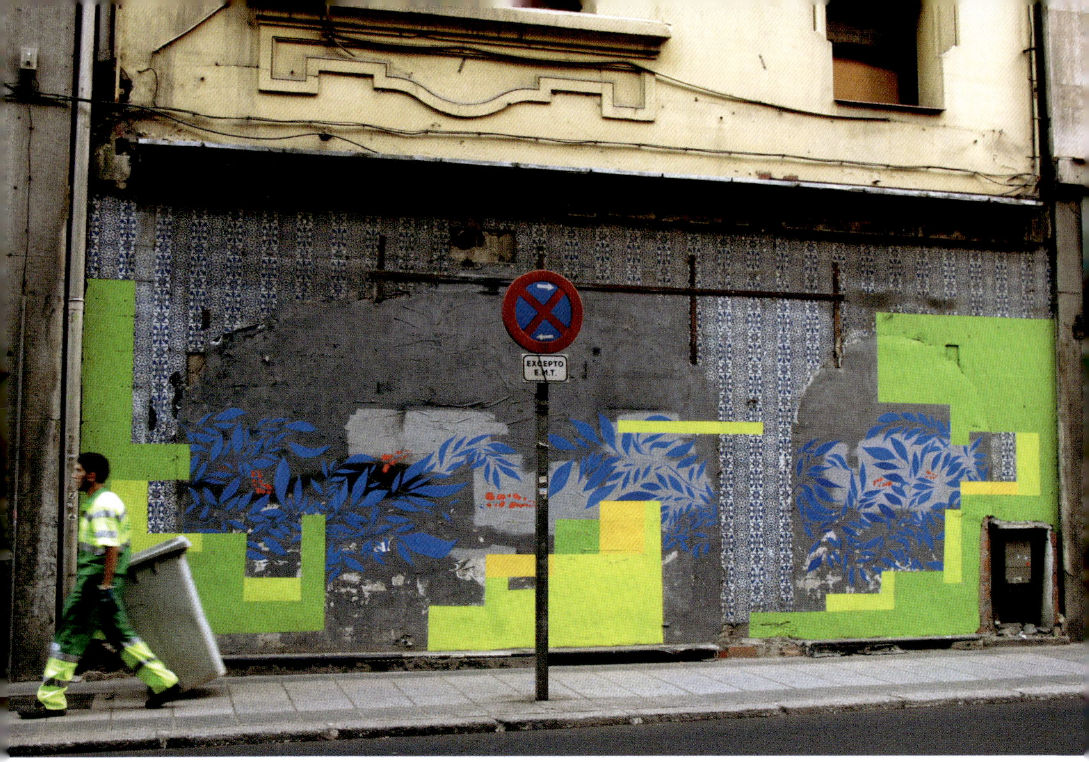

EXCEPTO
E.M.T.

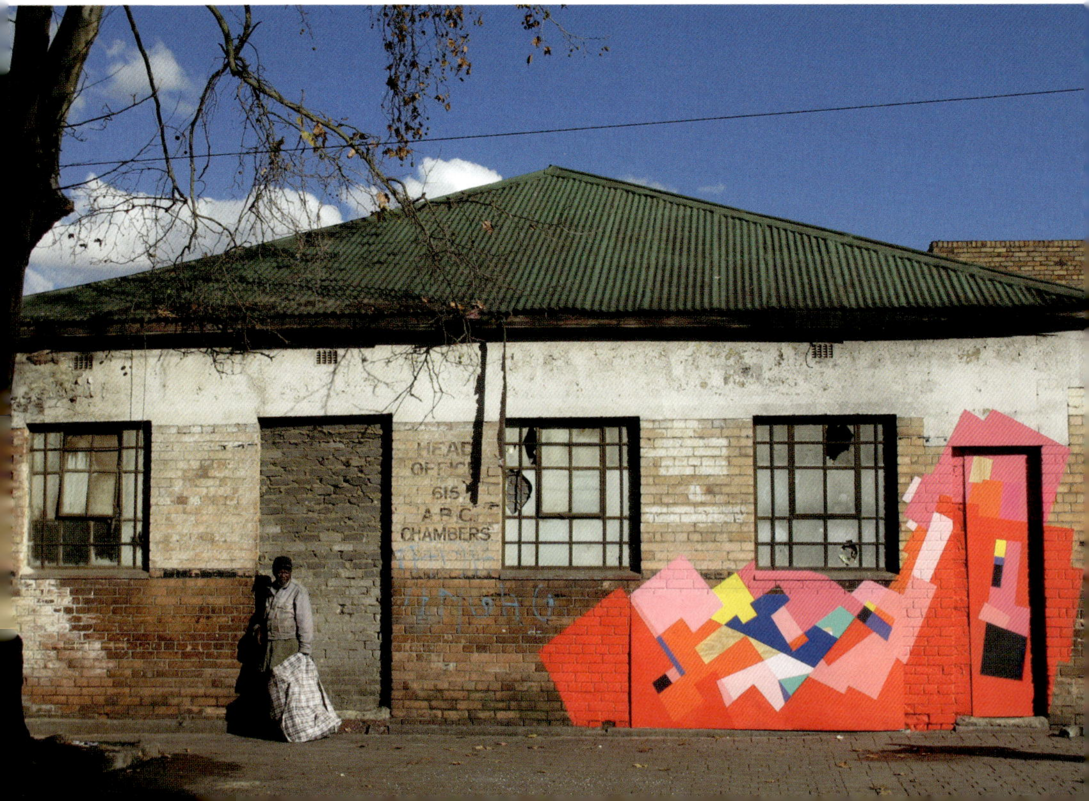

HEAD
OFFICE
615
A.P.C.
CHAMBERS

124 (*opposite, above*) **Nuria Mora**, *Untitled*, Madrid, Spain, 2010. The artist's recent works, which bring representations of natural elements into conversation with her infamous geometric shapes, beautifully emphasize, shape and breathe life into forgotten spaces.

125 (*opposite, below*) **Nuria Mora**, 'Estrella de Mar' project, Johannesburg, South Africa, 2010

126 (*right*) **Microbo**, *Untitled*, Belfast, Northern Ireland, 2010. Italian artist Microbo focuses on a marginal subject matter – microbes – in her fluid, detailed works. By enlarging them to human scale and portraying them as playful, intricate and indeed beautiful life forms, she both celebrates the minute organisms that infiltrate every facet of our lives and brings a hidden world to the forefront.

action through a dialogue with the architecture that supports it. My objective is to give value to the surface.' Indeed, her more recent work, which employs thicker blocks of colour as well as patterned and floral designs [124, 125], embraces the architecture, both emphasizing it and breathing life into it. The artist's intuition in terms of location, scale and colour infuses otherwise liminal spaces with brilliantly cheerful and visually pleasing designs.

While both Roadsworth and Nuria illuminate liminal spaces with decipherable imagery which activates an otherwise utilitarian or forgotten site, Italian artist Microbo's work deals with marginal subject matter: microbes. With microscopic organisms as the central characters of her practice, Microbo celebrates the first forms of life on earth in a grandiose manner. Portrayed as fluid, living creatures, the microbes are fashioned into animated forms which float on city walls [126]. Through her renditions of tangled tentacles, the artist suggests a complexity in the microbes' make-up that underlines the complicated and versatile beauty of our natural world. Like many street artists, Microbo's background as a graphic designer influences her pictorial compositions. Painted with

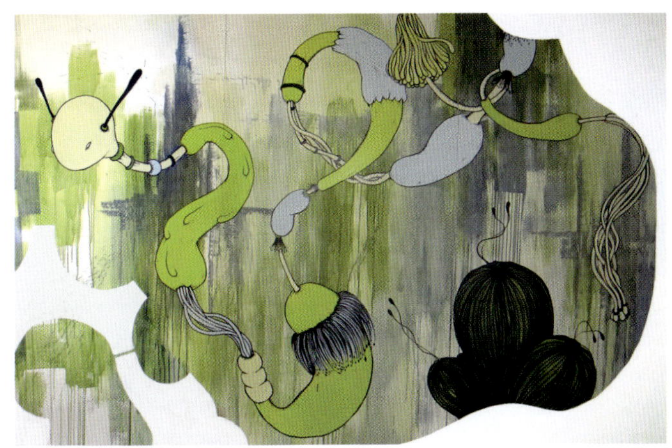

discernible outlines and tentacle-like bodies which emerge from the microbes' humanized heads, these large-scale caricatures of minute organisms invite reflection. Their depiction on city streets suggests that we live in their world, a world we know little about, but one that thrives in every facet of our lives.

Typically depicted in black and white or bluish grey, Microbo's detailed microbes both activate non-spaces and are themselves

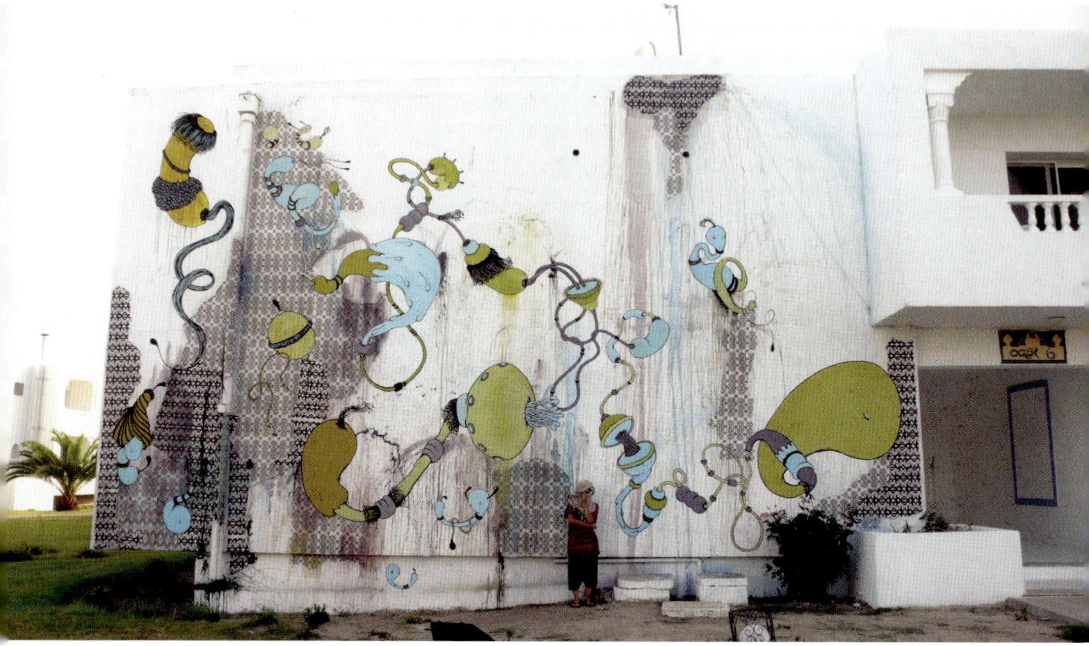

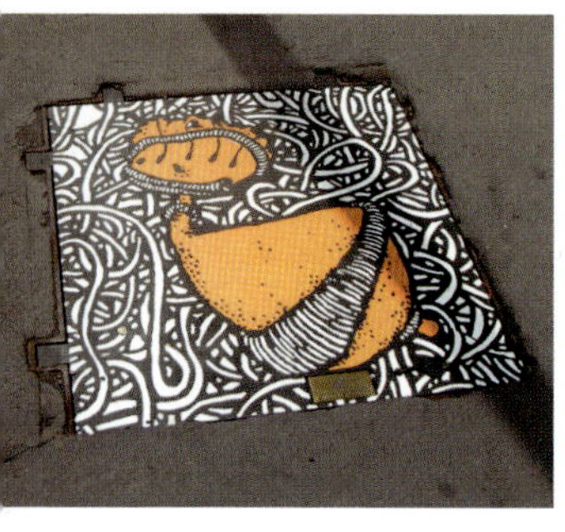

127 (*top*) **Microbo**, *Untitled*, Bizerte, Tunisia, 2009

128 (*above*) **Microbo**, *Chi C'è C'è*, Milan, Italy, 2009

compelling reminders of the forgotten societies of micro-organisms that impact our environments. Whether dancing fancifully on an appropriated wall (2009) [127] or occupying every inch of space on a manhole cover (2009) [128], they underline the reality that there is life everywhere. Any space, however marginal, is never static; as the artist shows us, it is always animated by organisms, even if we cannot see them.

But What Does It Do?

In the immediacy of the everyday, a city is continually remapped as it is navigated. Individuals, through their experience of a city, adopt the urban organization but also render it personal through their movements. Street art, as an element of everyday life, engages the contemporary city and reshapes places through human activity. Having evaluated street art in the context of a city as a performative, liminal, ephemeral art movement, one question – what does it do? – remains to be answered.

Both graffiti and street art integrate themselves into and at the same time disrupt the visual landscape of a city. The greatest differences between graffiti and street art in terms of function and meaning, however, lie in their respective pictorial vocabularies and hence the messages they might transmit.

While signature graffiti is essentially an affirmation of self within a network of initiates, street art, although it might also represent its maker, generally communicates a variety of ideas. Satirical, political, figurative and fun, street art stands in opposition to graffiti in its inclusivity. Signature graffiti traditions are so closely guarded and often associated with mischief and vandalism that they offer no real point of access for outsiders and are typically conceived as cryptic expressions working to distance people rather than draw them in. The major difference between graffiti and post-graffiti in terms of function thus rests in what the work visually imparts. By turning spaces into places, graffiti writers and street artists both read a city and write it. However, because – unlike most public art projects – the work of writers and street artists is illegal, it holds a particular position in the context of a city to emphasize the functionally private reality of public spaces. Using urban space to create non-profit, non-commissioned art, street artists go one step further by challenging the visual narrative of a city.

In cities as varied as Paris, Tokyo, Los Angeles, Bangkok and Perth, the French artist known as Invader marks city spaces

129 **Jace**, *Untitled*, Kuala Lumpur, Malaysia, 2009. The insertion of street art into unremarkable places accentuates the liveliness of a city – the fact that it is in constant motion, and thus subject to ongoing change. Jace's orange 'gouzou' character is graphically simple but instantly recognizable, offering moments of delight and shock in the most unlikely locations.

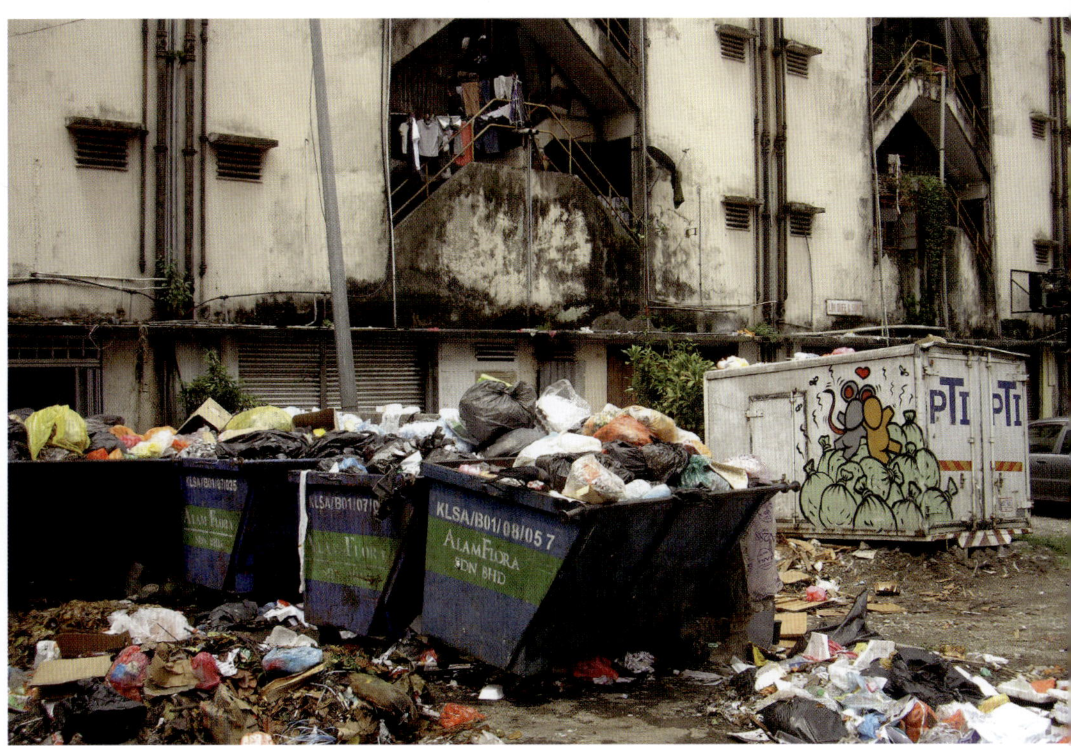

and thus effectively creates places with his unique brand of street art. His logos – characterized by pixelated mosaic tile representations of characters from 1970s Atari video games, primarily *Space Invaders* but also others such as *Pac-Man* and *Super Mario* – form part of a continually evolving urban narrative. The small coloured squares with which Invader fashions his characters are cemented onto locations chosen for their aesthetic or strategic value, and each piece is unique, with its own serial number identifying its series. Although the artist personalizes public spaces, he does so with a recognizably commercial aesthetic. As recreations of popular video game characters, Invader's mosaics function as both appropriations and subversions.

The artist's name not only describes his work visually, but also communicates his actions – he visually invades spaces. The word invasion signals a threat or attack; as such, it is especially well chosen to describe the work of a street artist whose interventions are illegal (invasive), yet whose imagery is light-hearted and non-threatening. With his invaders, the artist transplants virtual video game characters into reality and in so doing transforms the city itself into a video game. The invasions, carefully detailed on city maps that are available for purchase through the artist's website, are for the most part less spontaneous than one might imagine. When viewed on a map, the specific sites chosen for one series sometimes together form an image of one massive space invader, as in Montpellier (1999). Also, while many are in locations frequented by pedestrians, some are displayed in iconic sites, such as the artist's instalments beneath letters of the 'Hollywood' sign.

Affixed to surfaces in the built environment and typically out of reach, Invader's works are rarely removed by the authorities. Thus, they remain, especially in Paris where over five hundred pieces reside, as permanent evidence of the possibilities of unlawful urban interventions. Frequently rendered with sideways glances, both in populated and desolate spaces, Invader's characters give the impression that they are observing us and act as reminders that the urban environment is monitored by various surveillance measures. Whether they take up residence on a busy Los Angeles wall (2006) [130], peer through foliage in New York (2003) [131], look out over the Mediterranean Sea in Nice (2007) [132] or illuminate a stark Mombasa wall with some of Kenya's national colours (2005) [133], they seem to keep an ever watchful eye.

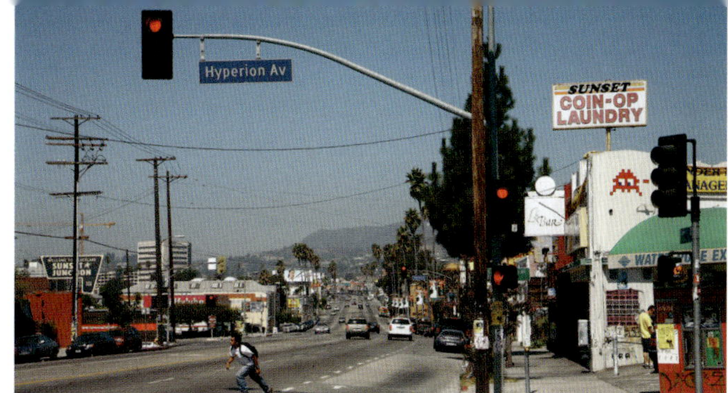

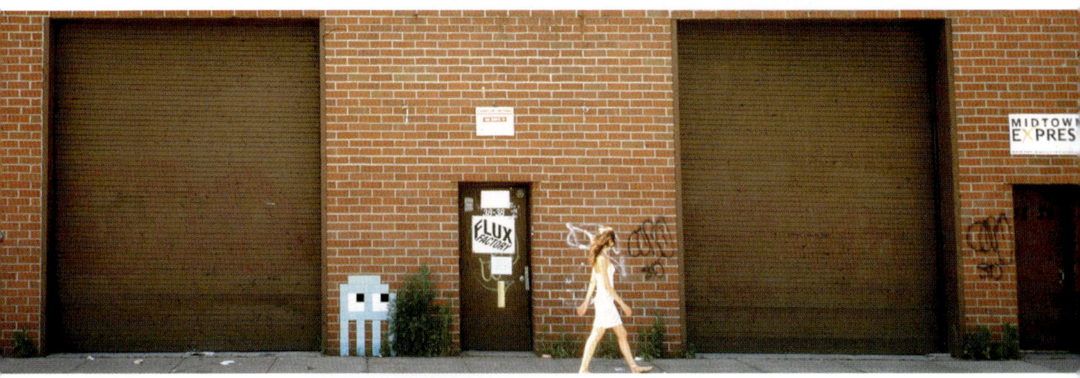

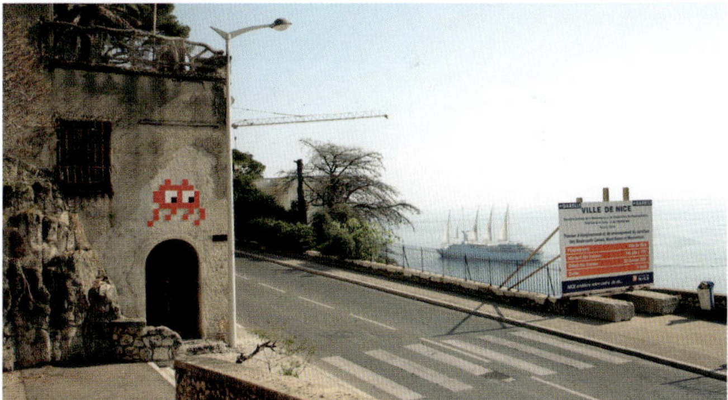

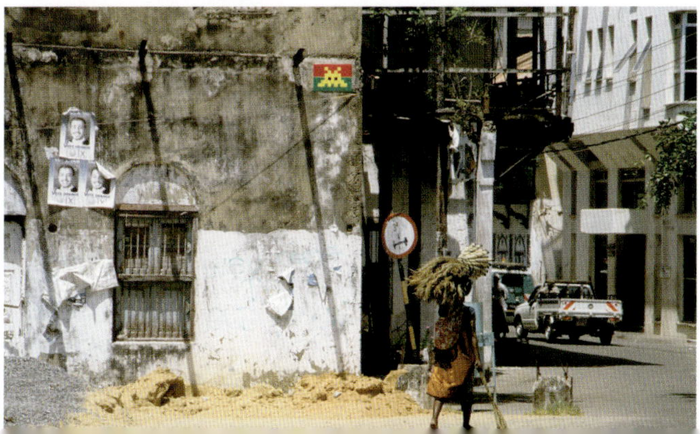

From top to bottom:
130 **Invader**, *Untitled*, Los Angeles, USA, 2006. As one of the most active street artists on the international scene, Invader demonstrates how a recurring character rearticulated in immeasurable ways and locations can nonetheless prove to be a meaningful addition to its appropriated home. Whether affixed to iconic landmarks or in desolate spaces, his characters seem to watch from afar and function as reminders of the many surveillance measures that characterize city life.

131 **Invader**, *Untitled*, New York City, USA, 2003

132 **Invader**, *Untitled*, Nice, France, 2007

133 **Invader**, *Untitled*, Mombasa, Kenya, 2005

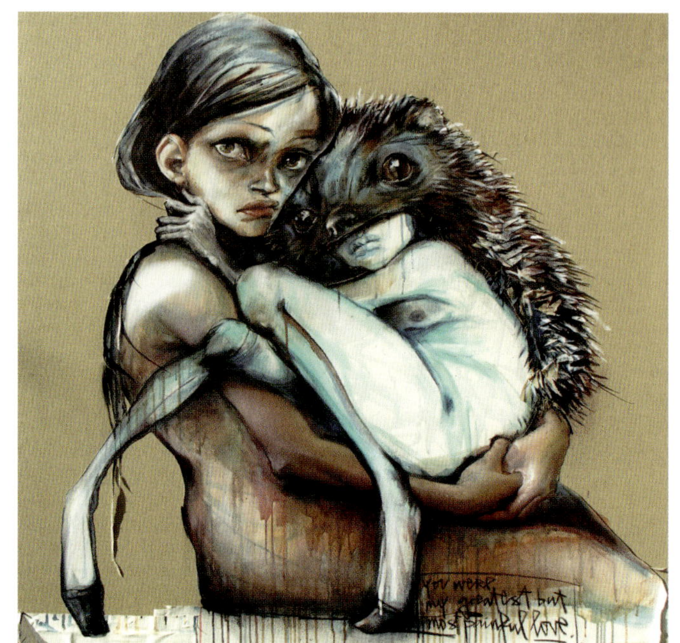

134 (*right*) **Herakut**, *You Were My Greatest But Most Painful Love*, 2010. Hera and Akut fuse their individual styles – one gestural, the other realistic – to create narrative scenes populated with human–animal hybrids. Although self-contained narratives, like snippets of a long story they tell haunting tales of longing, disappointment, contemplation and amusement, reflected through the earthy palette.

135 (*below*) **Herakut**, *You Teach What You Live*, 2007

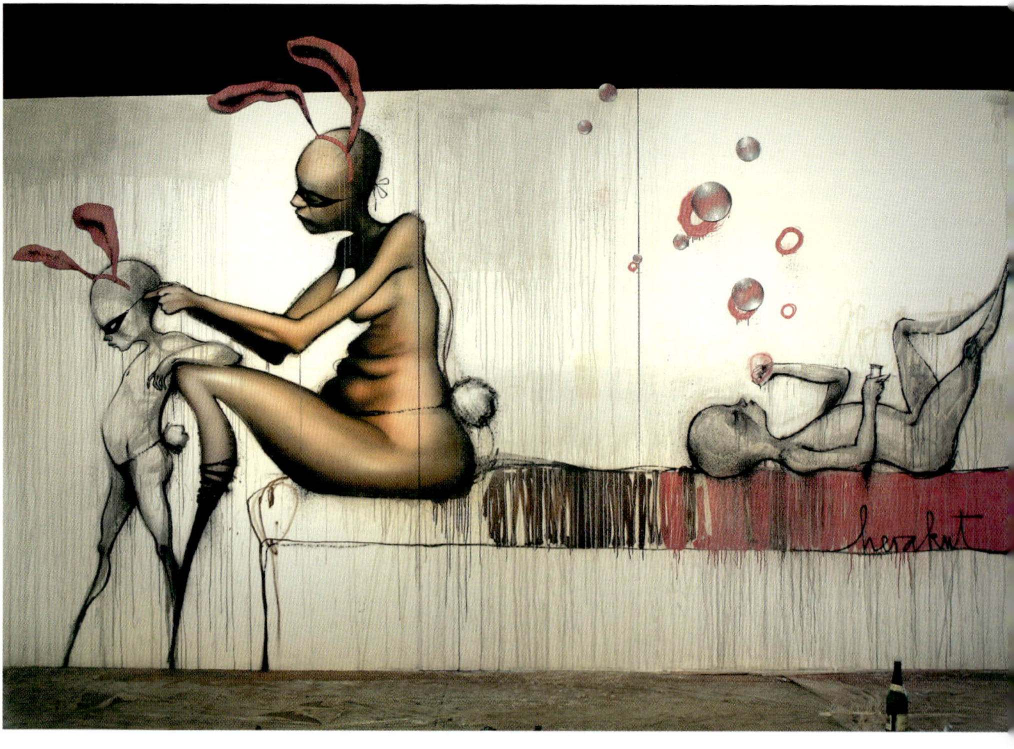

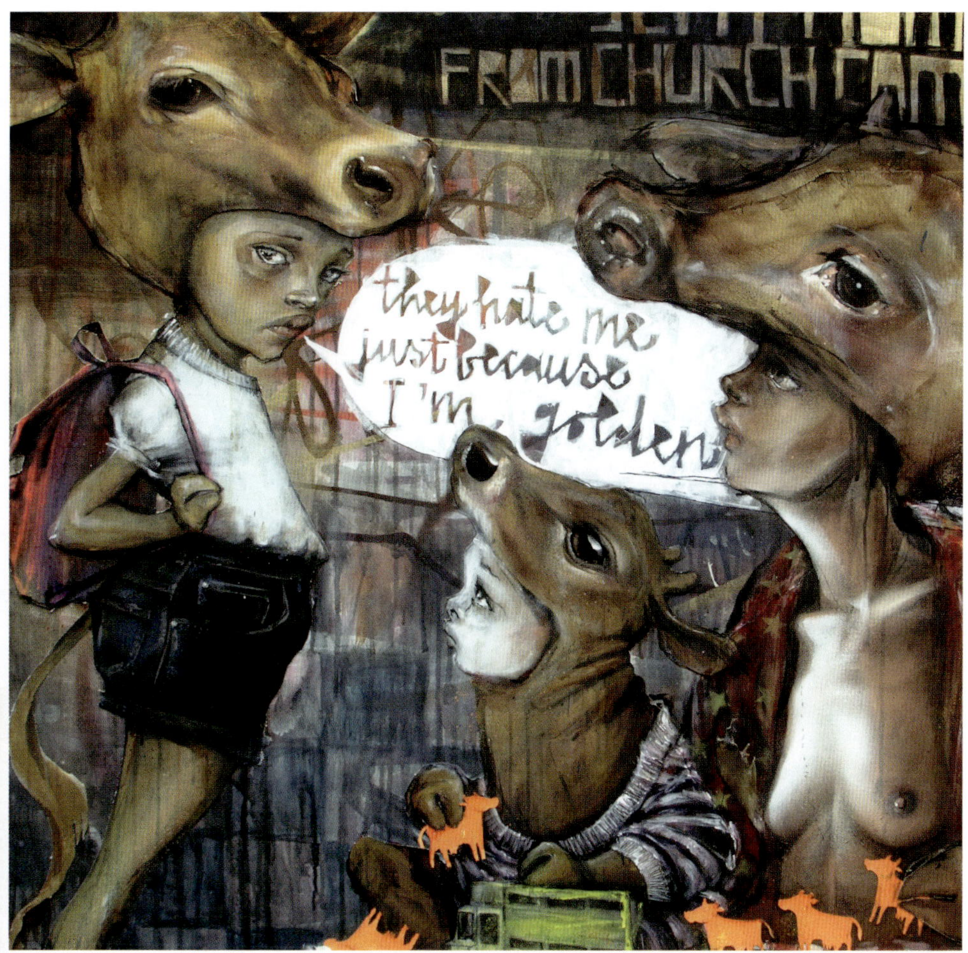

136 **Herakut**, *They Hate Me Just Because I'm Golden*, 2010. Often melancholic or sombre in mood, Herakut's pieces draw in the viewer through direct confrontation on the part of the protagonist and legible phrases that ignite contemplation. Multi-layered works such as this one, which not only combines text with imagery but also realism with symbolism, encapsulate Herakut's vision to invite the audience into a story that speaks to both reality and fantasy.

While the space invaders quietly reign over their assigned terrain, the work produced through the collaborative practice of German artists Hera and Akut, aka Herakut, is a great deal more confrontational. Populated with people, animals and text, the narrative scenes created by the pair perfectly fuse their individual styles and yet are simultaneously contemplative, eerie, grimy and haunting [134, 135, 136]. Visually in dialogue with one another, the artists generate a language that combines mythical elements with contemporary situations and is centred on story-telling. Akut's spray-painted realism combined with Hera's gestural figuration shape narratives that are self-contained but speak to the viewer. The serious tone of their work is reflected through the earthy palette as well as the

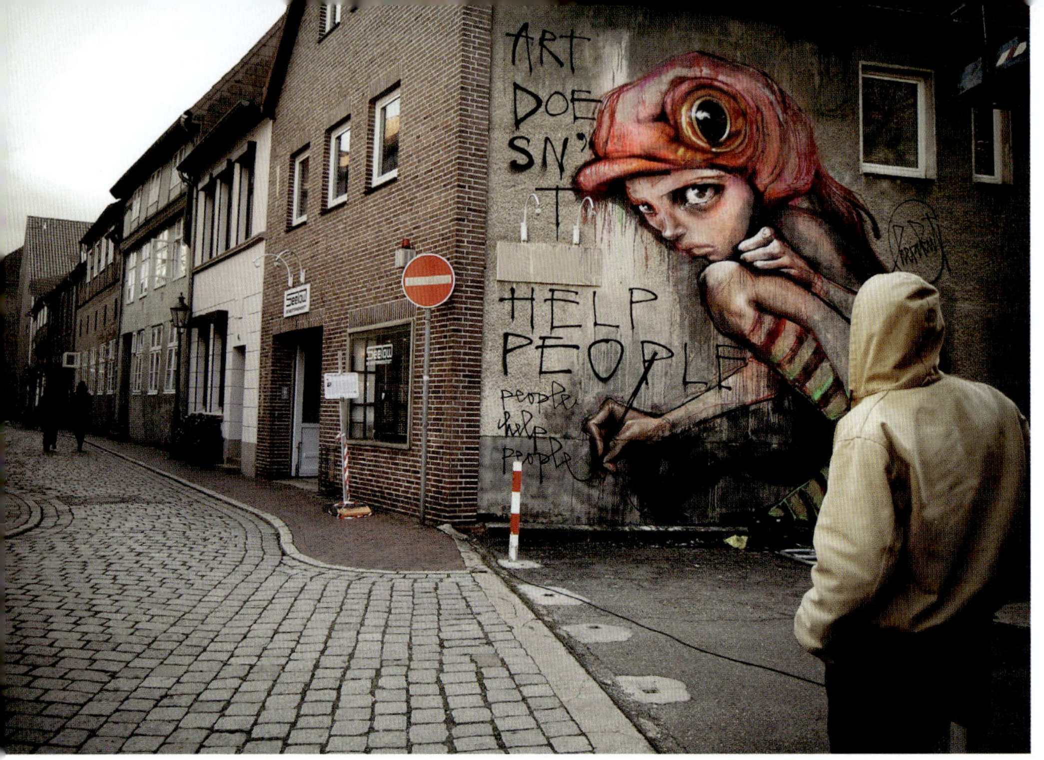

137 **Herakut**, *Art Doesn't Help People...*, Lüneburg, Germany, 2009

quiet contemplation and melancholic tension that are present in many of their pieces.

Part of the appeal of the individuals and figurative groupings portrayed in these scenes lies in their apparent indifference. Often they seem to make eye contact with the viewer but nonchalantly follow through with their activity [137]. As voyeurs of their world, the public is drawn into a situation that, whether light-hearted or sorrowful, is engrossing by virtue of the narrative it embodies. The visual dialogue between the artists in the creation of a piece is accentuated through the interactions between their characters – often children and parents – as well as the conversation in the work itself between image and text. Typically depicted with long limbs and animal heads atop their human heads, or even hooves and tails punctuating their human torsos, Herakut's characters are observably relaxed. The body language of the figures, often a little slumped in posture, coupled with a gestural and expressive painting style, infuses the pieces with an aura of familiarity, perhaps even comfort. The characters' large eyes, however, which display a sensibility that lies somewhere between distrust and confrontation, disturb the air of tranquillity. Like snippets of a long story, Herakut's narrative scenes are akin to fairy tales that are demystified when acted out in reality.

Although a tool for place-making and story-telling, street art can also work to raise social consciousness. Eco-tagger and originator of the reverse-graffiti project, British artist Paul 'Moose' Curtis has instituted a new wave of street art production. Instead of adding paint, paper and other materials to the cityscape, he creates art by carefully cleaning away layers of urban dirt. The idea of artfully cleaning the city is

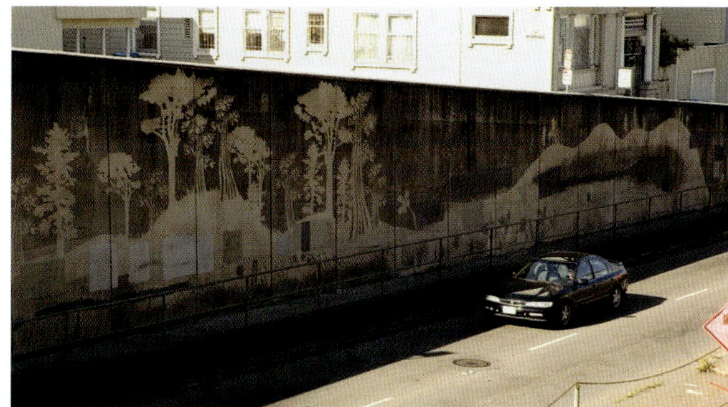

138 (*above*) **Moose**, *Untitled*, California, USA, 2008. The creation of street art is not always about the addition of artful elements into the cityscape. As Moose and other reverse-graffiti artists prove, it can also be about erasing the soot, dust and dirt already present in the city to form detailed compositions.

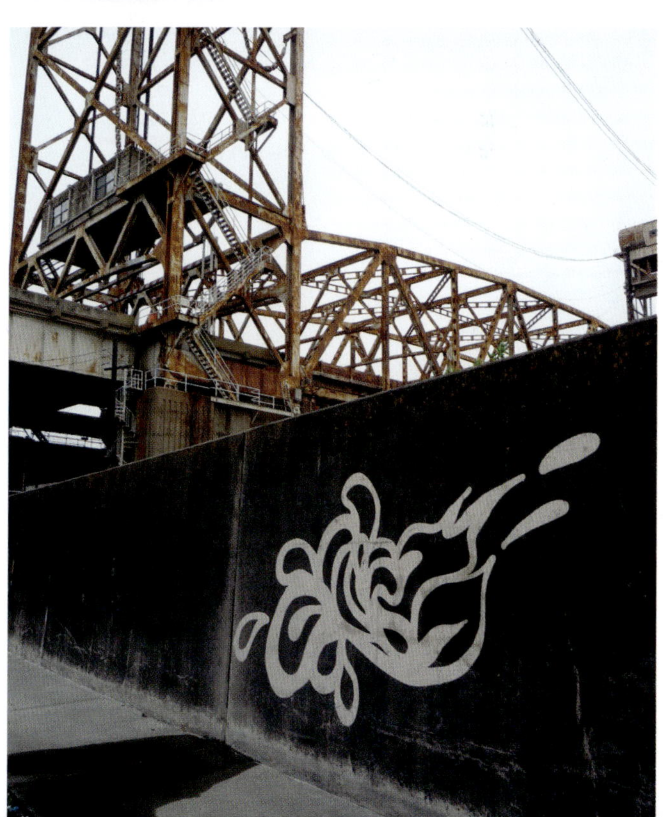

139 (*below*) **Moose**, *Untitled*, New Orleans, USA, 2009. Fashioning natural landscapes, abstract designs and other motifs on city walls by cleaning a given space allows for a fascinating reflection on the illegality of street art since, neither defacement nor destruction, this type of work involves effacement and restoration.

140 (*right*) **Moose**, *Untitled*,
Liverpool, UK, 2006

141 (*below*) **Moose**, *Untitled*,
Košice, Slovakia, 2009

142 (*opposite, above*) **Alexandre
Órion**, *Ossário*, Max Feffer
Tunnel, São Paulo, Brazil, 2006.
In this massive reverse-graffiti
project, Alexandre Órion
cleaned away dirt from the walls
of Brazilian tunnels to create
murals of skulls. The works act
as a commentary on the deadly
effects of pollution.

143 (*opposite, below*) **Alexandre
Órion**, *Ossário*, Ayrton Senna
Tunnel, São Paulo, Brazil, 2006

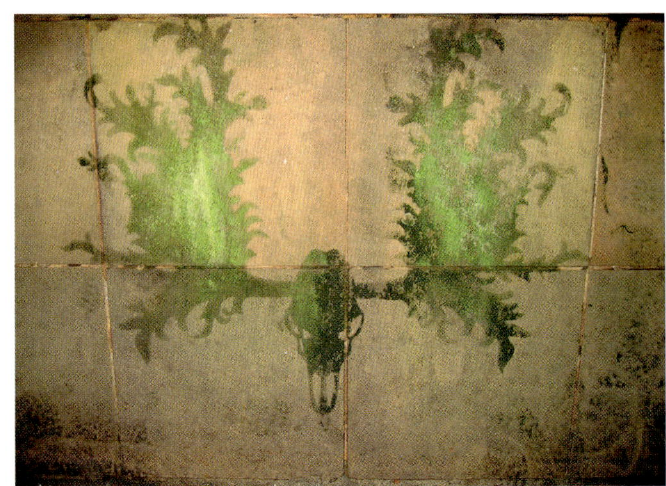

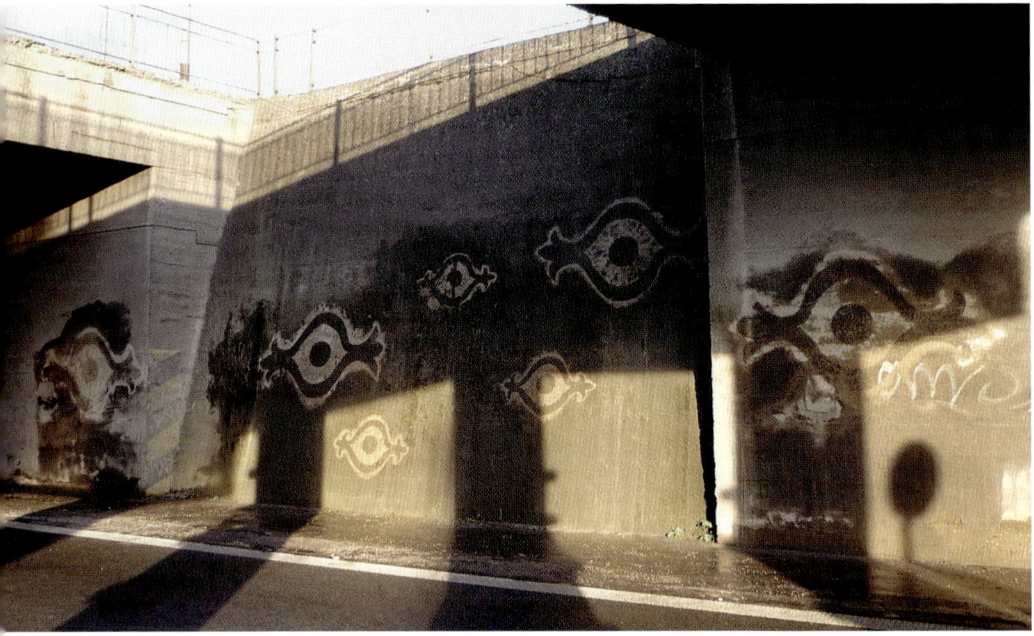

part of a project to promote environmental sustainability
and to emphasize the grime that we as populations produce.
Moose uses stencils along with organic cleaning agents and
recycled items such as moss, socks, lichen and shoe brushes to
create his pieces. Akin to the yarn bombing street movement,
the reverse-graffiti method occupies a grey area in terms of
illegality and stands in opposition to the imagery and traditional

materials of graffiti writing. Aerosol spray-paint continues to be harmful to the environment and human health, and working with the medium leaves a lasting mark. In contrast, the sort of surface restoration advocated by Moose inherently underlines environmentalism through the use of non-toxic materials. The artist's oeuvre includes fashioning a hillside forest on a bleak wall as a reminder of the natural world (2008) [138], fluid abstract designs [139], a skull head with organic, foliage-like antlers (2006) [140] and eye motifs (2009) [141].

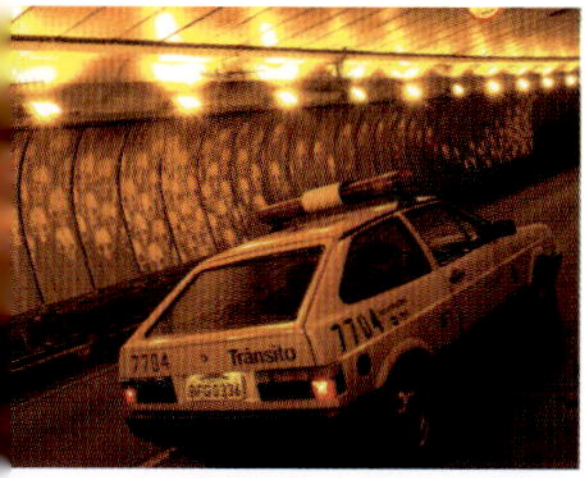

Concerned with the harmful effects of pollution, other artists such as Alexandre Órion also participate in the reverse-graffiti trend. The series of interventions named *Ossário* saw the artist use pieces of cloth to 'clean' immense tunnels in São Paulo by scraping off layers of grime and soot from car exhausts to depict a great number of skulls (2006) [142, 143]. After days

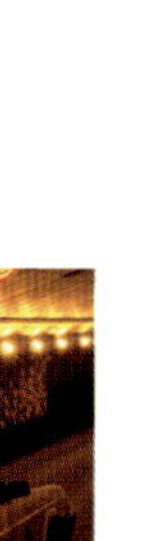

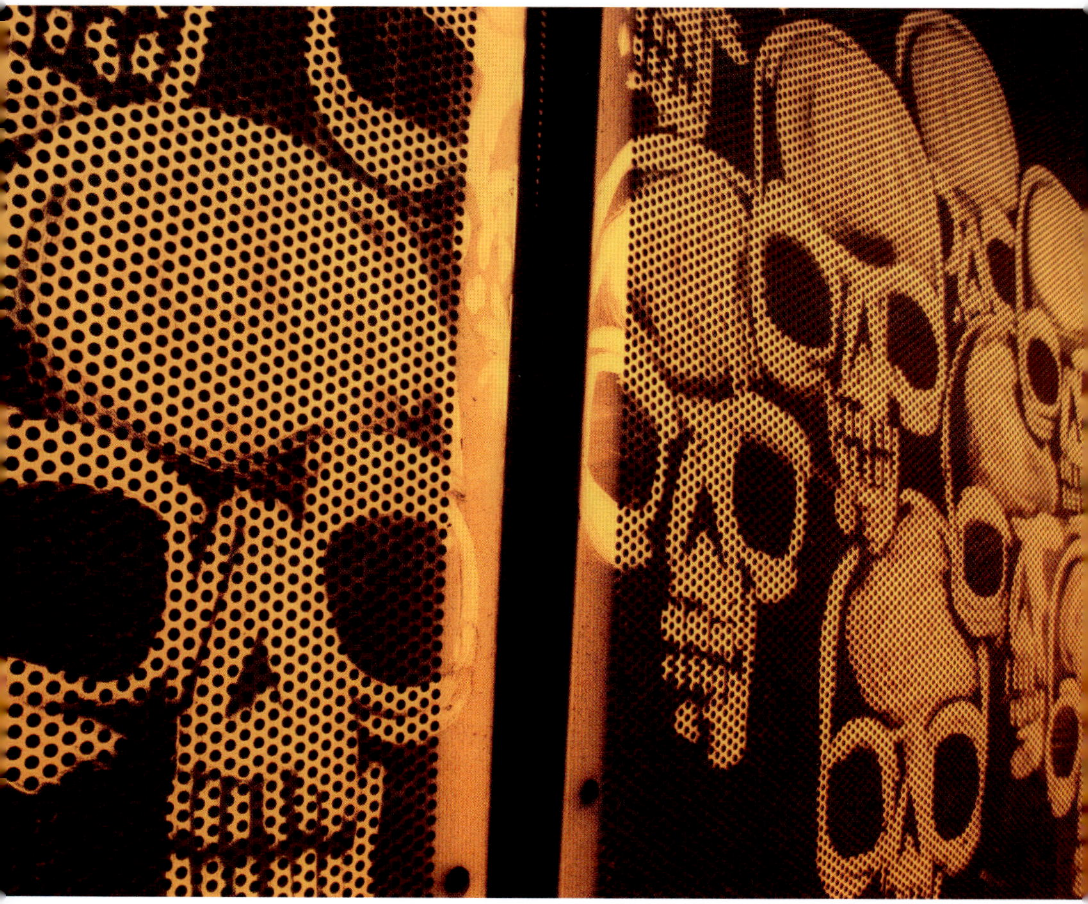

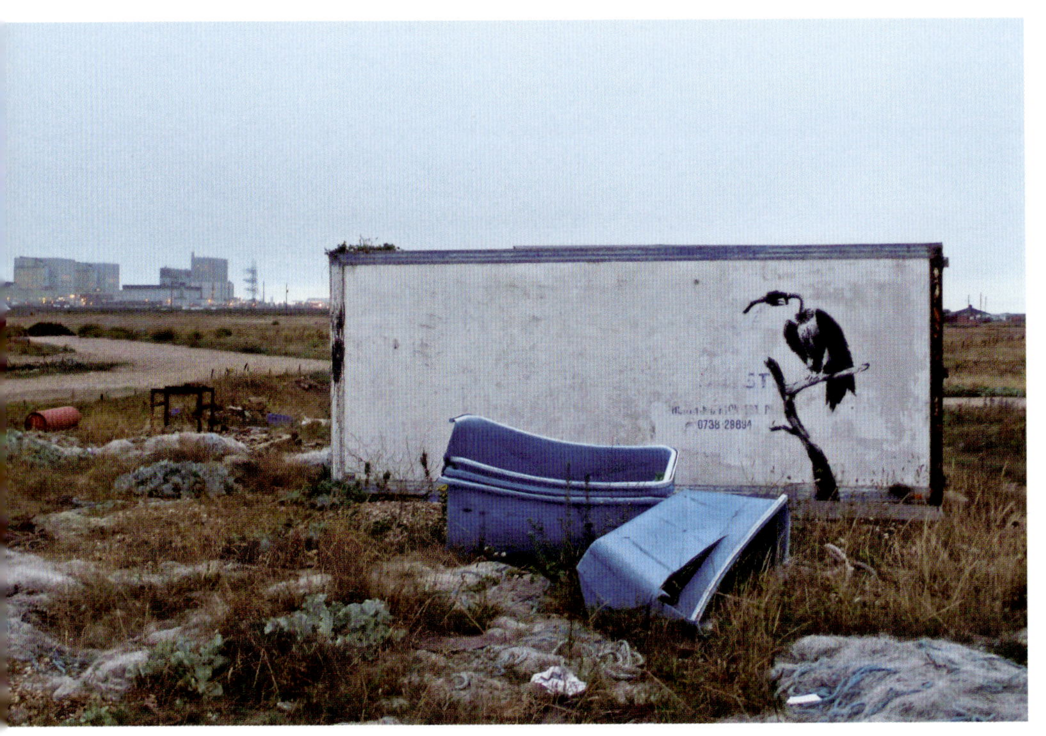

144 **Banksy**, *Untitled*, Dungeness, UK, 2010. A bird of prey that notoriously feeds on the dead proves the perfect body for Banksy's petrol-pump disguised as a vulture. Dungeness nuclear power station can be seen in the distance, forming a bleak but poignant backdrop.

of work, the Max Feffer Tunnel exhibited more than 3,500 hand-wiped skulls, which transformed the space into a sort of cemetery. This pungent reminder of death shaped by scrubbing away films of dirt explores the effects of pollution and the unbiased reminder that we, in one way or another, contribute to its production.

Same Work, Multiple Sites

Graffiti writers, especially through the dissemination of tags and throwies, effectively recreate the same work time and again as they navigate city streets. Although a writer's pieces can take on any number of creative articulations, they too are fundamentally an expression of the same name. Yet visually, it is impossible to categorize graffiti writing as recreations of the same work. Hand-drawn, the various elements of the work may look similar but they can never be exact duplicates.

Street artists, on the other hand, often display versions of the same work in numerous cities throughout the world and enrich the various renditions through context, seeking out the locations that best respond to or benefit from the pieces.

In this sense, street art is site-specific, regardless of whether a piece is permanent with a fixed address. Although some street artworks are inseparable from the sites they occupy, generally speaking street art can be understood as site-specific if the term 'site' is not contingent on a particular geographical location or if it is broadened to include types of sites, such as billboards, rooftops, walls, bridges, roads or simply city streets. Sometimes works are specifically chosen for already politicized locations, while other times they are put up in arbitrary places. In reality, the only physical or environmental specification for street art is that it is disseminated on the street. The urban domain is, by all accounts, the only condition necessary for the proliferation of art practices that respond to ordained imagery and create uncensored spaces of dialogue.

When working locally, artists might opt for sites that are especially significant to their experience of their own city. Whenever possible, they travel to locations where the urban art scene is booming, graffiti penalties are somewhat less severe, or interesting work is being made. The selected sites are, or become, arenas for social exchange, and aid in the construction of the world of street art as one that operates within the urban environment, but outside its sanctioned parameters. Much less overtly than signature graffiti writers, post-graffiti artists are influenced by each other's work. The street art communities that have arisen worldwide are dissimilar to graffiti crews, yet there is a definite network as well as a sense of collective venture, camaraderie and respect among urban painters.

Reproducing a particular piece in a number of contexts begs the question: if the same or a very similar work is diffused multiple times in varied places, is each variation meaningful in a different way? Indeed, this sort of seriality allows artworks to take on divergent meanings with each execution, making the work, because of its context, feel entirely different with every rendition. While the physical piece itself transforms by virtue of its existence in a permeable space, so do all the elements that support its exhibition. With time both the work and its context of display adapt to one another and thus translate the experience of movement and change through the visual gesture.

Above's stubby, upwardly pointed version of the arrow, an iconic symbol in graffiti and an integral part of many tags, stands on its own as his trademark. Whether an arrow is executed as a wooden block hanging from telephone wires or is painted

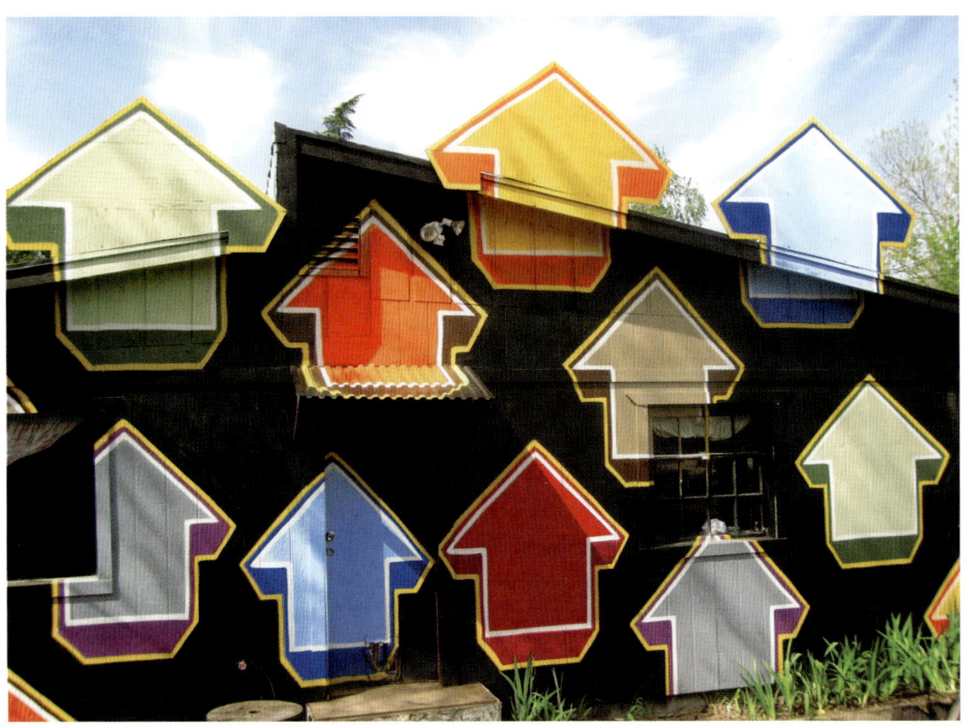

145 **Above**, *Arrow House*, California, USA, 2006. Above's trademark upwardly pointed arrow, a symbol close to any graffiti writer's heart, implies the notion of rising above and simultaneously encourages a glance towards the sky. This simple gesture works to momentarily disrupt one's trajectory and offers a moment of reflection.

on city walls [145], the American artist's message to 'rise above' populates cities worldwide. Painting or affixing arrows internationally allows him to reach a wide audience through a universal symbol and to encourage passers-by to reconsider their surroundings. A pedestrian who sees an arrow pointing up seemingly at nothing is likely to react by looking up and, through this response, is persuaded into a state of momentary reflection. Looking above, as the arrow suggests, proposes a different perspective from one's typical eye-level point of view when navigating the city. This simple change of viewpoint allows for an altered interpretation of a particular site.

Above's arrows typically transcend language but, when hung rather than painted, are occasionally adorned with a three- or four-letter word, one on each side. As the arrow swings and twirls in the wind, both words are revealed and thus disclose something about the work's particular location. In one piece in Istanbul, one side of the arrow read 'holy' and the other 'land' (2006) [146]. A symbol as iconic as the arrow functions in any city, which makes it possible to display versions of the same work time and again. Recently, the artist has evolved his

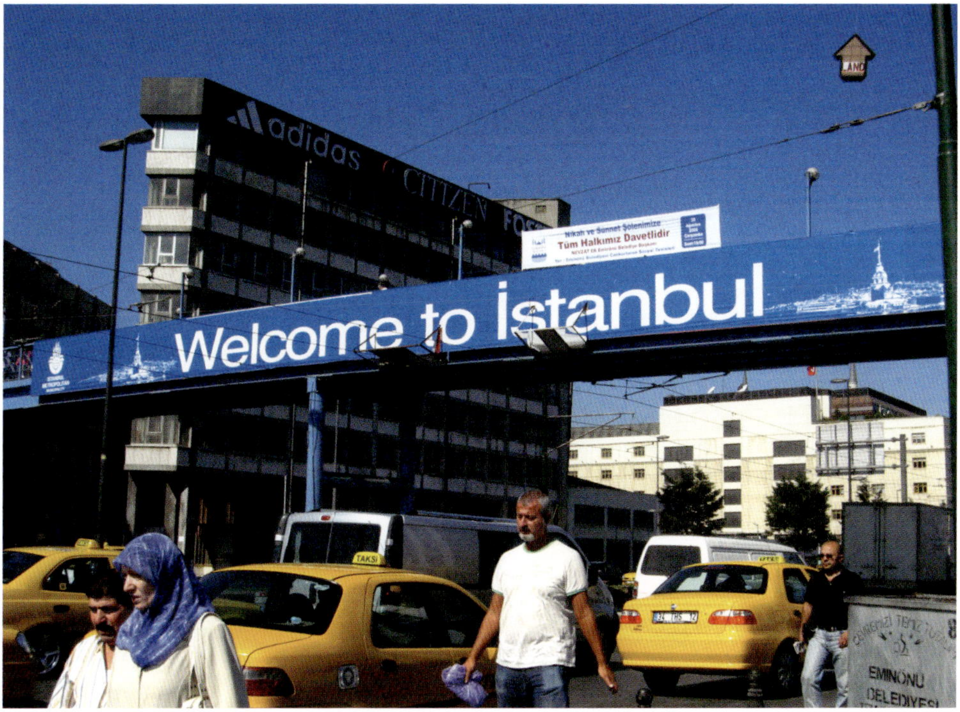

146 (*above*) **Above**, *Holy/Land*,
Istanbul, Turkey, 2006. Known
for his word-play wooden
arrow mobiles, Above affixes
his emblem in locations where
the words written on either side
of the arrow reveal something
about their appropriated home.
This one, in the heart of Istanbul,
reads Holy/Land.

147 (*right*) **Above**, *Help Thy
Neighbor*, Cuba, 2010. The
artist has recently evolved his
practice into colourful, figurative
stencilling. In this response to
the earthquake that devastated
Haiti in 2010, a young Cuban
boy sets out to offer help to
his neighbours in need, thus
advocating international aid relief.

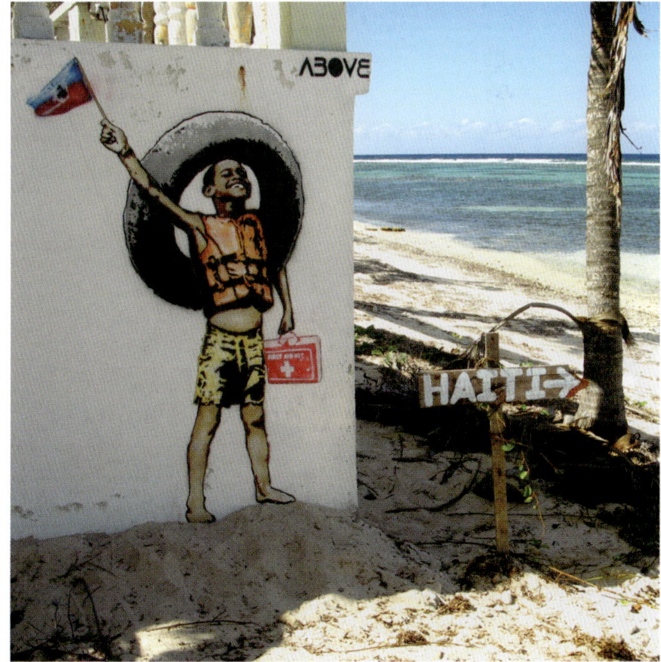

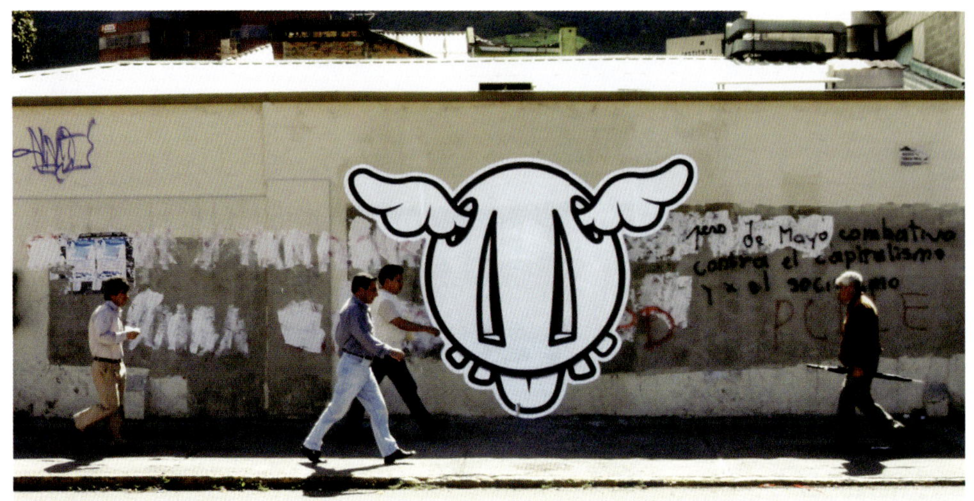

practice into colourful figurative stencilling, fashioning works that tend to be site-specific. *Help Thy Neighbor* (2010) [147], for example, shows a young Cuban boy ready to embark on an aid mission to Haiti to provide earthquake relief.

In another example of multiplicity, English artist D*Face works mainly with stencils, stickers, posters and sculpture, and positions his practice primarily as an alternative to the proliferation of advertising in the cityscape. His graphic imagery, based on the subversion of pop culture icons and the philosophy of mass marketing, is not only diverse in subject

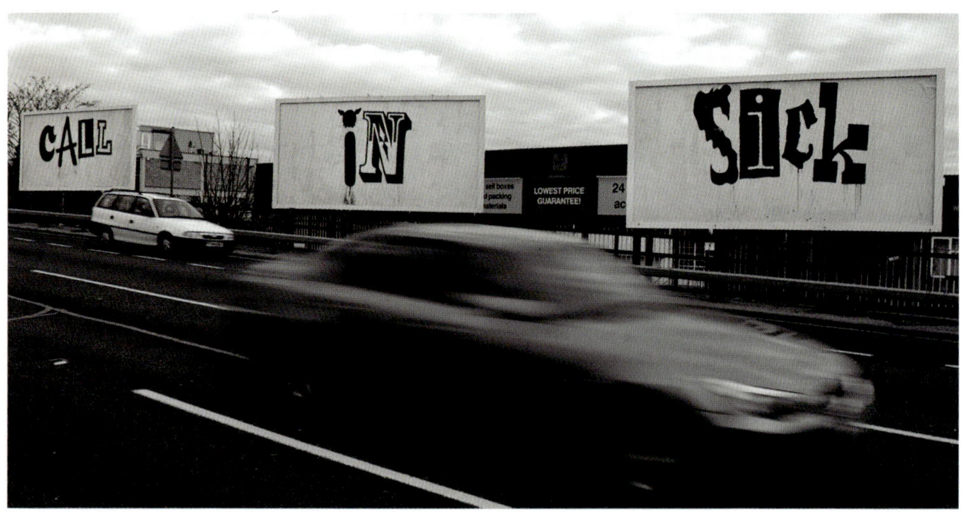

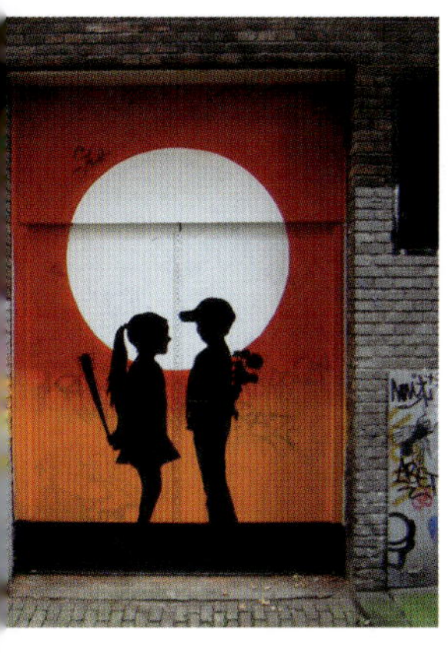

and style, but also ambitious in its range. By appropriating advertisements, images of celebrity figures, comic books and even currency, the artist essentially questions the state and direction of pop culture. With his series of dysfunctional characters, which resemble rowdy and radical Disney creatures, D*Face aims to jolt people out of their reverie. His brand of street art is concerned with using satirical, tongue-in-cheek strategies to navigate one's environment in an alternative way.

Through the proliferation of his best-known character, D*Dog [148], in innumerable places, the artist questions the ethos of modern society. As he explains: 'I wanted to encourage people not just to "see", but to look at what surrounds them and their lives, reflecting our increasingly bizarre popular culture, re-thinking and reworking cultural figures and genres to comment on our ethos of conspicuous consumption.' His use of multiple sites (in terms of physical locations) and material supports is typical of many street artists. Making art not only on the street but on everyday objects exposes the conversation between art and pop culture. The appropriation of three billboards urging citizens to 'call in sick' (2008) [149], a motto the artist revisits on numerous occasions on commercial billboards, is a simple yet effective message. The successful appropriation of a large advertising space to 'sell' a suggestion that is enticing to many members of the public rests in large part on the artist's direct style.

Dutch artist Fake's multi-coloured, detailed stencils are also reproduced in numerous locations and deal with a range of subject matter and imagery. His vivid, playful creations reveal a clear penchant for making people smile, from mischievous representations of young love (2010) [150] and the Hindu God Ganesha as a street artist (2009) [151] to a two-dimensional image of a young girl, turned somewhat three-dimensional through the drawing of a hopscotch game on the pavement (2009) [152]. Like Above and D*Face, Fake legibly signs his stencils, although he tends to incorporate the signature into the work, sometimes even as a brand, as in the case of the Fake spray-paint 'nectar' represented as a delicacy for hummingbirds in *Painting God and Canbird*. The straightforward nature of his pieces allows for transposition into all manner of places, with the capacity to speak to vast audiences.

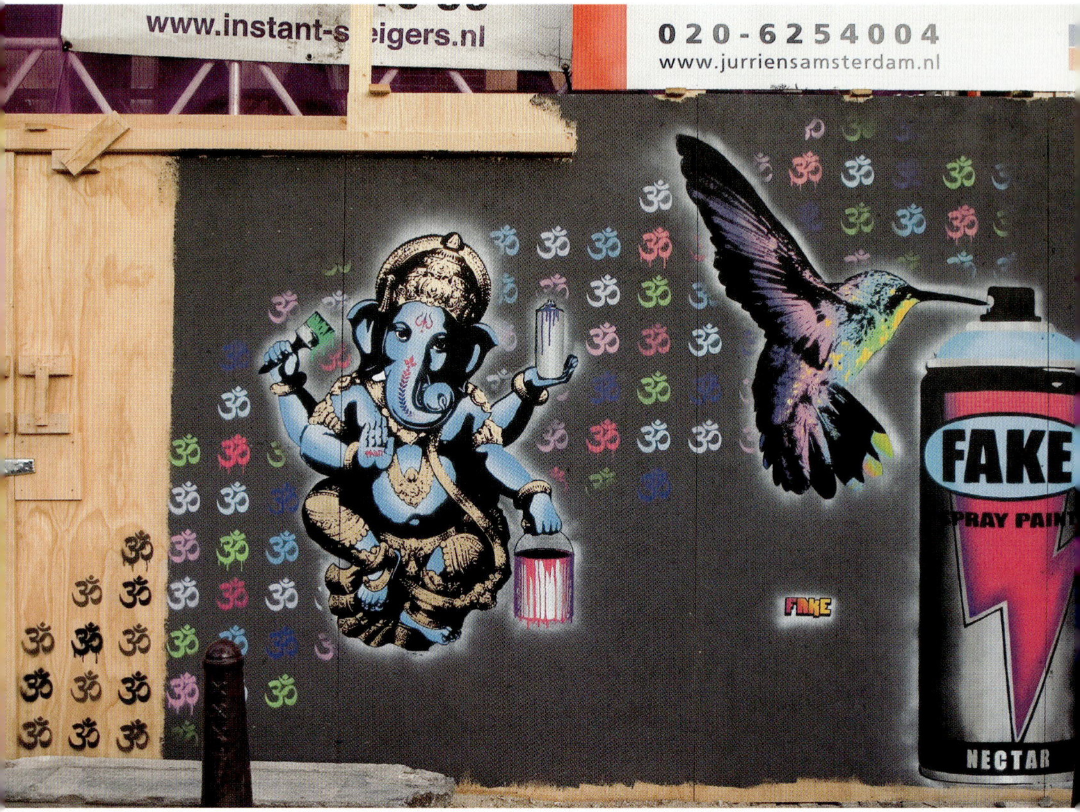

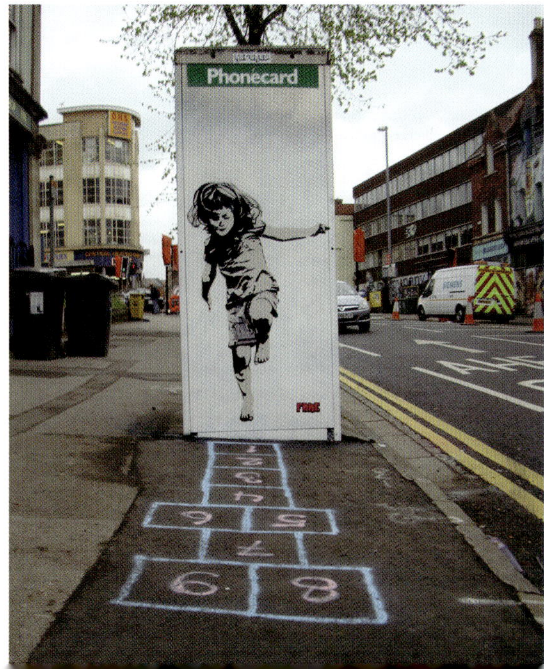

151 (*above*) **Fake**, *Painting God and Canbird*, Amsterdam, Netherlands, 2009

152 (*right*) **Fake**, *Hopscotch*, Bristol, UK, 2009

Location, Location, Location

Urban artworks together with their material support and surrounding landscape compose a specific context. In order to understand street art in situ, one must consider all the various elements that make up the work: not just the medium, surface, subject and setting, but also how the piece interacts with its environment (the media, architectural forms and signage that envelop it, for example, as well as local history or contemporary issues). The context is volatile and can be transformed repeatedly either through the artwork's removal or through further additions to the space by other artists. As it is altered through additions, erasures and any other signs of performance, the site and the piece live and thus play a part in street art culture. The work's engagement with its context therefore creates a particular space – it temporarily apprehends a discrete place.

Artists often choose their sites of dissemination both for visibility and for the relationship the artists might have with particular places. Montreal artist Roadsworth for many years circulated his work within only a small portion of the city's Plateau Mont-Royal neighbourhood. The streets that became his canvases were part of his daily commute and were thus most familiar and meaningful to the artist's experience of the city.

For other artists, such as JR, location provides the impetus for the work itself and dictates its imagery. Immense

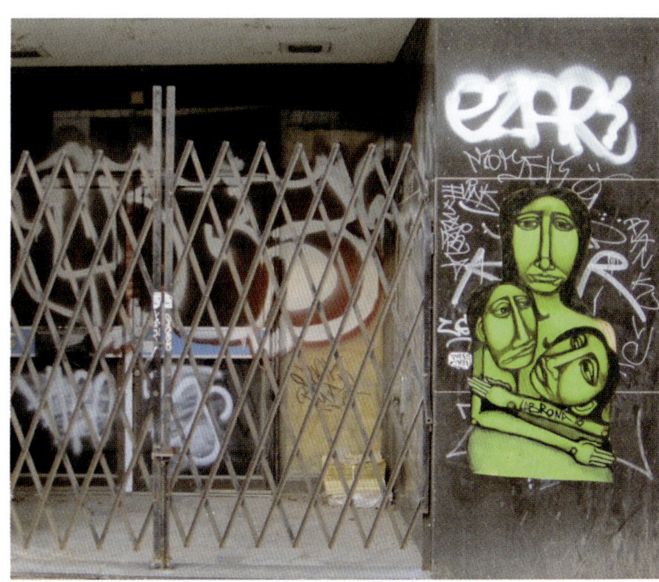

153 **Labrona**, *Street Hugs*, Montreal, Canada, 2010. The fact that graffiti breeds graffiti is essential to the survival of the culture since it is through visual communication that writers respond to each other's work and thus take over a particular location. Street artists sometimes share spaces occupied by graffiti and thus insert their work into visual street culture.

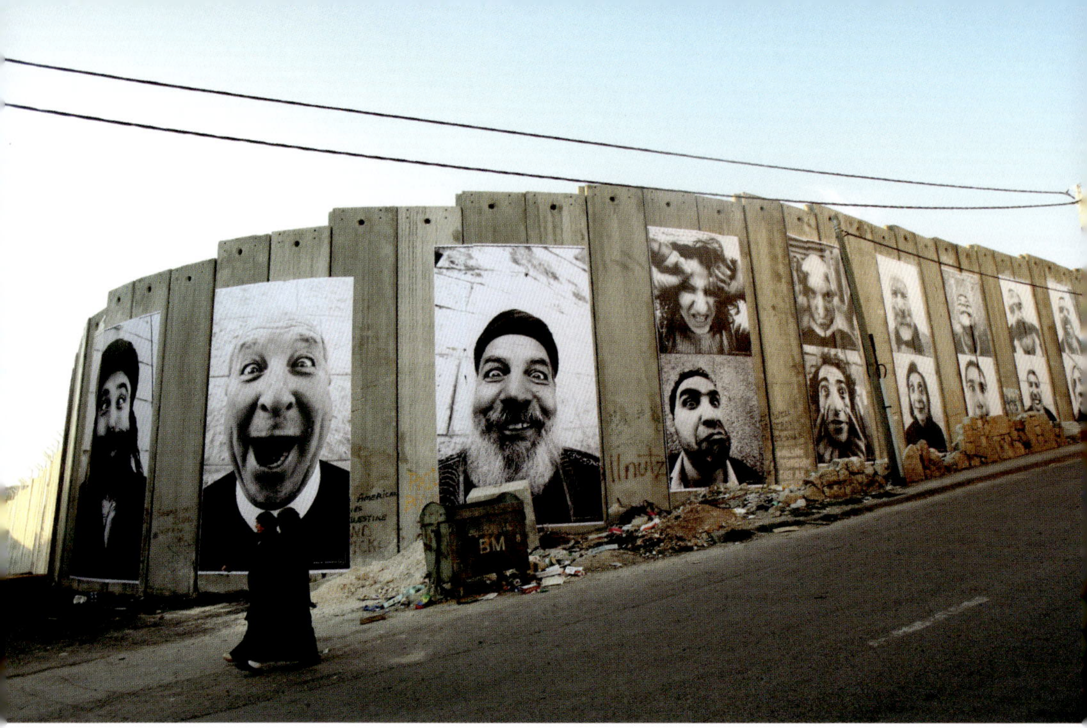

America
Palestine
BM

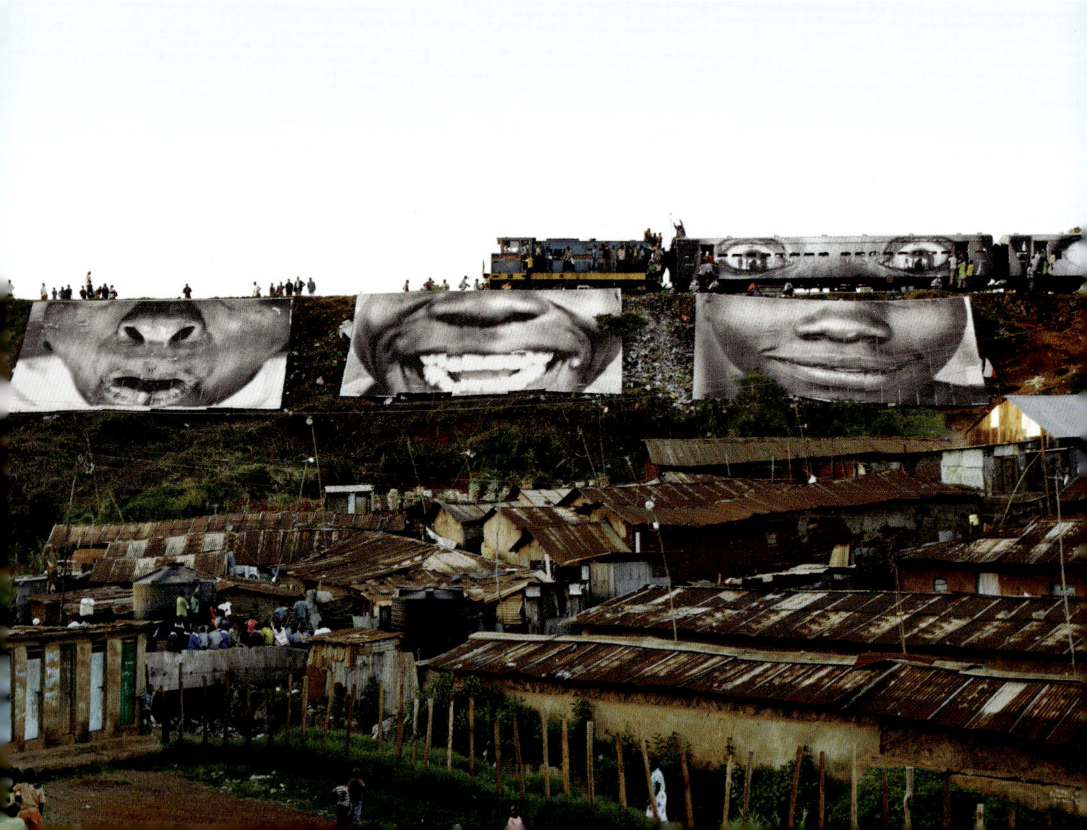

photographic posters depicting intimate portraits characterize the French artist's decade-long practice. The socio-politically motivated portraits, reflecting particular situations and places, are physically positioned amid those environments. Thus topography and political geography both inspire and become home to a particular project. Despite their monumentality, the photographs are incredibly accessible due to their genuine representations of real people in real situations.

With *Women* (2008) [155, 156], JR focused on female heroes in conflict situations, travelling to Africa, Brazil, India and Cambodia. Covering rooftops with portraits printed on waterproof material holds a double function of bringing art into unexpected places while involving the community in all aspects of production and diffusion, as well as sheltering fragile homes from heavy rains. Another project, *Wrinkles of the City* (2010) [116, 157], undertaken in Cartagena, Spain, and Shanghai, China, questioned the memory of a city and its inhabitants. The depiction of elderly residents on decaying, dilapidated and abandoned buildings communicates a very clear message of the passage of time and memory. One portrait from Shanghai [157], expertly framed by what is left of a decrepit building, resonates, especially through the sitter's quiet resolution and thoughtful sadness, with commemoration and remembrance. The modern skyline that frames this scene further accentuates the division between old and young, emphasized here through architecture and portraiture.

Through projects such as these, the French 'photograffeur' ingeniously proposes a different point of view of events, situations and populations represented in the mass media from a narrow, one-sided perspective. The scale of his pieces is significant not simply because such monumental portraits are typically reserved for celebrities advertising a film or a product, but also because it is confrontational. Representing real life through photographic portraiture provides stigmatized, stereotyped and marginalized communities with a voice. The photographs tell the story of the place they inhabit by representing its people in an authentic manner. At the same time, by focusing on similarities rather than differences, JR decategorizes his subjects. A good example of this aspect of his work is *Face2Face* (2006–7) [154], in which he populated both sides of the West Bank separation wall with juxtaposed portraits of Palestinians and Israelis who hold the same occupation on either side of the divide. The playful expressions of the sitters

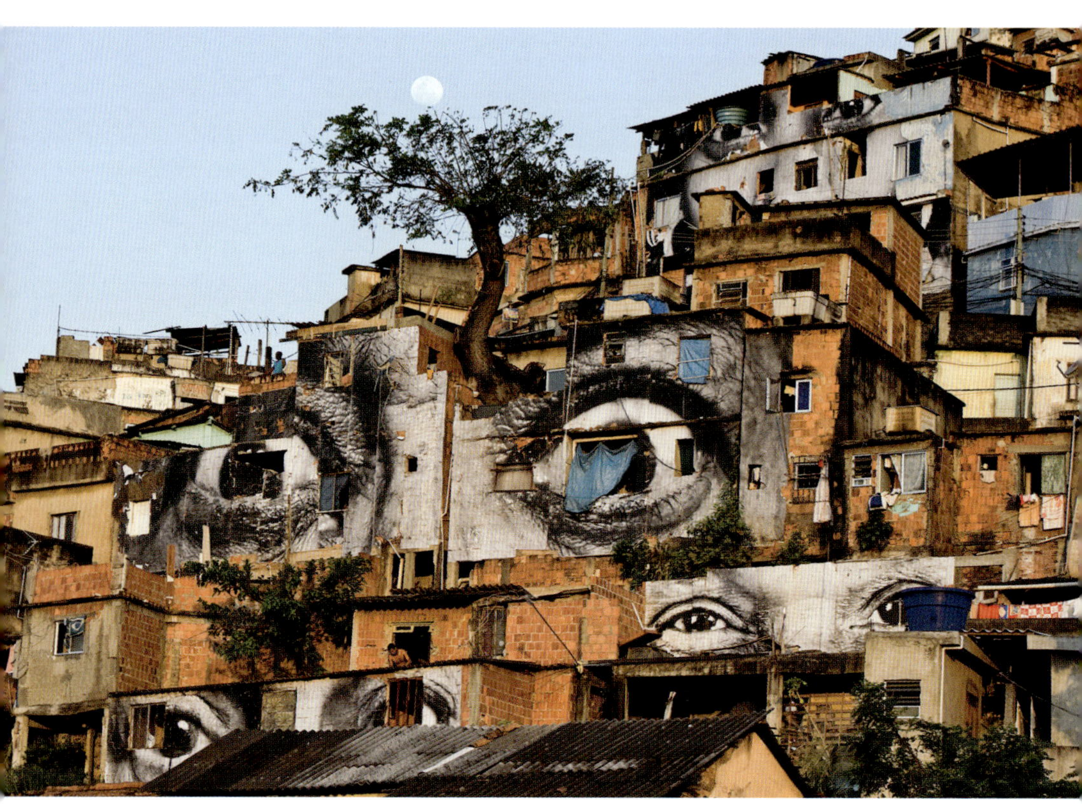

156 **JR**, *Women*, Rio de Janeiro, Brazil, 2008

add greatly to the contemplation of commonality in a situation of division.

In contrast to JR's reliance on location for artistic exploration, Canadian artist Omen's psychedelic portraits are not positioned in places that inspired the work. Nor is his choice of location motivated by political situations or social issues. Instead, the artist chooses sites that ensure high visibility and appropriate framing. Although Omen would describe himself as a graffiti writer, his art practice is not centred on the abstracted signature, but rather on the conceptual portrait. Working almost exclusively with spray-paint, the Montreal artist has been creating his unique brand of large-scale aerosol portraiture for over a decade. Surrealistically rendered faces morphing into each other and twisting onto themselves are characteristic of the artist's oeuvre [158]. Painted primarily in black, white and grey, Omen's work is remarkably accessible in its abstraction. Although his representations of faces are often troubling, melancholic and distressed, they are executed with a

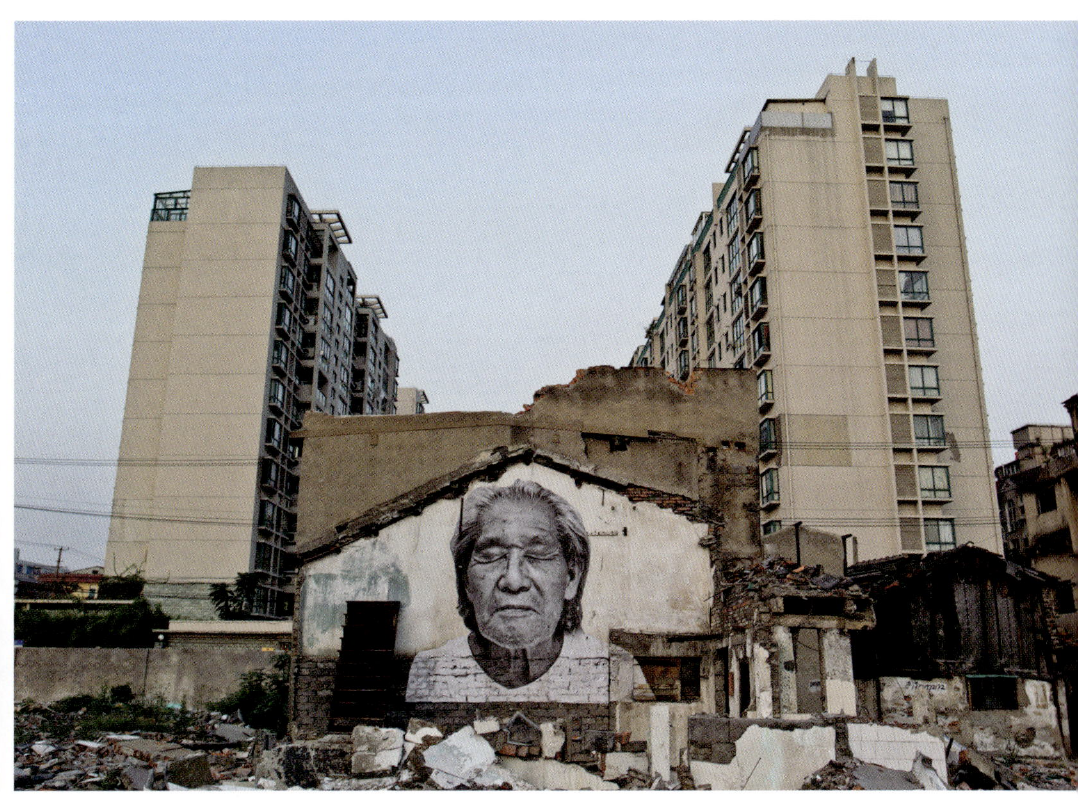

157 **JR**, *Wrinkles of the City*, Shanghai, China, 2010. Stretched across neglected or torn-down building façades, portraits of elderly residents speak to modern development but, with it, a disregard for the past. With these portraits, JR aims to give a voice to the history and life experience of a particular place and generations before us.

painterly flow and lyricism that draw in the viewer. The legibly signed portraits for which Omen is best known appear to fit seamlessly into their space of dissemination, and the location is thus rendered complete.

While most street artists are concerned with the physical, aesthetic or socio-political nature of their chosen locations, others aim to influence entire cities with their work. Brazil's Nina Pandolfo focuses on breathing life into São Paulo's cityscape through art. Dedicated to creating playful images for the city's children, she subverts the functionality and rampant commercialization of the city by introducing her vibrant images into its grimy, grey streets. The animal and female characters that the artist creates are less infantile than they may initially appear. Although they display an air of innocence, vulnerability and cuteness, their bodies are sexualized. With developed breasts and hips, her girls are women in their physical form, while their facial features are reminiscent of baby dolls [159]. Nina's practice addresses the changes from childhood to adulthood, as she

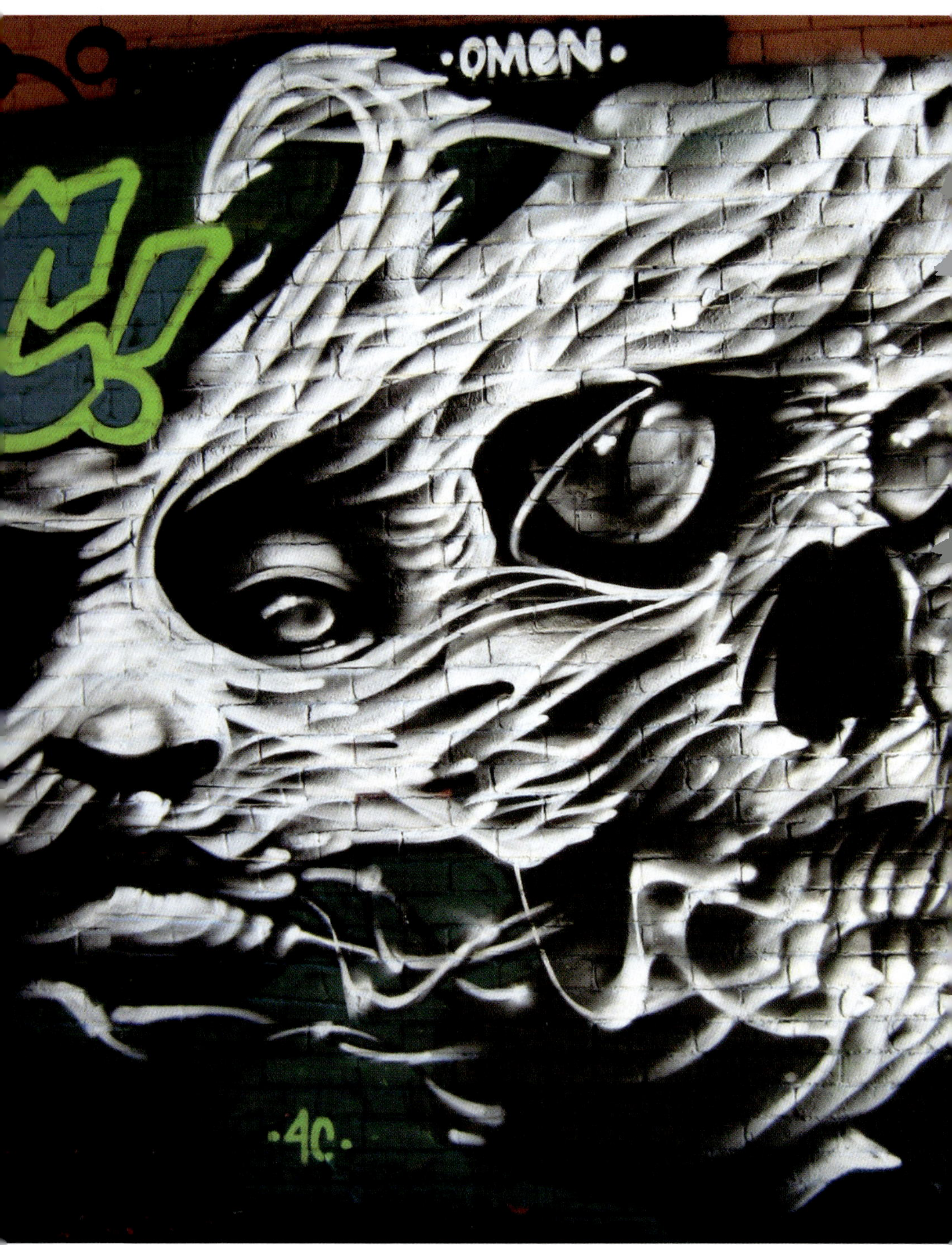
·OMEN·
.4C.

158 (*opposite*) **Omen**, *Untitled*, Montreal, Canada, 2009. Omen's psychedelic portraits take over their spaces of display through haunting, sometimes ominous imagery that remarkably holds the viewer's gaze.

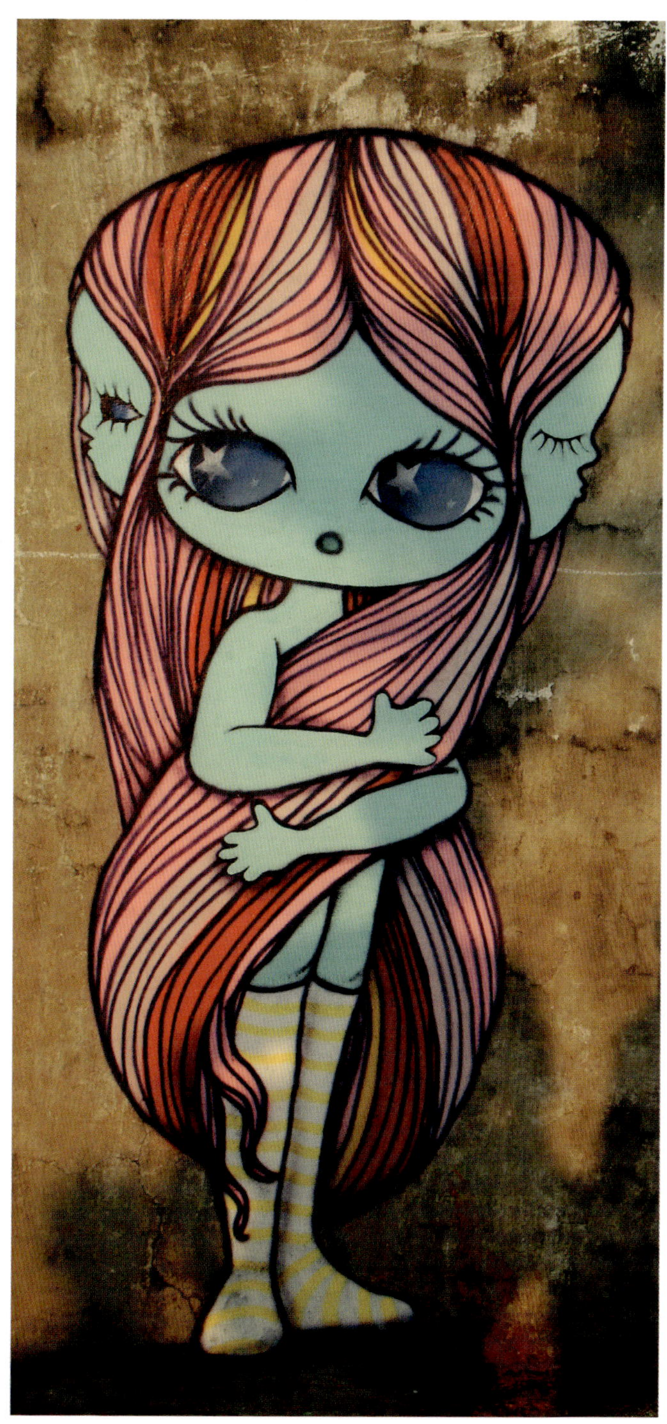

159 (*right*) **Nina Pandolfo**, *Untitled*, Mumbai, India, 2008. Colourful portraits of doll-like, wide-eyed children are part of Nina Pandolfo's enterprise to paint images that appeal to our inner-child.

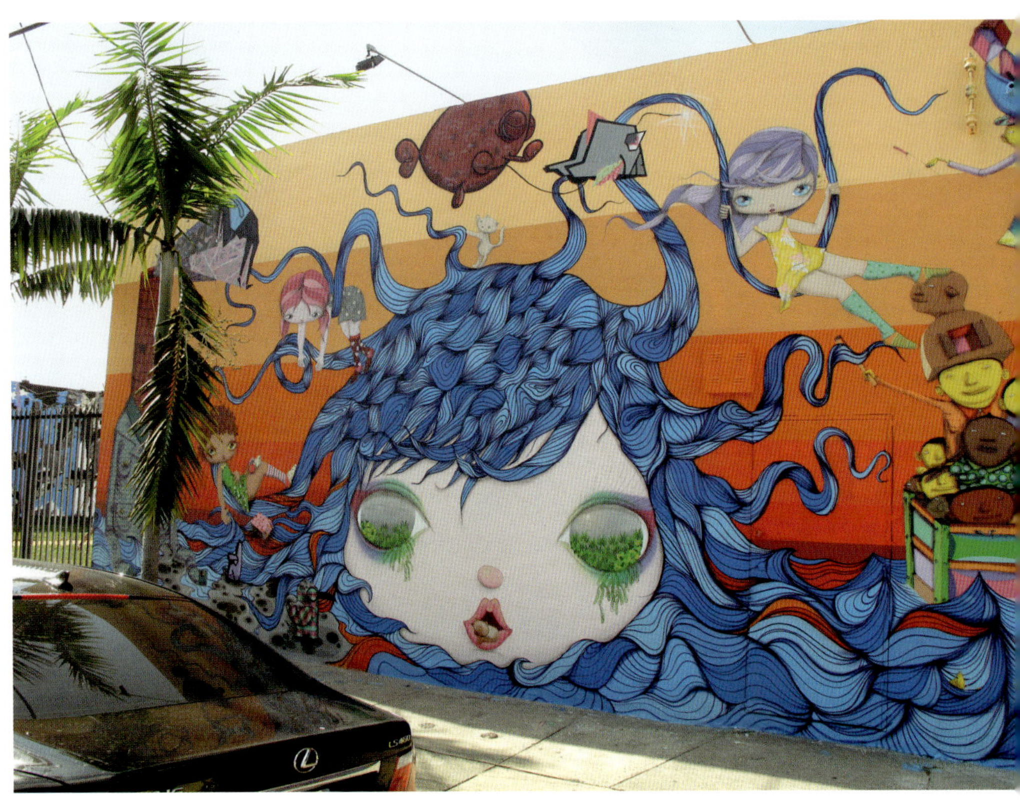

160 **Nina Pandolfo**, *Untitled*, Miami, USA, 2009. Nina's fanciful narrative scenes, abundant with play and wild imagination, facilitate escapism from an adult world that is otherwise full of responsibilities and consequences.

explains: 'When we were children we looked at problems and life in a different way, more positive; we dreamed more, we played more, and we enjoyed life more. But when we become adults we look at everything more seriously, we don't care about life's details, we don't play a lot, we don't dream…and we wanted to grow up quickly. This is terrible. We still need to enjoy, dream, do everything in a positive way… But of course, we have different visions about everything; we can't just close our "eyes".'

With oversized heads, large glassy eyeballs and tiny, sometimes nude torsos, Nina's characters create a rupture in the streets they populate. Their detailed, cartoonish renderings are emphasized by their colourful backgrounds, which together suggest a dream-like scenario [160]. More than an exploration of the physical changes from childhood to adulthood, Nina's pieces facilitate escapism. In the context of the city, her surrealistic characters transport the passer-by to a happier, gentler sort of universe, where the physicality of the city disappears and dreamy narratives are enacted.

The Material Support and the Work Itself

Beyond questions of where to place an artwork in the vastness
of a geographical region, many street artists are also concerned
with the materiality or the physical constitution of a particular
site. The material support is often integral to the work itself
and dictates the imagery and composition, or even establishes
the meaning of the piece. Banksy's project to produce a series
of paintings on the controversial security barrier around the
West Bank town of Bethlehem, as a comment on the Israeli-
Palestinian conflict, is a particularly pertinent example.

Adhering to the New York style of writing, Banksy began
producing graffiti during the 1980s before turning to stencils.
His art practice advocates a do-it-yourself attitude so as to
communicate unencumbered, culturally relevant messages.
For Banksy, the West Bank wall, as an extremely controversial
barrier, afforded the possibility for visual protest. The nine
characteristically satirical paintings that he created on the
Palestinian side of the barrier (2005) all echo the same agenda:
freedom and peace. Children are depicted gleefully playing with
buckets and spades beneath a tropical paradise [161], clutching
a bundle of balloons to float towards the top of the wall, or
kneeling at the base of a rope ladder that spans the barrier's
height. In other images, the artist transformed the wall into
an enormous living-room setting, complete with armchairs,
a coffee table, and a window looking out on a lush, idyllic
landscape [163]. In another example, the artist marked out a
section of the wall with a dotted line and scissors, as if to urge
people to cut along the line and slice open the divide [162].
Following his initial 2005 stunt, which prompted numerous
locally produced visual explorations on the wall, the artist
returned in 2007 to create another series of works as part of
the collaborative exhibition 'Santa's Ghetto Bethlehem'.

The site that the artist chose to adorn with his sardonic
imagery, already pregnant with meaning, was selected for its
transformative potential. The massive grey wall functions as
the ultimate canvas for street artists, who typically look for
frequented spaces in which to create their work, but as a
barrier awash with political tension it is an invaluable site. Both
as a structure and a symbol, it creates a politically repressive
situation against which artists can react. The creation of a
physical border is matched seamlessly with street art, itself
a transient reminder of the public/private divide. While
the histories of each are naturally dissimilar, a productive

161 **Banksy**, *Untitled*, West Bank barrier, 2005. Children, play and idyllic landscapes all echo Banksy's message of freedom and peace. Painted on the barrier wall around the West Bank town of Bethlehem, this series responds both to the oppressive physical structure and the socio-political situation that led to its erection.

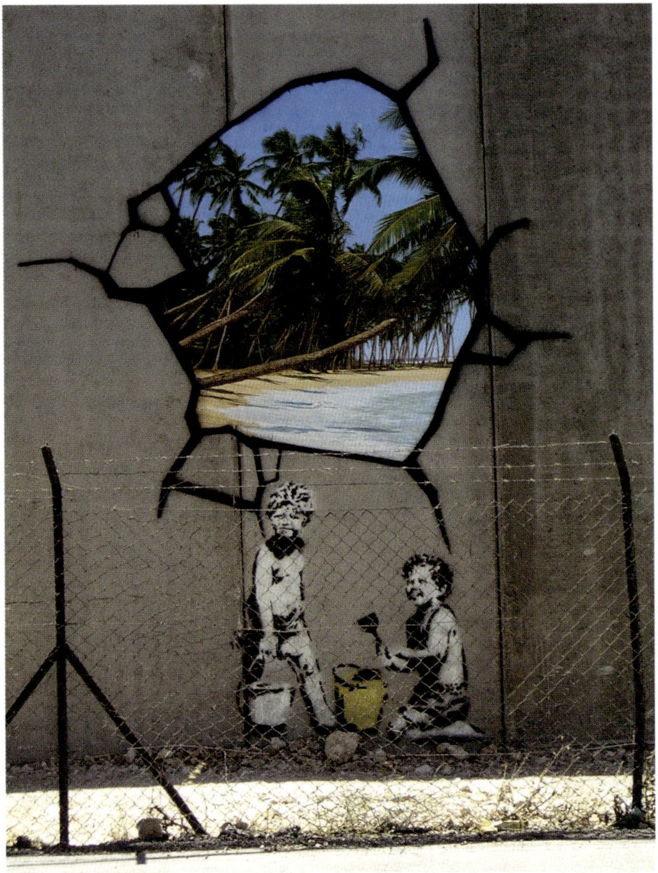

comparison can be made on the level of symbolic meaning. Both symbols of strife, their conjunction reflects the site's implication as a materially and spatially invasive structure. While Banksy's images are perhaps not overtly political when experienced out of context, they create a situation the artist is best known for: in their effortless, humorous imagery the works are suggestive. They suggest the obvious – that the wall is an oppressive structure, one that polarizes people and heightens a loss of peace and freedom. With the optical illusions created for this site-specific project, Banksy has succeeded in doing what he is revered for: crossing cultural borders with simple and accessible imagery.

Painting figurative images reminiscent of Cubism and German Expressionism, Canadian artist Labrona has established himself on the street art scene with his unique take on freight train

162 (*above*) **Banksy**, *Untitled*, West Bank barrier, 2005. This invitation to cut along the dotted line is the sort of simple yet witty and effective imagery for which Banksy is revered. Painting on a hostile structure both infuses the work with meaning and makes the artist's point of view clear.

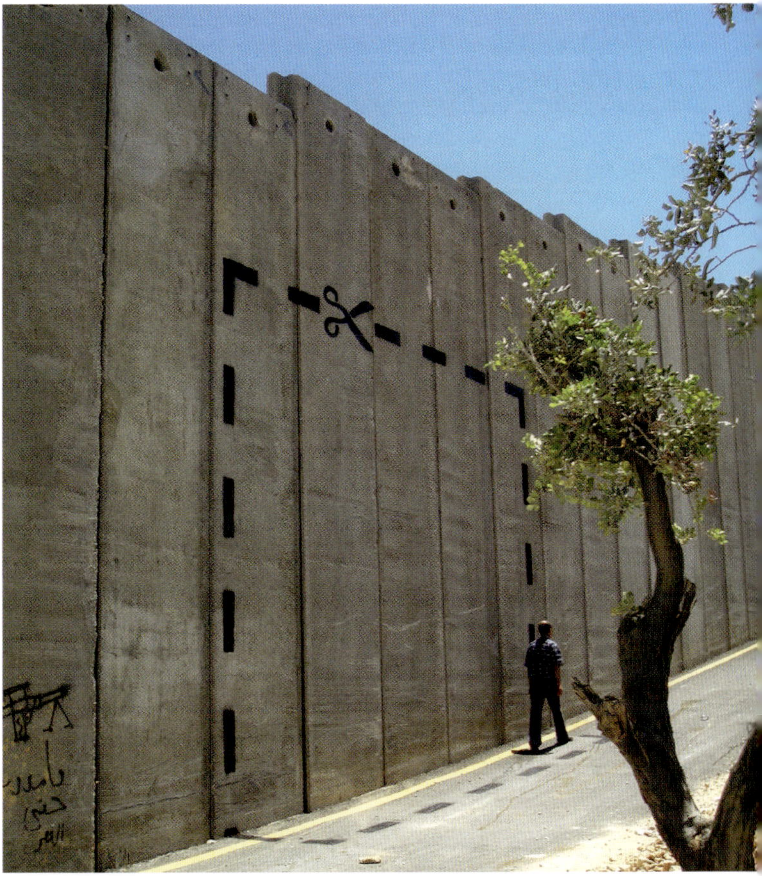

163 (*below*) **Banksy**, *Untitled*, West Bank barrier, 2005

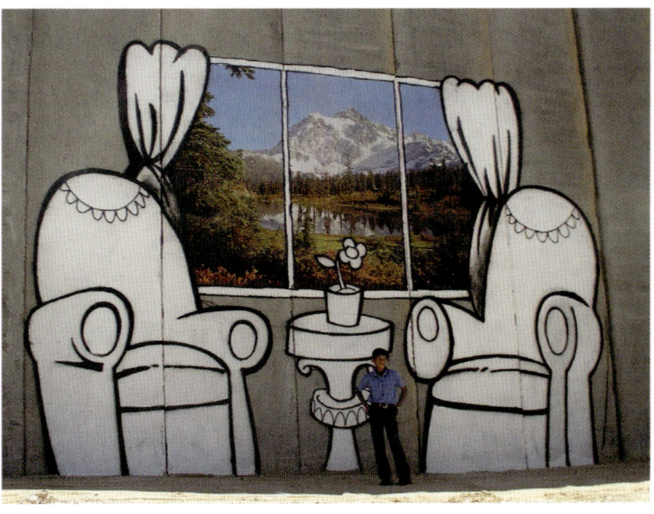

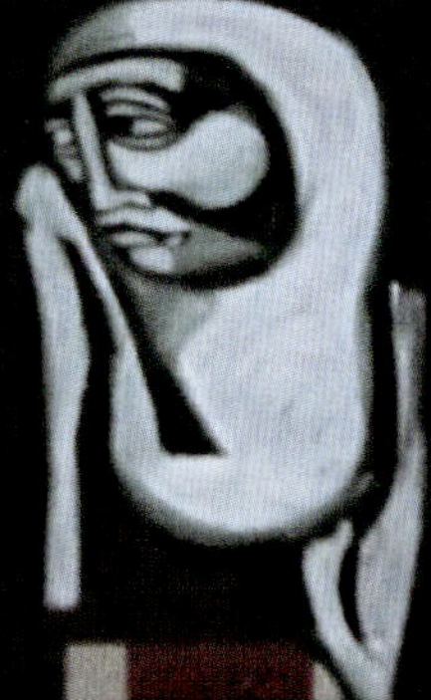

CANADIAN
PACIFIC
RAILWAY
CP
214
145
D LMT
201500
T WT
66500
PLATE
C
LABRONA
2010

art. For the artist, 'A train yard is like a forever-changing
outdoor art gallery.' Executed mostly with oil sticks, Labrona's
somewhat claustrophobic, melancholic compositions are
impeccably framed by their material support. The artist's
portraits, many of which are akin to sculptural busts in their
focus on the head and shoulders, create an air of mystery due
to the figures' down-turned eyes, distant gazes and overall
intensity [164]. The seriousness of his pieces is accentuated by
their composition on rusty, industrial freight trains. Painting
slightly withdrawn characters on a utilitarian, characterless
surface infuses his work with an introverted mood. When
Labrona's imagery appears in the urban sphere, it maintains a
feeling of reclusiveness. His figures, huddled together, create
a compact unit that stands apart from whatever physical and
visual elements surround the work. They seem lost, even
frightened [165]. On cargo trains, however, these bundles of
people are ideally positioned and reflect the severity of the

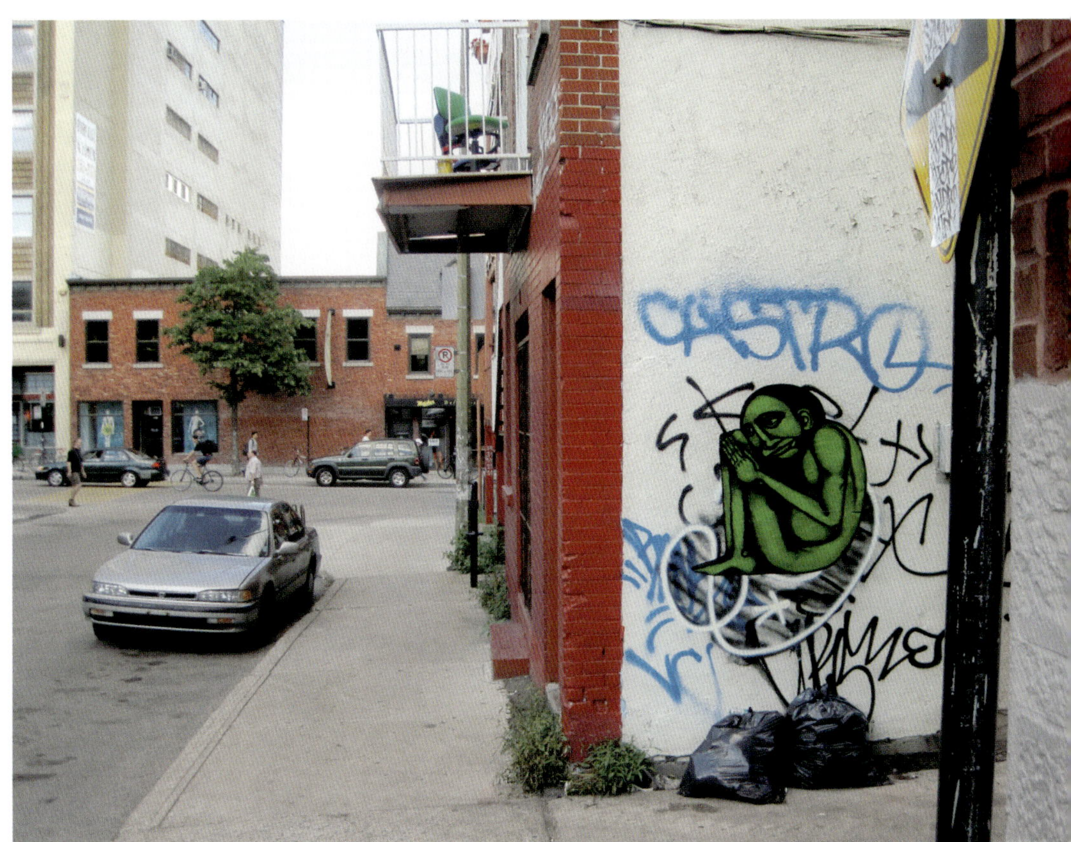

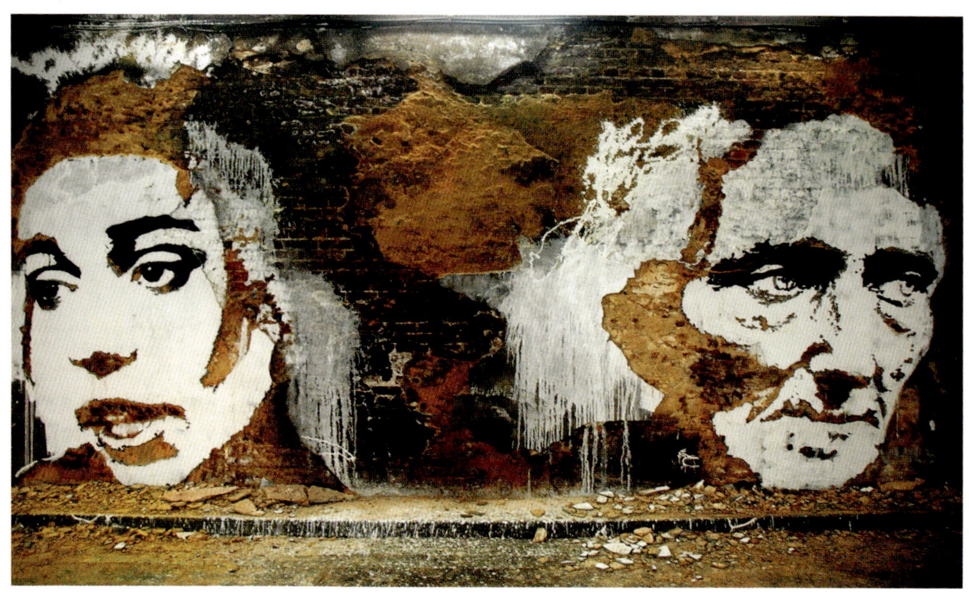

166 (*above*) **Alexandre Farto aka Vhils**, *Scratching the Surface*, London, UK, 2008. 'Scratching the surface' is both a pun and a reference to the artist's process of creation through techniques of destruction. Vhils literally chips away at his chosen surface so as to reveal evocative portraits.

167 (*right*) **Alexandre Farto aka Vhils**, *Scratching the Surface*, Grottaglie, Italy, 2009. At times, Vhils's portraits are so subtle and organically suited to the material surface that they seem to appear, ghost-like, through city walls.

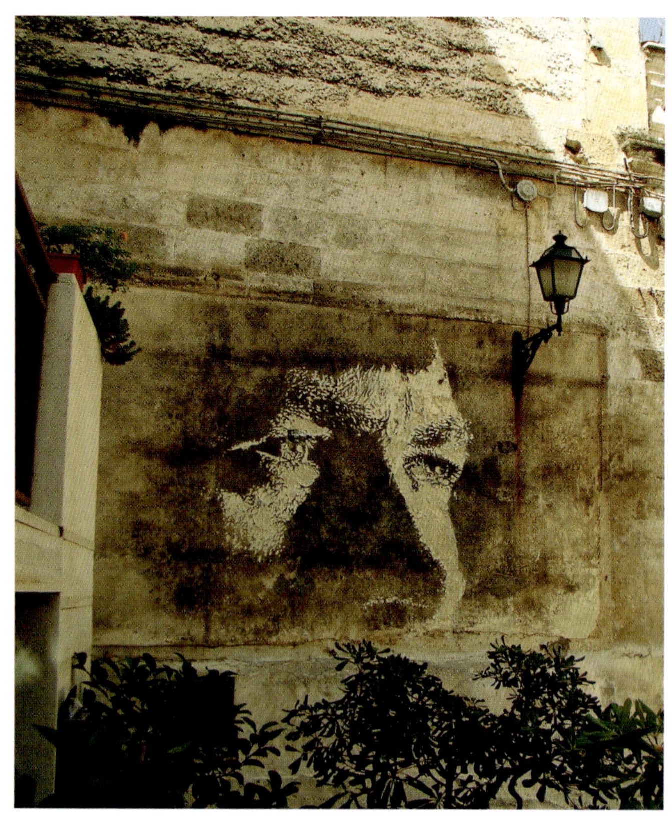

material surface. They are framed, supported and fit perfectly in their allotted spaces.

Whereas Banksy's work is often found on surfaces pertinent to his message, and Labrona's characters seem most comfortable on the side of a moving train, Portuguese artist Alexandre Farto, or Vhils ('the vitals') as he is known on the street art scene, remarkably manipulates a surface into the work itself. Best known for his distinctive large-scale depictions of faces, the artist works with materials already present on-site as well as bleach, ink, acid, spray-paint and construction tools. As opposed to layering the city with new pieces, he uncovers the formal lives of a chosen site by unveiling a wall's surface history to expose the complexity of urbanity. Delicately emotional and feverishly poetic, his pieces chronicle the biography of a particular wall.

Influenced by the revolutionary murals, paintings, slogans and stencils in his home country and their collision with advertising (in particular, the contradiction between decaying advertising

168 (*below*) **Alexandre Farto aka Vhils**, *Empty Faces*, Seixal, Portugal, 2007. Interested in uncovering the layers of a material surface, Vhils not only works directly on walls, but also on advertising posters to unleash faces produced through the layering of poster over poster.

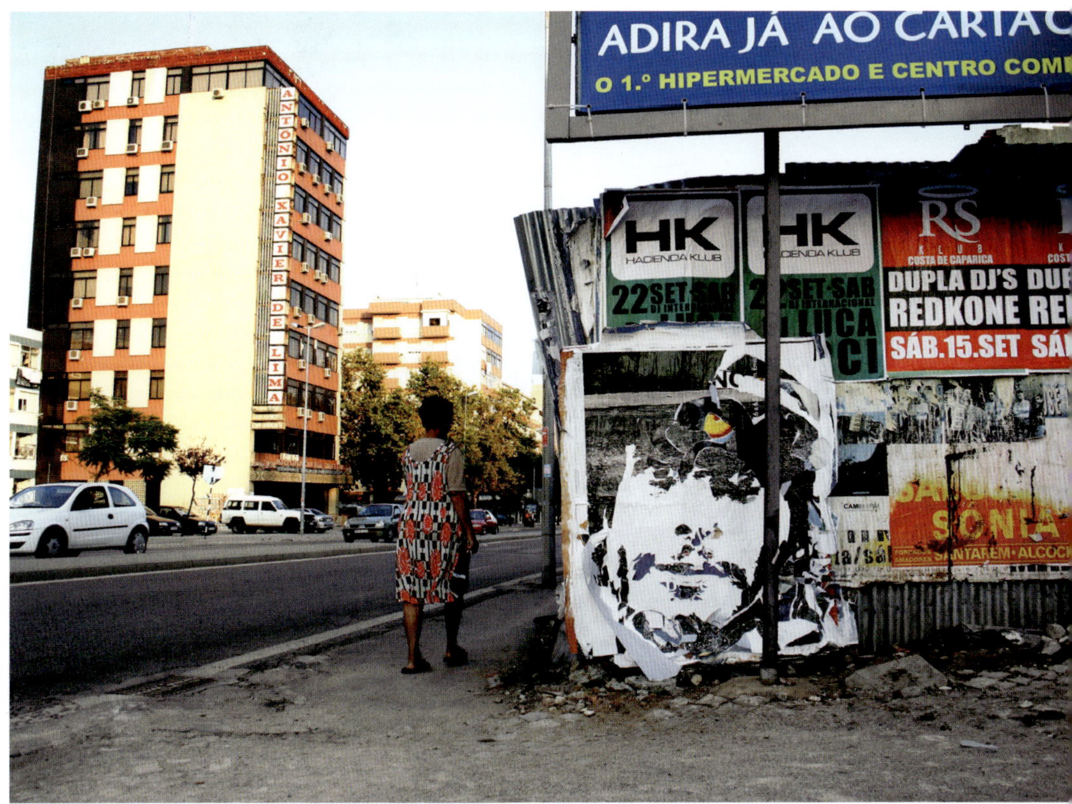

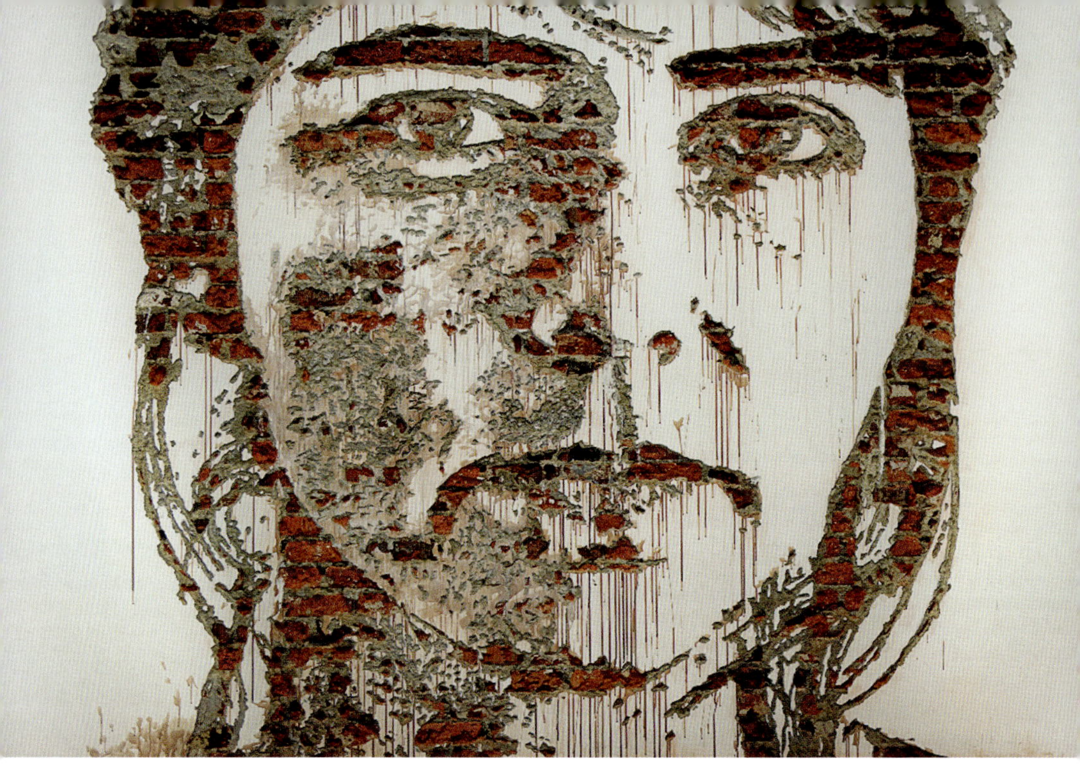

169 **Alexandre Farto aka Vhils**, *Viva la Revolución*, California, USA, 2009

campaigns and the revolutionary murals hidden beneath them), Vhils was inspired to focus on the various meanings attributed to a given space. This fascination with multiple layers led him to destroy in order to create, while emphasizing the process of change. He explains: 'Our social system is the product of this same process of layers, and I believe that by removing and exposing some of these layers, in fact by destroying them, we might be able to reach something purer, something of what we used to be and have forgotten all about. This is obviously in a symbolical sense. So I like to see it as a kind of archaeological work of dissecting the layers of history and time and exposing something which lies beneath all the noise, the clutter, the dirt, searching for an essence which has been lost somewhere along the way.'

Concerned with temporality, Vhils's practice is as much about the portraits he creates as it is about decomposition and destruction. His method is such that he cannot predict the layers he might uncover in a particular site. Some of his work pops out of its material surface as though it were an optical illusion, as seen in ill. 170 (2009) from the *Scratching the Surface* project. At one with its background, the face reveals itself

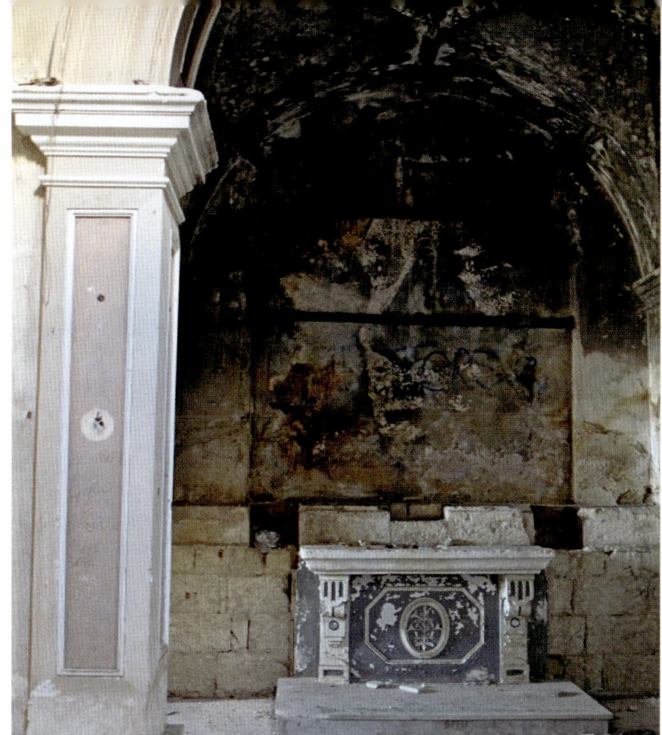

170 **Alexandre Farto aka Vhils**, *Scratching the Surface*, Grottaglie, Italy, 2009

faintly on the wall, like a ghost. Other works manifest as clear manipulations of layered imagery, as with the poster-portrait *Empty Faces* (2007) [168] in Portugal. Others, still, emerge from their material surface as though the removed layer freed the work from its dormancy [169]. Vhils's artwork suggests that a wall's metamorphosis through the addition of contemporary restorations has trapped some sense of history, and by unleashing his portraits, the artist personalizes a space through the process of destruction.

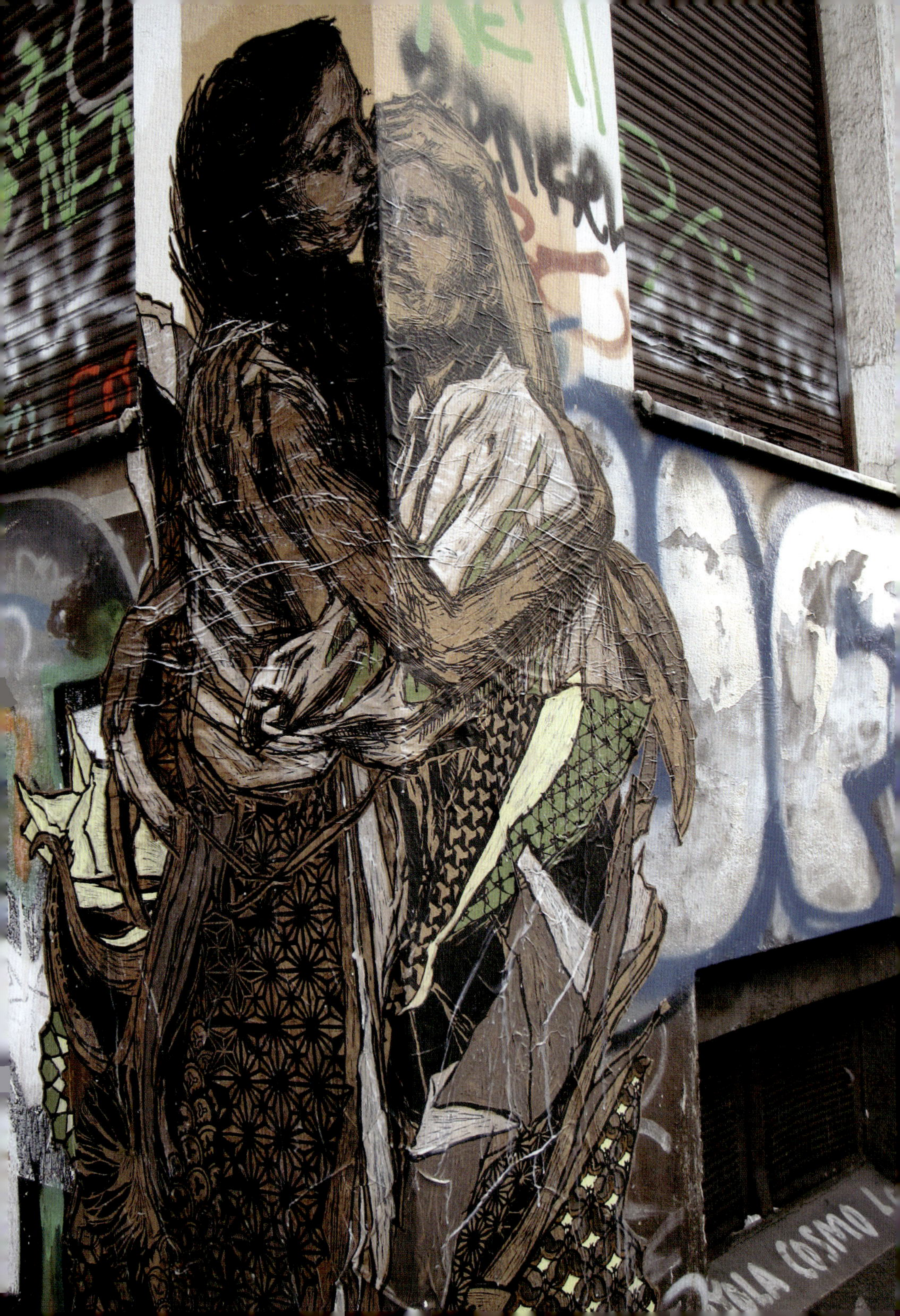

Chapter 5   Urban Visual Culture

Authorized and unauthorized public art projects, advertising campaigns, street signage and, more generally, the built environment characterize the visual structure of a city. Together these elements define the look and feel of a city and shape the urban landscape. All manner of art produced in a city responds to, interacts with or intervenes in particular spaces. Whether it is designed specifically for a space or appears there illegally, art in a city is a significant part of urban life and urban

171 (*opposite*) **Swoon**, *Alixa and Naima*, USA, 2009. Street art, like all other texts and images in the cityscape, contributes to the look and feel of a city. Its illegality, however, also allows its signs and symbols to speak to viewers in an unmediated, uncensored manner.

172 (*right*) **Microbo**, *Untitled*, Catania, Italy, 2010. Using the city as a canvas, street artists and graffiti writers tend to pay particular attention to the positioning of their work vis-à-vis its architectural support, material surface and all manner of structural elements.

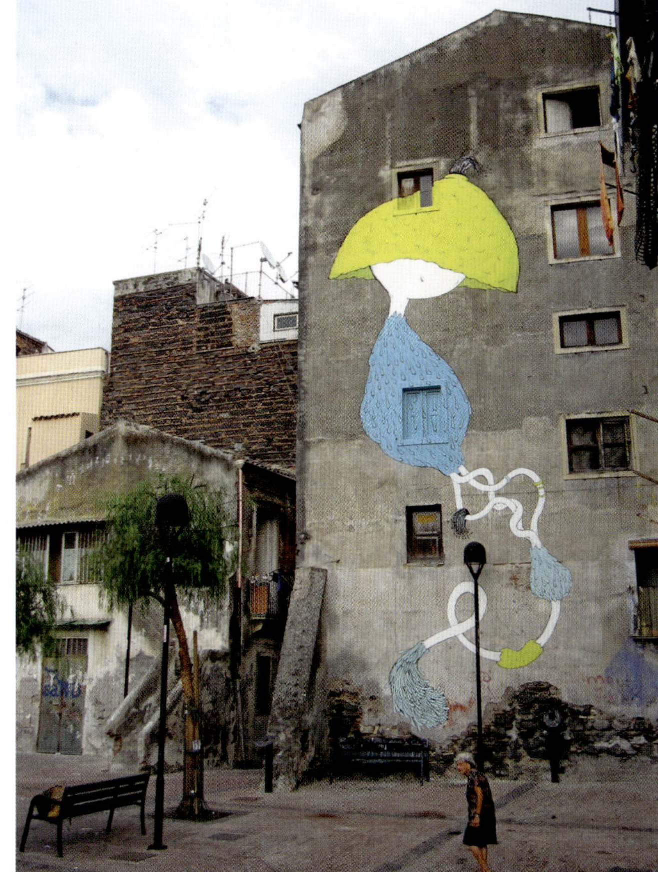

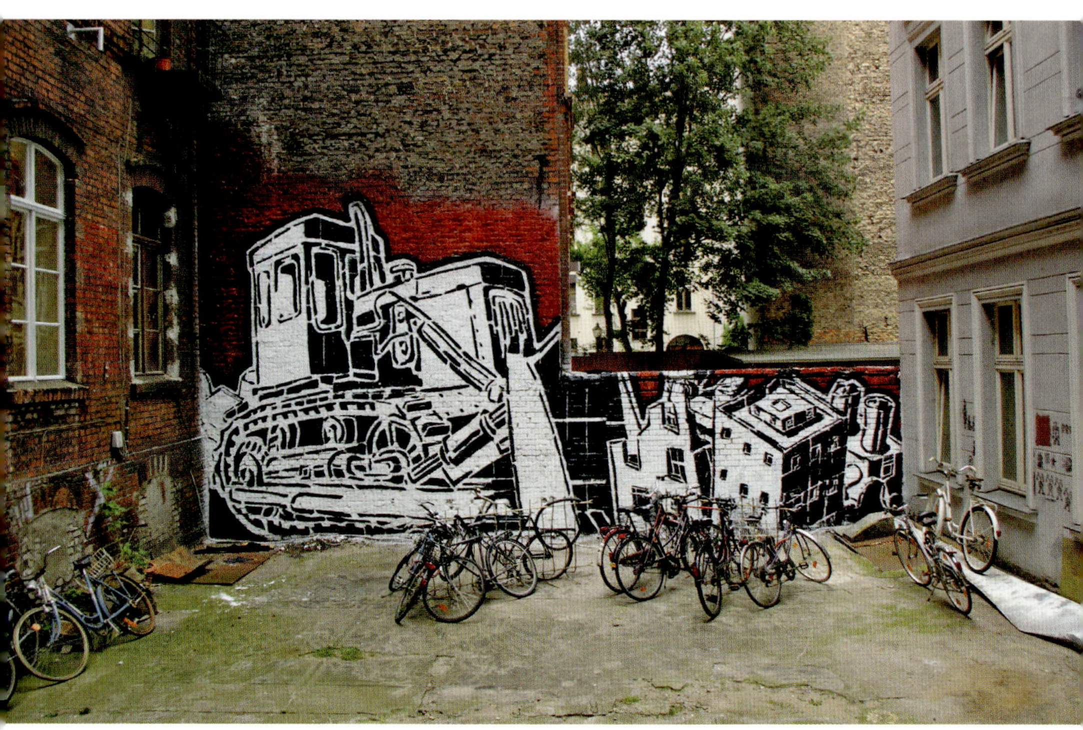

visual culture. The architectural landmarks of a city create one layer of meaning: one definition of space, one visual marker. Graffiti and street art imposed on a city's architectural grid propose other interpretations, definitions and experiences. As an ingredient in the culture of a city, graffiti and street art are invaluable objects of inquiry for art historians.

A space of production and consumption, the cityscape embodies immeasurable places. In our daily interactions with a city we encounter and experience any number of spaces designed for the general public. If there are places in a city reserved for advertisements propagated by corporations, then there are also places for art propagated by individuals. The images disseminated in our cities are bound to our reality – whether the reality is that we are consumers (advertisements), we have laws (road signs) or that we rebel (graffiti). Studying visual culture is thus a way of tapping into the images that circulate within a particular society, what they tell us about ourselves, and whom they represent.

Visual Culture and Art History

Graffiti and street art can be thought of in art-historical terms if the discussion is broadened to include images that are not classified as 'special' but rather as 'popular'. Graffiti and post-graffiti art are special in terms of their history and the breadth of their visual production, but because the objects that typify these art practices are not singular and because they are 'free', they also fall within the realm of popular art and street culture. Like commercial advertising and public art projects, graffiti and street art deliver a message in public space that, instead of promoting consumption, encourages personal expression, inquiry and free thought. On some level, most street writers and artists produce works as a way to participate in the creation of an alternative visual culture. While signature graffiti writing is more obviously motivated by youth looking to carve out a niche for themselves within their community and the city at large, for post-graffiti artists the motivation tends to be more politically guided. The work is not only a means of self-expression and a way to create opportunities for communication in a city, but also, most significantly, it is a negotiation of what participation in a city's visual culture represents.

Traditional art-historical studies focus on visual production that is first and foremost 'art', while visual culture studies examine visuality in a broader sense. In order to incorporate conventional art-historical themes within the myriad of other culturally relevant visual forms, many academic departments are fusing both fields together, so as to examine broader categories of images. Whereas art-historical research tends to emphasize form, content and the function of art within historical contexts, visual culture studies are more concerned with contemporary, everyday experiences of visual consumption. It follows, then, that the discipline of art history can either be perceived as a field within visual culture studies, or that art historians should, and in fact many do, expand their scope of research to include questions of visual culture. The work of many graffiti writers and street artists resonates with a similar undercurrent: their practices have developed through material, physical, conceptual and symbolic exchanges with cities. Reliance on the built and cultural environment of a city is a key ingredient of the work itself. Exploring graffiti and street art under the rubric of urban visual culture thus makes perfect sense.

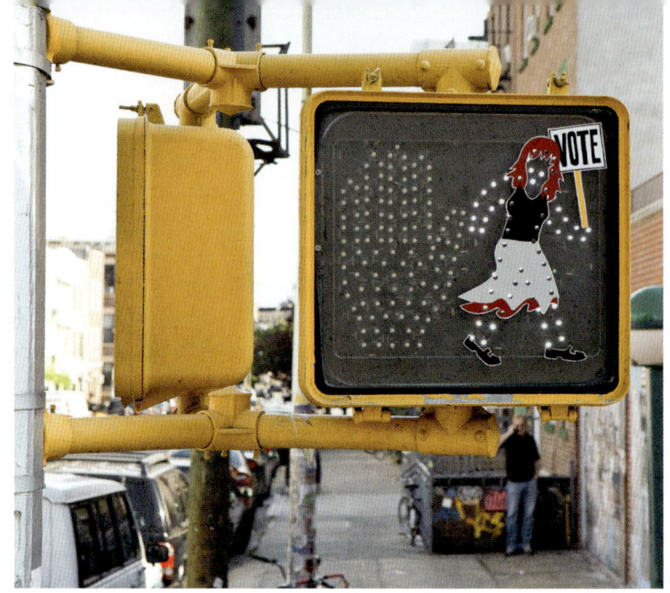

174 **Thundercut**, *Vote Walker*,
New York City, USA, 2008.
As opposed to promoting
consumption, graffiti and street
art encourage expression, inquiry
and free thought. With the
addition of custom-made vinyl
clothing to a pedestrian crossing
sign, Thundercut revitalize an
urban mainstay while promoting
the power of the vote.

The work of Brazilian twins Os Gêmeos has everything to do
with the culture of their city. Although they have become well
known in Europe and America thanks to their participation in a
variety of festivals, exhibitions, publications and films, their work
is very much tied to their hometown of São Paulo. Painting with
latex and rollers and outlining with spray-paint, as is common
for Brazilian street artists, the brothers disseminate their work
as a response to the reality of life in a country characterized
by social extremes. Their imagery, populated with expressive
characters [175], is distinctive in terms of style, technique,
colour and narrative. Brazil's isolation from the graffiti scenes
of the USA and Europe encouraged indigenous artists to be
inventive and develop original styles. Part-emulation and part-
originality, the Brazilian scene thus became an exciting mecca
for diversified techniques. By slowly moving away from more
traditional graffiti writing to the development of their now
trademark characters, the brothers found their own voice amid
the visual culture of the city.

Their yellow characters, dressed in a rich variety of colours
and textures, are generally composed in a similar way – their
rectangular torsos, balanced with only the thinnest extremities,
are topped with lemon-shaped heads which display flat features.
Although the eyes of both male and female representations are
pulled far apart, the men tend to have small, beady, half-opened
eyes, while the women's eyes are large and wide-opened.
Typically, the male characters are shown in mid-action, while

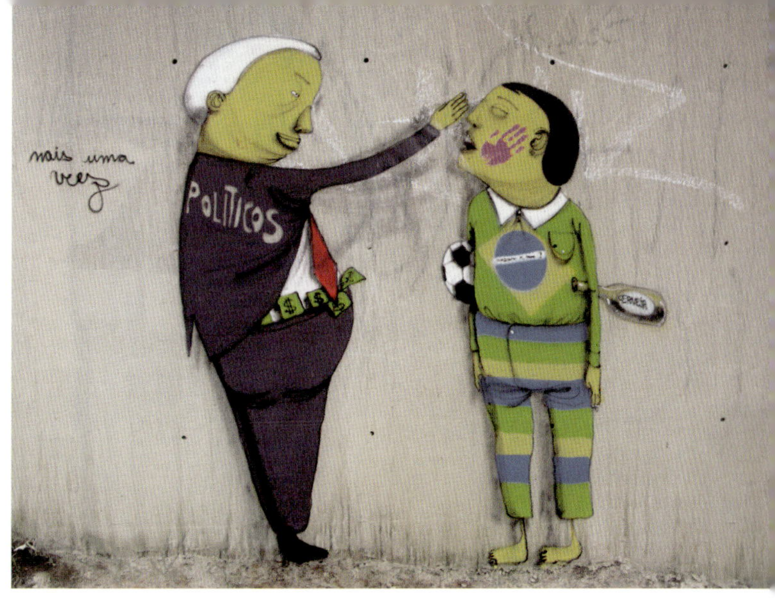

175 **Os Gêmeos** Clutching a football under one arm and a beer bottle under the other, the young man being slapped in the face by a beer-bellied, money-belted politician is a literal display of power and greed. The phrase next to the scene – 'mais uma vez' ('just once more') – suggests a revolutionary tone.

the women stand, kneel or sit in a quietly confrontational manner. The men are also largely depicted as causing havoc: robbing, rioting or terrorizing the neighbourhood. The narratives on which the brothers most often draw originate in Brazilian folklore as well as the everyday reality of living in a sprawling metropolis. Their art projects are largely dependent on the people they encounter in their city and reflect the culture of São Paulo. Their visual vocabulary is thus a function of the environment that their work inhabits.

While the city inspires many street art practices, so do iconic images from the history of art. Australian artist Psalm, for example, has created a series of small, multi-coloured stencils inspired by images from art history and pop culture. Psalm's legible tags, adorned with Buddhas (2005) [176], angels (2002) [177] or the protagonist from American pop artist Roy Lichtenstein's *Hopeless* of 1963 (2004) [178], are uniquely pop in their design. Small and self-contained, the artist's stencils highlight his name, while his characters use the letters of the name as a support. The interplay of Psalm's name and his imagery vividly emulates the otherwise symbolic dialogue between pop and street culture. Paralleling pop and street art is an effective way of pinpointing how both operate on the capitalist tradition of branding, thereby simultaneously contributing to and criticizing the culture of commodification. By adopting the images, strategies and entrepreneurial roles of the corporate world, pop artists joined collectors and

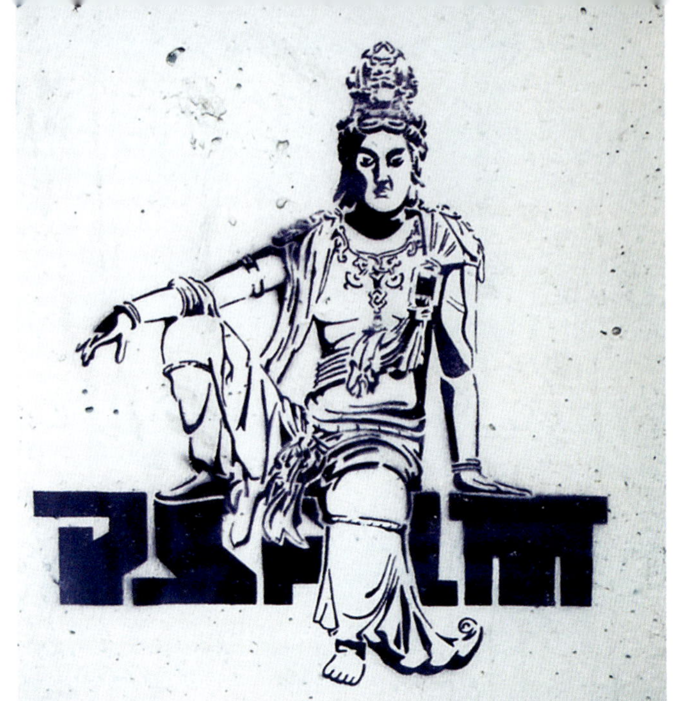

176 (*right*) **Psalm**, *Buddha*, Melbourne, Australia, 2005. Psalm's stencilled tag exemplifies the ongoing conversation between pop culture, street culture, and images from the art-historical canon.

177 (*below*) **Psalm**, *Angels*, Melbourne, Australia, 2002

178 (*bottom*) **Psalm**, *Roy*, Melbourne, Australia, 2004

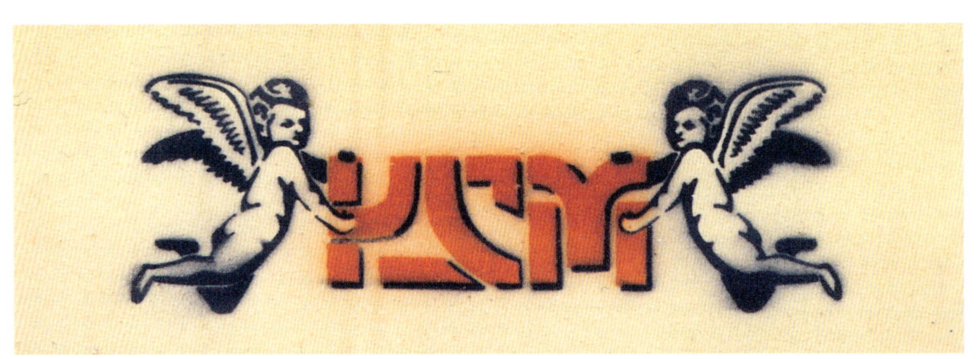

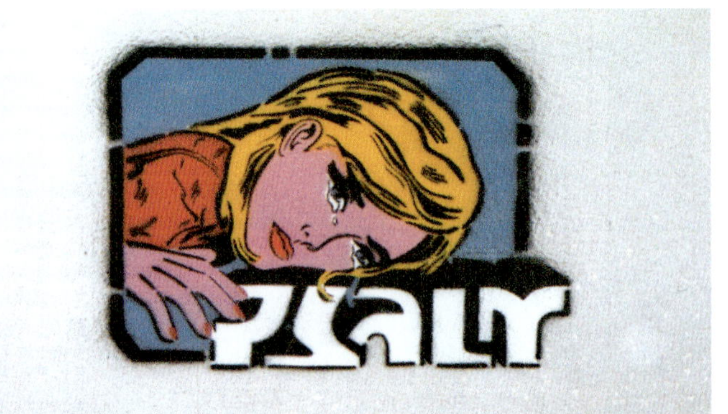

dealers in reinforcing an ethos of commodification in art and consumption in the wider society. By reproducing in their works the logos and products of the marketplace, adopting the presentational modes and techniques of advertising, and engaging in the cult of self-promotion, pop artists mimicked and contributed to the ideology of consumer culture. Street artists also often play on advertising strategies and imagery, and blur the distinction between the consumption of consumer goods and of fine art. Psalm's stencils emphasize the ongoing conversation between pop culture and the canonical art-historical movements.

While Psalm melds urban culture with art history to create iconic tags, Irish artist Conor Harrington references the history of art through his chosen medium and classical portrait style, but with a twist. Harrington's technique merges media – spray with oil paint – and styles – portraiture with gestural abstraction. His paintings, often of men (in recent works, specifically soldiers from Napoleon Bonaparte's era), resonate with both chaotic movement and controlled grace [179]. As Harrington explains: 'I'm interested in the dynamics

179 **Conor Harrington**, *Untitled*, New York City, USA, 2008. Working with both oil and spray-paint to produce portraits that are at once realistic and abstract means truly embracing historical traditions and contemporary styles. Conor Harrington's paintings reflect this sort of balanced opposition. The tension present in his work echoes modernity as a constant negotiation of images, texts, sounds and smells – a plethora of choice competing for consumer attention.

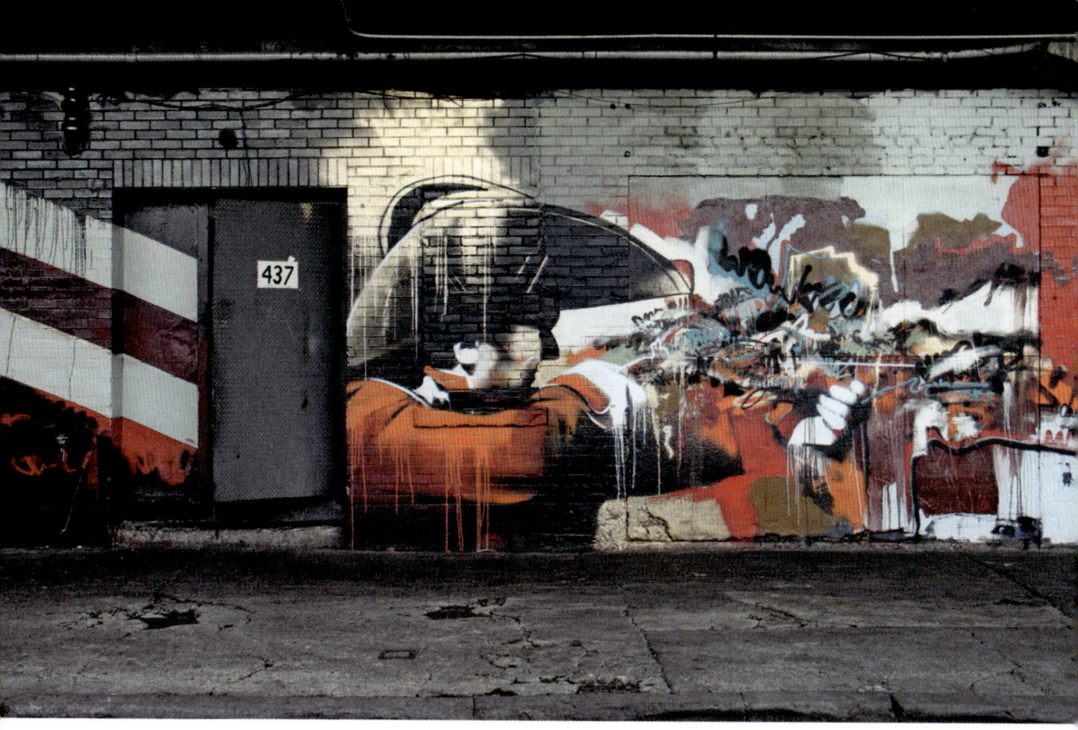

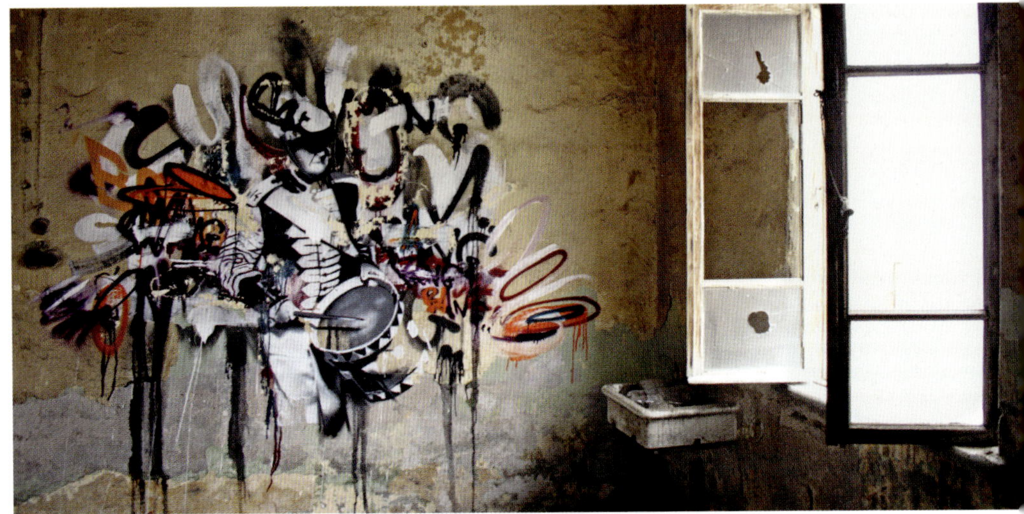

180 (*above*) **Conor Harrington**, *Untitled*, Tel Aviv, Israel, 2010

181 (*right*) **Conor Harrington**, *Untitled*, Grottaglie, Italy, 2009

182 (*opposite*) **Conor Harrington**, *Untitled*, Grottaglie, Italy, 2008

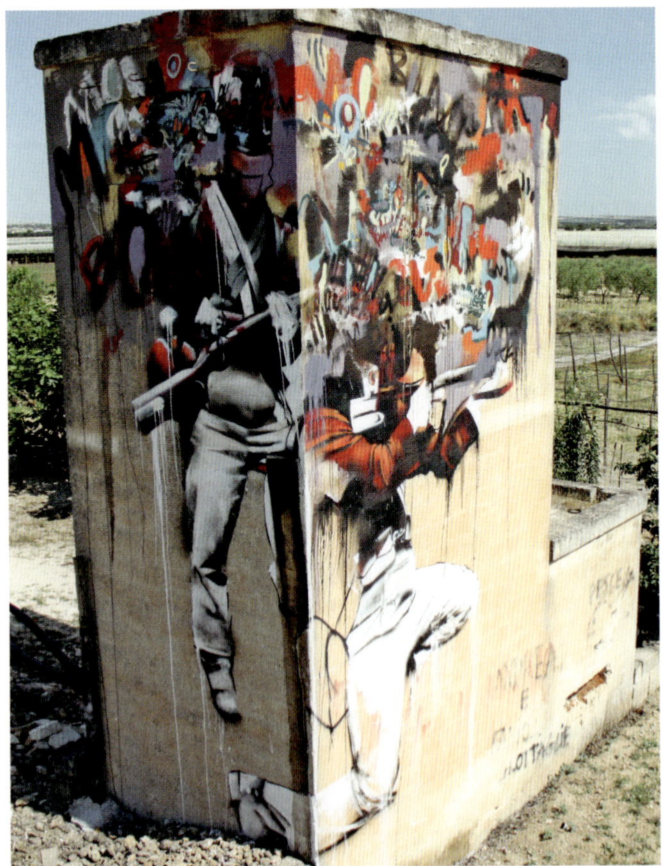

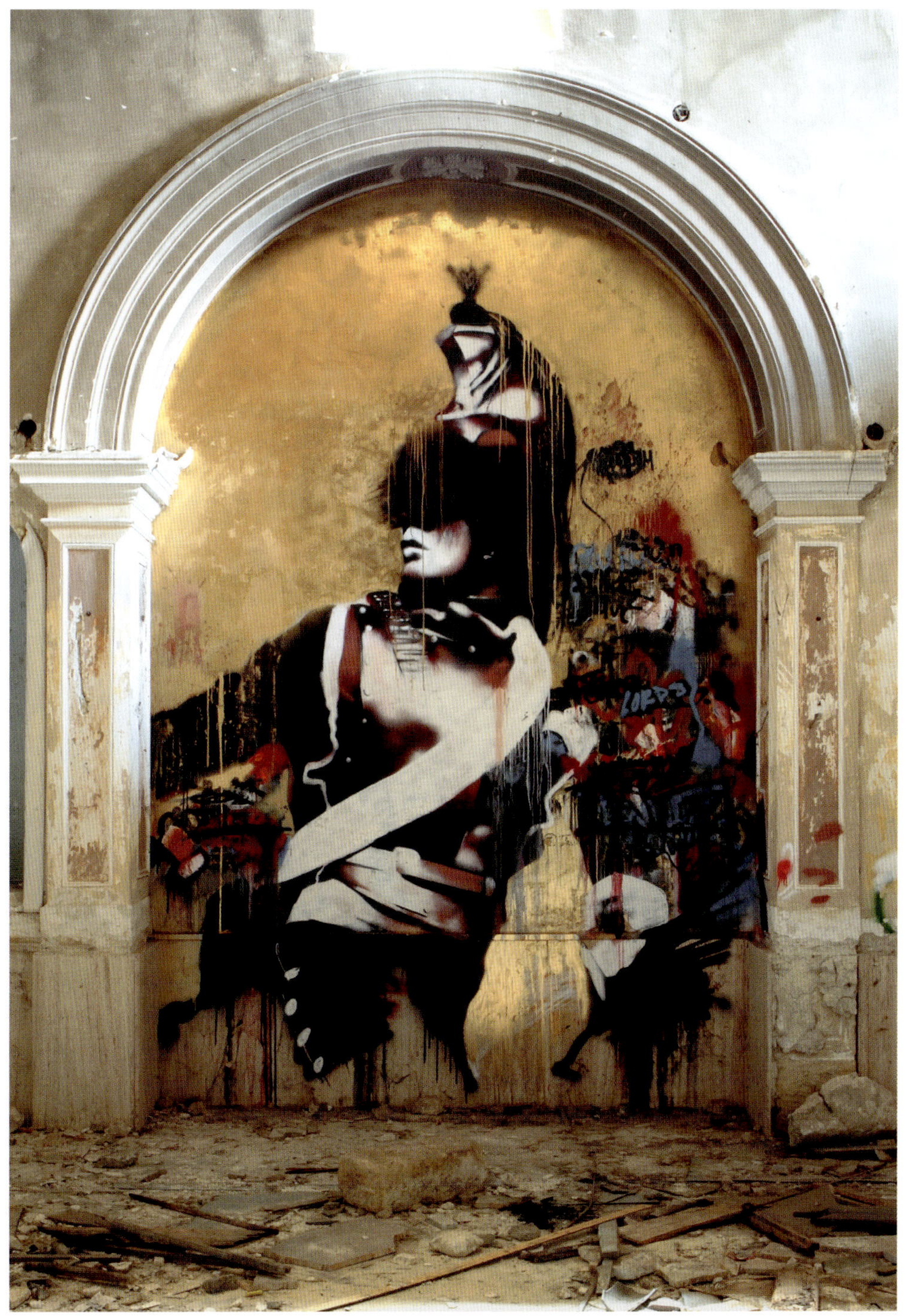

LORDS

between opposing elements.' Indeed, there is a great deal of tension in Harrington's work in terms of visual collisions and oppositions. Historical and contemporary portraits depicted in the traditional medium of oil paint live in a fragmented space – a space that reflects modern urban life.

The painted figures are slashed, drowned, sullied by illegible text, energetic lines, tags, dripping spray-paint and all manner of fragmentary elements [180, 181]. With their space invaded by contemporary media and disorderly abstraction, the people represented appear and disappear within the urban noise. Harrington's duality of both technique and subject is reflective of the modern information age as texts and images bombard our everyday and create a turmoiled narrative. The collision of street and fine art in Harrington's work, coupled with the artist's propensity to add elements to his pieces only to wipe them away, beautifully illustrates the re-mixed contemporary world [182].

Painting in a style that, if compared, stands in direct opposition to Harrington's, Japan's duo Kami and Sasu, known collectively as Hitotzuki, expertly fuse fluidity with solidity in their traditionally inspired motifs. Working with symmetrically balanced geometric shapes, typically representing flowers (Sasu), as well as pulsating, rhythmic waves (Kami), Hitotzuki complement each other's work to create a whole [183]. This

183 **Hitotzuki**, *Untitled*, Suzaka, Nagano, Japan, 2009. Painting together as Hitotzuki, Kami and Sasu combine their aesthetics to create rhythmic, geometrically balanced compositions, which are both ideally self-contained (Sasu's floral motifs) and fluidly never-ending (Kami's waves). Executed freehand, their remarkably symmetrical pieces reflect the natural world and traditional Japanese motifs rendered through a contemporary illegal art movement.

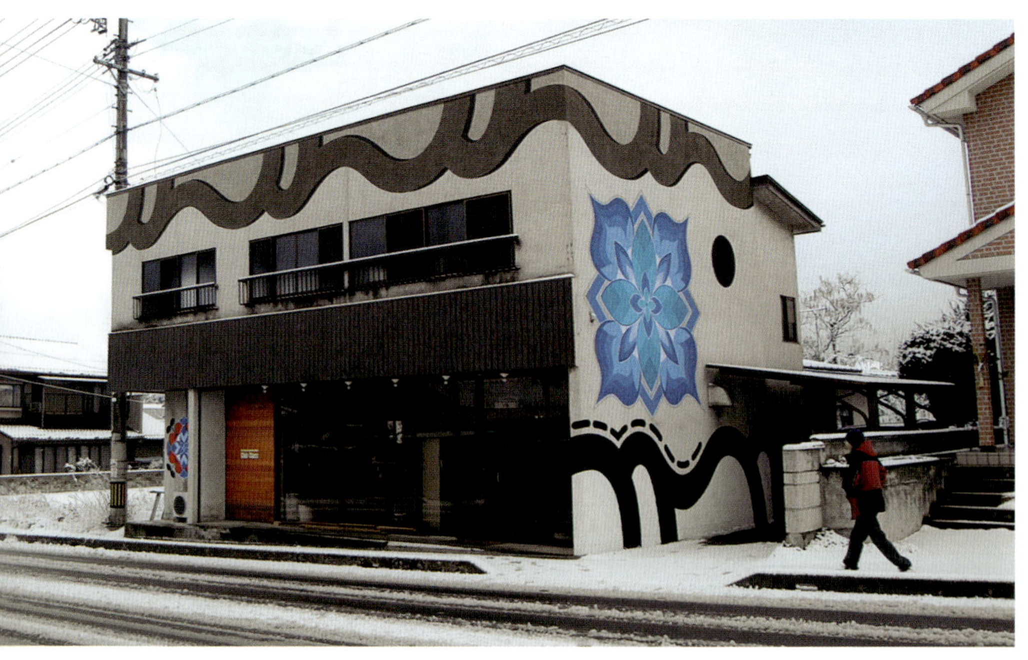

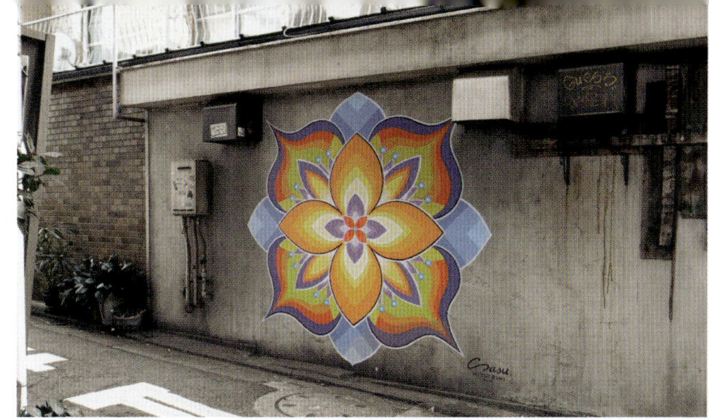

184 (*above*) **Sasu**, *To Remain Calm and Passionate*, Tokyo, Japan, 2009

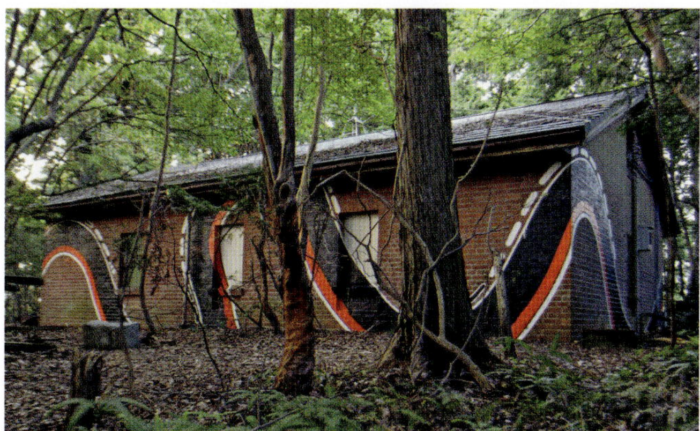

185 (*below*) **Kami**, *Past Memories and Present Self*, Kyoto, Japan, 2007

characteristic of being polar opposites of one another in style and yet fusing together to make a whole is reflected in their collective name, which stands for the sun and the moon. Executed freehand, their artworks display an accomplished understanding of the elements of art and design. Beyond the remarkably symmetrical balance of their pieces, their fusion of shapes from the natural world with traditional patterns gives rise to strikingly graceful images. Sasu's carefully created colourful, floral mandalas are self-contained designs [184]. With no discernible beginning or end, they are, as they would be in nature, independent and complete. In stark contrast, through their movement, Kami's lines disappear and reappear on their material surface [185]. Seemingly never-ending, they are reminders of the dynamism in the natural world. Working with latex and spray-paint, Hitotzuki vividly and yet discreetly point to the conversation between traditionalism and modernity.

Visual culture analysis provides access to a realm of creation positioned outside the art-historical canon. A study of urban visual culture, and specifically in this case, of illegal

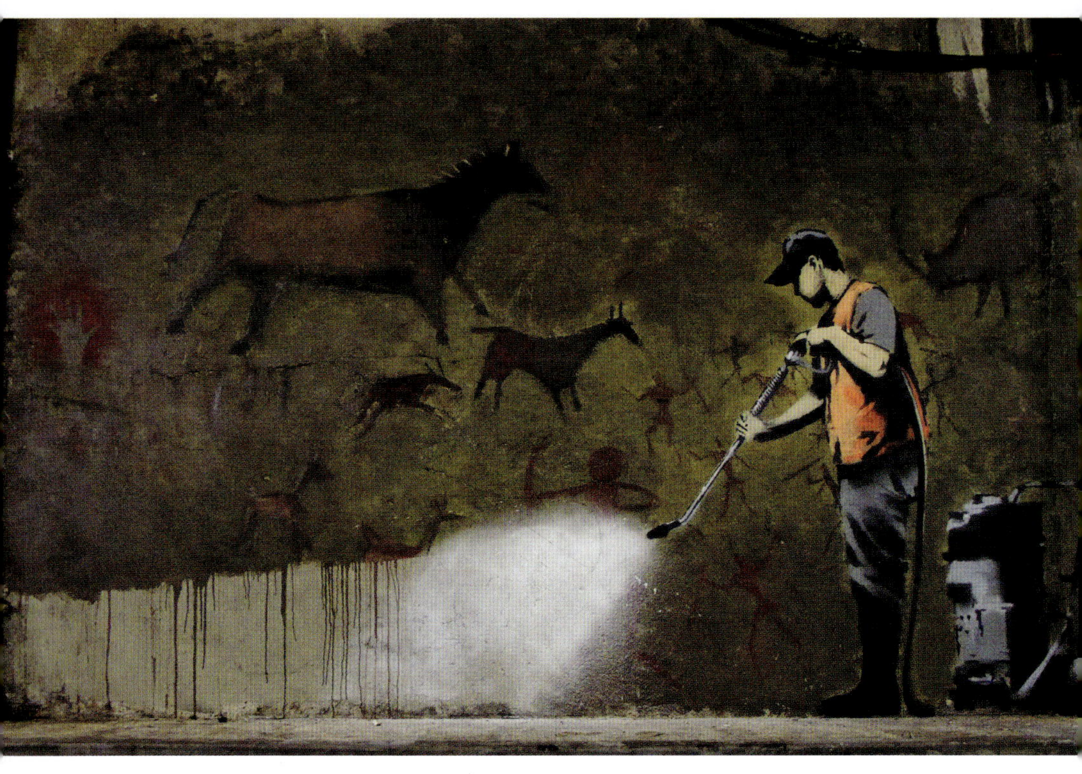

urban painting, signals the need for art history's expansion, so that it might reveal additional histories of art. Graffiti writing and urban painting reflect the fact that our lives have become shaped through contact with, and consumption of, images outside the field of art history. In a cross-media world, our experiences of culturally meaningful visual content appear in multiple forms, and as we have seen, these migrate between one another. Street art in particular, as an amalgamation of media and fields of visual imagery, concretely dematerializes the boundaries between art and non-art, or high and low art, through an accessible and culturally fertile imagery.

Over fifty years ago, Jasper Johns celebrated common objects, Robert Rauschenberg used mass-media images in his work, Roy Lichtenstein focused on comics as a central component of American popular culture, and Andy Warhol employed a pictorial vocabulary that reinforced the connection between icons of mass production and consumer culture. Through their varied practices, today's street artists echo many of the same ideals. Much like contemporary artists such as Jeff Koons, street artists are immersed in mass consumer culture and explore popular brand imagery and advertising to subvert their strategies. What today's urban visual culture suggests is that the propagation of illegal imagery is a true reflection and critique of and addition to an otherwise controlled art world.

Street Art off the Streets

While the urban domain is undoubtedly of primary significance for both the dissemination and experience of graffiti and street art, two other controversial realms exist – galleries and the internet. These sites play interesting roles as avenues for graffiti writers and street artists, yet they are problematic in terms of experiencing their work. Beyond commercial and non-profit exhibition spaces, a great number of writers and street artists are also exploring new channels through the creation of commercial products for a variety of brands or have founded their own companies and galleries. Others, such as Blu, are creating work on the street that takes on a new life through the medium of video.

Armed with a limited palette, paintbrushes and an obsessive interest in drawing and line, Italian artist Blu produces enormous murals which have most famously been transformed into video animations. Working with the physical space chosen for his imaginative creations, Blu visually tells stories contingent on simple representation and complex insinuation. The cartoonish, anthropomorphic tales that he fashions freehand, infused with monsters, battle scenes, human anatomy and death, read like a disturbingly provocative storybook. In his videos, which are disseminated through the artist's website (www.blublu.org) and on YouTube, Blu combines his street illustrations with hand-drawn animation using stop motion photography. The final products – works such as *Big Bang Big Boom* and *Muto* – live on the internet as a dynamic re-articulation of street painting. As such, the videos produce a record of his street work and facilitate the creation of entirely new works through a different medium.

These videos, complete with producers and original scores, transform street art into video art. The experience of art on the street is thus heavily mediated and rendered into one with options and control. Not only did the artist and those involved in the project create something whereby choices were made in terms of how the work would be viewed, but the audience itself has a great deal more control over their experience of the work. In other words, the work was first edited to meet the artist's requirements, but the technology that the audience uses to experience it allows for a personal viewing which can be paused, rewound, enlarged, etc. Creating animation narratives through large-scale street painting is a novel way of devising original projects, making technology a part of the process, and challenging the boundaries of street art production.

In addition to experimenting with different technologies, a great many graffiti and street artists also work with different consumer products. In fact, many have launched their own design companies and collaborate with numerous brands to infuse merchandise with their creations. French artist Fafi and her team of *fafinettes*, for example, make whimsical appearances on city streets [187] and on various products worldwide. A celebrated street artist, Fafi is also widely known for her commercial brand designs. Having created a fictitious world, the Carmine Vault, for her tantalizing female figures, and personalized each doll by name, personality and style, much in the vein of Barbie, Fafi has expertly turned her characters into veritable pop culture icons.

187 **Fafi**, *Untitled*, Paris, France, 2010. Many street artists who have developed their visual vocabularies around cartoonish characters have successfully segued their practices into commercial careers. The playfulness, accessibility and recognizability of their logos or characters facilitate a smooth transition into sales.

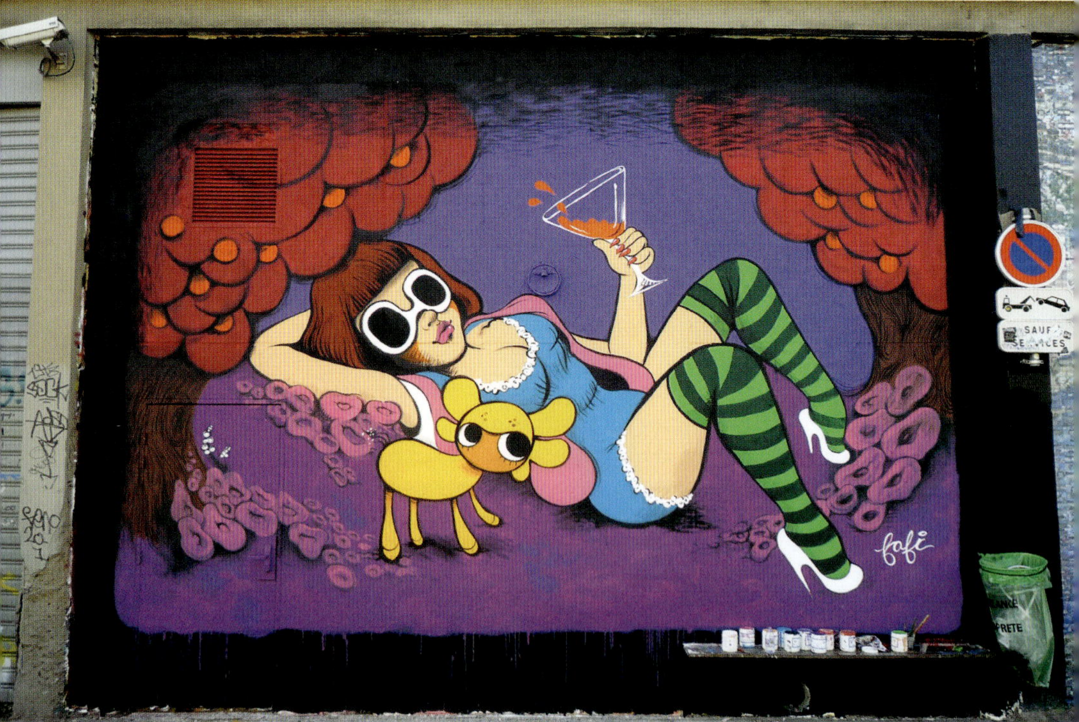

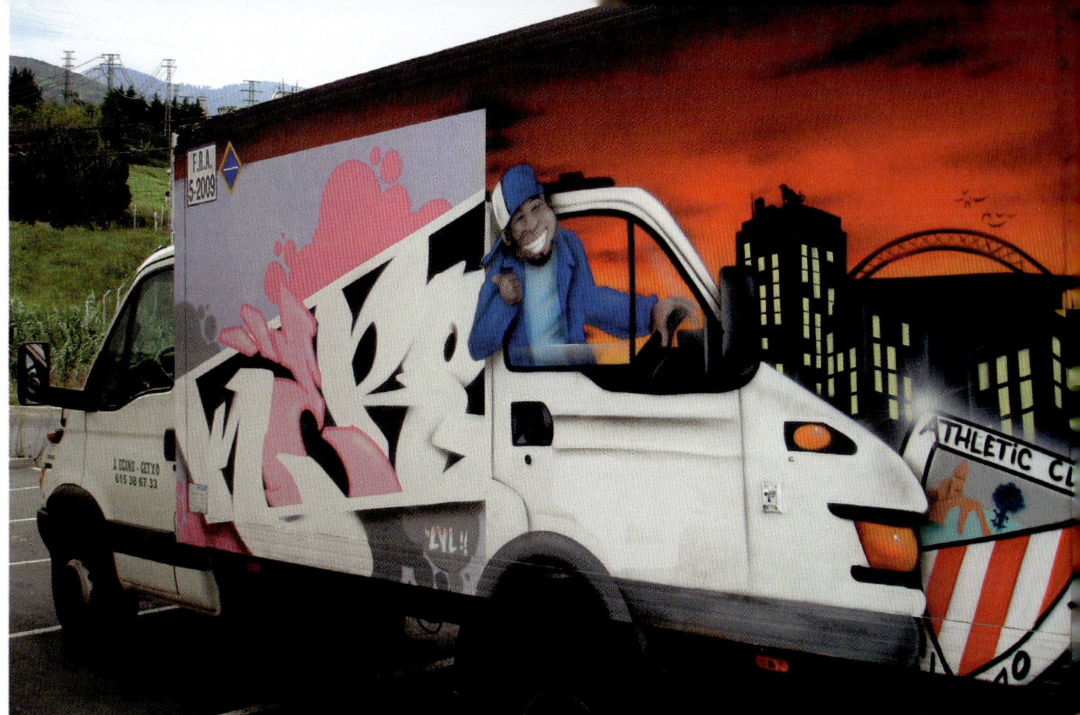

188 **Kero**, Bilbao, Spain, 2007. Graffiti writers such as Kero paint murals and work in design as well as illustration to earn a living. Many writers who have sustained illegal painting careers for a number of years often find ways to make a profit from their graffiti production while continuing to paint without permission.

Appearing as spokespeople for a number of international brands, such as MAC cosmetics and Adidas, the *fafinettes* provide a superb example not only of the predictably blatant anthem 'sex sells', but also of the transfiguration of street art into merchandise. Long before corporations jumped on the popularity of street art characters to help them market their products, they tapped into the art of graffiti writing to the same end. Graffiti has a long history of either being co-opted to sell products and events (a notable recent example being the logo of the 2012 London Olympics) and promote businesses or appropriated for various causes in order to appeal to youth and hipsters. Many graffiti writers such as Kero (Spain) willingly participate in marketing campaigns and create murals for local businesses [188]. Writers such as Kero earn a living from their graffiti practices by working in illustration as well as tattoo, clothing and advertising design. Some street artists also brand their characters, although they typically do so on their own terms through their own design companies.

Hawaii's Buff Monster made a name for himself in Los Angeles as a prolific street artist before dedicating his skills to numerous design projects. His atypically happy fluorescent pink monsters live in their own 'Lollipop Land' where ice cream abounds and

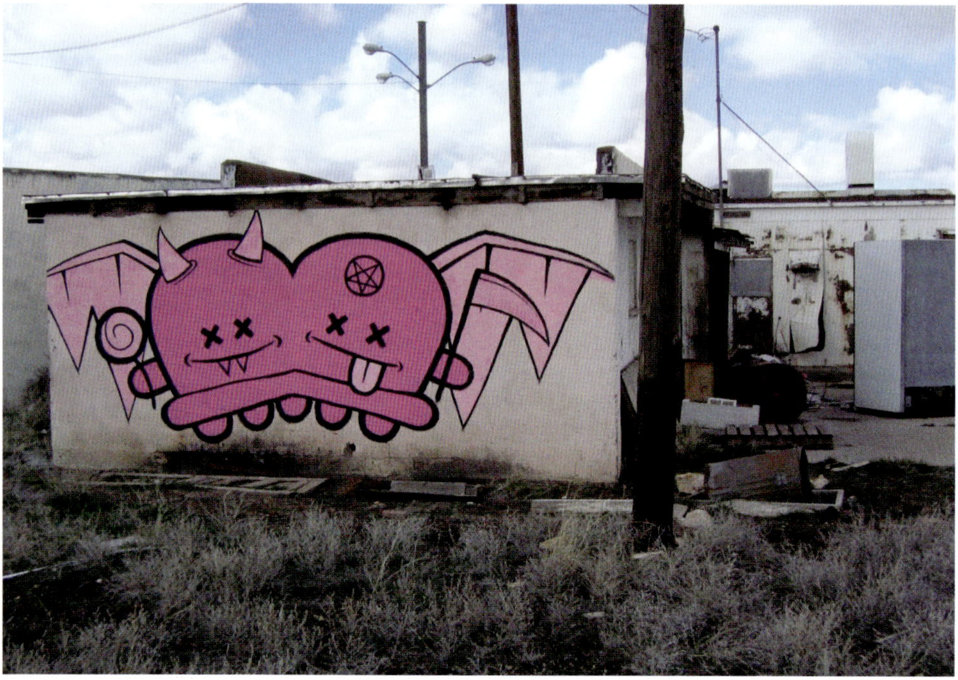

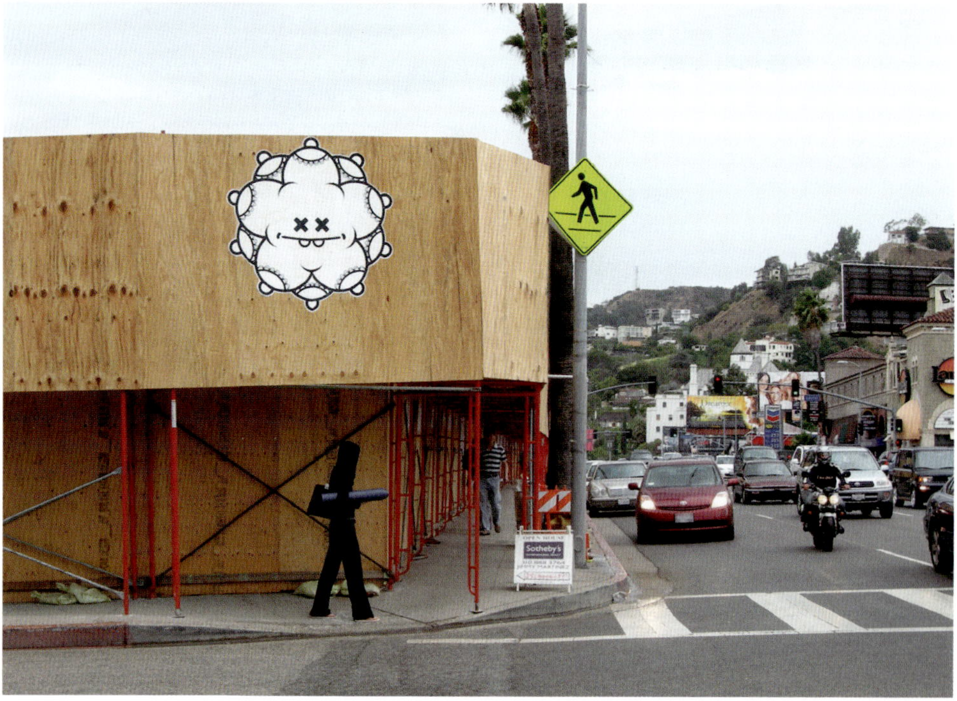

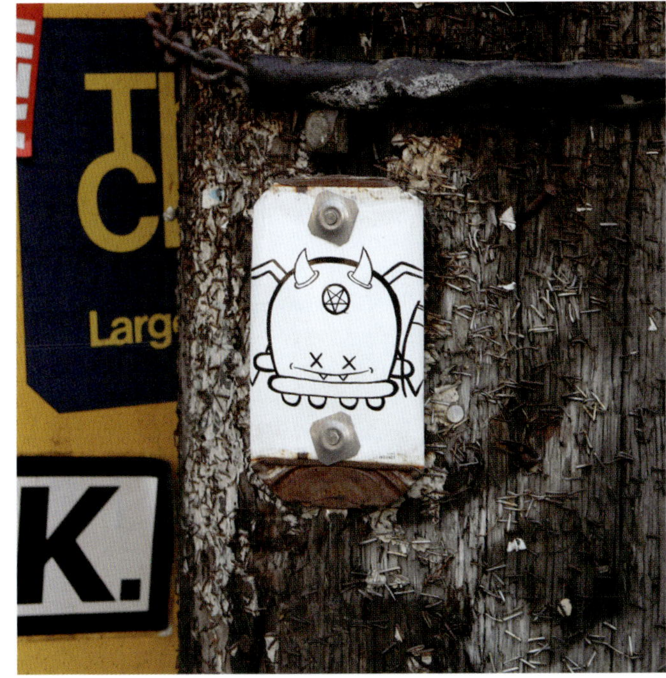

'pink is power'. Artists such as Fafi have also imagined entire worlds for their creatures, but Buff Monster's figures operate on a different plane from the playfully sexy *fafinettes*. Although the artist is absorbed with questioning the idiosyncratically LA notion of image and sex, his cheerful monsters are not overtly sexy in composition, design or mood. The colour pink, which the artist describes as 'a symbol of confidence, individuality and happiness', permeates many of his pieces and often creates a sense of opposition. In one piece that exemplifies this conflict (*c.* 2005) [189], twin monsters at once entice and repel. Whereas one holds a lollipop, the other bears a hatchet, and their bubbly pinkness is offset by fangs and horns. This is emblematic of Buff Monster's style – whether it is a monster symmetrically encapsulated by doily-like breasts (*c.* 2005) [190] or a tiny smiling winged demon on a flattened spray-paint can (2006) [191], his characters always explore the tension between allure and aversion. Transitioning into a career of designing collectable vinyl toys for MINDstyle and other major toy companies was an organic step for him.

In the Gallery

In the context of the gallery, street work necessarily becomes something else. Swoon explains: 'In the gallery setting I try to take advantage of that over-precious, protected space to create a small world. The work changes immensely because it is about creating a whole environment.' Whether experienced as a transposition or completely reworked to better suit the gallery environment, an artist's street practice transforms materially, spatially and visually when performed indoors.

Generally speaking, graffiti writers tend to be against the formal exhibition of their work. The fact that graffiti developed on the street and loses a sense of dynamism in an enclosed space is an argument many support. Furthermore, many writers view graffiti as a rebellion against a system of consumption, and the fact that their work is free and illegal is essential to their participation in the subculture. Moving into the commercial gallery market is often simply disrespected. Still, over the past twenty years numerous progressive graffiti exhibitions have provided writers with new avenues for their work. As opposed to early graffiti shows, contemporary exhibitions often challenge traditional modes of display and involve the writers in the curatorial process.

For street artists, there exists a consensus of sorts in terms of participation in gallery exhibitions. Vexta explains that gallery spaces give her 'a chance to create things that are more complex and intricate...it's completely different from making work for the street'. The difference, which continues to be criticized as negative by some artists and critics, is in fact positive for many. For his part, Roadsworth explains that, gallery or not, his interest lies in doing work that intervenes or integrates within a given space: 'I find that any and every space and/or situation has different possibilities and challenges.' Obviously, street art is no longer street art when displayed indoors. Some people from within as well as outside the street art culture object to this very disparity. Yet, perhaps in a more defined way than traditional graffiti writers, many street artists who participate in indoor exhibitions have been successful because of their concentrated efforts to make work that is beyond the scope of their street practices.

Today, post-graffiti exhibitions rarely rely on frames or conventional display strategies. Instead, the work is often presented directly on the walls in a chaotic manner – one that might be perceived as a replication of the busyness of city life.

Interestingly, while the space of the gallery typically dictates a particular mode of presentation and appeals to a specific audience, welcoming street work indoors largely disrupts these criteria. While some artists such as Miss Van use the gallery to create more detailed pieces, which push her practice forward both conceptually and technically, others, such as Swoon, employ the space to construct environments that lie somewhere between both the spaces of the street and those of the gallery.

Since her first gallery exhibition, Miss Van's practice has noticeably evolved, especially with the work she has done for the Magda Danysz Gallery in Paris. In the gallery, the artist found the time to expand her aesthetic vocabulary. As opposed to the crisp outlines and simple forms that characterize her street work, on canvas the artist's dolls have become much more detailed renditions of soulful expressions and precise modelling. The graphic lines have given way to a lighter, unstable aesthetic, which renders the dolls more ambiguous and expressive. In works for the exhibition 'Atame' (2007), for example, Miss Van's preoccupation with hair as a powerful feminine weapon is a mature exploration of femininity and sexuality [192]. At the same time, the recurring fascination with playful, erotic images of women and animals remains at the forefront of her practice.

192 **Miss Van**, 'Atame' (2007) works on show at the 'Lovestain' exhibition, Stolen Space, London, UK, 2009. After years of painting her doll characters on city streets, Miss Van has evolved her aesthetic vision within exhibition spaces. Some street artists utilize the gallery venue to advance their practices both conceptually and technically.

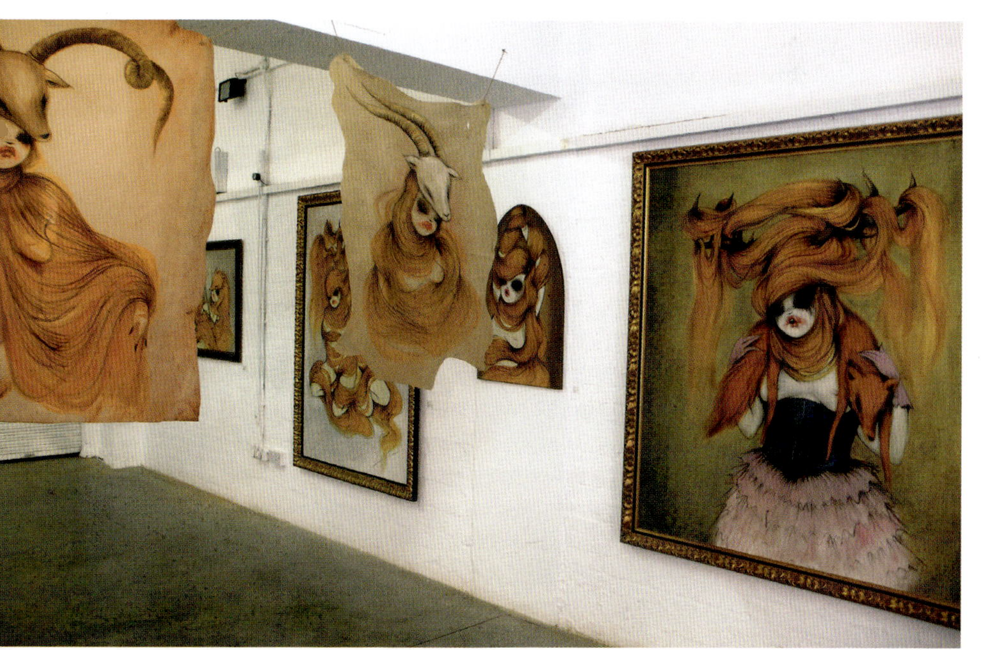

With the canvases prepared for this show, Miss Van's works function on a different plane from her street work – one where the artist is in control of the environment her dolls inhabit. In the exhibition space, some of the works were hidden behind heavy velvet drapes, which offered the visitor a private and intimate viewing experience, unattainable in the urban environment. The dolls, rendered more like goddesses than the playthings for which the artist is known on the street, transformed the space into one of heightened sexuality as well as fragility. Besides their softer quality, Miss Van's dolls have become quieter for this exhibition – a characteristic accentuated through a major deviation, their closed eyes. Whereas in the cityscape the artist's dolls display a menacing stare, in the context of this exhibition the girls float in blindness. Although a lot less inspired by comic strips and much more hauntingly fragile, the artist's 'Atame' show is still consistent with her overall aim to suggest fantasies.

In a similar vein, Swoon chooses to 'benefit and take advantage of the use of a roof' in her exhibitions. However, unlike Miss Van's carefully arranged portraits prominently displayed on gallery walls, Swoon's work is scattered and at times hidden throughout the exhibition space. The artist uses the gallery as a supplementary medium for giant installations – projects unrealistic in the spaces of a city. After a year of construction, in late 2008 Swoon unveiled a project for Deitch Studios on the East River in Long Island City. The 'Swimming Cities of Switchback Sea' exhibition combined seven floating sculptures or handmade boats, fashioned by Swoon and seventy-five of her friends, with the installation itself. The ambitious project merged floating sculptural cities, created out of found materials and scrap wood, performance and portraiture, set within majestically organized scenes of urban decay. The boats travelled down the Hudson River, through New York's harbour to Long Island City, where they docked at the exhibition space. The thick ropes that were used to anchor the boats at the site of the gallery fed into Deitch Studios and led up to the show's central piece – a massive sculpture of two sisters, an image the artist has re-used on the street.

The rest of the exhibition space displayed an extraordinary number of pieces intertwined with found objects and constructed architectural forms. The installation, which was divided by an imagined flood line, depicted images and portraits that derive from the sea below the line, and city

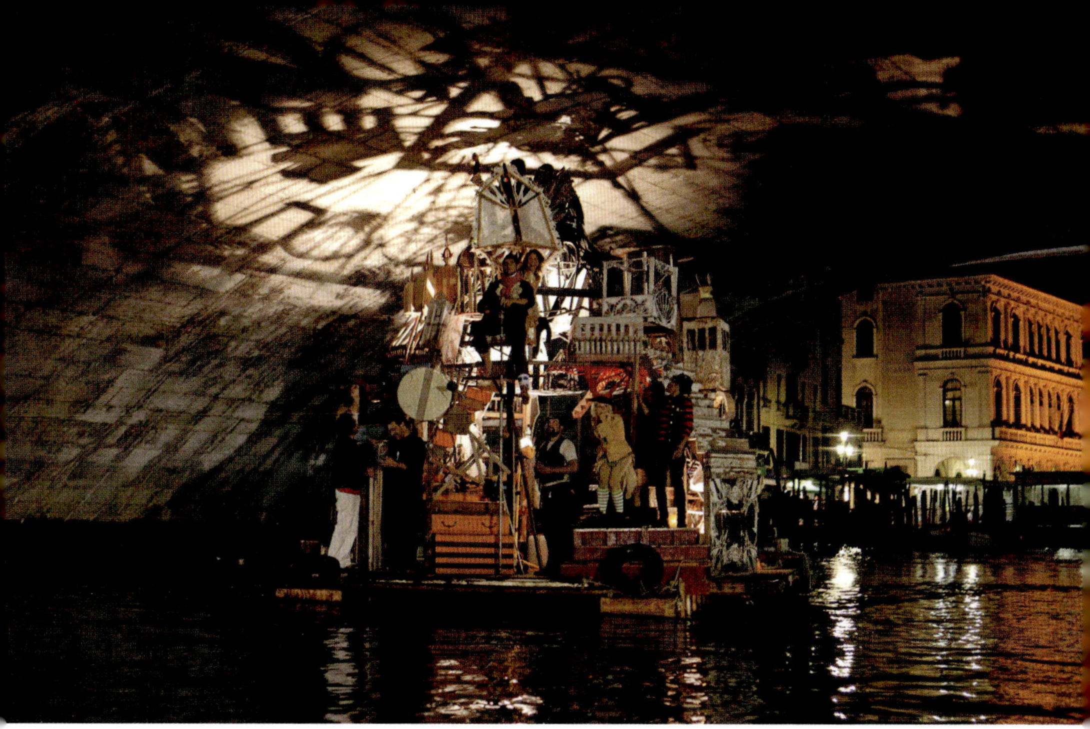

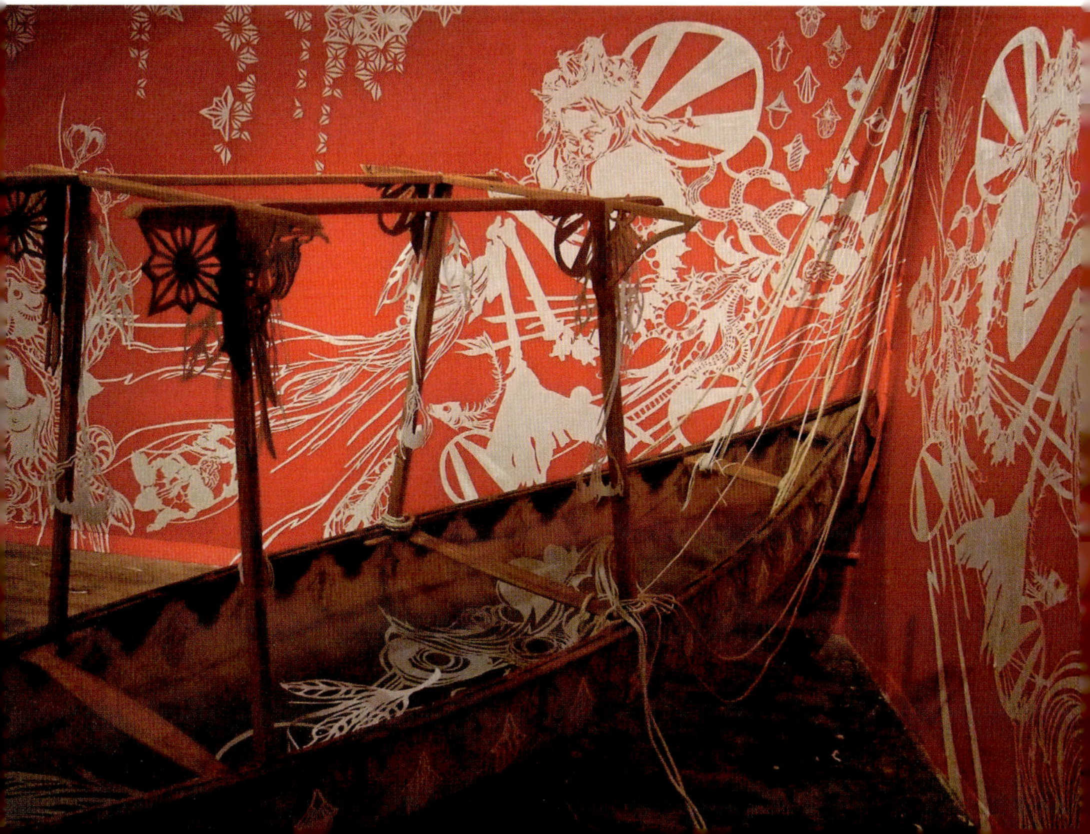

narratives above it. Swoon's fanciful sea creatures have also found their way onto the streets and into other exhibitions (as indeed, in terms of shows, have her floating sculptural cities) [193, 194]. The fragility and incredibly textured and detailed representations of people, elements from the natural world, and cities in many ways echo the atmosphere of urbanity, but also forge an entirely unique way of conceptualizing the city's chaos. Swoon's street practice is in no way diminished through this sort of exhibition. In fact, juxtaposed in the artist's handmade city, her portraits reverberate a new level of consciousness in her work.

On the Internet

In addition to their dissemination in formal exhibition spaces, the interpretation of graffiti and street art is further complicated through the appearance of these art forms in photographs and on the internet. While photography and graffiti or street art practices often go hand in hand, the graffiti photograph infrequently alerts us to the work's physical location. As a matter of fact, the background is most often incidentally present in the frame. This dynamic of graffiti's photographic representation is both understandable and problematic; understandable because, frequently taken by the artists, the photographs rarely serve as anything more than a record of the work. For artists who take photographs to document their work, the context is seldom the primary focus. Rather, the pictures record the aesthetic character of the piece – its detailed composition. However, in the absence of the work's relationship to its place of diffusion, the piece's material presence in a particular site is obscured. Consequently, the record of the work exists, but in a sort of void where site and time are obsolete. This dislocation prevents a complete reading of the piece, since unless we actually experience the work live, we do not have access to its impact in or experience of a particular urban context.

Our experience of graffiti or street art, often encountered at a distance, especially via photographs posted online, is thus incomplete, but this does not render it insignificant. Practically, photographs of graffiti are the most valuable foundation on which the movement thrives and, indeed, evolves. Were it not for the numerous photograph-based publications and websites focused on graffiti, the movement would quite literally have been lost. Since the work's lifespan in the urban context is limited, it is predominantly through photography that we have access to this art form's global history. Graffiti photographs are a primary resource for the study of style and technique and for recording and sharing one's work with colleagues and people around the world.

Since documenting the movement through photographs has become the primary means by which the work becomes known, in a way the document constitutes the work itself, which blurs the line between event and account, between object and experience. Certainly, experiencing graffiti or street art through the medium of photography in many ways authenticates the work, as does diffusing those photographs in cyberspace and through published materials. Photographs of 1970s New York trains that were forever memorialized in books now also appear online. Many old-school writers who represent iconic personas in graffiti's history, such as Blade [49], Lady Pink and Lee [47], have developed websites that both immortalize their pieces on subways and act as venues for the dispersal of their contemporary work. Websites that are specific to the preservation of graffiti's history, in a sense, carry on the legacy of early writing and have made an enormous contribution to what graffiti has become. The sheer number of pages dedicated to graffiti – including artcrimes.com, bombingscience.com, at149st.com and visualorgasm.com – suggests that writers are sharing styles and ideas, and developing friendships without necessarily meeting in person. The formation of this legal alternative has fuelled the growth and evolution of the global graffiti culture.

There are both positive and negative aspects to disseminating graffiti and post-graffiti art online. On the one hand, the use of the internet promotes a sense of inclusion through distribution, which for artists means invitations to participate in projects and exhibitions and a much wider audience base. On the other, while the work can be accessed by a greater number of people, by virtue of the medium, it also distances the viewer from it. By mediating a personal engagement with the work, the internet dilutes the viewing experience. The true gift of graffiti and street art as an element of surprise, encountered accidentally, vanishes. Roadsworth considers the internet a valuable tool in the dissemination of his art, but he also recognizes its problematic 'authority': 'You could alter a photo in Photoshop (an example comes to mind where someone faked the tagging of Air Force One using Photoshop), put it on the net and claim

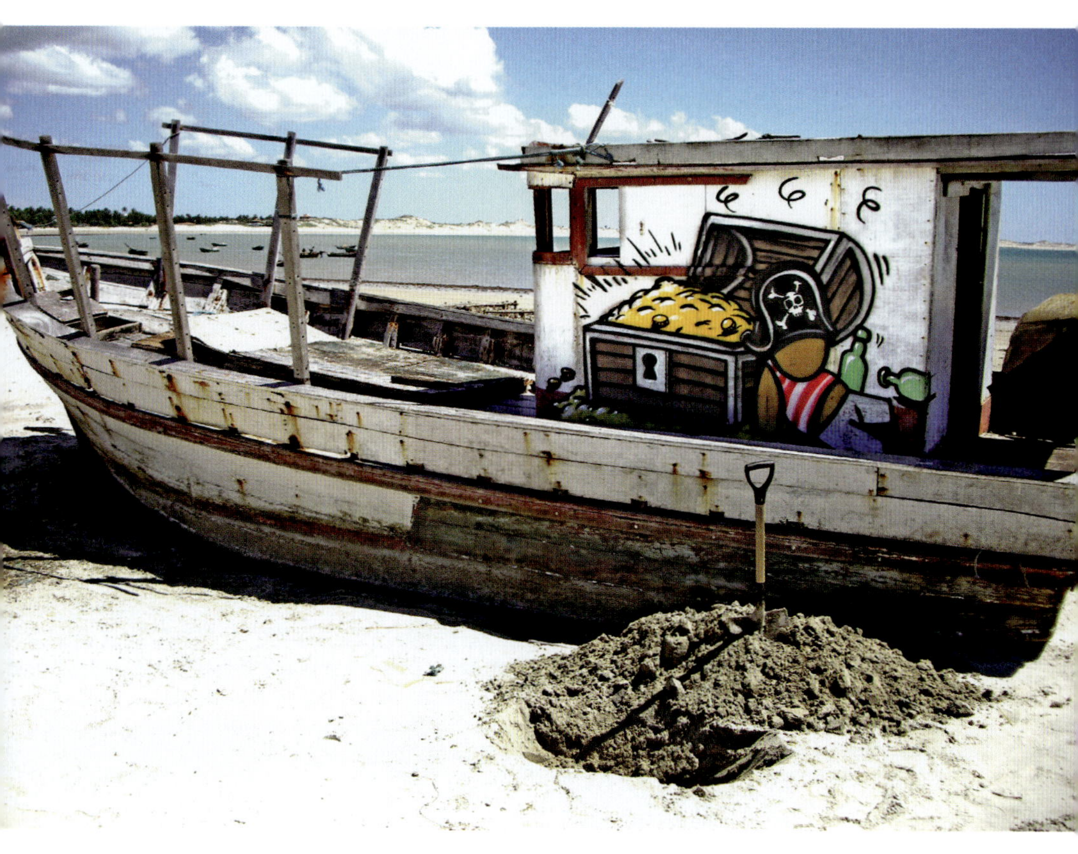

195 (*above*) **Jace**, *Untitled*, Icaraí de Amontada, Brazil, 2008. Street artists who live in remote places away from major cosmopolitan cities, such as Réunion Island's Jace, rely on the internet to make themselves known. Interestingly, Jace often includes a great deal more context in the photographic frame than other street artists, most likely because his works appear in unusual locations.

196 (*opposite, above*) **Jace**, *Untitled*, Réunion Island, 2002

197 (*opposite, below*) **Jace**, *Untitled*, Réunion Island, 2007

that you are a street artist. Or you could hit one or two spots (they could be in your own backyard), take a picture and put it on the internet, and give an impression that you are a street artist that gets up. I think the internet is an amazing tool and it has been beneficial to me, but it is also interesting how it can be used to represent "reality".' The artist's sentiment is one echoed time and again among graffiti and street artists who simultaneously value the internet and criticize it for complicating and, at times, trivializing these art forms.

One artist who has flourished online is Jace. After years of traditional graffiti writing, Jace, wanting to assert his individuality, developed his 'gouzou' character, displaying it most famously in his hometown of Saint-Pierre, Réunion Island. His graphically simple and stylistically identifiable character has cemented him as a well-known artist on the urban art scene. After working with the same character for almost twenty years, he still finds ways to delight, shock and

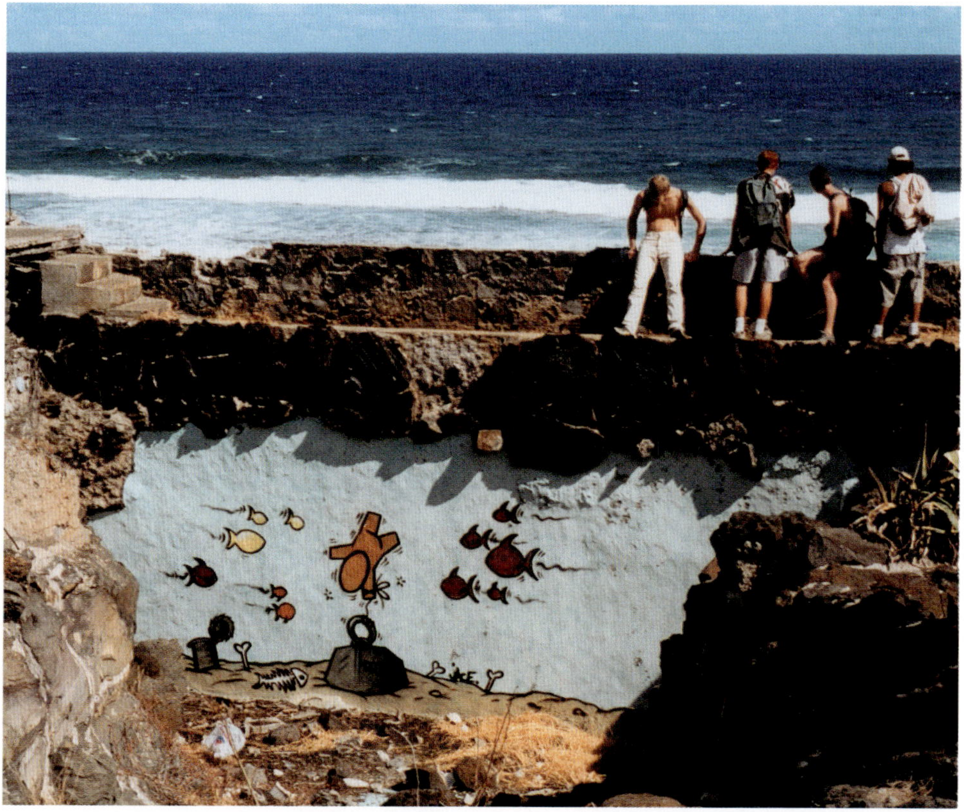

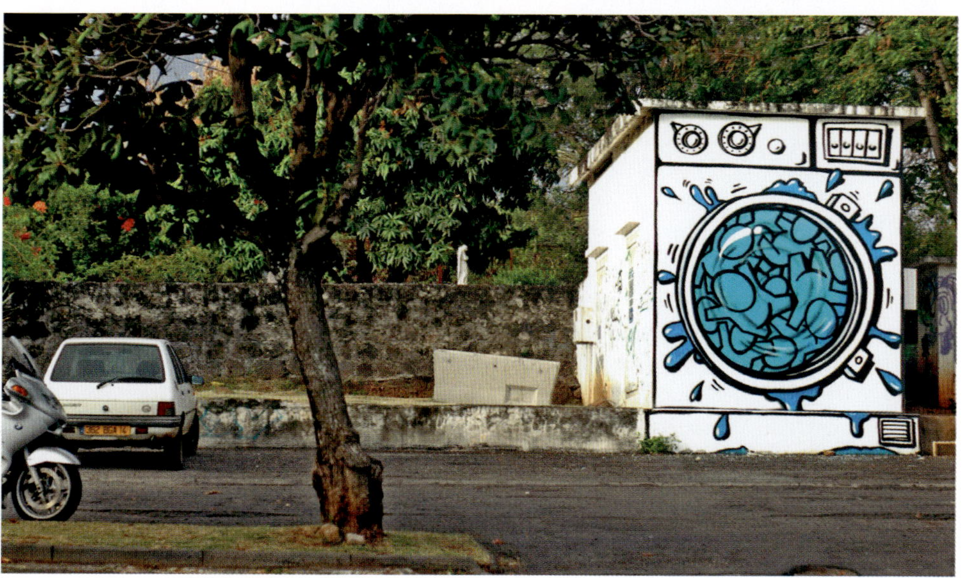

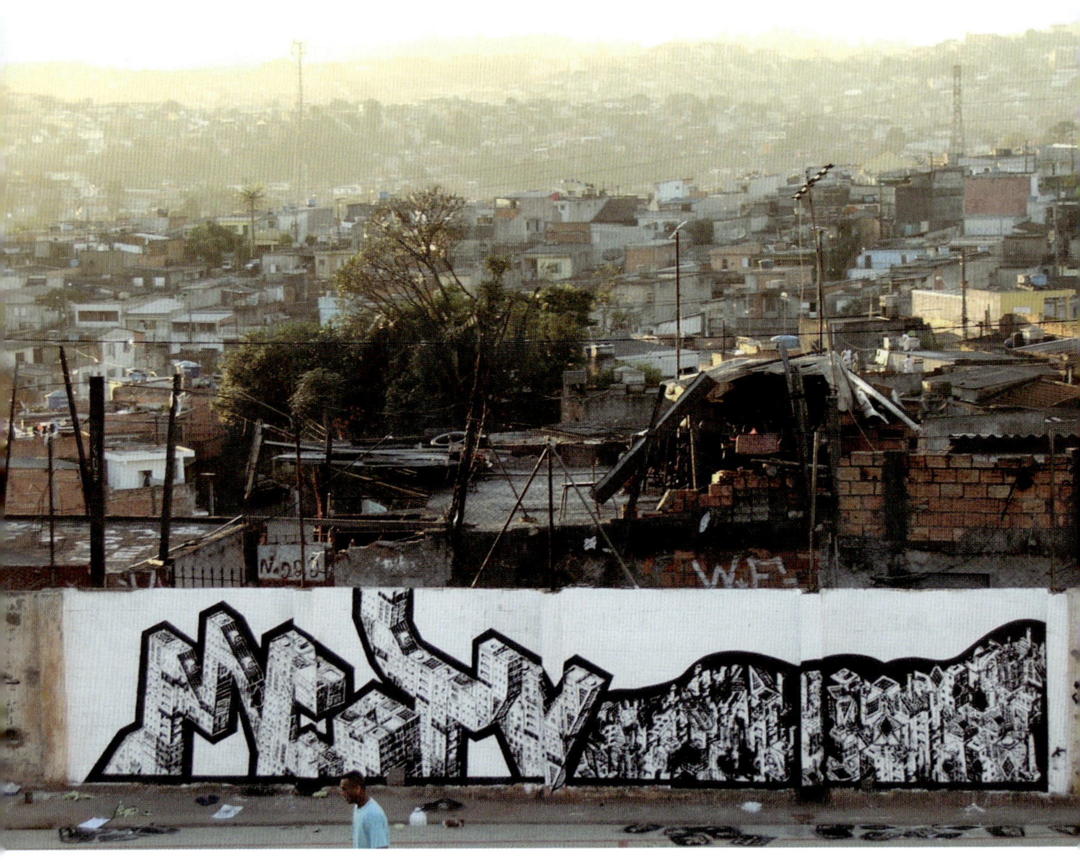

198 **Mariusz Waras aka M-City**, *M-City 123*, São Paulo, Brazil, 2007. Waras's aesthetic vocabulary is reliant on the built environment both as context and object. By reproducing industrial cities on physical city walls, the artist points to urbanity as a construct: orderly and sterile from afar and pulsating with anomalies in its details.

impress by diffusing his gouzous in the most unlikely places, acting out hilariously improbable scenarios. Gouzou is typically faceless, gender-neutral and orange. Whether dangling from cliffs, leaning against a treasure chest on a beach (2008) [195], being tied to a weight on the seabed (2002) [196] or getting cleaned in a washing machine (2007) [197], gouzou is always represented in a jovial, colourful way.

Although Jace has exhibited gouzous in many corners of the world, he is best known on Réunion Island where even the official tourism website promotes his work as an attraction, which is quite uncharacteristic for an illegal art form. Further afield, Jace's works are primarily disseminated in countries and cities not especially recognized as graffiti-centres, such as Le Havre, Budapest, Mayotte, Bali, Madagascar, Mauritius and Hong Kong. The internet is thus an especially valuable tool for experiencing his work. Notable too is the fact that photographs

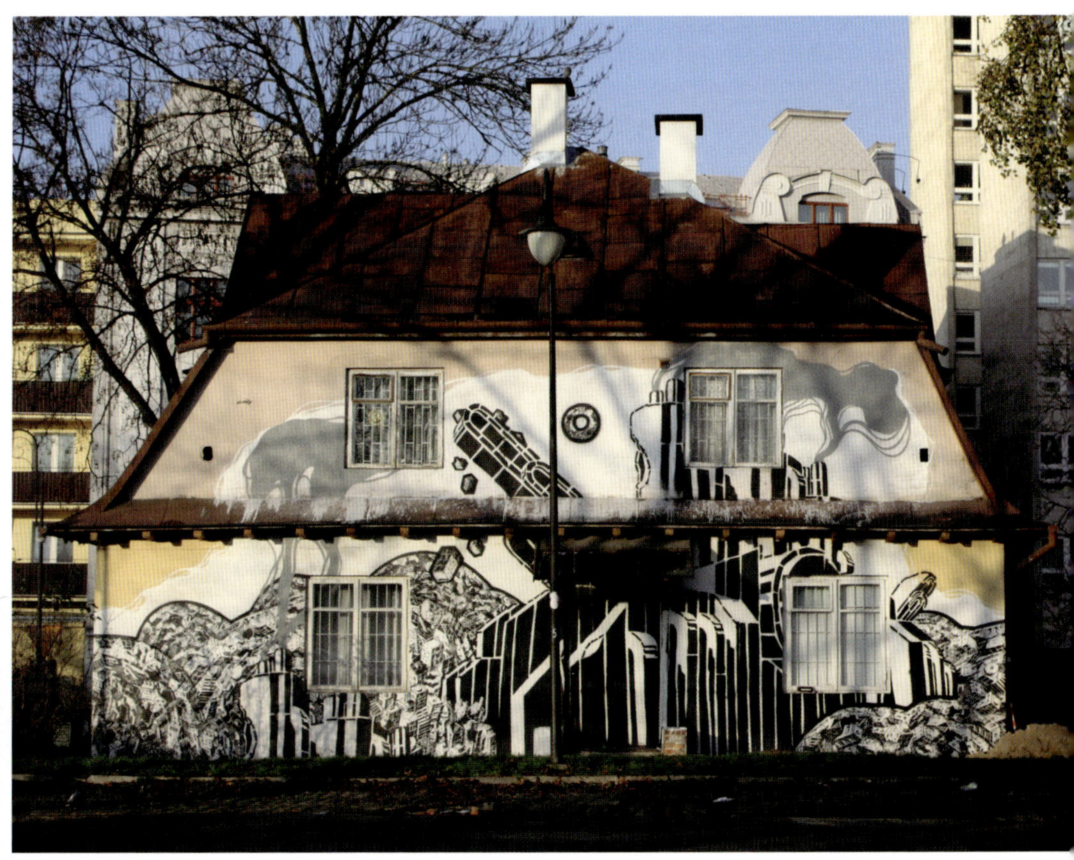

of the artist's pieces include a far greater sense of context, perhaps because of their 'exotic' locations. Whereas the majority of street artists display their art in busy urban centres, by virtue of where he is situated, this is not the case for Jace. The photographs available on Jace's website thus in a way stand in for the work itself as the main access point to his creations.

Some artists, such as Swoon, represent portraits of city-dwellers on city walls. The work of Polish artist Mariusz Waras, aka M-City, focuses on the architectural feel and design of the cityscape. In other words, instead of portraits of people, he stencils huge representations of cities on city walls. His black-and-white constructions of industrial spaces are graphically designed into chaotic and fragmented sites that are simultaneously orderly and vividly emblematic of city life [198, 199]. For M-City, the city is akin to a factory: systematically productive. Having grown up in the northern port city of Gdańsk, the artist was influenced by the remnants of the massive industrial shipyards where today abandoned factories, cranes and cargo containers abound. An interest in geometric lines and urban design has prompted M-City to make work that is at once stark and incredibly detailed. While from afar his pieces seem to depict only clusters of buildings, the closer one moves to the work, the more details are exposed. The confrontation with the work is thus akin to an actual experience and navigation of a city.

The artist's interest in the organization of urban space is accentuated through his website. Visiting www.m-city.org means participating in the virtual creation of urbanity. On the site, using the artist's 'city constructor' tool, the elements that make up M-City's stencils are individualized and separated into categories that the viewer can drag and drop into a city model, components of which can also be shifted and reorganized. The left-hand column includes all manner of 'buildings', 'infrastructure' and 'people', as well as elemental shapes and unexpected large-scale figures: robots, dinosaurs, astronauts. These elements, when dragged into the pre-designed model of urbanity on the right-hand side, can be further adjusted – brought to the forefront or sent to the back, for example. Through his website, M-City provides navigators with access both to his stencilled images and his participatory vision of urban organization.

Other artists such as Invader use the model of the interactive website to echo the meaning of their work on the street. His site, www.space-invaders.com, is programmed to operate much like a video game in that the 'player' is alerted to a new invasion (a new site of dissemination), and with the cursor must locate the 'invader' (the tiled artwork) on a photograph in the tradition of *Where's Wally?* (*Where's Waldo?*), and click on it in order to move on to the next level (photograph). Looking through images of Invader's work, and thus playing a game where the score is kept and levels are reached, is a novel way to access his worldwide practice.

These and other comprehensive sites suggest that graffiti and street art are becoming 'internetized', meaning that the amount of written, visual and personalized information found on the internet surpasses the possibilities of an individual's actual engagement with these art traditions. In a way, the internet is not only a source of information about graffiti and street art, but is also swiftly becoming the primary vehicle for an encounter with the work. Thus, the discourse around the graffiti subculture and the post-graffiti movement is moving into the virtual realm – a realm that unifies those who have access to it, but fundamentally distances its users from physical experiences with the works themselves.

Reclaiming the Streets: Remixing, Culture Jamming and Subvertising

Through the action of writing their names on city streets, graffiti writers essentially reclaim the public sphere. The practice of writing is one that is not as observably politically motivated as much street art, in terms of visuals and slogans, yet the very defiant act of getting up is in essence one of rebellion and reclamation. Graffiti writers are largely in it for themselves, but because their actions are exercised in the city, ultimately their visual culture communicates resistance and subversion.

Street artists, on the other hand, often quite obviously play on the commercialization of space in order to produce meaning through their work. Were it not for the privatization of public space, street art – produced on the outskirts of prime advertising locations – would not so readily impart satirical or reactionary ideas. Since space is continually in a state of production, it embodies endless opportunities for modification

200 **Herakut** Whether politically minded or not, street artists and graffiti writers are effectively reclaiming public space through the illegal act of making art in places that are not specifically designated for creation.

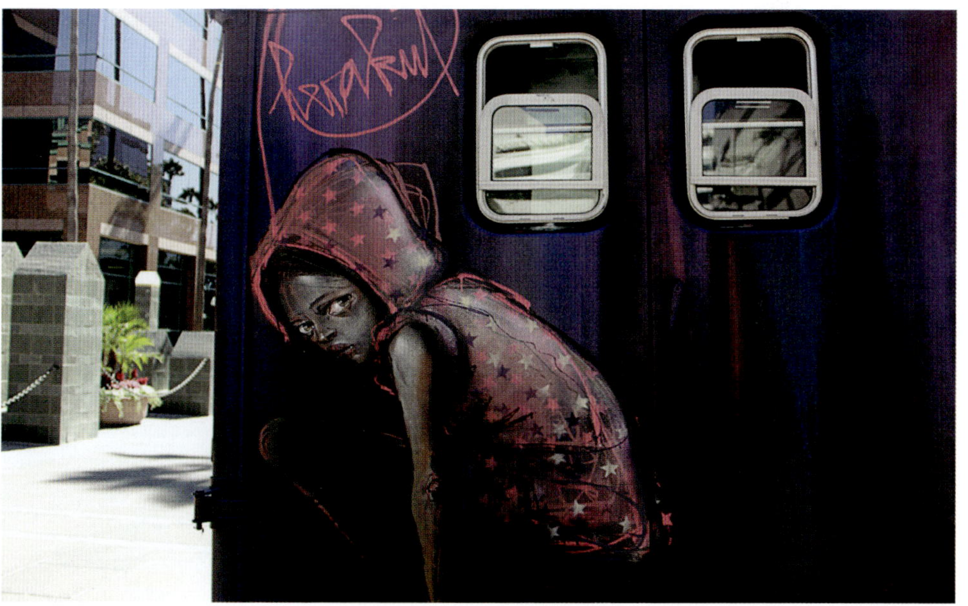

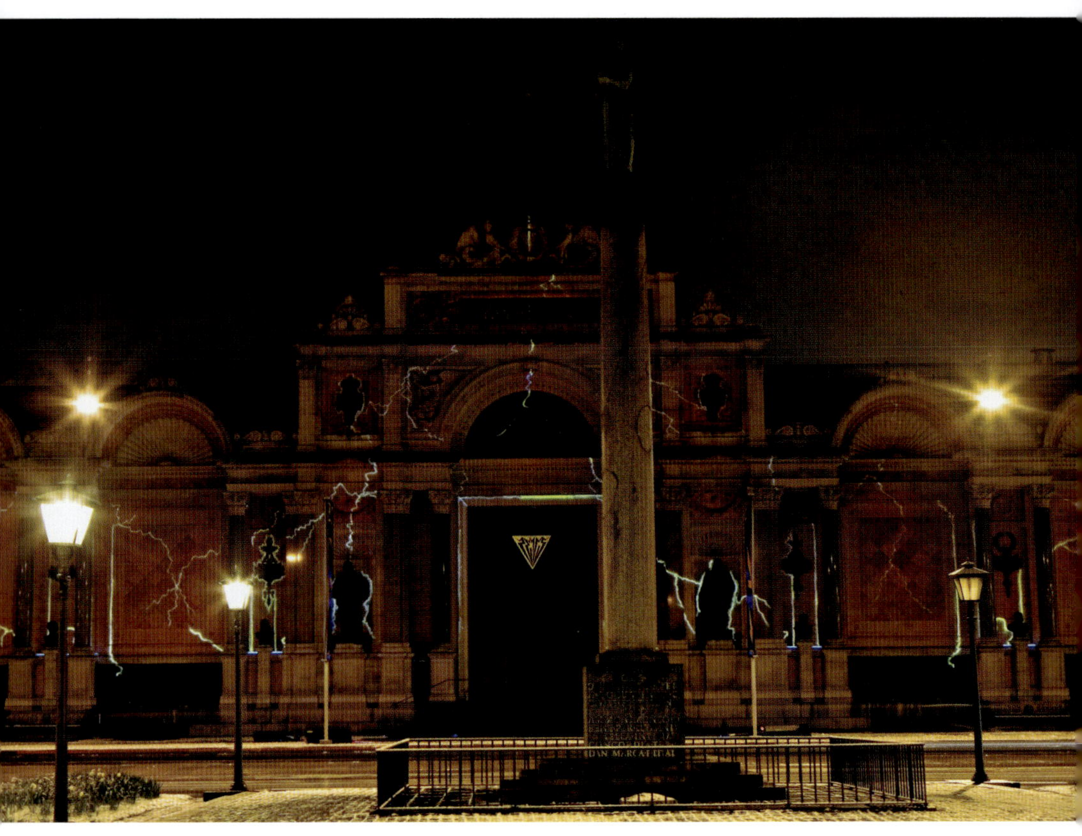

201 **Zevs**, *Invisible Graffiti*, Glyptotek Museum, Copenhagen, Denmark, 2008. Interested in the ephemeral and intangible, Zevs painted with invisible ink that can only be seen through UV-filtered light. In this way, his creations appear solely under the cover of night, while during the day his graffiti is undetectable.

and signs of resistance. By personalizing public spaces and reworking prominent advertising areas, street artists are critically examining the experience of contemporary urban life. Just as streets are transformed into spaces through people's movement, street art, through its physical interaction with city spaces, alters the urban fabric via its material impermanence and the imaginative narratives and spirited dialogues it fosters.

Visual imagery in a city is predominantly composed of advertisements displayed prominently in prime locations. Acting either as counter-advertisements or additions to sanctioned imagery in a city, post-graffiti art functions as a necessary opposition to corporate representations of how a city is visually organized – what does and does not belong. It does so at times directly on or next to authorized imagery, and at times in neglected spaces. Like the city itself, street art is in motion. By disseminating their work on the street, artists emphasize a number of obscured urban realities: that much of what may

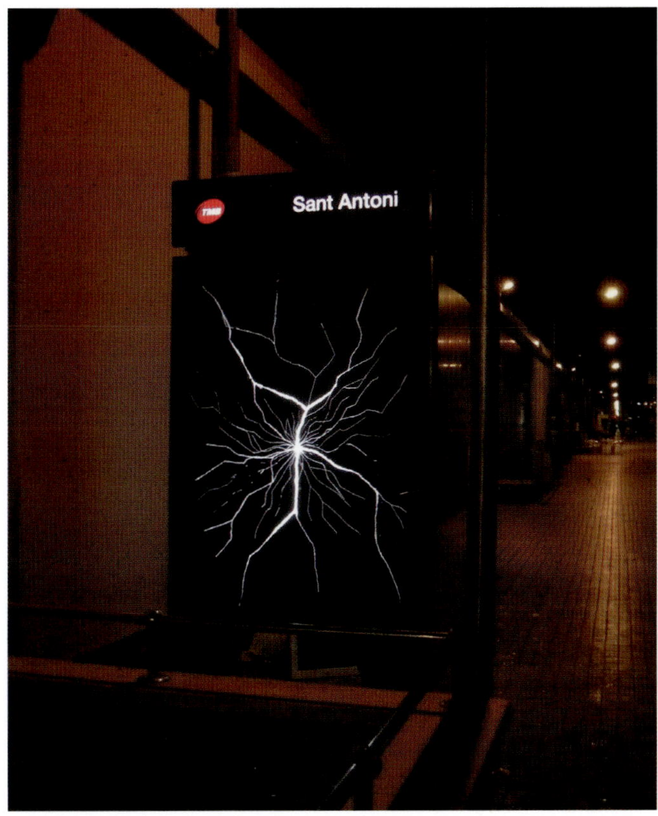

202 **Zevs**, *Graffiti Illumination*, Barcelona, Spain, 2010. The 'Graffiti Illuminations' series necessitates light boxes scattered throughout the city as a starting point. Zevs layers the neon lights with thick black paint and subsequently scratches out representations of lightning, thus obscuring the boxes' function and simultaneously transforming them into art projects.

seem to be public is in fact private space, and that unauthorized public art contributes as much to the production of space and a city's visual culture as sanctioned projects.

With his 'Electric Shadows', Zevs explored the idea of incorporating the human hand into existing objects, such as benches and bins. In a more political series entitled 'Visual Attacks' (2001), he targeted another urban mainstay: advertising posters. By spray-painting red, dripping spots on models' foreheads or eyes in various advertisements, including Gap, Yves Saint Laurent and Eau de Rochas, the artist 'assassinated' the campaigns. In another series, 'Invisible Graffiti' (*c.* 2006–10) [201], he wrote graffiti with invisible ink that could be seen only at night through UV-filtered light. Similar projects include 'Graffiti Illuminations' (*c.* 2006–10) [202], whereby light sources were painted black and representations of lightning were subsequently scratched on, and the use of high-pressure water jets to create 'clean graffiti' ('Proper Graffiti', *c.* 2006–8) [203].

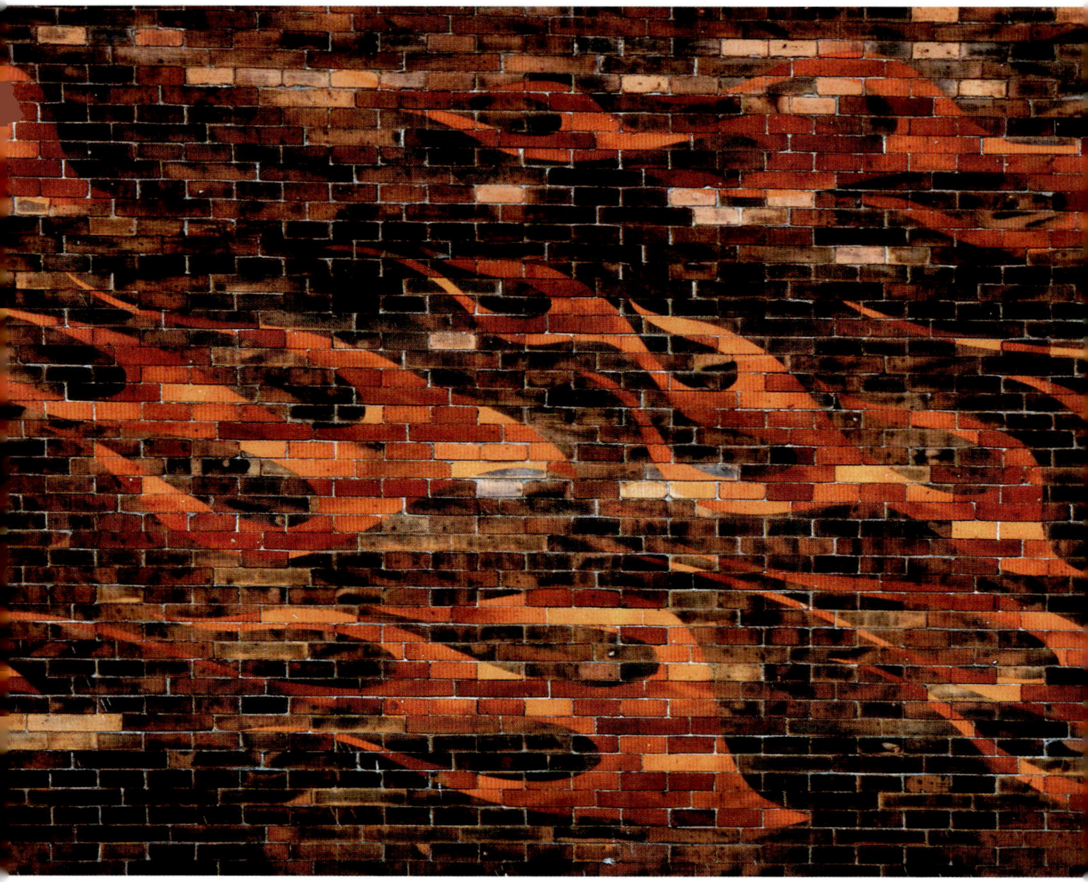

203 (*above*) **Zevs**, *Flaming*, 'Proper Graffiti' series, Copenhagen, Denmark, 2008. Using a high-pressure jet, Zevs cleans dirty city walls into words and images and thus reverses the standard notion of graffiti soiling a clean surface.

204 (*right*) **Zevs**, *Nike Liquidated Logo*, Berlin, Germany, 2005. By painting well-known logos in their original colours and letting the paint drip to create the illusion that the logo is melting, Zevs effectively communicates the idea of liquidating the power ascribed to branding, marketing and consumption.

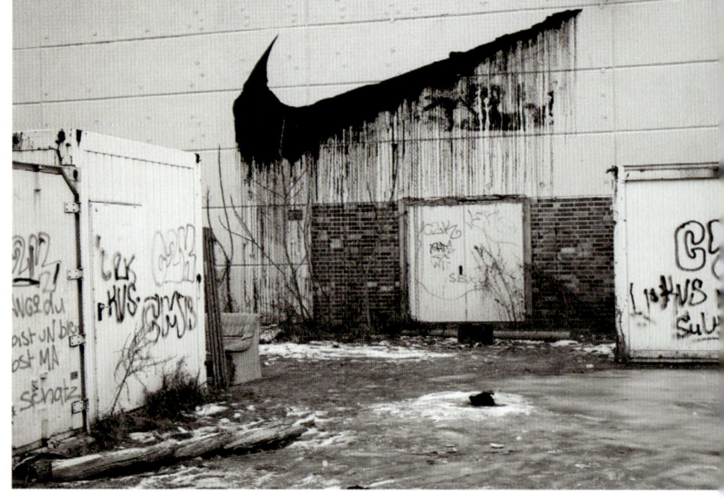

Recently Zevs has also taken to 'melting' recognizable brand logos (*c.* 2000–8). As McDonald's golden arches drip yellow paint and Nike's swoosh becomes a *Liquidated Logo* (2005) [204], the artist's visual protest is clear: to turn corporate advertising strategies on their head and thus to question their function in urbanity. Explaining this process, Zevs says: 'Of course, there is a graffiti aesthetic to my art, but I primarily play with the visual effect. I use the original colours and re-paint the logo with excess. By pouring paint over them, the logo dissolves in front of the viewer's eyes, drawing attention to, and visually disturbing the recognizable and omnipresent trademark. By doing so, I try to investigate the logo's visual power. It's a simple gesture, just as in Aikido when you reverse the power and change the flow of energy.'

The idea of re-mixing advertising strategies through sampling or creating parodies of advertisements by subvertising is a popular practice among activists and artists who operate anonymously or under pseudonyms. Of course a street artist's logo or character, like a graffiti writer's tag, can be read as a form of advertising given that similar strategies are involved, even if instead of a product, it is the idea of self-expression and creativity being sold. The practice of culture jamming – in other words disrupting corporate and cultural institutions (of which subvertising is a key component) – is a much more direct way to answer back to those who have financial, and by extension visual, control over cityscapes. By altering corporate logos, re-interpreting advertisements and generally playing with the meaning of visual forms in the city, artists effectively empower the public in their experience of their environment and challenge the status quo.

Some artists such as American street artist Ron English have, since the 1980s, criticized consumption culture on a massive scale. By reworking iconic brands in his distinctively witty style, English integrates his pieces into otherwise transparent spaces of sale: commercial advertising billboards. By appropriating celebrated art-historical images and widely known corporate symbols, the artist creates his special brand of 'POPaganda' – the term he uses to describe his signature style of cultural mash-ups. Working on privatized spaces in the public sphere allows English to subvert their function by manipulating prominent brands from the role of selling to facilitating inquiry. The *Camel Jrs* billboard (1992) [205], for example, relies on the essence of the familiar mascot for the Camel brand cigarette,

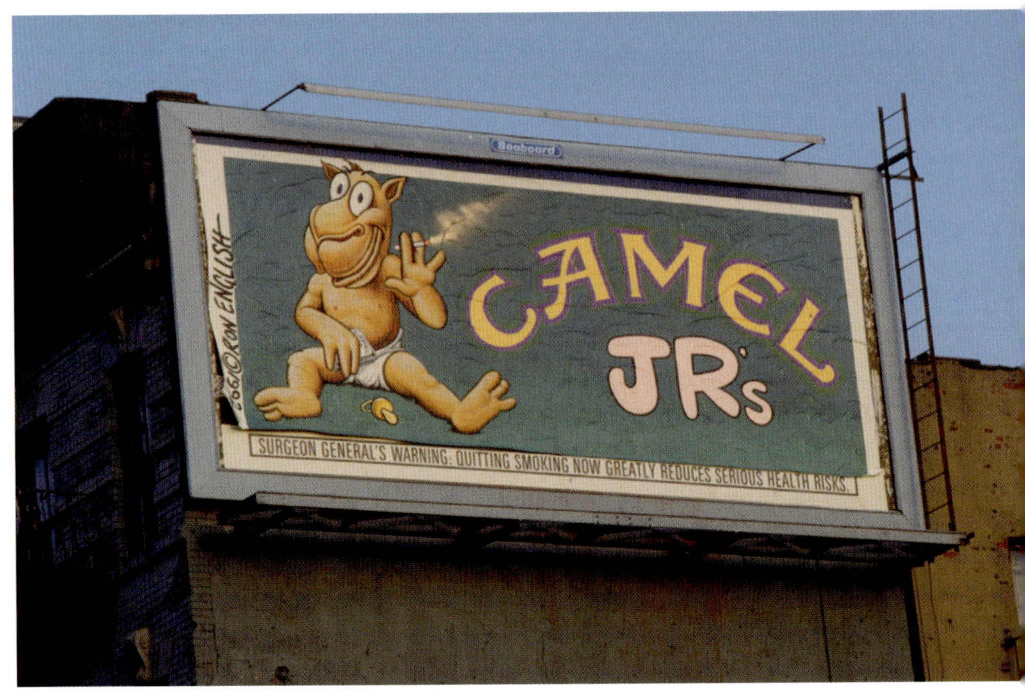

205 **Ron English**, *Camel Jrs*, New York City, USA, 1992. The father of 'POPaganda', Ron English has been reworking iconic brands so as to question the culture of consumption and advertising for over thirty years. Turning brand slogans, mascots and logos on their heads through the appropriation of billboards is one of English's most successful and long-standing projects.

but to advocate non-smoking. In another instance, the artist's *We Deceive, You Believe* Fox News billboard (2008) [206] plays on Fox's recognizable logo and font-type to question its credibility. English aims to challenge the culture and strategies of advertising, but also to promote the possibilities of free speech by creating his own fake 'brands' such as the children's cereal *Sugar Smack* (2010) [207].

Urban Painting Today

The overwhelming pervasiveness of this art genre worldwide proves that urban painting is a defining art movement of the twenty-first century. Not limited by style, content, context, message or media, it is truly international. The intersection between graffiti and post-graffiti is conceived in a number of ways: empirically by writers and artists, and spatially through the exhibition of these art forms in a city. While for some artists, such as Pez, writing graffiti was essential to their eventual experimentation with different modes of street art, for others the evolution is not so readily observable. Pez's fish functions and is disseminated in the same tradition as tagging; the difference is of course visual, in that a fish in a variety

206 (*above*) **Ron English**, *We Deceive, You Believe*, Colorado, USA, 2008

207 (*below*) **Ron English**, *Sugar Smack*, New York City, USA, 2010. The insertion of a fake brand, 'Sugar Smack', among other well-known breakfast cereals in a grocery store is typical of the subversive and interventionist projects that many politically minded street artists take on. This sort of project allows renegade artists to work within a popular visual language for the purpose of sabotage.

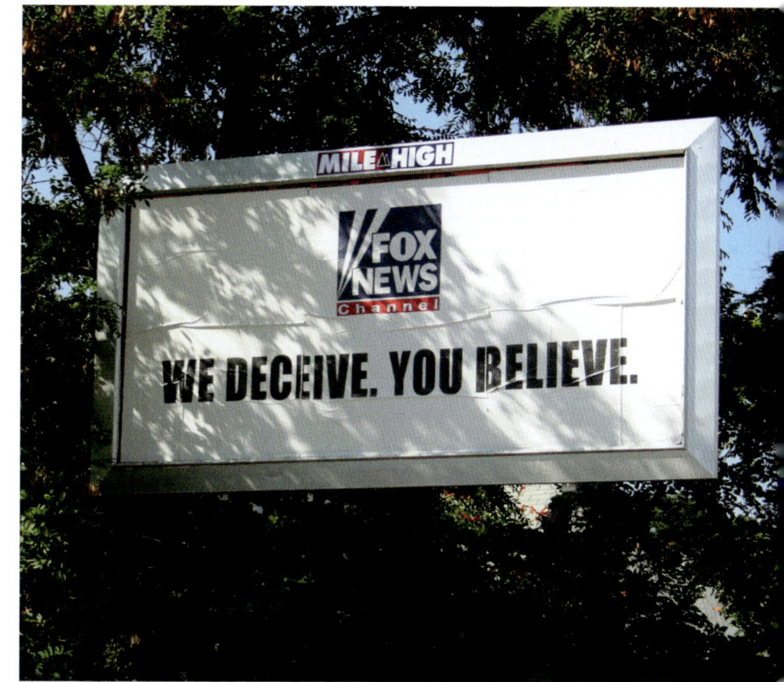

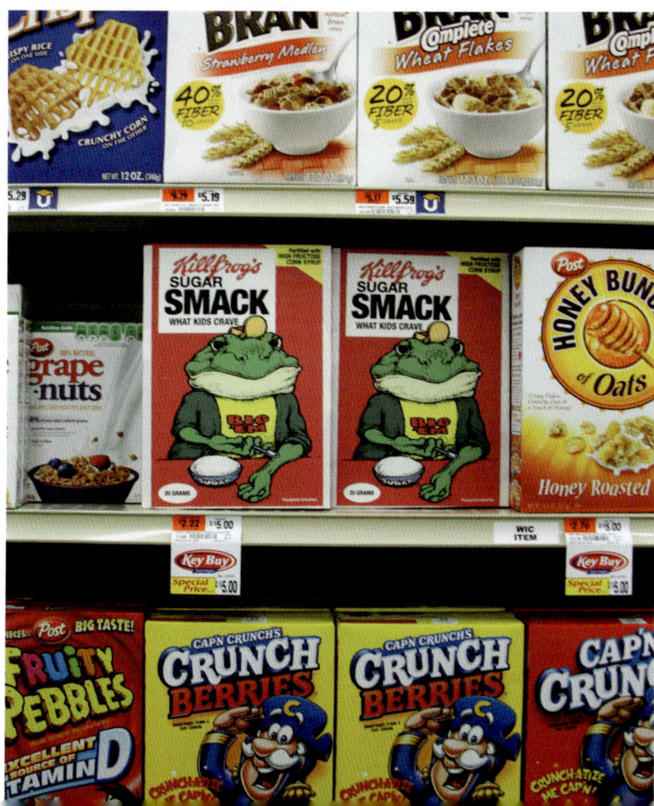

of playful executions stands in for a signature. Roadsworth, who identifies with the signature graffiti movement in terms of his moniker and social circle, remarks that his connection to graffiti is 'as much an identification as it is a reaction to it'. In truth, his practice is visually distant from graffiti and thus functions in a distinct way. Like Roadsworth, Vexta has a social graffiti connection but finds the graffiti world 'a bit too boycore and internalized'. Street artists and graffiti writers share the same framework of urbanity for the execution of their pieces, but their visual languages and their communities differ to such extents that the experience of their work culminates in completely different appreciations.

For cultural historians and art theorists, the most compelling facet of graffiti and post-graffiti practices should reside in this very reality: these movements operate as dynamic reflections of and additions to peoples' experiences of city life and visual culture. As such, they are unmediated, uncensored, visual dialogues that in their production incorporate the materials and spaces of a city, as well as the personal and culturally driven encounter between artist and audience. Creating art on the street is a powerful initiative for reasons that move beyond non-conformism and rebellion. Art on the street not only reaches the largest possible audience, but also sets trends and establishes new directions for the creative gesture. Street artists rely on comprehensible, explicit and popular pictorial codes, and this uniquely positions their practices to comment on contemporary issues.

For art historians, graffiti and street art provide an ideal avenue through which to question some of the discipline's canonical categories such as style, subject and signature. For a field of study that accesses its objects of inquiry first through form, content, style and medium, and second through their social context, meaning, artist, patron and viewer, the graffiti and post-graffiti movements provide extraordinarily rich narratives. Uncovering the socio-political intentions of these movements, and investigating the works formally and contextually, proves fundamental to the works themselves and to their viewers. Graffiti cultures, as sophisticated forms of communication, both shape and are shaped by their social contexts. Engaging with the graffiti and street art movements with a critical, art-historical eye reveals not only the impetus for their creation, but also our responsibility as viewers to allow the objects to speak while we uncover their function.

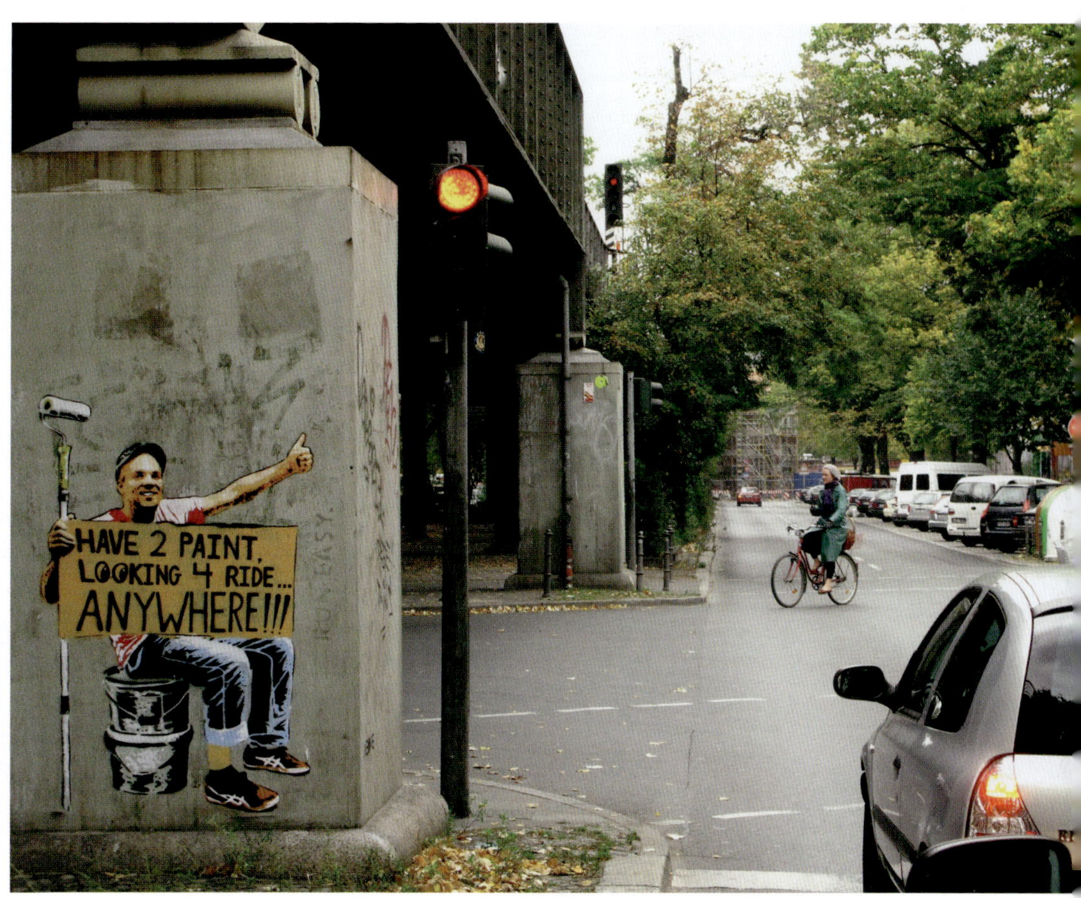

208 **Above**, *Looking 4 Ride… Anywhere*, Berlin, Germany, 2010. As with graffiti writing, creating art on the street can become an addictive obsession. Many artists relish locating the perfect context for their work and travel internationally, at their own expense, to create art that is not supposed to be there, in spaces that are not supposed to matter.

The categories of style, subject and signature – or who made it and who paid for it – are exceptionally pertinent to the study of works of art that fully fit into art-historical ways of seeing, but simultaneously disrupt these fundamental classifications. Style is a key element of graffiti analysis. Personal, regional and period styles characterize art-historical inquiries, and these groupings are extremely relevant for graffiti writers as well. Distinctive individualizations of a common visual vocabulary account for stylistic breakthroughs or discrepancies; geographical adaptations allow for the proliferation of a number of varied scenes associated with one international network; and reading pieces within the framework of a specific time facilitates the study of stylistic and technical developments. The categories of subject and signature prove immeasurably more complicated for an analysis of graffiti within the discipline

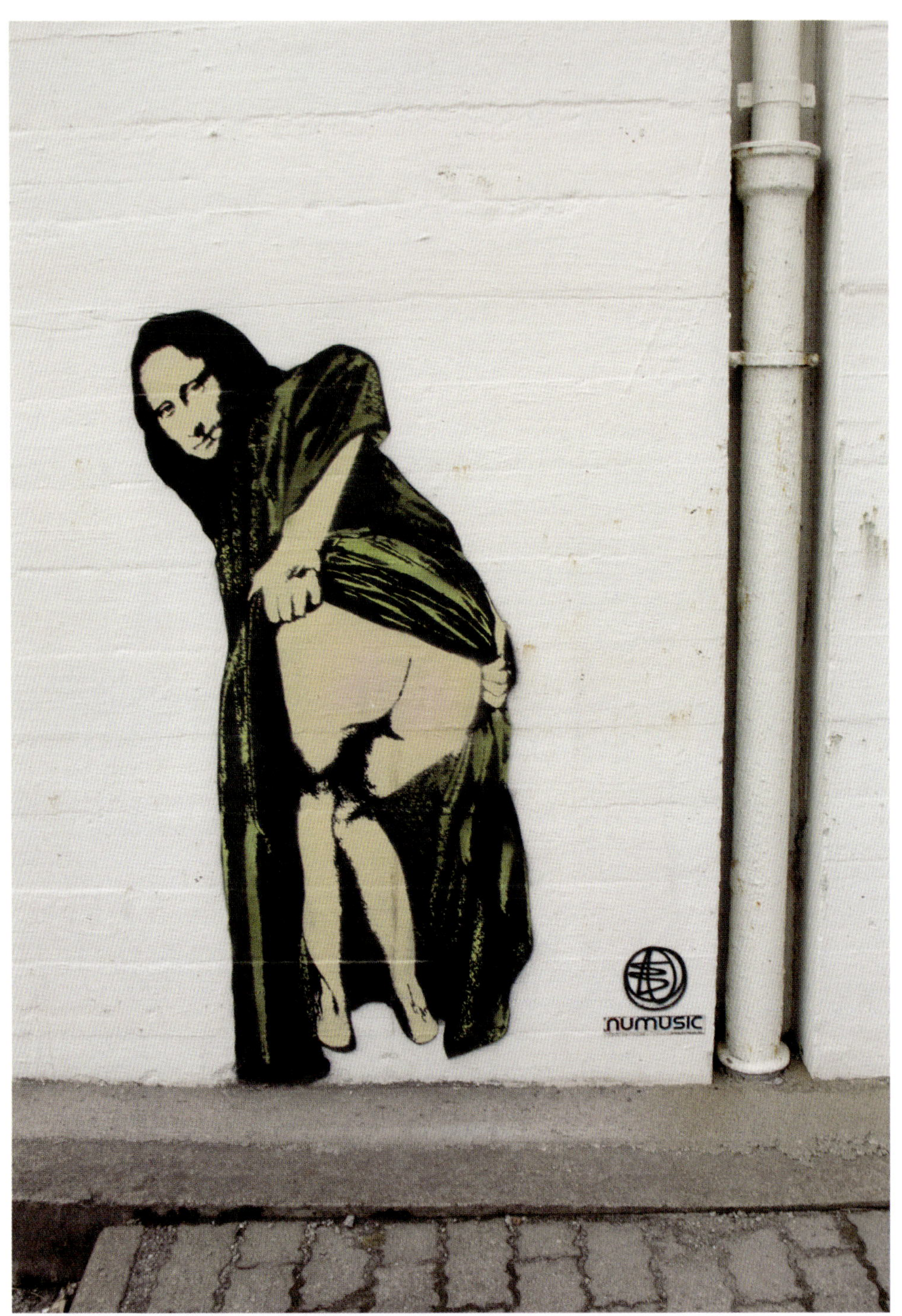

numusic

of art history, namely because the signature is the subject. A formal graffiti analysis, focused on line, colour, composition, form, volume, technique, material, texture and space, discloses writers' styles and thus their approaches towards their subject matter — their signatures.

The study of post-graffiti art practices allows art historians to scrutinize a movement that truly mirrors a global artistic community: one that in the twenty-first century ideally reflects the future of art and art history. As the traditional boundaries of artistic creations loosen, the study of art expands to examine practices of appropriation, neo-expressionism and conceptualism, craft and feminist art, a return to the body and figures, public art, as well as digital and installation pieces. The post-graffiti movement has a place within these dialogues as an exploration of our cultural landscape using an amalgamation of both traditional and new media and imagery. As unwarranted performative gestures, street art practices provide a counterbalance to the commercial and sanctioned images that populate the cityscape, and respond to increasingly fertile explorations of public space. These projects foster exchanges with the built environment, commercial imagery, canonical movements within the history of art, and urban, street cultures. As such, post-graffiti practices epitomize contemporary visual culture. Street art creates an alternative city narrative which pushes boundaries, refutes consumerism and essentially questions the role of art and artists in contemporary societies.

Today, numerous museums and galleries display the work of artists who are part of the ongoing development of contemporary art as it intersects with the street, animation, popular culture and the visual language of cities. These artistic ventures hint at the crossovers between the cultural forms shaping the streets and the questions that persist in the contemporary art world. Creating new avenues for expression, street artists negotiate the world not only at their own expense but also in a way that is palatable, reflective, fun, political and, most of all, raw and free.

209 **Nick Walker**, *Moona Lisa*, Norway, 2006. Re-imagining iconic images from the art-historical canon is a tradition among many street artists. This sort of work assures recognizability and thus accessibility, while simultaneously making a playful comment on the history of art and street art's place within it.

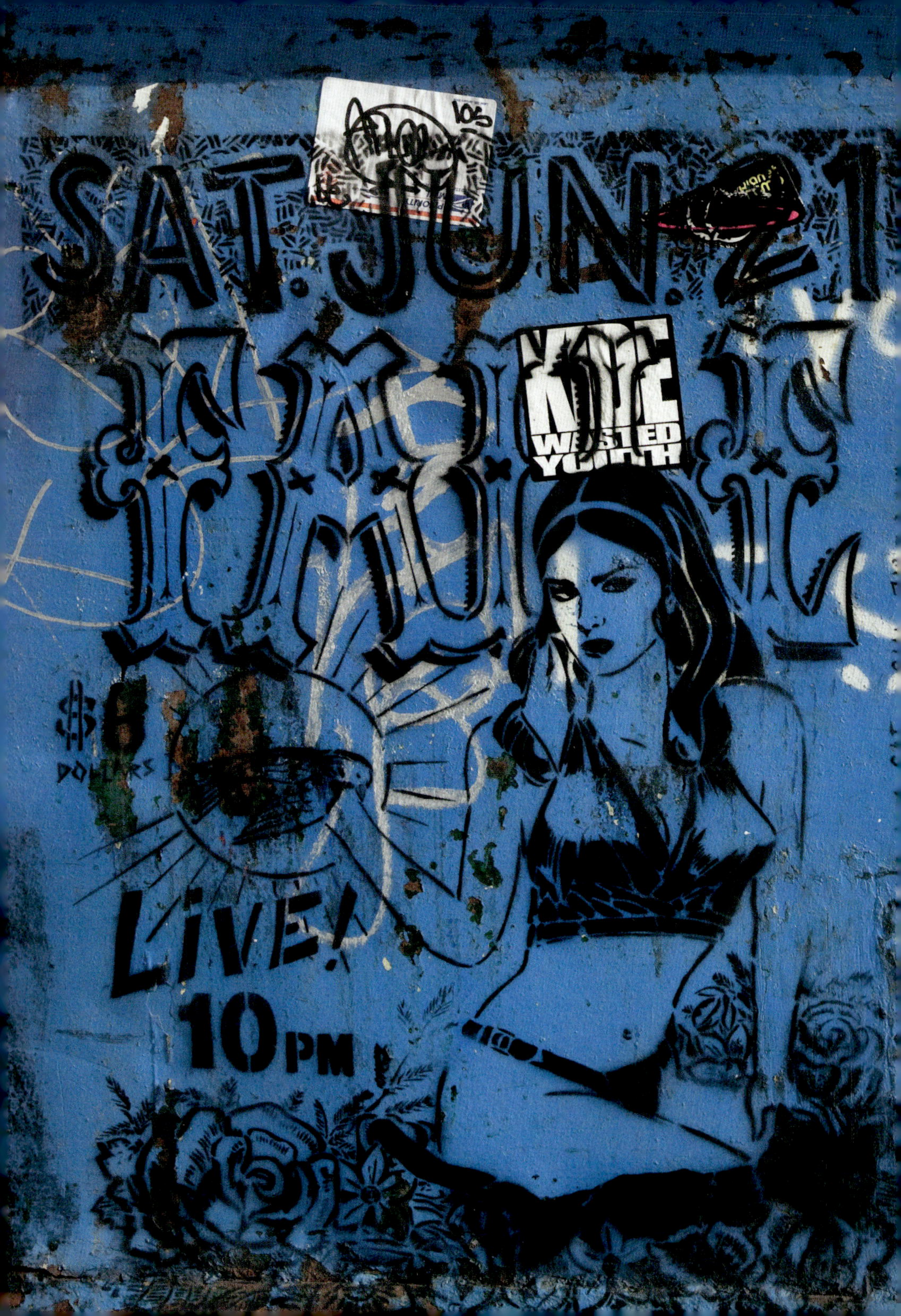

SAT. JUN. 21
LIVE!
10 PM
$8 DOLLARS
WASTED YOUTH

Artists' Websites

Above (USA) www.goabove.com
Banksy (UK) www.banksy.co.uk
Jean-Michel Basquiat (USA) www.basquiat.com
Blek le Rat (France) http://bleklerat.free.fr
Blu (Italy) www.blublu.org
Buff Monster (USA) www.buffmonster.com
Chas (Netherlands) www.flickr.com/chasloveletters
D*Face (UK) www.dface.co.uk
Does (Netherlands) www.digitaldoes.com
Eine (UK) www.einesigns.co.uk
Ron English (USA) www.popaganda.com
Fafi (France) www.fafi.net
Faile (USA, Canada) www.faile.net
Shepard Fairey (USA) www.obeygiant.com
Faith47 (South Africa) www.faith47.com
Fake (Netherlands) www.fakestencils.com
Graffiti Research Lab (USA) www.graffitiresearchlab.com
    and www.evan-roth.com
Keith Haring (USA) www.haring.com
Conor Harrington (Ireland/UK-based)
    www.conorsaysboom.wordpress.com
Herakut (Germany) www.herakut.de
Hitotzuki (Japan) www.hitotzuki.com
Invader (France) www.space-invaders.com
Jace (Réunion Island) www.gouzou.net
JR (France) www.jr-art.net
Kero (Spain) www.keroart.com
Knitta Please (USA) www.magdasayeg.com
Koralie (France/USA-based) http://kogaylou.free.fr
M-City (Poland) www.m-city.org
MadC (Germany) www.madc.tv
Microbo (Italy) www.microbo.com
Miss Van (France/Spain-based) www.missvan.com
Nuria Mora (Spain) www.nuriamora.com
Mosstika (Hungary/USA-based) www.mosstika.com
Omen (Canada) www.omen514.com
Alexandre Órion (Brazil) www.alexandreorion.com
Os Gêmeos (Brazil) www.osgemeos.com.br
Pez (Spain) www.el-pez.com
Puppet (Sweden) www.puppetindustries.com
Roadsworth (Canada) www.roadsworth.com
Slider (Germany) www.bandits-dresden.de
Thundercut (USA) www.thundercut.com
Vexta (Australia) www.vexta.com.au
Vhils (Portugal) www.alexandrefarto.com
Nick Walker (UK) www.theartofnickwalker.com

Dan Witz (USA) www.danwitz.com
Zevs (France) www.gzzglz.com

See also:
www.artcrimes.com
www.at149st.com
www.bombingscience.com
www.lost.art.br/nina
www.lost.art.br/nunca
www.symbollix.com
www.visualorgasm.com
www.woostercollective.com

Select Bibliography

—'Art of Destruction: Interview with Vhils',
Urbanartcore.eu, 27 April 2010:
www.urbanartcore.eu/vhils-act-of-destruction

—'Brazilian Street Artist Nunca', trans. by Ines Amaro,
Ideaseek.com, 2007: http://ideaseek.blogspot.com/2007/10/
brazilian-street-artist-nunca.html

—'The World Gouzous', Réunion Island website:
http://reunion.runweb.com/lang-EN-page-1114-2V-
page,Welcome-to-the-world-of-Gouzous.html

Acconci, Vito, 'Leaving Home: Notes on Insertions into the
Public', in Florian Matzner (ed.), *Public Art: A Reader*, pp. 28–34.
Ostfildern-Ruit: Hatje Cantz, 2004.

Agnew, John, and James Duncan (eds), *The Power of Place: Bringing
Together Geographical and Sociological Imaginations*. Boston
(Mass.) and London: Unwin Hyman, 1989.

Andino, Sandra, *The Production of Graffiti Writing in El Barrio
of North Philadelphia*. PhD dissertation, Temple University,
Philadelphia (Pa.), 2001.

Ardenne, Paul. *Un art contextuel, création artistique en milieu
urbain*. Paris: Flammarion, 2002.

Armajani, Siah, 'Public Art and the City', in Florian Matzner (ed.),
Public Art: A Reader, pp. 66–72. Ostfildern-Ruit: Hatje Cantz,
2004.

Augé, Marc, *Non-Places: Introduction to an Anthropology of
Supermodernity*, trans. by John Howe. London and New York:
Verso, 1995.

Austin, Joe, *Taking the Train: How Graffiti Art Became an Urban
Crisis in New York City*. New York and Chichester: Columbia
University Press, 2001.

Bain, Alison, 'In/visible Geographies: Absence, Emergence,
Presence, and the Fine Art of Identity Construction',
Tijdschrift voor Economische en Sociale Geografie, vol. 95,
no. 4, Royal Dutch Geographical Society (KNAG),
September 2004, pp. 419–26.

Banksy, *Wall and Piece*, London: Century, 2005.

Barber, Bruce, 'Cultural Interventions in the Public Sphere', in
Annie Gérin and James S. McLean (eds), *Public Art in Canada:
Critical Perspectives*, pp. 371–401. Toronto and London:
University of Toronto Press, 2009.

Barker, Martin, and Anne Beezer (eds), *Reading into Cultural
Studies*. London and New York: Routledge, 1992.

Barthel, Jennifer, *The Perceptions of Graffiti in Ottawa: An
Ethnographic Study of an Urban Landscape*. MA dissertation,
Carleton University, Ottawa, 2002.

Bauwens, Malika, 'Le street art faut le mur', *Beaux Arts Magazine*,
December 2008, pp. 54–65.

Beauchamp, Geneviève, *Le graffiti comme sous-culture
contemporaine: pratique anarchique et marginale ou microcosme
de la société moderne?* MA dissertation, Université de
Montréal, Montreal, 2005.

Becker, Howard S., *Art Worlds*. Berkeley (Calif.) and London:
University of California Press, 1982.

—*Doing Things Together: Selected Papers*. Evanston (Ill.):
Northwestern University Press, 1986.

—'L'oeuvre elle-même,' in Jean-Olivier Majastre and Alain
Pessin (eds), *Vers une sociologie des oeuvres*, pp. 449–63. Paris:
L'Harmattan, 2001.

—*Outsiders: Studies in the Sociology of Deviance*. New York: Free
Press, 1963.

Belcher, Michael, *Exhibitions in Museums*. Washington, DC:
Leicester University Press and Smithsonian Institution,
1991.

Bennett, Tony, 'The Political Rationality of the Museum', in
The Birth of the Museum: History, Theory, Politics, pp. 64–88.
London and New York: Routledge, 1994.

Bhabha, Homi K. (ed.), 'The Other Question: Stereotype,
Discrimination and the Discourse of Colonialism', in
The Location of Culture, pp. 64–88. London: Routledge, 1994.

Bilodeau, Denyse, *Les murs de la ville: les graffitis de Montréal*.
Montreal: Liber, 1996.

Blackshaw, Ric, and Liz Farrelly, *The Street Art Book: 60 Artists in
their Own Words*. New York: Collins Design, 2008.

Borden, Iain, *Skateboarding, Space and the City: Architecture and the
Body*. Oxford: Berg, 2001.

Bou, Louis, *Street Art: The Spray Files*. New York: Collins Design,
2005.

Boudreau, Laura, 'The New Beautiful City: A Divided Highway',
Spacing.ca, 2005: http://spacing.ca/art-roadsworth.htm

Bourdieu, Pierre, *Sociology in Question*, trans. by Richard Nice.
London and Thousand Oaks (Calif.): Sage, 1993.

Bousteau, Fabrice, 'JR à Paris', *Beaux Arts Magazine*, October
2009, pp. 120–25.

Brake, Mike, *Comparative Youth Culture: The Sociology of Youth
Cultures and Youth Subcultures in America, Britain and Canada*.
London: Routledge and Kegan Paul, 1985.

Bret, Schulte, 'Propaganda that Sticks – and Pays; Obey Giant
Campaign Wrestles with Consumer Culture', *Toronto Star*,
10 September 2002.

Broadhurst, Susan, *Liminal Acts: A Critical Overview of Contemporary
Performance and Theory*. London and New York: Cassell, 1999.

Brown, J., 'Appropriation: Appropriate?', *ARTnews*, vol. 108, no. 4,
2009, p. 46.

Bryson, Norman, 'Visual Culture and the Death of Images', in 'Responses to Mieke Bal's "Visual essentialism and the object of visual culture"', *Journal of Visual Culture*, vol. 2, no. 2, 2003, pp. 229–32.

'Buff Monster', buffmonster.com: www.buffmonster.com/bio.php

Burnham, Scott, 'Customised City', Iconeye.com, August 2007: www.iconeye.com/index.php?option=com_content&view=article&id=2365&Itemid=64

Buskirk, Martha, *The Contingent Object of Contemporary Art*. Cambridge (Mass.) and London: MIT Press, 2003.

Carlson, Marvin A., *Performance: A Critical Introduction*. New York: Routledge, 2004.

Cartwright, Lisa, and Stephen Mandiberg, 'Obama and Shepard Fairey: The Copy and Political Iconography in the Age of the Demake', *Journal of Visual Culture*, vol. 8, no. 2, 2009, pp. 172–76.

Carvajal, Pedro (director), *Popaganda: The Art and Crimes of Ron English* (documentary), 2005.

Castleman, Craig, *Getting Up: Subway Graffiti in New York*. Cambridge (Mass.) and London: MIT Press, 1982.

—'The Politics of Graffiti', in Murray Forman and Mark Anthony Neal (eds), *That's the Joint!: The Hip-Hop Studies Reader*, pp. 21–28. New York and Oxford: Routledge, 2004.

Cepeda, Raquel (ed.), *And It Don't Stop: The Best American Hip-Hop Journalism of the Last 25 Years*. New York: Faber and Faber, 2004.

Chaffee, Lyman G., *Political Protest and Street Art: Popular Tools for Democratization in Hispanic Countries*, vol. 40. Westport (Conn.) and London: Greenwood Press, 1993.

Chalfant, Henry, and James Prigoff, *Spraycan Art*. London: Thames & Hudson, 1987.

Chapman, Matt, 'REVERSE GRAFFITI: Clean Green Street Art | Inhabitat – Green Design Will Save the World', Inhabitat.com, 1 November 2007.

Chmielewska, Ella, 'Framing Temporality: Montreal Graffiti in Photography', in Annie Gérin and James S. McLean (eds), *Public Art in Canada: Critical Perspectives*, 2009, pp. 438–79. Toronto and London: University of Toronto Press, 2009.

Christie, Nancy Lynne, *Graffiti: What You Know is What You Get*. MA Ed. dissertation, Mount Saint Vincent University, Halifax (Nova Scotia), 1999.

Clarke, John, 'Style', in Stuart Hall and Tony Jefferson (eds), *Resistance through Rituals: Youth Subcultures in Post-war Britain*. London: Hutchinson for the Centre for Contemporary Cultural Studies, University of Birmingham, 1976.

Cohen, Albert, *Delinquent Boys: The Culture of the Gang*. Glencoe (Ill.): Free Press, 1955.

Cohen-Cruz, Jan (ed.), *Radical Street Performance: An International Anthology*. London and New York: Routledge, 1998.

Colgrove, Sarah, 'Graffiti Artist Faces 53 Counts of Vandalism', *The McGill Daily* (Montreal), vol. 94, no. 32, 31 January 2005.

'Conor Harrington', Lazarides: www.lazinc.com/artists/conor-harrington

Cooper, Martha, and Henry Chalfant, *Subway Art*. London: Thames & Hudson, 1984.

Cresswell, Tim, *Place: A Short Introduction*. Oxford: Blackwell, 2004.

Cybriwsky, Roman, and David Ley, 'Urban Graffiti as Territorial Markers', *Annals of the Association of American Geographers*, vol. 64, no. 4, December 1974, pp. 491–505.

D*Face, 'Why?': www.dface.co.uk/why

Davis, James, *Skateboarding is Not a Crime: 50 Years of Street Culture*. New York: Firefly Books, 2004.

Davvetas, Demosthenes, 'Lines, Chapters, and Verses', in Larry Warsh (ed.), *Jean-Michel Basquiat: The Notebooks*, pp. 28–31. New York: Art + Knowledge, 1993.

De Certeau, Michel, *The Practice of Everyday Life*, trans. by Steven Rendall. Berkeley (Calif.) and London: University of California Press, 1988.

Decker, Andrew, 'The Price of Fame', *Art News*, vol. 88, no. 1, 1989, pp. 96–101.

Deitch, Jeffrey, '1981: The Studio of the Street', in *Jean-Michel Basquiat 1981: The Studio of the Street*, pp. 8–13. Milan: Charta and New York: Deitch Projects, 2007.

—'Why the Dogs Are Barking', *Keith Haring*, pp. 17–20. New York: Tony Shafrazi Gallery, 1982.

Demers, Jeanne, *Graffiti et loi 101*. Montreal: VLB, 1989.

—Josée Lambert and Line McMurray, *Montreal graffiti*. Montreal: VLB, 1987.

Deutsche, Rosalyn, *Evictions: Art and Spatial Politics*. Cambridge (Mass.): MIT Press, 1996.

—'Public Art and Its Uses', in Harriet F. Senie and Sally Webster (eds), *Critical Issues in Public Art: Content, Context, and Controversy*, pp. 158–70. New York: Icon Editions, 1992.

—'The Question of "Public Space"', 1998. Paper presented at the 8th Annual American Photography Institute National Graduate Seminar: www.thephotographyinstitute.org/journals/1998/rosalyn_deutsche.html

Dimitriadis, Greg, *Performing Identity/Performing Culture: Hip Hop as Text, Pedagogy, and Lived Practice*. New York and Oxford: P. Lang, 2005.

Docuyanan, Faye Marie, *Inscribing at the Crossroads of Culture and Crime: Graffiti in Place and on Property in Urban Los Angeles*. PhD dissertation, University of California, Berkeley (Calif.), 2002.

Dolan, Jill, *Utopia in Performance: Finding Hope at the Theater*. Ann Arbor (Mich.): University of Michigan Press, 2005.

Doran, Anna, 'Swoon', *Time Out New York*, no. 512, 21–27 July 2005.

Doss, Erika, *Twentieth Century American Art*. Oxford: Oxford University Press, 2002.

Duncan, Carol, *Civilizing Rituals: Inside Public Art Museums*. London and New York: Routledge, 1995.

Duvignaud, Jean, *The Sociology of Art*, trans. by Timothy Wilson. New York: Harper & Row, 1973.

Edelman, Murray J., *From Art to Politics: How Artistic Creations Shape Political Conceptions*. Chicago (Ill.) and London: University of Chicago Press, 1995.

Eine, 'Eine', *Swindle Magazine*, issue 16: http://swindlemagazine.com/issue16/eine

Emmerling, Leonhard, *Basquiat*. Cologne and London: Taschen, 2003.

English, Ron: www.popaganda.com/blog1.php/about

Escobar, Ticio, 'Identity and Myth Today', in R. Araeen, S. Cubitt and Z. Sardar (eds), *The Third Text Reader on Art, Culture and Theory*, pp. 144–51. London and New York: Continuum, 2002.

Fairey, Shepard, 'Manifesto', 1990: http://obeygiant.com/about

—'Banksy', *Swindle Magazine*, issue 8: http://swindlemagazine.com/issue08/banksy

—'Space Invader', *Swindle Magazine*, issue 3: http://swindlemagazine.com/issue03/space-invader-2

Faith47, biography sent to author, 20 September 2010.

Fauquet, Joël-Marie, and Hennion, Antoine, *La grandeur de Bach: l'amour de la musique en France au XIXe siècle*. Paris: Fayard, 2000.

Ferrell, Jeff, *Crimes of Style: Urban Graffiti and the Politics of Criminality*. Boston (Mass.): Northeastern University Press, 1996.

Finkelpearl, Tom, 'Introduction: The City as Site', in Tom Finkelpearl (ed.), *Dialogues in Public Art*, pp. 52–60. Cambridge (Mass.): MIT Press, 2001.

Flannery, Claire, 'Art on the Road Fails to Appeal to Montreal Officialdom', *Circa Art Magazine*, 7 March 2005: www.recirca.com/artnews/396.shtml

Francis, Richard, *Jasper Johns*. New York: Abbeville Press, 1984.

Fraser, Marie, 'Sur l'expérience de la ville', in Marie Fraser, Diane Gougeon and Marie Perrault (eds), *Sur l'expérience de la ville: interventions en milieu urbain*, pp. 13–42. Montreal: Optica, 1999.

—and Marie-Josée Lafortune, *Artists' Gestures*. Montreal: Optica, 2001.

Gablik, Suzi, *Has Modernism Failed?* London: Thames & Hudson, 1984.

Ganz, Nicholas, *Graffiti World: Street Art from Five Continents*. London: Thames & Hudson, 2004.

—*Graffiti Woman: Street Art from Five Continents*. London: Thames & Hudson, 2006.

Garcia, Brian Paul, *Conceptual Street Art as a Means of Democratic Participation*. PhD dissertation, University of Southern California, Los Angeles, 2006.

Gastman, Roger, Darin Rowland and Ian Sattler, *Freight Train Graffiti*. London: Thames & Hudson, 2006.

Gauthier, Louise, *Writing on the Run: The History and Transformation of Street Graffiti in Montreal in the 1990s*. PhD dissertation, New School for Social Research, New York, 1998.

Gavin, Francesca, *Street Renegades: New Underground Art*. London: Laurence King, 2007.

Gérin, Annie, and James S. McLean (eds), *Public Art in Canada: Critical Perspectives*. Toronto and London: University of Toronto Press, 2009.

Gibson, James J., *The Ecological Approach to Visual Perception*. Boston (Mass.): Houghton Mifflin, 1979.

Ginwright, Shawn A., *Black in School: Afrocentric Reform, Urban Youth, and the Promise of Hip-Hop Culture*. New York: Teachers College Press, 2004.

Gioni, Massimiliano, 'An Interview with Olu Oguibe', *Third Text*, no. 47, Summer 1999, pp. 51–57.

Goffman, Erving, *Asylums*. Harmondsworth: Penguin, 1968.

Gorsek, Christopher Stanley, *The Effect of Informal Social Control on the Presence and Geographic Distribution of Graffiti on City Streets*. PhD dissertation, Portland State University (Oreg.), 2004.

Gottlieb, Lisa, 'Graffiti Art and Facet Analysis', *Graffiti Art Styles: a Classification System and Theoretical Analysis*, pp. 63–64. Jefferson (NC): McFarland, 2008.

Grody, Steve, *Graffiti L.A.: Street Styles and Art*. New York: Abrams, 2006.

Guevara, Nancy, 'Women Writin' Rappin' Breakin'', in William Eric Perkins (ed.), *Droppin' Science: Critical Essays on Rap Music and Hip Hop Culture*, pp. 49–62. Philadelphia (Pa.): Temple University Press, 1996.

Habermas, Jürgen, 'The Public Sphere: An Encyclopedia Article (1964)', *New German Critique*, vol. 1, no. 3, 1974, pp. 49–55.

Hager, Steven, 'Afrika Bambaataa's Hip-Hop', in Raquel Cepeda (ed.), *And It Don't Stop: The Best American Hip-Hop Journalism of the Last 25 Years*, pp. 12–26. New York: Faber and Faber, 2004.

—*Hip Hop: The Illustrated History of Break Dancing, Rap Music, and Graffiti*. New York: St Martin's Press, 1984.

Hall, Stuart, 'Cultural Identity and Diaspora', in Nicholas Mirzoeff (ed.), *Diaspora and Visual Culture: Representing Africans and Jews*, pp. 21–33. London and New York: Routledge, 2000.

Hayden, Dolores, 'Claiming Urban Landscapes as Public History', *The Power of Place: Urban Landscapes as Public History*. Cambridge (Mass.) and London: MIT Press, 1995.

Hazzard-Donald, Katrina, 'Dance in Hip Hop Culture', in William Eric Perkins (ed.), *Droppin' Science: Critical Essays on Rap Music and Hip Hop Culture*, pp. 220–35. Philadelphia (Pa.): Temple University Press, 1996.

Hebdige, Dick, 'Posing…Threats, Striking…Poses: Youth, Surveillance, and Display', in Ken Gelder and Sarah Thornton (eds), *The Subcultures Reader*, pp. 288–99. London: Routledge. 1997.

—*Subculture: The Meaning of Style*. London: Methuen, 1979.

Hein, Hilde, *Public Art: Thinking Museums Differently*. Lanham (MD) and Oxford: Altamira Press, 2006.

—'What is Public Art?: Time, Place, and Meaning', *The Journal of Aesthetics and Art Criticism*, vol. 54, no. 1, Winter 1996, pp. 1–7.

Heinich, Nathalie, *La sociologie de l'art*, Collection Repères, no. 328. Paris: Editions La Découverte, 2004.

—*Le triple jeu de l'art contemporaine: sociologie des arts plastiques*. Paris: Minuit, 1998.

—and Pollack, Michael, 'From Museum Curator to Exhibition Auteur: Inventing a Singular Position', in Reesa Greenberg, Bruce W. Ferguson and Sandy Nairne (eds), *Thinking About Exhibitions*, pp. 231–50. London and New York: Routledge, 1996.

Heller, Scott, 'What Are They Doing to Art History?', in John C. McEnroe and Deborah F. Pokinski (eds), *Critical Perspectives on Art History*, pp. 289–95. Upper Saddle River (NJ): Prentice Hall, 2002.

Hennion, Antoine, *La passion musicale: une sociologie de la médiation*. Paris: Métailié, 1993.

Hetherington, Kevin, *Expressions of Identity: Space, Performance, Politics*. London and Thousand Oaks (Calif.): Sage, 1998.

'Hitotzuki': www.hitotzuki.com

Hoban, Phoebe, *Basquiat: A Quick Killing in Art*. New York: Viking, 1998.

Hochtritt, Lisa J., *Creating Meaning and Constructing Identity Through Collaborative Art Practices Among Urban Adolescents*. EdD dissertation, Columbia University Teachers College, New York, 2004.

Hoffmann, Jens, and Joan Jonas, *Perform*. London: Thames & Hudson, 2005.

Holmes, Pernilla, 'Report Card: Jean-Michel Basquiat', *Art Review*, vol. 53, no. 6, 2002, p. 77.

Hooper-Greenhill, Eilean, *Museums and the Interpretation of Visual Culture*. London: Routledge, 2000.

Hundertmark, Christian, *The Art of Rebellion 2: World of Urban Art Activism*. Mainaschaff: Publikat, 2006.

Iveson, Kurt, *Publics and the City*. Oxford and Malden (Mass.): Blackwell, 2007.

Januszczak, Waldemar, 'Blek le Rat, the Man Who Gave Birth to Banksy', *The Sunday Times*, June 2008.

Jenkins, Sacha, 'The Writing on the Wall: Graffiti Culture Crumbles into the Violence it Once Escaped', in Raquel Cepeda (ed.), *And It Don't Stop: The Best American Hip-hop Journalism of the Last 25 Years*, pp. 288–99. New York: Faber and Faber, 2004.

Jones, Sam, 'Spray Can Prankster Tackles Israel's Security Barrier', Guardian.co.uk, 5 August 2005: www.guardian.co.uk/world/2005/aug/05/israel.artsnews

JR, 'JR', 2005: http://jr-art.net

Kammen, Michael, *Visual Shock: A History of Art Controversies in American Culture*. New York: Knopf, 2006.

Kaplan, Flora E. S., 'Exhibitions as Communicative Media', in Eileen Hooper-Greenhill (ed.), *Museums, Media, Message*, pp. 37–57. London: Routledge, 1995.

Kaye, Nick, *Site-specific Art: Performance, Place, and Documentation*. London: Routledge, 2000.

Keyes, Cheryl L., *Rap Music and Street Consciousness*. Urbana (Ill.): University of Illinois Press, 2002.

Kiriakos, Iosifides, *Mural Art: Murals on Huge Public Surfaces around the World: From Graffiti to Trompe L'œil*. Mainaschaff, 2008.

Kitwana, Bakari, *The Hip Hop Generation: Young Blacks and the Crisis in African American Culture*. New York: Basic Civitas Books, 2002.

Kleiner, Fred S., and Christin J. Mamiya, *Gardner's Art Through the Ages: The Western Perspective*, 12th edition. Belmont (Calif.) and London: Thomson Wadsworth, 2006.

Knelman, Joshua, 'Graffiti Goes Six-figure Legit', *The Globe and Mail*, 4 August 2007.

Kosuth, Joseph, 'Public Text', in Florian Matzner (ed.), *Public Art: A Reader*, pp. 188–98. Ostfildern-Ruit: Hatje Cantz, 2004.

Krauss, Rosalind, *The Originality of the Avant-Garde and Other Modernist Myths*. Cambridge (Mass.) and London: MIT Press, 1985.

Kuball, Mischa, '"And, it's a Pleasure…"/The Laboratory of Public Space', in Florian Matzner (ed.), *Public Art: A Reader*, pp. 290–98. Ostfildern-Ruit: Hatje Cantz, 2004.

Kwon, Miwon, *One Place After Another: Site-Specific Art and Locational Identity*. Cambridge (Mass.) and London: MIT Press, 2002.

—'Public Art and Urban Identities', *European Institute for Progressive Cultural Policies (EIPCP) Multilingual Webjournal*: http://eipcp.net/transversal/0102/kwon/en

'Labrona (Canada)', Carmichael Gallery: http://carmichaelgallery.com/artists/labrona.shtml

Lachmann, Richard, 'Graffiti as Career and Ideology', *The American Journal of Sociology*, vol. 94, no. 2, 1988, pp. 229–50.

Lacy, Suzanne (ed.), 'Fractured Space', in Arlene Raven (ed.), *Art in the Public Interest*, pp. 287–301. Ann Arbor (Mich.) and London: UMI Research Press, 1989.

—*Mapping the Terrain: New Genre Public Art*. Seattle (Wash.): Bay Press, 1995.

—'Seeing Mud Houses', in Kym Pruesse (ed.), *Accidental Audience: Urban Interventions by Artists*, pp. 69–74. Toronto: off\site collective, 1999.

Lamarche, Bernard, 'Les artistes de la bonbonne à l'oeuvre – Le graffiti aux Foufs', 6 August 2002: www.ledevoir.com/2002/08/06/6603.html

Latour, Bruno, *Laboratory Life: The Construction of Scientific Facts*. Princeton (NJ): Princeton University Press, 1986.

—*La science en action: introduction à la sociologie des sciences*. Paris: Gallimard Folio, 1995.

Le Coroller, Franck, *Les graffeurs de Montréal: penser la mobilité dans la construction du social*. MSc dissertation, Université de Montréal, Montreal, 2004.

Lefebvre, Henri, *The Production of Space*. Oxford and Cambridge (Mass.): Blackwell, 1991.

—'Space: Social Product and Use Value', in J. W. Freiberg (ed.), *Critical Sociology: European Perspectives*, pp. 285–96. New York: Irvington Publishers and London: Wiley, 1979.

Lejtenyi, Patrick, 'Roadsworth Busted', *Mirror*, vol. 20, no. 25, 9–15 December 2004: www.montrealmirror.com/2004/120904/front.html

Lemoine, Stéphanie, and Julien Terral, *In situ: un panorama de l'art urbain de 1975 à nos jours*. Paris: Editions Alternatives, 2005.

Linker, Kate, 'Post-Graffiti', *Art Forum*, vol. 22, no. 3, 1984, p. 92.

Lippard, Lucy, 'Foreword to the 1998 Edition', in Eva Cockcroft, John Pitman Weber and James Cockcroft (eds), *Toward a People's Art: The Contemporary Mural Movement*. Albuquerque (N. Mex.): University of New Mexico Press, 1998.

—'Moving Targets/Moving out', in Arlene Raven (ed.), *Art in the Public Interest*, pp. 209–28. Ann Arbor (Mich.) and London: UMI Research Press, 1989.

Loar, Peggy, 'Pondering the Products of Propaganda: Art and Thought on the Periphery', *The Journal of Decorative and Propaganda Arts*, no. 16, 1990, pp. 40–53.

Lobel, Michael, *Image Duplicator: Roy Lichtenstein and the Emergence of Pop Art*. New Haven (Conn.) and London: Yale University Press, 2002.

Lucie-Smith, Edward, 'The Writing on the Wall', *Art Review*, vol. 48, no. 3, 1996, pp. 20–22.

McCormick, Kimberly A., 'Tag, you're it': A Critical Discourse Analysis of the Dominant Culture and Albuquerque's Graffiti Co-culture. PhD dissertation, University of New Mexico, Albuquerque (N. Mex.), 2004.

Macdonald, Nancy, *The Graffiti Subculture: Youth, Masculinity and Identity in London and New York*. New York: Palgrave Macmillan, 2002.

MacNaughton, Alex, *London Street Art*. Munich and London: Prestel, 2006.

MacPhee, Josh, *Stencil Pirates: A Global Study of the Street Stencil*. New York: Soft Skull Press, 2004.

Magana, Lainya, 'MISS VAN', *Juxtapoz*, no. 90, July 2008, pp. 66–79.

Mahsun, Carol Anne (ed.), *Pop Art: The Critical Dialogue*. Ann Arbor (Mich.) and London: UMI Research Press, 1989.

Mailer, Norman, 'The Faith of Graffiti', *Esquire*, vol. 81, no. 5, 1974, pp. 77–88.

Mamiya, Christin J., *Pop Art and Consumer Culture: American Super Market*. Austin (Tex.): University of Texas Press, 1992.

Manco, Tristan, *Stencil Graffiti*. London: Thames & Hudson, 2002.

—*Street Logos*. London: Thames & Hudson, 2004.

—*Street Sketchbook*. London: Thames & Hudson, 2007.

—*Street Sketchbook: Journeys*. London: Thames & Hudson, 2010.

—Lost Art and Caleb Neelon, *Graffiti Brasil*. London: Thames & Hudson, 2005.

Mark, Lisa Gabrielle, 'The Secret Life of the City', in Kym Pruesse (ed.), *Accidental Audience: Urban Interventions by Artists*, pp. 15–19. Toronto: off\site collective, 1999.

'Mars-1 + Jr, Herakut, Thomas Keeley, Louie Cordero, Ryohei Hase', *Juxtapoz*, no. 97, February 2009.

Martin, Randy, 'Artistic Citizenship, Introduction', in Mary Schmidt Campbell and Randy Martin (eds), *Artistic Citizenship: A Public Voice for the Arts*, pp. 1–22. New York and London: Routledge, 2006.

Martinez, Hugo, *Graffiti NYC*. Munich and London: Prestel, 2006.

Masboungi, Ariella, *Penser la ville par l'art contemporain*. Paris: Project Urbain/Editions de la Villette, 2003.

Merle, Florence, *The International Graffiti Movement: Mixed Metaphors and Aesthetic Disruption*. PhD dissertation, Princeton University, Princeton (NJ), 1998.

Miles, Malcolm, *Art, Space and the City: Public Art and Urban Futures*. London and New York: Routledge, 1997.

—*Cities and Cultures*. London and New York: Routledge, 2007.

—*Urban Avant-Gardes: Art, Architecture and Change*. London and New York: Routledge, 2004.

Miller, Ivor L., *Aerosol Kingdom: Subway Painters of New York City*. Jackson (Miss.): University Press of Mississippi, 2002.

Miller, Marc H. (narrator), *Graffiti, Post-Graffiti*, video recording from 'Art/New York' series, no. 21. New York: Inner-Tube Video, 1984.

Mirzoeff, Nicholas, *Bodyscape: Art, Modernity and the Ideal Figure*. London and New York: Routledge, 1995.

—*An Introduction to Visual Culture*. London and New York: Routledge, 1999.

Mitchell, Don, *The Right to the City: Social Justice and the Fight for Public Space*. New York: Guilford Press, 2003.

Mitchell, Tony (ed.), *Global Noise: Rap and Hip-Hop Outside the USA*. Middletown (Conn.): Wesleyan University Press, 2001.

Mitchell, W. J. T. (ed.), 'Introduction: Utopia and Critique', *Art and the Public Sphere*, pp. 1–5. Chicago and London: University of Chicago Press, 1992.

—'Showing Seeing: A Critique of Visual Culture', in Michael Ann Holly and Keith Moxey (eds), *Art History, Aesthetics, Visual Studies*, pp. 231–50. Williamstown (Mass.): Sterling and Francine Clark Art Institute, 2002.

Moore, Mandy, and Prain, Leanne, *Yarn Bombing: The Art of Crochet and Knit Graffiti*. Vancouver: Arsenal Pulp Press, 2009.

Naar, Jon, *The Birth of Graffiti*. Munich and London: Prestel, 2007.

Neelon, Caleb, 'Miss Van', Magda Danysz Gallery website: www.magda-gallery.com/ang/missvantexte.htm

—'Miss Van', *Swindle Magazine*, issue 9: http://swindlemagazine.com/issue09/miss-van

Nguyen, P., 'Alexandre "Vhils" Farto', *Juxtapoz*, no. 103, August 2009, pp. 62–75.

'Nina Pandolfo', Art Asylum Boston website: http://artasylumboston.wordpress.com/nina-pandolfo

Novakov, Anna (ed.), *Veiled Histories: The Body, Place, and Public Art*. New York: San Francisco Art Institute: Critical Press, 1997.

'Nuria Mora', *Subaquatica*, 4 November 2007: www.subaquatica.com/en/index.php/2007/11/04/nuria-mora

Oosterbaan, Warna, 'The Images of Visual Culture: Assumptions, Definitions, and Reality', in Frits Gierstberg and Warna Oosterbaan (eds), *The Image Society: Essays on Visual Culture*, pp. 11–21. Rotterdam: NAi Publishers, 2002.

Pearlman, Alison, *Unpacking Art of the 1980s*. Chicago (Ill.): University of Chicago Press, 2003.

Pereira, Sandrine, *Graffiti*. Paris: Fitway, 2005.

Perkins, William Eric, 'The Rap Attack: An Introduction', in William Eric Perkins (ed.), *Droppin' Science: Critical Essays on Rap Music and Hip Hop Culture*, pp. 1–45. Philadelphia (Pa.): Temple University Press, 1996.

Perry, Imani, *Prophets of the Hood: Politics and Poetics in Hip Hop*. Durham (NC): Duke University Press, 2004.

Perullo, Alex, and John Fenn, 'Language Ideologies, Choices, and Practices in Eastern African Hip Hop', in Harris M. Berger and Michael Thomas Carroll (eds), *Global Pop, Local Language*, pp. 19–53. Jackson (Miss.): University Press of Mississippi, 2003.

Pez, interview with author, 15 October 2007.

Phelan, Peggy, in Lynda Hart and Peggy Phelan (eds), *Acting Out: Feminist Performances*. Ann Arbor (Mich.): University of Michigan Press, 1993.

Philby, Charlotte, 'Blek le Rat: This is not a Banksy', *The Independent*, 19 April 2008.

Phillips, Susan, *Wallbangin': Graffiti and Gangs in L.A.* Chicago (Ill.) and London: University of Chicago Press, 1999.

Pough, Gwendolyn D., *Check it While I Wreck it: Black Womanhood, Hip Hop Culture, and the Public Sphere*. Boston (Mass.): Northeastern University Press, 2004.

Powers, Stephen, *The Art of Getting Over: Graffiti at the Millennium*. New York: St Martin's Press, 1999.

Pricco, Evan, 'Conor Harrington: "The Next Big Thing"', *Juxtapoz.*, no. 93, October 2008, pp. 54–67.

Prigoff, James, foreword in Steve Grody, *Graffiti L.A.: Street Styles and Art*. New York: Abrams, 2006.

Proctor, Lenore Feltman, *Graffiti Writers: An Exploratory Personality Study*. PsyD dissertation, Pace University, New York, 1991.

Prou, Sybille, and King Adz, *Blek Le Rat: Getting Through the Walls*. London: Thames & Hudson, 2008.

Pruesse, Kym (ed.), *Accidental Audience: Urban Interventions by Artists*. Toronto: off\site collective, 1999.

Quinones, Lee George, *New Horizons*. London: Riverside Studios, 1985.

Rahn, Janice, *Painting without Permission: Hip-Hop Graffiti Subculture*. Westport (Conn.) and London: Bergin & Garvey, 2002.

Reiss, Jon, 'Blek le Rat', *Swindle Magazine*, issue 11: http://swindlemagazine.com/issue11/blek-le-rat

Ricard, Rene, 'The Radiant Child', *Art Forum*, vol. 20, no. 12, 1981, pp. 35–43.

Roadsworth, interview with author, 12 October 2007.

Roberge, Marie, *L'art sous les bombes*. Outremont (Quebec): Lanctôt éditeur, 2004.

Romanik, Barbara, *Graffiti (legal wall slashin')*. MA dissertation, University of New Brunswick, Canada, 2004.

Rose, Tricia, *Black Noise: Rap Music and Black Culture in Contemporary America*. Middletown (Conn.): Wesleyan University Press, 1994.

Rosenblum, Robert, 'Pop Art and Non-Pop Art', in Steven Henry Madoff (ed.), *Pop Art: A Critical History*. Berkeley (Calif.) and London: University of California Press, 1997.

Roth, Evan, 'Graffiti Analysis': http://evan-roth.com/graffiti_analysis/ga_about.html

—'Graffiti Taxonomy': http://evan-roth.com/graf_taxonomy/graf_tax_01.php

Rushing, Rebecca, *Illegal Expression*. MS dissertation, Utah State University, Logan (Ut.), 2000.

Saul, Julie, 'Post-Graffiti, Sidney Janis Gallery', *Flash Art*, vol. 116, no. 3, 1984, pp. 38–39.

Sayeg, Magda: www.magdasayeg.com/about_knitta_please_magda_sayeg.html

Schiller, Marc, 'Swoon', *Swindle Magazine*, issue 4: http://swindlemagazine.com/issue04/swoon

Schwartz, Brie, 'Artist Draws Attention to Bethlehem', CNN.com, 12 December 2007: www.cnn.com/2007/WORLD/meast/12/03/banksy.bethlehem

Semple, Kirk, 'Lawbreakers, Armed with Paint and Paste: Underground Artists Take to the Streets', *The New York Times*, 9 July 2004: http://query.nytimes.com/gst/fullpage.html?res=9400E0DC133BF93AA35754C0A9629C8B63

Shields, Rob, 'Intersections in Cultural Policy: Geographic, Socioeconomic and Other Markers of Identity', *Canadian Ethnic Studies Journal*, vol. 35, no. 3, 2004, pp. 150–64: http://findarticles.com/p/articles/mi_hb039/is_/ai_n29061365?tag=artBody;col1

—*Places on the Margin: Alternative Geographies of Modernity*. London and New York: Routledge, 1991.

Sholette, Gregory G., 'Interventionism and the historical uncanny…Or: can there be revolutionary art without the revolution?', in Nato Thompson and Gregory Sholette (eds), *The Interventionists: Users' Manual for the Creative Disruption of Everyday Life*, pp. 133–43. Cambridge (Mass.) and London: MIT Press, 2004.

Siddiqui, Jasmin, and Falk Lehmann, *Herakut: The Perfect Merge*. Publikat, 2008.

Simpson, Charles R., *SoHo: The Artist in the City*. Chicago (Ill.): University of Chicago Press, 1981.

Sloan, Johanne, 'At Home on the Street: Public Art in Montreal and Toronto', in Johanne Sloan (ed.), *Urban Enigmas: Montreal, Toronto, and the Problem of Comparing Cities*, pp. 213–38. Montreal: McGill-Queen's University Press, 2007.

Smallman, Jake, and Carl Nyman, *Stencil Graffiti Capital: Melbourne*. New York: Mark Batty Publisher, 2005.

Snyder, Gregory J., *An Ethnography of Post-Subway Graffiti in New York City and the Formation of Subculture Careers*. PhD dissertation, The New School, New York, 2003.

Soteriou, Helen, 'Exclusive Interview: Blek le Rat on Homelessness', *Juxtapoz*: www.juxtapoz.com/Features/exclusive-interview-blek-le-rat-on-homelessness

'Space Invaders' for Atari 2600 (1980), Mobygames.com: http://mobygames.com/game/space-invaders-

Spicer, Valerie, *Couch Surfing in Vancouver: An Aggregate Study of the Vancouver Graffiti Suspect Network*. MA dissertation, Simon Fraser University, Canada, 2005.

Stewart, Jack, *Subway Graffiti: An Aesthetic Study of Graffiti on the Subway System of New York City, 1970–1978*. PhD dissertation, New York University, New York, 1989.

Sudbanthad, Pitchaya, 'New York, New York: Paper Faces, Paper Cities', *The Morning News*: www.themorningnews.org/archives/new_york_new_york/paper_faces_paper_cities.php

—'Personalities: Roundtable: Street Art', *The Morning News*: www.themorningnews.org/archives/personalities/roundtable_street_art.php

Sutherland, Peter, and Revs. *Autograph: New York City's Graffiti Writers*. New York: PowerHouse Books, 2004.

Swoon, interview with author, 25 October 2007.

Taylor, Gary, *Buying Whiteness: Race, Culture, and Identity from Columbus to Hip Hop*. New York: Palgrave Macmillan, 2005.

Thompson, Robert Farris, 'Hip Hop 101', in William Eric Perkins (ed.), *Droppin' Science: Critical Essays on Rap Music and Hip Hop Culture*, pp. 211–19. Philadelphia (Pa.): Temple University Press, 1996.

Tokodi, Edina, 'The A's To Our Q's: Edina Tokodi (aka Mosstika)', 16 November 2008. Interview by Wooster Collective: http://www.woostercollective.com/2008/11/16-week

Tschinkel, Paul, and Marc H. Miller (directors), *Jean-Michel Basquiat: An Interview*, video recording from 'Art/New York' series, no. 30A. Interview by Marc H. Miller. New York: Inner-Tube Video, 1982.

Turley, Alan C., *Urban Culture: Exploring Cities and Cultures*. Upper Saddle River (NJ): Pearson/Prentice Hall, 2005.

Turner, Victor, 'Are There Universals of Performance in Myth, Ritual, and Drama?', in Richard Schechner and Willa Appel (eds), *By Means of Performance: Intercultural Studies of Theatre and Ritual*, pp. 8–18. Cambridge: Cambridge University Press, 1990.

—*Dramas, Fields, and Metaphors: Symbolic Action in Human Society*. Ithaca (NY) and London: Cornell University Press, 1974.

—*The Ritual Process: Structure and Anti-Structure*. Chicago (Ill.): Aldine Publishing Company, 1969.

Varnedoe, Kirk, and Adam Gopnik, *High & Low: Modern Art, Popular Culture*. New York: Museum of Modern Art, 1990.

Verena, 'Zevs: Visual Kidnapping', *PingMag*, 11 August 2008: http://pingmag.jp/2008/08/11/zevs-visual-kidnapping

Vergo, Peter, 'The Reticent Object', in Peter Vergo (ed.), *The New Museology*, pp. 41–59. London: Reaktion, 1989.

Vexta, interviews with author, 28 January and 18 March 2008.

Wacławek, Anna, *Exhibiting Hip-Hop Graffiti*. MA dissertation, University of Sydney, Australia, 2003.

Walde, Claudia, *Sticker City: Paper Graffiti Art*. London and New York: Thames & Hudson, 2007.

Walker, Nick: www.theartofnickwalker.com/biog

Walsh, Michael, *Graffito*. Berkeley (Calif.): North Atlantic Books, 1996.

Weizman, Eyal, 'Strategic Points, Flexible Lines, Tense Surfaces, Political Volumes: Ariel Sharon and the Geometry of Occupation', *The Philosophical Forum*, vol. 35, no. 2, Summer 2004, pp. 221–44.

Wilson, Elizabeth, 'Against Utopia: The Romance of Indeterminate Spaces', in Amy Bingaman, Lise Sanders and Rebecca Zorach (eds), *Embodied Utopias: Gender, Social Change and the Modern Metropolis*, pp. 256–63. London and New York: Routledge, 2002.

Witz, Dan, *Dan Witz: In Plain View: 30 Years of Artworks Illegal and Otherwise*. Berkeley (Calif.): Gingko Press, 2010.

—'Q&A with Dan Witz', *Vandalog*, 22 June 2010: www.danwitz.com/index.php?article_id=394

Wright, Andrew Jeffery, 'Barry McGee; TWIST', *Swindle Magazine*, issue 14: http://swindlemagazine.com/issue14/barry-mcgee

Yapondjian, Maria Arshalouis, *Using the Four Elements of Hip-Hop as a Form of Self-expression in Urban Adolescents*. PsyD dissertation, University of Hartford (Conn.), 2005.

Ziffer, Daniel, 'Illegals Come in From the Cold', on Theage.com.au, 6 October 2004: www.theage.com.au/articles/2004/10/05/1096949485055.html

Zijlmans, Kitty, 'One Image is not Like Another: Art History and Current Visual Culture', in Frits Gierstberg and Warna Oosterbaan (eds), *The Image Society: Essays on Visual Culture*, pp. 69–77. Rotterdam: NAi Publishers, 2002.

Zolberg, Vera L., *Constructing a Sociology of the Arts*. Cambridge and New York: Cambridge University Press, 1990.

Notes and Sources of Quotations

p. 7 The Tate Modern exhibition, simply entitled 'Street Art', ran from 23 May until 25 August 2008 and brought together the work of Blu, JR, Faile, Sixeart, Os Gêmeos and Nunca.

p. 70, quote: http://swindlemagazine.com/issue11/blek-le-rat

p. 75, quote: http://obeygiant.com/about

p. 77, quote: http://swindlemagazine.com/issue16/eine

p. 80, quote: interview with author

p. 83, quote: http://ideaseek.blogspot.com/2007/10/brazilian-street-artist-nunca.html

p. 86, quotes: interview with author

p. 88, quote: www.danwitz.com/index.php?article_id=394

p. 95, quote: http://evan-roth.com/graf_taxonomy/graf_tax_01.php

p. 95, quote: http://evan-roth.com/graffiti_analysis/ga_about.html

p. 96, quote: interview with author

p. 104, quotes: interview with author (18 March 2008)

p. 106, quote: interview with author (28 January 2008)

p. 107, quote: www.theartofnickwalker.com/biog

p. 118, quote: interview with author

p. 119, quote: www.subaquatica.com/en/index.php/2007/11/04/nuria-mora

p. 124 The premise of *Space Invaders* (the game) is as follows: 'Earth is under attack from rows of bomb dropping aliens, and you need to defend it! Your goal is to earn points by shooting the aliens before they can land.' 'Space Invaders' for Atari 2006 (1980), MobyGames, www.mobygames.com/game/space-invaders-

p. 137, quote: www.dface.co.uk/why

p. 146, quote: http://artasylumboston.wordpress.com/nina-pandolfo

p. 151, quote: www.carmichaelgallery.com/artists/labrona.shtml

p. 154, quote: www.urbanartcore.eu/vhils-act-of-destruction

p. 163, quote: www.lazinc.com/artists/conor-harrington

p. 173, quote: www.buffmonster.com/bio.php

p. 174, Swoon quote: interview with author

p. 174, Vexta quote: interview with author (28 January 2008)

p. 174, Roadsworth quote: interview with author

p. 176, quote: http://swindlemagazine.com/issue04/swoon

p. 176 'The Swimming Cities of Switchback Sea' exhibition ran from 7 September to 19 October 2008 in Deitch Studios, 4–40 44th Drive, Long Island City, New York

p. 179, quote: interview with author

p. 182 See 'The World Gouzous', http://reunion.runweb.com/lang-EN-page-1114-2V-page,Welcome-to-the-world-of-Gouzous.html

p. 189, quote: http://pingmag.jp/2008/08/11/zevs-visual-kidnapping

p. 192, Roadsworth quote: interview with author

p. 192, Vexta quote: interview with author (28 January 2008)

List of Illustrations

p. 2 Nick Walker, *Ratatouille*, New York City, USA, 2008. Courtesy of the artist. **1** Baker, *Untitled*, 2008. Courtesy of the artist. **2** Above, *Because Now I'm Worth It*, Paris, France, 2010. Courtesy of the artist. **3** Thundercut, *Thundercut*, New York City, USA, 2004. Courtesy of the artists. **4** Puppet, *Graffiti Girl*, 'Classics' series, Spain, 2009. Courtesy of the artist. **5** Cool Earl and Cornbread, Philadelphia, 1960s. Courtesy of Roman Cybriwsky. **6** D*Face, *Dog Tag*, Ecuador, 2010. Courtesy of the artist. **7** Puppet, Sweden, 2011. Courtesy of the artist. **8** Evan Roth, *Graffiti Analysis*, 'Media Facades Festival', Berlin, Germany, 2010. Courtesy of Ruthi Zuntz. **9** Kero, Berlin, Germany, 2007. Courtesy of the artist. **10** Chas, Kumasi, Ghana, 2011. Rollerpaint and spray-paint, c. 2 m (6½ ft) high by 4 m (13 ft) wide. Courtesy of the artist. **11** MadC, Leipzig, Germany, 2009. Spray-paint on brick wall. **12** Zephyr and Noc167, New York City, USA. Courtesy of Henry Chalfant. **13** Kero, *lavidalooka*, Bilbao, Spain, 2010. Courtesy of the artist. **14** Puppet, *Golden Times*, Sweden, 2009. Courtesy of the artist. **15** D*Face, *Concrete Can*, London, UK, 2008. Courtesy of the artist. **16** Baker, 2007. Courtesy of the artist. **17** Baker, 2008. Courtesy of the artist. **18** Baker, 2008. Courtesy of the artist. **19** Baker, 2008. Courtesy of the artist. **20** Vexta, Bogotá, Colombia, 2009. Courtesy of Hogar. **21** Demer, Col and Kasso, New Jersey, USA, 2010. Courtesy of Demer. **22** Dan Witz, *Untitled*, 'Skateboarders Are Graffiti' series, New York City, USA, 2005. Courtesy of the artist. **23** Eine, *Sell the House, the Kids, the Wife, It's Bonus Time* (detail), London, UK, 2010. Courtesy of the artist. **24** Shepard Fairey, *Power & Equality*. Courtesy of the artist/ObeyGiant.com. **25** Fafi, *Untitled*, Mexico City, Mexico, 2010. Courtesy of the artist. **26** Shepard Fairey, *Duality of Humanity*, c. 2008. Courtesy of Geoff Hargadon. **27** Banksy, *Untitled*, Israel, 2007. Courtesy of Pest Control Office. **28** Banksy, *Untitled*, Detroit, USA, 2010. Courtesy of Pest Control Office. **29** Roadsworth, *Male Plug*, Baie-Saint-Paul, Canada, 2007. Courtesy of the artist. **30** Vexta, *Neon Bird*, Bogotá, Colombia, 2009. Courtesy of the artist. **31** Jace, *Untitled*, Réunion Island, 2008. Courtesy of the artist. **32** Pez and Flying Fortress, *Ams Dragons*, Amsterdam, Netherlands, 2010. Courtesy of Pez. **33** Invader, *Untitled*, New York City, USA. 2007. Courtesy of the artist. **34** Swoon, *Temple and Alixa and Naima*, Tokyo, Japan, 2009. Courtesy of the artist. **35** Miss Van, *Mascaras 8*, 2010. Courtesy of the artist. **36** Mosstika, *Dumbo*, New York City, USA, 2008. Courtesy of the artist. **37** Os Gêmeos, *The Youth Are No Longer Young*. Courtesy of the artists. **38** Puppet, *Blue Graffiti With B-boy*, 'Classics' series, Germany, 2009. Courtesy of the artist. **39** Banksy, *Untitled*, London, UK, 2009. Courtesy of Pest Control Office. **40** Swet. Courtesy of the artist. **41** Does, Bondi Beach, Sydney, Australia, 2010. Spray-paint. Courtesy of the artist. **42** Kies, Santa Pola, Spain, 2010. 2.5 m (8 ft) high by 6 m (20 ft) wide. Courtesy of the artist. **43** Dondi, *Children of the Grave Return, Part 2*, New York City, USA, 1980. Courtesy of Henry Chalfant. **44** New York subway, USA, 1972. © AP/Press Association Images. **45** New York subway, USA, 1972. © AP/Press Association Images. **46** Kase2 and El Kay, New York City, USA, 1981. Courtesy of Henry Chalfant. **47** Lee, *Sherlock*, New York City, USA, 1978. Courtesy of Henry Chalfant. **48** Crash, New York City, USA. Courtesy of Henry Chalfant. **49** Blade and Comet, New York City, USA. Courtesy of Henry Chalfant. **50** Slider, *Bandits 4 Life*, Dresden, Germany, 2010. 3 m (10 ft) high by 15 m (49 ft) wide. Courtesy of the artist. **51** Banksy, *Untitled*, London, UK, 2009. Courtesy of Pest Control Office. **52** Keith Haring, New York City, USA, 1983. © Laura Levine/Corbis. **53** Conor Harrington, *Surveillance*, London, UK, 2009. Courtesy of Ian Cox. **54** Blek le Rat, *Computerland*, Paris, France, 2007. Courtesy of Sybille Prou. **55** Thundercut, *Out of Here*, New York City, USA. 2006. Courtesy of Mark Jenkins. **56** Blek le Rat, *The Man Who Walks Through Walls*, London, UK, 2008. Courtesy of Sybille Prou. **57** Blek le Rat, *Napoleon and his Sheep*, Paris, France, 2003. Courtesy of Sybille Prou. **58** Blek le Rat, *Florence Aubenas*, Paris, France, 2005. Courtesy of Sybille Prou. **59** Blek le Rat, *Homeless in San Francisco*, California, USA, 2010. Courtesy of Sybille Prou. **60** Magda Sayeg, *Untitled*, Paris, France,

2007. Courtesy of Bergere de France. **61** Magda Sayeg. Courtesy of the artist. **62** Magda Sayeg, *Untitled*, Texas, USA, 2010. Courtesy of Denise Prince. **63** Magda Sayeg, *Untitled*, Tilburg, Netherlands, 2008. Courtesy of the artist. **64** Magda Sayeg, *Untitled*, New York City, USA, 2008. Courtesy of Dan Fergus. **65** Shepard Fairey, *Untitled*. Courtesy of the artist/ObeyGiant.com. **66** Shepard Fairey, *Giant Cured All My Obedience Problems*. Courtesy of the artist/ObeyGiant.com. **67** Zevs, *Public Bench*, 'Electric Shadows' series, Paris, France, 2000. Courtesy of the artist. **68** Zevs, *Subway*, 'Electric Shadows' series, Paris, France, 2000. Courtesy of the artist. **69** Eine, *Anti Anti Anti*, London, UK, 2010. Courtesy of the artist. **70** Eine, *Happy*, London, UK, 2010. Courtesy of the artist. **71** Koralie, *Untitled*, Paris, France, 2010. Courtesy of Mr Eone. **72** Faith47, *All Shall Be Equal Before the Law*, Eastern Cape, South Africa, 2009. Courtesy of the artist. **73** Faith47, *A Silent Nation*, Cape Town, South Africa, 2008. Courtesy of the artist. **74** Faith47, *The Hunted*, São Paulo, Brazil, 2010. Courtesy of the artist. **75** Faith47, *The People Shall Share in the Country's Wealth*, Cape Town, South Africa, 2010. Courtesy of the artist. **76** Nunca. Courtesy of the artist. **77** Alexandre Órion, *Metabiotica 05*, São Paulo, Brazil, 2003. Courtesy of the artist. **78** Mariusz Waras aka M-City, *M-City 233*, Florence, Italy, 2009. Courtesy of the artist. **79** Swoon, *Portrait of Silvia Elena*, San Francisco, USA, 2008. Courtesy of the artist. **80** Swoon, *Girl from Ranoon Province*, Philadelphia, USA, 2010. Courtesy of the artist. **81** Dan Witz, *Untitled*, 'Birds 2000' series, New York City, USA, 2000. Courtesy of the artist. **82** Dan Witz, *Untitled*, 'In Plain View' series, New York City, USA, 2009. Courtesy of the artist. **83** Dan Witz, *Untitled*, 'Ugly New Buildings' series, New York City, USA, 2008. Courtesy of the artist. **84** Thundercut, *Tourist Walker*, New York City, USA, 2009. Courtesy of the artists. **85** Thundercut, *Graph Walker*, New York City, USA, 2008. Courtesy of Thomas Moore. **86** Blek le Rat, *Untitled*, Arizona, USA, 2007. Courtesy of Sybille Prou. **87** Mosstika, *Coney Island Moss*, New York City, USA, 2008. Courtesy of the artist. **88** Mosstika, *Brooklyn Moss Rabbit*, New York City, USA, 2009. Courtesy of the artist. **89** Mosstika, *Wunderbaum*, New York City, USA, 2009. Courtesy of the artist. **90** Mosstika, *Metro*, New York City, USA, 2008. Courtesy of the artist. **91** Faile, *Untitled*, New York City, USA, 2010. Courtesy of the artists. **92** Faile, *Save Your Stilettos, Faile's a Comin'*, New York City, USA, 2010. Courtesy of the artists. **93** Evan Roth, *Graffiti Taxonomy: 'S'*, New York City, USA, 2004. Courtesy of the artist. **94** Evan Roth, *Graffiti Analysis: 'Hell'*, New York City, USA, 2005. Courtesy of the artist. **95** Buff Monster, *Untitled*, Los Angeles, USA, 2010. Courtesy of the artist. **96** Shepard Fairey, *Zapatista Woman*. Courtesy of the artist/ObeyGiant.com. **97** Koralie and Supakitch, *Untitled*, San Sebastián, Spain, 2007. Courtesy of Koralie. **98** Koralie, *Untitled*, San Sebastián, Spain, 2007. Courtesy of the artist. **99** Miss Van, *Untitled*, Barcelona, Spain, 2006. Courtesy of the artist. **100** Koralie and Fafi, *Untitled*, New York City, USA, 2008. Courtesy of Koralie. **101** Alexandre Órion, *Metabiotica 3*, São Paulo, Brazil, 2004. Courtesy of the artist. **102** Alexandre Órion, *Metabiotica 14*, São Paulo, Brazil, 2004. Courtesy of the artist. **103** Alexandre Órion, *Metabiotica 18*, São Paulo, Brazil, 2005. Courtesy of the artist. **104** Psalm, *Bedtime for the Workaholic*, Melbourne, Australia, 2005. Courtesy of the artist. **105** Vexta, *We Are Creatures of the Wind*, Bogotá, Colombia, 2009. Courtesy of Hogar. **106** Vexta, *Ghetto Make-out*, Melbourne, Australia, 2009. Courtesy of the artist. **107** Vexta, *Welcome to Australia*, Melbourne, Australia, 2004. Courtesy of Joe Armao. **108** Nick Walker, *The Empire's State*, 'The Morning After' series, 2008. Courtesy of the artist. **109** Nick Walker, *Chihuahua*, Los Angeles, USA, 2009. Courtesy of the artist. **110** Nick Walker, *Brat*, California, USA, 2009. Courtesy of the artist. **111** Nick Walker, Rome, Italy, 2009. Courtesy of the artist. **112** D*Face, *I Need A Riot*, London, UK, 2010. Courtesy of the artist. **113** Dan Witz, *Untitled*, 'WHAT THE %$#@ (WTF)' series, New York City, USA, 2010. Courtesy of the artist. **114** Omen, *Untitled*, Montreal, Canada, 2009. Courtesy of omen514.com. **115** Ron English, *Udderly Unique*, San Francisco, USA, 2005. Courtesy of the artist. **116** JR, *Wrinkles of the City*, Cartagena, Spain, 2010. Courtesy of the artist. **117** Mariusz Waras aka M-City, *M-City 104*, Gdynia, Poland, 2007. Courtesy of the artist. **118** Roadsworth, *Asphalt Fetish*, Montreal, Canada, 2004. Courtesy of the artist. **119** Roadsworth, *Bullets for Oil*, Montreal, Canada, 2001. Courtesy of the artist. **120** Roadsworth, *Attention All Drivers*, Montreal, Canada, 2004. Courtesy of the artist. **121** Roadsworth, *Asphalt Glory*, Montreal, Canada, 2004. Courtesy of the artist. **122** Roadsworth, *Fall Leaves*, Toronto, Canada, 2008. Courtesy of the artist. **123** Nuria Mora and El Tono, *Untitled*, Arraial d'Ajuda, Brazil, 2001. Courtesy of Nuria Mora. **124** Nuria Mora, *Untitled*, Madrid, Spain, 2010. Courtesy of the artist. **125** Nuria Mora, 'Estrella de Mar' project, Johannesburg, South Africa, 2010. Courtesy of the artist. **126** Microbo, *Untitled*, Belfast, Northern Ireland, 2010. Courtesy of the artist. **127** Microbo, *Untitled*, Bizerte, Tunisia, 2009. Courtesy of the artist. **128** Microbo, *Chi C'è C'è*, Milan, Italy, 2009. Courtesy of the artist. **129** Jace, *Untitled*, Kuala Lumpur, Malaysia, 2009. Courtesy of the artist. **130** Invader, *Untitled*, Los Angeles, USA, 2006. Courtesy of the artist. **131** Invader, *Untitled*, New York City, USA, 2003. Courtesy of the artist. **132** Invader, *Untitled*, Nice, France, 2007. Courtesy of the artist. **133** Invader, *Untitled*, Mombasa, Kenya, 2005. Courtesy of the artist.

134 Herakut, *You Were My Greatest But Most Painful Love*, 2010. Courtesy of the artists, **135** Herakut, *You Teach What You Live*, 2007. Courtesy of the artists. **136** Herakut, *They Hate Me Just Because I'm Golden*, 2010. Courtesy of the artists. **137** Herakut, *Art Doesn't Help People...*, Lüneburg, Germany, 2009. Courtesy of the artists. **138** Moose, *Untitled*, California, USA, 2008. Courtesy of Laura Morton. **139** Moose, *Untitled*, New Orleans, USA, 2009. Courtesy of the artist. **140** Moose, *Untitled*, Liverpool, UK, 2006. Courtesy of the artist. **141** Moose, *Untitled*, Košice, Slovakia, 2009. Courtesy of the artist. **142** Alexandre Órion, *Ossário*, Max Feffer Tunnel, São Paulo, Brazil, 2006. Courtesy of the artist. **143** Alexandre Órion, *Ossário*, Ayrton Senna Tunnel, São Paulo, Brazil, 2006. Courtesy of the artist. **144** Banksy, *Untitled*, Dungeness, UK, 2010. Courtesy of Pest Control Office. **145** Above, *Arrow House*, California, USA, 2006. Courtesy of the artist. **146** Above, *Holy/Land*, Istanbul, Turkey, 2006. Courtesy of the artist. **147** Above, *Help Thy Neighbor*, Cuba, 2010. Courtesy of the artist. **148** D*Face, *D*Dog*, Ecuador, 2010. Courtesy of the artist. **149** D*Face, *Call In Sick*, London, UK, 2008. Courtesy of the artist. **150** Fake, *Fake Love*, Amsterdam, Netherlands, 2010. Courtesy of the artist. **151** Fake, *Painting God and Canbird*, Amsterdam, Netherlands, 2009. Courtesy of Hans Hendriks. **152** Fake, *Hopscotch*, Bristol, UK, 2009. Courtesy of the artist. **153** Labrona, *Street Hugs*, Montreal, Canada, 2010. Courtesy of the artist. **154** JR, *Face2Face*, West Bank barrier, 2007. Courtesy of the artist. **155** JR, *Women*, Nairobi, Kenya, 2008. Courtesy of the artist. **156** JR, *Women*, Rio de Janeiro, Brazil, 2008. Courtesy of the artist. **157** JR, *Wrinkles of the City*, Shanghai, China, 2010. Courtesy of the artist. **158** Omen, *Untitled*, Montreal, Canada, 2009. Courtesy of omen514.com. **159** Nina Pandolfo, *Untitled*, Mumbai, India, 2008. Courtesy of the artist. **160** Nina Pandolfo, *Untitled*, Miami, USA, 2009. Courtesy of the artist. **161** Banksy, *Untitled*, West Bank barrier, 2005. Courtesy of Pest Control Office. **162** Banksy, *Untitled*, West Bank barrier, 2005. Courtesy of Pest Control Office. **163** Banksy, *Untitled*, West Bank barrier, 2005. Courtesy of Pest Control Office. **164** Labrona, *Freight Train North America*, 2010. Courtesy of the artist. **165** Labrona, *Green Hugs*, Montreal, Canada, 2010. Courtesy of the artist. **166** Alexandre Farto aka Vhils, *Scratching the Surface*, London, UK, 2008. Courtesy of the artist. **167** Alexandre Farto aka Vhils, *Scratching the Surface*, Grottaglie, Italy, 2009. Courtesy of the artist. **168** Alexandre Farto aka Vhils, *Empty Faces*, Seixal, Portugal, 2007. Courtesy of the artist. **169** Alexandre Farto aka Vhils, *Viva la Revolución*, California, USA, 2009. Courtesy of Geoff Hargadon. **170** Alexandre Farto aka Vhils, *Scratching the Surface*, Grottaglie, Italy, 2009. Courtesy of the artist. **171** Swoon, *Alixa and Naima*, USA, 2009. Courtesy of the artist. **172** Microbo, *Untitled*, Catania, Italy, 2010. Courtesy of the artist. **173** Mariusz Waras aka M-City, *M-City 128*, Berlin, Germany, 2007. Courtesy of the artist. **174** Thundercut, *Vote Walker*, New York City, USA, 2008. Courtesy of Thomas Moore. **175** Os Gêmeos. Courtesy of the artists. **176** Psalm, *Buddha*, Melbourne, Australia, 2005. Courtesy of the artist. **177** Psalm, *Angels*, Melbourne, Australia, 2002. Courtesy of the artist. **178** Psalm, *Roy*, Melbourne, Australia, 2004. Courtesy of the artist. **179** Conor Harrington, *Untitled*, New York City, USA, 2008. Courtesy of the artist. **180** Conor Harrington, *Untitled*, Tel Aviv, Israel, 2010. Courtesy of Andy Telling. **181** Conor Harrington, *Untitled*, Grottaglie, Italy, 2009. Courtesy of the artist. **182** Conor Harrington, *Untitled*, Grottaglie, Italy, 2008. Courtesy of Ciro Quaranta. **183** Hitotzuki, *Untitled*, Suzaka, Nagano, Japan, 2009. Courtesy of the artists. **184** Sasu, *To Remain Calm and Passionate*, Tokyo, Japan, 2009. Courtesy of the artist. **185** Kami, *Past Memories and Present Self*, Kyoto, Japan, 2007. Courtesy of the artist. **186** Banksy, *Untitled*, London, UK, 2008. Courtesy of Pest Control Office. **187** Fafi, *Untitled*, Paris, France, 2010. Courtesy of the artist. **188** Kero, Bilbao, Spain, 2007. Courtesy of the artist. **189** Buff Monster, *Untitled*, New Mexico, USA, c. 2005. Courtesy of the artist. **190** Buff Monster, *Untitled*, Hollywood, USA, c. 2005. Courtesy of the artist. **191** Buff Monster, *Untitled*, San Francisco, USA, 2006. Courtesy of the artist. **192** Miss Van, 'Lovestain', Stolen Space, London, UK, 2009. Courtesy of the artist. **193** Swoon, *Swimming Cities of Serenissima*, Adriatic Sea, 2009. Courtesy of Tod Seelie. **194** Swoon, 'Miss Rockaway', New York City, USA, 2007. Courtesy of the artist. **195** Jace, *Untitled*, Icaraí de Amontada, Brazil, 2008. Courtesy of the artist. **196** Jace, *Untitled*, Réunion Island, 2002. Courtesy of the artist. **197** Jace, *Untitled*, Réunion Island, 2007. Courtesy of the artist. **198** Mariusz Waras aka M-City, *M-City 123*, São Paulo, Brazil, 2007. Courtesy of the artist. **199** Mariusz Waras aka M-City, *M-City 181*, Lublin, Poland, 2008. Courtesy of the artist. **200** Herakut. Courtesy of the artists. **201** Zevs, *Invisible Graffiti*, Glyptotek Museum, Copenhagen, Denmark, 2008. Courtesy of the artist. **202** Zevs, *Graffiti Illumination*, Barcelona, Spain, 2010. Courtesy of the artist. **203** Zevs, *Flaming*, 'Proper Graffiti' series, Copenhagen, Denmark, 2008. Courtesy of the artist. **204** Zevs, *Nike Liquidated Logo*, Berlin, Germany, 2005. Courtesy of the artist. **205** Ron English, *Camel Jrs*, New York City, USA, 1992. Courtesy of the artist. **206** Ron English, *We Deceive, You Believe*, Colorado, USA, 2008. Courtesy of the artist. **207** Ron English, *Sugar Smack*, New York City, USA. 2010. Courtesy of the artist. **208** Above, *Looking 4 Ride...Anywhere*, Berlin, Germany, 2010. Courtesy of the artist. **209** Nick Walker, *Moona Lisa*, Norway, 2006. Courtesy of the artist. **p. 196** Faile. Courtesy of the artists.

Page numbers in *italic* refer to illustrations

2Hot 15
2Many 15

Above 133–6
  Arrow House 133–4, *134*
  Because Now I'm Worth It 8
  Help Thy Neighbor 135, *136*
  Holy/Land 134, *135*
  Looking 4 Ride…Anywhere *193*
Acconci, Vito 110
advertising, and graffiti 186, *187*, 189–91
Akut 127–9
  see also Herakut
animation narratives 169–70
'Anti Design Festival' (2010) *78*
anti-graffiti alliance, New York 50, 54
arrows 15, 19, 46, *47*, 133–4, *135*
art history, and graffiti 159–69, 192, *193*, *194*, 195
Asia 15
Aubenas, Florence 69, 71

Baker 23, *24*
  Untitled (2008) *6*
Banksy 8, 33–4, 147–9, 153
  Untitled (Detroit, 2010) 34, *34*
  Untitled (Dungeness, 2010) *132*
  Untitled (Israel, 2007) 33, *33*
  Untitled (London, 2008) *168*
  Untitled (London, 2009) 44, *44*, *57*
  Untitled (West Bank barrier, 2005) *148*, 149
Barbara62 48, *51*
Basquiat, Jean-Michel 60, 62–3

billboards *114*, 137
biting 28
blackbooks 22, *24*
Blade *52–3*, 179
Blef 15
Blek le Rat 70–1, 74
  Computerhead 67
  Florence Aubenas 69, 71
  Homeless in San Francisco 69, 71
  The Man Who Walks Through Walls 68, 71
  Napoleon and his Sheep 68, 71
  The Spaceout Cowboy 91
Blu 169
  Big Bang Big Boom 169
  Muto 169
brand designs by street artists 170–1
brand logos, sampling *188*, 189–91
Buff Monster 171, 173
  Untitled (Hollywood, c. 2005) *172*, 173
  Untitled (Los Angeles, 2010) 97
  Untitled (New Mexico, c. 2005) *172*, 173
  Untitled (San Francisco, 2006) 173, *173*
burners 18
Burnham, Scott 7

caps, spray-paint 20
cartoon characters 39
Caru 15
Case2 18
characters *11*, 24, 38–41, *125*, 137
Chas *17*
city as context 84–90
Col 27
Comet *52–3*

communication, visual *16*, 80–1, *82*, 96, 128
community representation 79–83
contrasting 92
Cool Earl 12, *12*
Cope2 15
Cornbread 12, *12*
Cortez, Diego 59
Crash 18, 49, *52–3*, 62
crews 26–7, *27*
crowns 46, *47*
culture jamming 189–91
Curtis, Paul 'Moose' 129–31

D*Face 136–7
  Call In Sick 136, *137*
  Concrete Can 22
  *D*Dog* 136, *137*
  Dog Tag 14
  I Need A Riot *111*
Daze 18, 62
decriminalization of graffiti 58–61
Deitch Studios, Long Island City 176
Demer 27
Does 46, *46*
Dondi 15, 49
  Children of the Grave Return, Part 2 48–9, *49*
drips 47
'Duality of Humanity' exhibition (2008) 32
Duro 18

eco-tagging 129–31
Eine 74, 76–8
  Anti Anti Anti *78*, 78
  Happy 78, *79*
  Sell the House, the Kids, the Wife, It's Bonus Time 29, *30*
Eins, Stefan 59
El Kay 49, *52–3*
El Tono, *Untitled* (Arraial d'Ajuda, 2001) *119*, 119

English, Ron
  Camel Jrs 189–90, *190*
  Sugar Smack 190, *191*
  Udderly Unique *114*
  We Deceive, You Believe 190, *191*
Eva62 14

Fafi 170–1, 173
  Untitled (Mexico City, 2010) 30, *31*
  Untitled (New York City, 2008) *100*
  Untitled (Paris, 2010) 170, *170*
Faile 92–3
  Save Your Stilettos, Faile's a Comin' 93, *94*
  Untitled (New York City, 2010) 93, *94*
Fairey, Shepard 74–5
  Andre the Giant 'Obey' image *31*, 74, *74*, 75
  Duality of Humanity 32, *32*
  Giant Cured All My Obedience Problems 75, *75*
  Power & Equality 30, *31*
  Zapatista Woman 97
Faith47 80
  All Shall Be Equal Before the Law 81, *81*
  The Hunted 81, *82*
  The People Shall Share in the Country's Wealth 81, *82*
  A Silent Nation 80–1, *82*
Fake 137
  Fake Love 137, *137*
  Hopscotch 138
  Painting God and Canbird 137, *138*
Falco 15
Farto, Alexandre see Vhils
Fashion Moda, New York 59
Flying Fortress, *Ams Dragons* 37
Fun Gallery, New York 59

galleries, and graffiti 58–61, 169, 174–8, 195
gangs and graffiti 43
going over 27–8
Goldsworthy, Andy 91, 110
Graffiti Research Lab (GRL) 15, 93, 95
Great & Bates 15

haloes 46, 47
handskills 22
Haring, Keith 61, 61, 62–3
Harrington, Conor 163–6
    Surveillance 64
    Untitled (Grottaglie, 2008) 165
    Untitled (Grottaglie, 2009) 164, 166
    Untitled (New York City, 2008) 163, 163
    Untitled (Tel Aviv, 2010) 164, 166
Hera 127–9
    see also Herakut
Herakut 127–9, 185
    Art Doesn't Help People 128, 128
    They Hate Me Just Because I'm Golden 127, 128
    You Teach What You Live 126, 127
    You Were My Greatest But Most Painful Love 126, 127
hip-hop graffiti 56–8
Hitotzuki 166–7
    Untitled (Suzaka, 2009) 166

identity politics 102–11
'III Communication' (2003) 7
illegality of graffiti 54–5, 91, 96
In 16, 26
internet, and graffiti 169, 178–85
Invader 37, 80, 123–4, 184
    Untitled (Los Angeles, 2006) 124, 125
    Untitled (Mombasa, 2005) 124, 125
    Untitled (New York City, 2003) 124, 125
    Untitled (New York City, 2007) 38, 38
    Untitled (Nice, 2007) 124, 125
Iz the Wiz 15, 49

Jace 37, 180–3
    Untitled (Icaraí de Amontada, 2008) 180, 182

Untitled (Kuala Lumpur, 2009) 123
Untitled (Réunion Island, 2002) 181, 182
Untitled (Réunion Island, 2007) 181, 182
Untitled (Réunion Island, 2008) 36, 37
JR 139–42
    Face2Face 140, 141
    Women (Nairobi, 2008) 140, 141
    Women (Rio de Janeiro, 2008) 142
    Wrinkles of the City 115, 141, 143
Julio204 14

Kami 166–7, 166
    Past Memories and Present Self 167, 167
    see also Hitotzuki
Kase2 49, 52–3
Kasso 27
Kero 16, 171, 171
    lavidalooka 18, 20–1
Kies 46, 47
Kill3 see In
kings 26, 28, 50
Knitta Please 70, 71–2, 71
Koch, Edward 50, 54
Koons, Jeff 168
Koralie 101
    Untitled (New York City, 2008) 100
    Untitled (Paris, 2010) 80, 80
    Untitled (San Sebastián, 2007) 98

Labrona
    Freight Train North America 148–51, 150
    Street Hugs 139
Lady Pink 49, 54, 62, 179
Laser Tag 15, 95
layering 28, 92
Lee see Quinones, Lee
Lee163d 18, 48, 51
lettering styles 16, 19, 45–7
Lichtenstein, Roy 168
    Hopeless 161
Lindsay, John 50
location 96, 112, 114–19, 132–3, 139–46
logos 36, 37–8, 124
    sampling brand logos 188, 189–91
Lum, Ken 109–10

M-City see Waras, Mariusz
MadC 17
Magda Danysz Gallery, Paris 175
Mare139 15, 18
marker pens 21–2
Martinez, Hugh 58
material support 147–55
Matta-Clark, Gordon 110
'Meeting of Styles New Jersey' (2010) 27
Microbo 121–2
    Chi C'è C'è 122, 122
    Untitled (Belfast, 2010) 121, 121, 157
    Untitled (Bizerte, 2009) 122, 122
Miss Van 39, 40, 98–101, 175–6
    'Atame' exhibition (2007) 175, 175–6
    'Lovestain' exhibition (2009) 175
    Mascaras 8 40, 40
    Untitled (Barcelona, 2006) 98, 99, 100
Mode2 39
Moose 129
    Untitled (California, 2008) 129, 131
    Untitled (Košice, 2009) 130, 131
    Untitled (Liverpool, 2006) 130, 131
    Untitled (New Orleans, 2009) 129, 131
Mora, Nuria 118–21
    'Estrella de Mar' project 120, 121
    Untitled (Arraial d'Ajuda, 2001) 119, 119
    Untitled (Madrid, 2010) 120, 121
Mosstika 91, 92
    Brooklyn Moss Rabbit 92, 92
    Coney Island Moss 92, 92
    Dumbo 41, 41
    Metro 92, 93
    Wunderbaum 92, 93

Naco 15
Nation of Graffiti Artists (NOGA) 58
natural world and graffiti 91–2, 117, 118, 129–31
neo-graffiti 29–32, 96
new genre public art 66, 79
New York 12, 16, 43
    early tags 14
    graffiti in galleries 58–61

revitalization of pieces 18
train graffiti 26, 48–54
'New York/New Wave' (1981) 59
Noc167 18
non-spaces 114–19
nozzles, spray-paint 20
Nunca 81, 83, 83

Obama, Barack 74
Olympics, London (2012) 171
Omen 142–3
    Untitled (Montreal, 2009) 113, 142, 144
Órion, Alexandre 101–2, 131–2
    Metabiotica 05 84
    Metabiotica 14 101, 103
    Metabiotica 16 101, 102
    Metabiotica 18 101, 103
    Ossário 130, 131–2
Os Gêmeos 39, 40, 160–1, 161
    The Youth Are No Longer Young 40–1, 41
overexposure 16
overlapping 45, 92

paint see spray-paint
Pandolfo, Nina 143–6
    Untitled (Miami, 2009) 146, 146
    Untitled (Mumbai, 2008) 145
PB5 26
Pelsinger, Jack 58
pens, marker 21–2
performing street art 96–102
Pez 37–8, 190
    Ams Dragons 37, 37
Phase2 16, 19
Philadelphia 10, 12, 43
photography and graffiti 178–9
piecebooks 22, 24
pieces 18–19
plagiarism 28
'plop' art 66
pop artists 161, 163
pop culture 47–8, 162
'POPaganda' 189, 190
post-graffiti art movement 29–32, 96, 133, 159, 186, 192, 195
'Post Graffiti' exhibition (1983) 59–60
Powderly, James 95
Prisco 15
Psalm 161–3
    Angels 161, 162

Bedtime for the Workaholic 104
Buddha 161, *162*
Roy 161, *162*
PS1 Gallery, New York 59
public art, street art as 65–72, 110
public spaces, art in 72–8
punctuation 46
Puppet 14, *15*
Blue Graffiti With B-boy 42
Golden Times 19, *21*
Graffiti Girl 11

queens 26
Quinones, Lee 26, 39, 50, *52–3*, 54, 179
quotation marks 15

reproducing street art 132–7
reverse-graffiti project 129–31
Revolt 15, 18
roads, graffiti on 116–18
Roadsworth 34, 115–18, 121, 192
Asphalt Fetish 116, *118*
Asphalt Glory 117, *118*
Attention All Drivers 117, *118*
Bullets for Oil 116, *118*
Fall Leaves 117, *118*
and the internet 179–80
location of work 139, 174
Male Plug 34, *35*
Roth, Evan 95
Graffiti Analysis 15, 32
Graffiti Analysis: Hell 95, *95*
Graffiti Taxonomy 95, *95*
rules of graffiti artists 27–8

'Santa's Ghetto Bethlehem' (2007) 147
Sasu 166–7, *166*
To Remain Calm and Passionate 167, *167*
see also Hitotzuki
Sayeg, Magda 70, 71–2, 72
Untitled (New York City, 2008) 72, *73*
Untitled (Paris, 2007) 71, 72
Untitled (Texas, 2010) 72, *72*
Untitled (Tilburg, 2008) 72, *73*
Scharf, Kenny 60
Seen 39, 49
shadows, use of 76
Sidney Janis Gallery, New York 59–60

signature graffiti writing 30, 123, 159
and layering 28
origins of 10, 12–13
sketchbooks 22, *24*
Slider, *Bandits 4 Life* 55, *55*
space 112–22
spray-paint 19–21, 22, 32, 142
stars 15, 46
status 27, 28, 44, 45
StayHigh149 15
stencils 33–6, 80
style 44–8, 193
subcultures 13, 29, 45, 55
subway graffiti *18*, 26 48–54
Supakitch, *Untitled* (San Sebastián, 2007) 98
SuperKool223 18, 48, *51*
'Survey Select' exhibition (2010) 40
Swet 45, *45*
Swoon 80, 84–6, 89, 96, 183
Alixa and Naima 39, *39*, 156
Girl from Ranoon Province 86, *87*
'Miss Rockaway' exhibition (2007) *177*, 178
Portrait of Silvia Elena 85, *87*
street art in galleries 174, 175, 176
Swimming Cities of Serenissima 177, *178*
'Swimming Cities of Switchback Sea' exhibition (2008) 176
Temple 39, *39*
symbols 46

tags and tagging *10*, 21
origins of 12, *12*, 14–16
on trains 48, 49, *51*
Takil83 14
Tate Modern, London 7
Tats Cru 15
throwies (throw-ups) 16, 18, 26, 50, 95
Thundercut 84, 89
Graph Walker 90, *90*
Out of Here 67
Thundercut 10
Tourist Walker 90, *90*
Vote Walker 160
'Walker' series 89–90, *90*
'Times Square Show' (1980) 59
tips, spray-paint 20
Tokodi, Edina see Mosstika
tools of the trade 19–25, 32
TopCat126 19

toys 26, 28, 50
Tracy168 18, 19, 49
train graffiti *18*, 26, 48–54, *150*
trompe-l'œil 88, 89

United Graffiti Artists (UGA) 58–9
urban painting 28–32, 41, 190–5
urban visual culture 156–95

Van, Miss see Miss Van
Vexta 25, 104–7, 109, 192
Ghetto Make-out 105, 106
Neon Bird 35, 36
street art in galleries 174
We Are Creatures of the Wind 104, *105*
Welcome to Australia 34, 36, 106–7, *107*
Vhils 153–4
Empty Faces 153, 155
Scratching the Surface (2008) 152
Scratching the Surface (2009) 152, 154–5, *155*
Viva la Revolución 154, 155
Vicious Styles crew 27
visual communication *16*, 80–1, *82*, 96, 128
visual culture and art history 159–69

Walker, Nick 107–9, *110*
Brat 109, *109*
Chihuahua 109, *109*
The Empire's State 108, 109
Moona Lisa 194
Waras, Mariusz 183–4
M-City 104 115
M-City 123 182, 183
M-City 128 158
M-City 181 183, 184
M-City 233 85
Watson, Theo 95
websites, and graffiti 178–85
White761 15
Witz, Dan 84, 86, 88–9
'Birds 2000' series 88, *88*
'In Plain View' series 88, 89
'Skateboarders Are Graffiti' series 29, *29*
'Ugly New Buildings' series 89, *89*
'WHAT THE %$#@ (WTF)' series *112*
Wodiczko, Krzysztof 109
writing style 44–8

yarn bombing 71, 72

Zephyr 15, 18, *18*
Zevs 74, 75–6, 187–9
'Electric Shadows' series (*Public Bench, Subway*) 76, *76, 77*
'Graffiti Illuminations' series 187, *187*
'Invisible Graffiti' series 186, 187
Nike Liquidated Logo 188, 189
'Proper Graffiti' series (*Flaming*) 187, 188
'Visual Attacks' series 187